THE PUBLIC NATURE OF PRIVATE VIOLENCE

THE DISCOVERY OF DOMESTIC ABUSE

MARTHA ALBERTSON FINEMAN
ROXANNE MYKITIUK

Routledge · New York, London

Published in 1994 by

Routledge
29 West 35th Street
New York, NY 10001

Published in Great Britain by

Routledge
11 New Fetter Lane
London EC4P 4EE

Library of Congress Cataloging-in-Publication Data

The Public nature of private violence / edited by Martha Albertson
  Fineman and Roxanne Mykitiuk.
    p.   cm.
  Includes bibliographical references.
  ISBN 0-415-90844-2 (hb)—ISBN 0-415-90845-0 (pbk)
    1. Family violence—United States. 2. Family violence—Government
policy—United States. 3. Family violence—Law and legislation—
United States. I. Mykitiuk, Roxanne.
HQ809.3.U5P83   1994
306.87—dc20   94-4591
                                                                      CIP

British Library Cataloguing-in-Publication Data also available.

THE PUBLIC NATURE OF PRIVATE VIOLENCE

From Martha: To Lillian and other wonderful little girls who deserve a better world than that into which they have been born.

From Roxanne: For my grandmothers, Anna Mykitiuk and Anna Mathison, who have been sources of encouragement and love.

Contents

SECTION III / INTERNATIONAL AND COMPARATIVE PERSPECTIVES ON DOMESTIC VIOLENCE

SECTION IV / POLICY POSTSCRIPT

Acknowledgments

We would like to thank Cynthia Hewett, who contributed time, energy, and her considerable administrative skills in organizing the Feminism and Legal Theory Workshop session from which the bulk of these papers arose. She also assisted in preparation of the manuscript, and kept us relatively on time with deadlines. Shari Crossfield's assistance in organizing and running the workshop was also invaluable. It is fair to say that this volume, indeed the progress of the entire Feminism and Legal Theory Project at Columbia, would not have been possible without the contributions of these two wonderful women, whose grace and humor smoothed many a rough spot. We would also like to thank Isabel Karpin and Jeremy Paltiel who made important suggestions during the editorial process, and were always ready to lend a hand when an extra one was needed. Kim Cordero also provided valuable assistance, retyping manuscripts and compiling the initial bibliography and table of cases.

Preface

by Martha Albertson Fineman

Many of the chapters in this volume were first presented as working papers at one of the Feminism and Legal Theory Workshops I conduct at Columbia University Law School. During the course of this particular workshop, I was struck by the complexity and density reflected in the combined presentations of the legal issues surrounding violence against women and children. Some of the presenters seemed most involved in attempts to reconceptualize the whole topic of "domestic" violence—what, in the title to this volume, is labeled "private" violence.[1] Others were concerned with criticizing or developing specific legal solutions or proposing concrete policy responses. Still others explored topics often considered "taboo" in some more generalized feminist discussions, such as the appropriate legal response to the violence women perpetuate against children or against each other and the dilemmas for attorneys who defend them.

As it developed, the workshop had some distinctive aspects that enriched the nature and direction of the discussions. Most significantly, the papers, in addressing domestic violence as primarily a legal as well as a feminist issue, moved away from the psychological and emotional dimensions of the problem, and focused on the assessment of the direction and development of the law. This focus is important. The legal (or public) ramifications of the problem of domestic violence are often obscured in feminist discussions attuned to the plight of individual women and children living in the context of abusive situations. The papers at the workshop assumed law as a vital and central component in shaping as well as defining the nature of what constitutes domestic violence.

The initial papers have been supplemented by the inclusion in this volume of additional chapters and introductions. *En masse*, the collected contributions consider a wide range of issues relating to private violence.

The chapters not only reveal the evolving patterns; they also reflect some of the tensions within feminist legal theory over the appropriateness of tactics and strategies as lawyers and academics interested in the role of law in society grapple with the public dimension of the phenomena of violence. While not all the ramifications of private violence are addressed, and not all potential voices are represented in this collection, there has been an attempt to broaden the inquiry beyond what is, and who are, typically found in discussing "domestic" violence. Women from different perspectives speak from these pages on a topic of general feminist concern. Like the topic itself, the authors are located across racial, class, ethnic, and sexual orientation boundaries and bring diverse perspectives to the issues.

The collection is also diverse and comprehensive on the legal issues. While the focus of this collection is on "the law," different legal systems are considered in the various analyses. The attention to different legal perspectives presents a collection that has cross-legal-cultural diversity, showing differences among similar legal systems' treatment of the issues as well as differences in stages of awareness and formal response to the whole question of domestic violence.

The very range and nature of the multiple diversities conscientiously represented in this collection may make it seem a bit fragmented at places. Some fragmentation seems the inevitable result of the necessary expansive scope of the collection. It is hoped that the introductions help to tie the papers in each section together, and that the total, overall impression is coherent in this multifaceted feminist legal consideration of this pervasive social problem.

In the way of general introduction, I would like to comment on the specific relationship of law and the domestic. In addition, it is useful to make a few points about the limits of law as a tool for societal transformation.

Law and the Domestic—Intimates and Families

When societal norms are in a state of flux (as they certainly are in regard to matters of sexual intimacy and gender relations) the law tends to become identified as a significant site of contest. Competing societal factions seek to codify their worldview, thereby giving legitimacy to the stories they tell about what are appropriate ideals and values. Policy formation and law reform in this regard are inevitably political or, at least, tend to develop in a politicized environment. This is significant because it means that the lawmaking (or law-interpreting) process often becomes a highly charged, symbolic endeavor signaling who wins and who loses in an ongoing battle over larger societal definitions and directions.

Furthermore, as we have recently seen in the context of presidential politics, when politicians and public figures speak of undefined "family values," rhetorical battles do not have to culminate in actual physical violence to be virulent and vicious. In such instances the stakes seem high to the participants, with the explicit subject matter under immediate consideration understood or experienced as merely the tip of a larger, ideologically potent iceberg. This is certainly the case with legal debates surrounding issues of "domestic" violence. Submerged barely below the surface in these debates are fears about the future of families and the direction of relations between the sexes in a world in which feminists argue that intimacy is potentially lethal to women.

The feminist concern with the dangers of intimacy should also serve to remind us that the contemporary "war" in which we are engaged—the battle to redefine the role of women and, simultaneously, the future of the traditional family—is being fought not only over the domestic sphere, but *in* it. It therefore is appropriate to include in the preface to this volume some reference to the traditional family and its role and function within the larger society. The parameters of this institution, traditionally set aside as paradigmatically "private," have historically defined a more or less bright line across which state or "public" intervention and regulation are considered problematic.

The lines between public and private spheres have become less clear in recent decades, however. Our collective notions about the family have been contested, and what had been received as wisdom is often recast as outdated, unrealistic, or inappropriately biased. As our ideas about family and marriage have been challenged by political and intellectual forces that focus on individuals, not entities, and reference concepts such as equality and freedom, tensions are generated on many different levels. These tensions erupt in legal and cultural institutions as well as in specific families, provoking heated debates about the need for and extent of possible reforms.

Fears for the traditional, heterosexual, hierarchical (patriarchal) family, though greatly overreactive, are not unfounded. For over twenty-five years the American family had been the object of so called "second-wave" feminist criticism and attack. The family constructed in this discourse was sometimes cast as a potentially violent and dangerous social institution, marred by long-standing power imbalances and the specter of gender domination.[2] These feminist critiques of the family have had some significant impact in regard to recent law reforms. No longer can violence between intimates easily remain invisible and ignored. Laws explicitly forbid child abuse, marital rape and other violence historically considered normal, or at least inevitable and excusable, because it also was "domestic." In addition, and affecting all families, the veil of privacy has been partly pulled aside, revealing the hierarchical nature of the family and its conceptual core of common-law inequality. In response to feminist agitation (and after much time and effort) the language of the law regulating the domestic has changed.

The very structure of marriage has been reformulated to present an egalitarian idea. On a formal legal level issues may no longer be resolved according to explicitly patriarchical assumptions. Tasks and responsibilities associated with families have ceased to be allocated in law on the basis of gender, with the husband deemed the "head" of the household with obligations to support a wife and children over whom he exercised control, and who correspondingly owed him obedience and, on the wife's part, sexual and other domestic services.

Marriage is no longer formally an appropriate defense to a charge of rape, and battering of one's sexual partner is technically punishable by law. On an abstract level, the law has adopted a "gender-neutral" stance. Our rhetorical model is now based on the marital "partnership" of husband and wife. Gone from our formal, official discourse is the hierarchical organization of the common-law marriage described so graphically by Blackstone under the doctrines of "unity" and "merger." Married women during this century gained the legal rights to own property and make contracts. Female subservience is no longer assumed, nor our inherent incompetence for the business and market world seriously asserted and used as a basis for exclusion. Wives and mothers are equally responsible for the economic well-being of their families, and are no longer presumed by virtue of their sex to be the preferred parent in custody disputes.

Linguistic changes often do not reflect "real" changes (and seldom compel them), however. The rhetorically revised roles must still be understood as an ideological construct implicated in and fashioned by traditional power relationships within the institutions of family and state. The historical organization and operative assumptions about traditional family relationships obscured the state-sanctioned power imbalance inherent in the institution. The status of "father," "husband," "head of household" needed no formal explication of the power the status held.

In considering the empirical data on the operation of the family, the inescapable conclusion—rhetoric aside—is that gender divisions persist, and inequality abounds. For example, women continue to bear what I call the "burdens of intimacy"—the "costs" of "inevitable dependency"[3]— in our society. The societal functioning of the family as the core institution for raising and caring for children means that attempts to recast family roles cannot be viewed in isolation from other social forces that serve to distort, impede, or prevent change.

The family as an institution has historically served important practical and ideological functions in our society. For centuries, it stood alone as the formal and institutionalized manifestation of condoned sexual intimacy, a cultural monopoly currently under attack. It has also operated as the social institution in which the dependency of the very young and, sometimes, the elderly and ill can be referred, confined, and thus hidden and ignored. The family functions as a complementary institution to the state, alleviating its direct economic responsibility for its citizens.

The "evolutionary dialogue" associated with renegotiation of family relationships reveals the inescapably political (in the largest sense of that word) and ideological nature of change. Changes quite often generate controversy and provoke resistance. Traditional stories are met with alternative visions, and as a result are modified, restated, and reintroduced into the ongoing debates. Ultimately the collected and conflicting stories we tell about families in our society reveal a great deal about how we view and understand the worlds in which we operate. New stories may be fashioned, but the emerging alternative narratives do not always challenge the basic operation of the *status quo*. As adherence to the historic family form has begun to wither away, the complementary power relationships embedded in the traditional family have had to be made explicit in order to be preserved.

In divorce law newly wrought designations of the "rights" and/or "responsibilities" associated with the gender-neutral status of "spouse" and "parent" ensure male control will survive the end of the marital relationship. Traditional assumptions, refashioned for a no-fault divorce world, are articulated as ongoing economic support obligations along with coerced continued access to and control over ex-wife and child. Marital rape is no longer shielded from prosecution, but juries fail to convict even when prosecutors can be persuaded to pursue such crimes. As the essays in this volume attest, quite often women also bear the brunt of societal changes that engender fear and precipitate lashing out in response to male perceptions of losses of power and position.

The Limits of Law

One final point of caution for the uninitiated who view law as having significant potential to transform society and curtail individual behavior. In regard to the role of law in addressing private violence, many of the chapters illustrate that there are some serious questions about the extent to which law can realistically carry the major burden of reform. "Domestic" violence is located within our larger (and seemingly uncontrollable) violent society. "Domestic" violence could be said to reflect our peculiar American commitment to force as a primary tool of persuasion and reaction—a tendency revealed in everything from the Gulf War to the war on drugs (or guns or poverty or whatever—the relevant word being "war").

While general political and ideological hurdles are alone formidable, it is also important to remember that there are independent limitations on law and legal institutions. Most significant for a feminist is the reliance in law on the processes of classification and bureaucratization. The law is a system of rules and/or norms, many of which are designed to have universal application, all of which have potential application beyond any specific set of circumstances. Therefore, the process of lawmaking relies on the generation of broad generalizations about groups or classes of things and people at the legislative level. On the individual case level, law is also a process of classification—courts make decisions using analogies and distinctions within the context of precedent and *stare decisis,* tieing "like things" together in a web of consistent and coherent doctrine.

Classification, inevitable though it might be, is nonetheless a process that is susceptible to criticism because it will invariably both include inappropriate cases and exclude appropriate ones. As classification involves line-drawing and assessments of similarity and difference, it seems clear that both as a process and in terms of fashioning responses, classification should be understood to be of a political nature. Those who have disproportionate power will disproportionately influence lawmaking and implementation.

Even if one believes in the abstract possibility of change and progress, it is not likely that widespread redistribution of power within families or between women and men will be accomplished by mere legal restructuring. Law is more reflective than constitutive of social realities, tracking closely to existing power alignments. Law is a very crude instrument with which to fashion and further social policy—much better at fashioning prohibition and determining punishment than it is at creating affirmative incentives for behavior. In either case, whether developed to structure incentives or to define punishments for certain behavior, law is most effective when it tracks societal norms and values about which there is strong agreement. Therefore, it is no surprise that law incorporates dominant stereotypes, and replicates existing ingrained inequities.

The inherent failures of law are exaggerated when there is no consensus about reform (or even about the nature of the problem). When it comes to violence among intimates, even feminists argue with each other. Debates within feminism on issues such as agency and victimization are evident in this collection, for example. Disagreements are public, often vicious, in regard to the nature and extent (even the existence) of differences between women and men, while the assertion and acceptance of significant differences among women seems at times to threaten the possibility of cohesive and coherent political action under a feminist banner. Also reflecting divisions (or a desire to avoid them) are the silences of many feminists on social and legal issues such as child abuse or lesbian battering where women are uncomfortably implicated as perpetuators of violence.

The possibility of consensus seems elusive at present. Nonetheless, from a feminist perspective, focused on the material and legal position of women in our society, the nature and operation of the coercive power of law is cause for immediate concern. The critiques of law of private violence in this volume have an air of urgency (perhaps desperation) because the power of the system is so explicitly and immediately threatening to women and harmful to children.

Notes

1. "The term "domestic violence" is the one most commonly employed to describe incidents of familial or intimate battering. In the title to this collection, however, the term chosen to modify violence is not "domestic" but "private." "Domestic," defined as "having to do with the home or family: as domestic happiness" (*Webster New World Dictionary of the American Language, College Edition* (1964), p. 432) seems a less politically focused word than "private," which refers to those things "belonging to oneself, not public or of the state." (*Id.*, p. 1159). Historically, the domestic has referenced an idealized family unit functioning in a protected and secluded manner, appropriately shielded from public view. Private encompasses that, but also references activity beyond the home, the purely domestic that historically has not been open to, intended for control or even consideration by the public, the powerful, the political. The purpose of this volume is to highlight and call into question the historic dichotomy between public and private, which so often excludes and hides the mistreatment of women and children both in and outside families.

2. Paradoxically, within feminist discourse also, the family was often recast as potentially the most fulfilling site of intimacy—the intimate base that allowed the construction of a complete life if it was based on principles of equality and sharing.

3. As a definitional note, "burden" is *not* the same as oppression. I use the term to clearly signify that there are costs associated with what women typically do in regard to caretaking in our society. Their labors may provide "joy," but they are also burdensome and have material costs and consequences. Not to recognize them as "burdens" is to ignore the costs and to continue to make women's labor invisible, condoning the fact that it is also uncompensated.

   A second definitional point is that dependency is "inevitable," in that it flows from the status and situation of being a child and often accompanies aging, illness, or disability. In this sense dependency will always be with us (and always has been with us). Furthermore, caretakers are dependent too—a derivative dependency derived from their roles as caretakers and the need for resources they generate.

To point out that the costs of caretaking associated with these dependencies continue in our society to be allocated to women should not be misunderstood to be an argument about essentialism. The allocation is accomplished and reinforced by the culture and our ideology of the family as a functioning institution. Nonetheless, to label something as a social construct does not mean it will be easy to change.

Section I

Images of Violence

Introduction

by Susan F. Hirsch

Each chapter in this section acknowledges significant changes over the past two decades in the legal treatment of private violence. Feminist activists and legal practitioners have been instrumental in effecting these changes: they developed legal definitions of private violence that better reflected women's experiences, pursued the prosecution and punishment of violent men, and helped women to empower themselves. Feminist theory has been integral to combatting private violence, as scholars analyzed how the abuse of women is endemic in patriarchal societies and how institutions such as the law tend to support men's violence. These efforts offered many women new images of lives without violence.

The contributors below carefully scrutinize these developments, focusing on concepts and images that have gained currency as the foundations for conceptualizing private violence. They explore what it has meant to develop theory and practice around "the battered woman," "the rape victim," and "the cycle of violence." When initially deployed, these foundational constructs were powerful tools for changing consciousness and providing new policy directions, yet they elided other ways of seeing the problems and imagining solutions. Theories built on particular images always mask or foreclose others. And the images themselves are at risk of turning perverse, as illustrated by painful, paradoxical examples: a battered woman who loses custody of her children because, in the eyes of the law, her injuries preclude her from providing for them adequately; a rape victim who is assumed by police, prosecutors, and judges to be more credible or more injured than another because of her race, class, or occupation. Troubled by these and similar examples, the authors in this section dare to ask: What are the limitations, perversions, and blind spots of the premises that underlie contemporary legal efforts against private violence?

Questioning the fundamental assumptions of a theory or practice is an awesome undertaking. Some deem it politically unwise to expose deficiencies and thereby risk undermining successes. Others insist that such questioning is politically indispensable. Writing of feminist theory's tendency to posit problematic foundations, Judith Butler justifies interrogating even the most basic assumptions:

> ... foundations function as the unquestioned and the unquestionable within any theory. And yet, are these "foundations," that is, those premises that function as authorizing grounds, are they themselves not constituted through exclusions which, taken into account, expose the foundational premise as a contingent and contestable presumption. (Butler 1992, p. 7)

Butler implies that no foundations, not even basic assumptions about women's subjectivity or subordination, should be left unquestioned in the effort to develop politically effective theory. This logic applies to feminist theories of private violence. Accordingly, the political challenge is to expose the foundations of efforts against private violence—identifying what they exclude and scrutinizing the political trajectoriers they chart.

The contributors to this section question the foundations of scholarship and advocacy on private violence by interrogating fundamental concepts like coverture, privacy, violence, agency, victimage, identity, and power, and the images of women's lives that they support. As importantly, they discard some concepts, refashion and redeploy others, and search for innovative ideas and images in new places and among people previously ignored. Recognizing that the law tends to encode foundations in statutes and precedents, these contributors acknowledge the contingency and contestability of all fundamental concepts. They assume that the concepts they embrace will play different roles in different legal and cultural contexts. An ongoing process of positing and questioning foundations becomes for them a strategy for re-imaging women's lives and for refining law's role as a weapon against private violence.

For Isabel Marcus, the concept of "violence" as it relates to women's lives desperately needs "reframing." She looks first at the roots of domestic violence, finding them firmly planted in nineteenth-century legal doctrines such as coverture, which subordinated a wife to her husband. The recent rhetoric of marital equality conceals how coverture continues to operate in the "attitudes, beliefs, and practices" surrounding contemporary marriage. When husbands claim that they beat their wives just to remind them "who's in charge," they betray assumptions about hierarchy and control in marriage that reinscribe coverture. Ingrained cultural notions that support violence in intimate relationships are also perpetuated through the language of law and the language of feminist activism. For example, Marcus finds the term "domestic violence" inadequate for several reasons, including its status in relation to violence *unmodified*. Exposing the inadequacies of current foundational terms and proposing alternatives is central to developing better political and legal strategies for ending violence against women.

Marcus's reframing of domestic violence proceeds from her belief that "[h]ome is the most unsafe place for women," not just in countries with a history of coverture, but globally. Conversations with women in India, China, Poland, and elsewhere convinced her of the need for a global approach. Identifying domestic violence as a violation of international human rights accords offers a strategy potentially more powerful than current remedies in that it "move[s] beyond . . . Western political theory[; it incorporates a] vision which substitutes a global 'our' for a narrower 'my' rights." Developing a perspective that claims universality yet respects cultural difference is a challenge for law, one that requires new foundational terms with international resonance. By describing domestic violence as "terrorism," Marcus emphasizes its devastating social and psychological consequences, and highlights its resemblance to political terrorism. The parallel is striking when one considers how, in terrorism of each type, the fear of the next attack can overwhelm the life of its target. In specifying "terrorism in the home," Marcus makes a brave and provocative leap to a new foundation from which she asks fresh political questions.

By contrast, Elizabeth Schneider revisits a familiar legal concept: "privacy." Since *Griswold,* the right to privacy has been used to keep the state out of many intimate relationships, yet this distancing means that marital violence is sometimes left unregulated. Although in recent years domestic violence has gained recognition as a social problem requiring legal intervention, privacy still operates as an "ideological rationale" for denying the extent of violence or for refusing to protect abused women. But privacy has many meanings. While some support violence and perpetuate gender inequality, others are potentially liberating for women. Schneider looks to the opinions of Justice Douglas for interpretations of privacy that emphasize an individual's autonomy and independence, and uses these affirmative aspects of privacy to frame a new feminist agenda against woman abuse.

Schneider's chapter draws attention to the public/private continuum, a theme of this volume. Activisits in the battered women's movement were instrumental in defining woman abuse as a public, rather than a private, problem and in demanding public remedies. But, because notions of public and private are "deeply gendered" in ways that support patriarchy, these activists encountered frequent subversion of their efforts. For example, as the movement itself gained political legitimacy and adopted bureaucratic organization, activists' early, hard-edged discourse linking domestic violence to systemic gender inequality became muffled by talk of serving individual clients and seeking mediated or therapeutic solutions. This example suggests that no social movement can control the definition or treatment of violence, especially when the new visions it offers challenge existing gender relations. Schneider recognizes that her own attempt to redeploy privacy as an affirmative concept serving women's interests will need strong fortification to counter patriarchy's persistent backward tug into the unprotected "privacy" of the home.

Martha Mahoney takes on two foundational dichotomies—victim/agent and stay/separate—showing how they function in tandem to construct paradoxical choices and positions for women in violent relationships. The political effort to depict battered women as legitimate "victims" of violence has circumscribed the permissible actions of women seeking relief. As Mahoney argues: "victimization implies the one-way exercise of power, harm without strength; agency implies freedom from victimization." The victim/agency dichotomy traps battered women. Many have difficulty denying their agency, especially given the centrality of personal autonomy as a cultural ideal. The problem is exacerbated by the law's contradictory demand for women to perform some agentive acts (for instance, caring for their children). They must also choose between staying with or separating from an abusive partner, and the wrong choice can undermine their victim status or expose them to further violence. As Mahoney demonstrates, the law's tendency to treat the stay/separate dichotomy as analogous to victim/agent exacerbates the false opposition of each and leads inevitably to the question: Why didn't she leave? Battered women rarely have an answer that satisfies legal or social expectations.

A central deficiency of the legal application of the dichotomies described above is that they fail to depict the "dualism and resistance" that characterize battered women's lives. For Mahoney, the solution lies in understanding why the law sees victimage and agency as mutually exclusive and, more significantly, in moving beyond such dichotomies to reconceptualize private violence itself. Depicting violence in marriage as a struggle for "power and control," she deflects attention away from the battering incidents to which a woman is expected to respond as a stereotypic victim/nonagent. Her approach "makes visible" not only the many kinds of "violence" used to exert power and control, but also the full range of strategies that women use to resist abuse and refashion their intimate relationships. Through this framework, women appear as active agents when they take a "leap of faith" and decide to stay in a relationship. When used in treatment programs and prosecutions, the power/control model offers a refreshing direction that maps the realities of women's lives more closely and envisions them as agents, even within contexts of oppression. As Mahoney's examples demonstrate, this approach challenges contemporary legal discourse which rarely incorporates "a complex account of women as both oppressed and struggling."

Kimberlé Crenshaw develops a new concept—"intersectionality"—to counteract the tendency in work on private violence to marginalize the experiences of women of color. Intersectionality entails developing analyses of violence that, rather than focusing exclusively on gender, address the effects of race, class, culture, and other hierarchies that operate simultaneously. Crenshaw begins by examining structural intersectionality, in effect, how people are positioned within intersecting structures of subordination. Concerned with the differential effect of violence on those women positioned at the bottom of multiple hierarchies, she describes how immigrant women's experiences of domestic violence are generally ignored. In addition, failure to appreciate the convergence of categories means that black women are frequently marginalized in feminist efforts to develop remedies. Crenshaw's analysis illuminates the ever-present power of categorical identity in social life, providing numerous examples of how people are treated as category members rather than by virtue of their actions. Racist and sexist assumptions continue to have dramatic implications for the prosecution of rape, delineating who is a legitimate victim or perpetrator and which rapes—based on the race of those involved—are more heinous. When Crenshaw demonstrates that such assumptions pervade even progressive scholarship about rape, it becomes clear that adopting an intersectional analysis is absolutely critical.

Intersectionality also has a more specifically political dimension. Crenshaw documents how, for African-Americans, the politics of community integrity in the face of racism preclude acknowledging the extent of intracommunity domestic violence. Feminist attempts to fight domestic abuse in an "antiracist" way are similarly problematic. By treating all communities as equally affected by domestic violence, some feminists ignore how the higher incidence in minority communities impacts on women. Ultimately, these political divergences make it difficult for women of color to develop accurate understandings of the violence in their lives. Black feminists, like Crenshaw, are challenged by such political conundrums, feeling the pull of multiple concerns, discourses, and strategies. Crenshaw meets this challenge through her intersectional perspective. For example, applying this perspective to cultural representations that demean black women by depicting them as victims of sexual violence, Crenshaw demonstrates how complex messages about gender and race can be effectively analyzed and countered.

Crenshaw makes the important point that representations of women as victims of violence can operate as counternarratives, undermining legal and political efforts against woman abuse as well as the stories of battered women themselves. The other contributors also acknowledge the power of media images to shape cultural understandings of violence. The normative projects that they outline rely on publicizing images of violence against women in ways that will effect social change and legal reform. Yet this strategy is complicated by the tendency for images to take on problematic meanings as they are used. Recent public awareness of "stalking" as a crime has been facilitated through extensive media attention, yet most representations reinforce the alluring image of stalking as an obsession with a celebrity (Mahoney). The contributors are well aware that, although images are mediated publicly, they are often consumed privately, in ways that decontextualize and distort what women face.

When images of violence cross cultural or national borders, the problem of interpretation becomes especially acute. Several contributors invite this challenge as they develop analyses with global reach and remedies that include previously marginalized women. They provoke some critical questions: What images and foundations will a broader, more international perspective rely on? How should we interpret images of violence against women with very different cultural experiences? Will we develop projects that assist all women or will we get caught in misinterpretations and stereotypes?

The problem of reproducing stereotypes was especially evident in the international press coverage of an incident of violence against women that occurred in Kenya. In July of 1991, major U.S. newspapers reported that young men at St. Kizito Secondary School raped seventy-one female students in a midnight attack on a dormitory. Eleven young women were crushed to death in the onslaught. Journalists in the U.S. explained the incident as reflecting "traditional" and "tribal" attitudes that support the sexual exploitation of African women. In long analyses, full of generalizations about tribal practices lingering in the midst of modernization, the media accounts veered close to blaming Kenyan women themselves for their oppression and, by intimation, for the St. Kizito incident. A female school official who attempted to explain the incident by saying "the boys didn't want to kill, they only wanted to rape" was vilified by a U.S. press that ignored the desperation behind her struggle to assess responsibility for the horrific event. Extensive media coverage generated a set of stereotypic images: wild, tribal African men; silent, abused, (complicit?) African women; and liberal Western feminists offering the "appropriate" rational condemnation.

I argue elsewhere that the St. Kizito incident should not be understood as a regressive cultural ritual, though that image certainly plays well in the mainstream international press (Hirsch 1994). My analysis examines how Kenyans, including the Kenyan media, identified the multiple causes of the incident. Rather than emphasize primordial tribal custom, they attributed the tragedy to struggles for power of several kinds in a postcolonial nation: intense, nationwide student dissatisfaction with educational and employment opportunities often expressed through violence against school property, school personnel, and each other; the state's increasing militarization and authoritarianism; and rapidly changing gender roles and rules about sexuality, especially in relatively new contexts like coeducational schools. Taken together, these factors link the incident to a patriarchy that secures its force through state domination, class oppression, and the dynamics of gender. By reducing the analysis to "traditional abuse of women," Western accounts, though "feminist," erase or obscure the multiple origins of private violence and other misogynistic acts.

My critique of media accounts of the St. Kizito incident is not meant to imply that cross-cultural examples can only be understood by those intimately familiar with the context. Rather, I want to emphasize that we can all develop responsible analyses of such incidents by attending to the strategies laid out by the contributors to this section. Several specific examples should suffice. First, the authors encourage us to interrogate any foundational constructs. With respect to St. Kizito, we must question basic conceptualizations of rape, violence, and sex in the context of Kenyan law, daily life, and feminist practice. The concept of privacy also plays a pivotal role. How to interpret violence in a dormitory—and how to prevent it—is a problem relevant to violence on our own campuses. Second, we should always assume the intersectionality of power. Patriarchy never stands alone; state and global politics are usually complicit too. The St. Kizito incident must therefore be understood as bearing a relation to other incidents of violence in Kenyan schools and against other state institutions. I do not mean to diminish the sexism that motivated the young men to rape their female colleagues, but rather I seek to link it to other acts of terroristic destruction. Finally, we need to insist that any accounts of violence against women make an effort to explore women's lives and perspectives. We should evaluate with heightened scrutiny any representations in which "all the stereotype buttons get pushed at once" (Crenshaw). The young women at St. Kizito school are silent in the media accounts, and their experiences are unexplored. By distancing these women, we learn little about how their lives are similar to or different from our own or those of women in other places. Developing a feminist response is thus that much more difficult.

By reframing and redeploying the foundational concepts and images associated with violence, the following chapters give us new tools to use in scrutinizing the St. Kizito incident and others that might at first seem unfamiliar. In addition, they offer new, contingent foundations and strategies to counter instances of private violence in contexts closer to the places we call home.

Reframing "Domestic Violence": Terrorism in the Home

by Isabel Marcus

Prologue: Encounters Across Cultures

During a recent conversation with a university health center doctor, I volunteered that I was teaching a law school seminar on violence in the home; the doctor's voice became quite animated. "You know," she said "we now realize that this is a serious problem for a far greater number of students than we ever thought. We believe that the rash of psychosomatic conditions like headaches and stomach pains which students report before winter and spring breaks as they prepare to return to their family home are connected with violence there—against them, against a sibling or a parent. They don't talk about it directly; they feel helpless. Only within the past year or so have we recognized the connection between the ailments and the students' situation. And we don't know what to do about it."

Not long after this conversation I noticed that the *Buffalo News* contained a prominent story with the headline "Rise in domestic violence getting extra attention from city police. After more than 20,000 incidents in a year, a special panel is formed" (*Buffalo News*, 3 October, 1992, p. A1). Accompanying the story was a graph which indicated that, despite the decrease in Buffalo's population between 1981 and 1992, the number of "domestic trouble" emergency calls increased steadily during this period. In fact, the numbers rose from 12,659 to 20,799 by the end of the decade. Registering her shock, one of my neighbors remarked "of course we know that there is some domestic violence in our city, but this—this is something different and horrifying!"

"Why the domestic *unrest*?" (author's emphasis) the same news story asked. An odd framing of the issue, I thought to myself. A term with possible political connotations of widespread dissatisfaction and disarray—social rather than individual—conveying the need perhaps for con-

11

structive remedial measures to *quell* it. Regrettably, the police response to this query is the conventional superficial descriptive one—a litany of "frictions" are invoked—money or close quarters or such "provocations" and "picayune actions" as taking the last piece of pie from the refrigerator or a misunderstood tone of voice. It is clear from this story that the police focus on real or imagined "grievances" or "provocations"; the ensuing violence is minimized or trivialized. Lost or submerged is the fact that, in a rising number of relationships premised on love, trust, and respect, death by hammering, strangling, or stabbing, as well as many serious injuries, are frequent occurrences. There is an unsettling parallel between this presumably well-intentioned newspaper analysis and the claims of batterers, who often recount elaborate narratives stressing a partner's allegedly "provocative" words or behavior to excuse or deny their own violence.

Many people who know about my involvement with issues of violence in the home reported their initial surprise and shock as they read the story. I am pleased that the newspaper has publicized the issue. But I worry over the fact that the story does not contain a probing discussion of the convictions, beliefs, and conventions in our society that allow men to inflict this terror on their partners, and then to deny or to rationalize their behavior.

Everywhere I have travelled, violence against women in that supposedly safe place, the home, is present. Mind you, it is not readily discussed. Often it emerges only after a probe or query. But I always have found the violence acknowledged. Rarely is it identified and addressed directly as "violence." Never have I heard it called "terror." Usually it is characterized by such euphemistic terms as "keeping order" or "discipline" or "reminding" women of their responsibilities and obligations to their husbands.

But in fact, the phenomenon of violence against women in the home, which, in Buffalo, is considered ordinary and mundane, yet, when occurring in other different and "exotic" societies, is remarked upon as "uncivilized," is marked by greater similarities than differences; though we may wish to attribute "differences" to it for the purpose of enhancing or refining our own sense of superiority. For me this recognition and understanding of the pervasiveness of violence against women in many different societies, the extent of the denial of both its existence and incidence, and the need for naming it in order to break the silence has meant that I can no longer experience the world in the same way.

I scan the local newspaper in Bombay, in Calcutta, in Delhi, in Madras. In each paper I find tucked away remarkably similar small news items. Mrs. X was standing in front of her kerosene stove and cooking a meal for her husband; her sari caught on fire; her husband attempted to rescue his wife but unfortunately his efforts were unsuccessful. The first time I see such a story, I read it as news; the next time I read a similar story involving another couple, I make a mental note of the parallels in the brief accounts of each woman's death; the third time I happen on an account of yet another woman's "unfortunate" death, I cannot move past the article; I cannot put the newspaper down. I catch my breath. Thereafter, each day I scan the local newspaper first to determine if there is a reported incident of yet another woman's death, another formulaic account of what the Indian press identifies as a "dowry death." (A newly married woman whose husband and/or family are dissatisfied with the dowry she has brought to the marriage is doused with kerosene and ignited.) Note that this happens to young women, before they bear children, before they assume all the burdens of child-rearing which Indian culture assigns to women. Such women are easily replaceable; their deaths will not create problems for household management.

As I travel around India and lecture about women's rights and international human rights, I notice time and time again that as soon as I raise issues of silencing women through violence in the home in many societies, including my own, there is a palpable and perceptible level of discomfort. Male jurists and reporters in the audience are quick to retort "But what about the divorce rate in your society? Shame!" The first time this happens, I am taken aback by such a *non sequitur*. Then I come to recognize a pattern. It is either a denial response or a justification of the violence. That I have been critical of my own country as well is irrelevant. It is my raising the subject of violence in the home and my connecting it to the silencing of women which is so threatening.

While the men in the audience are vocal and dominate the question-and-answer period, the women watch closely. After I finish my talk, however few their number, they cluster around me. They tell me stories about violence against Indian women in their homes; sometimes they thank me for raising the issue. No woman denies its existence; no woman justifies or excuses it.

In January 1990 I am in Peshawar, the fabled Northwest Frontier of Pakistan. By now I have accustomed myself to the fact that, unlike many other societies I have visited, if I wander around big city markets in Pakistan I will probably not see large numbers of women either selling or buying. But until now, I have not been challenged, accosted, or harassed during my forays.

Before I am to make the official rounds, I have several hours to myself. I inform the driver that he can leave me off at the hotel on the outskirts of the city, and that I will take a taxi to the market. A look of alarm crosses his face. "Oh, please, no Sir (I am often addressed with this honorific). You may not do this." I look down at my arms and legs. They are fully covered. I pull out my shawl and wrap it around me, trying to signal that I understand the need for modesty. Still he shakes his head. Once again I try to convey my respect for the local norms and mores. I rewrap myself in the shawl, draping it over my head as well. "May I go now?" I inquire. "No, Sir, please, it is not possible. Here in Peshawar you may not walk on the streets without a man."

We drive downtown, past streets with men strolling along, Kalashnikov rifles slung bandolier-fashion across their shoulders. There is no woman, even veiled, in sight. I ask the driver if we may stop so that I can look in a rug shop. He nods his head. As we emerge from the car, partly because I see a shop down the street with a beautiful brass urn outside and partly to reject the oppressive feeling of constraint, I start walking down the street before him, so that he will have to catch up. Several men come toward me. They are large and armed. They glare at me; their jaws tighten; they move so that they occupy the dusty sidewalk and I am pushed into the roadway. They mutter in a menacing tone that surely sounds like a curse or an imprecation. I ask the driver who is still running to catch up with me if he heard what they said. He averts his eyes. "It is not possible to tell a woman what they said. Please, Sir, let us enter this shop." I persist in my questioning. "At least tell me whether what they said is connected with my being a 'European' foreigner or being an unveiled woman." "Oh, a woman, Sir!"

The next day I lecture to the university law faculty and students. Eighty or ninety young men walk into the room where, over in the far right-hand corner, seven or eight young women with headscarves sit. At the end of my by now fairly standard talk, which focuses on violence as a means of silencing women and denying them any expectation of citizenship, I ask for questions. A number of young men raise their hands. "But what about the divorce rate in your country?" I suppress the desire to laugh at this *deja vu*. I try to answer the query and to move back into the topic of violence against women. No one will respond; the young women lower their eyes. They know.

Afterwards, the women cluster around me. One of them whispers, "You know we have dreadful laws which punish women. We must observe Islam, but these laws and the cruelty are not religion. Many women are beaten and they cannot complain. If they do, they will be thrown into prison and violated there by the guards." She stops abruptly as one of the professors approaches.

I, along with three other female colleagues, invite our ten Chinese female students to coffee and dessert at a hotel in Beijing near the campus, where we are teaching a group of Chinese law professors and lawyers. We sit down after the obligatory polite chatter. Many of the women are nervous; it is clear that they have never been in such a place; nor is it common for professors to invite their students out to a restaurant. We scan the dessert menu; it is replete with a list of chocolate creations accompanied by glossy photos—not food with which many Chinese are likely to be familiar. As the desserts arrive I notice some of the women looking around the table nervously; they are waiting for one of us to use a fork. Some glance dubiously at the items they have ordered. More laughter and polite exclamations are in order to create a safe social space. Only then can we begin to talk about ourselves.

I talk about the status of women in the United States, and refer to the issue of violence against women as a serious problem. Then I mention that in my travels in India and Pakistan I learned about "dowry deaths," as well as the other violence against women. I remark on the difference between my discussions with North American, Indian, and Pakistani men who deny the extensiveness of this violence, and with women in all three countries who, without exception and without hesitation, have provided me with a plethora of horror stories.

Suddenly, one of the Chinese women blurts out "you know we Chinese have an old tradition of beating women." The other women around the table nod. "It still happens in the rural areas," someone chimes in. "Not only in the countryside," says another. "It occurs in urban areas, in big cities among all sorts of people. I know women who have been beaten by their husbands and no one helps them."

It is a warm spring evening in Krakow, Poland. As a visiting professor at Jagiellonian University I have been asked to meet with a handful of young Polish women who identify themselves as feminists. The previous evening, at what I hoped was an opportune moment in a dinner party conversation with colleagues from the Faculty of Law, I raised the issue of violence against Polish women in their homes. I was met by a round of robust denials. "Poles are gallant towards women; Mary, the mother of Jesus, is Queen of Poland." Hard upon these remarks was a round of qualified and partial admissions. "Yes, of course, such violence unfortunately sometimes occurs in the rural areas; peasants are still a backward lot. And, of course, there is a problem with alcoholism in Poland."

At the student gathering the tenor is quite different. A handful of earnest young women talk about the violence, especially against their mothers, that they have witnessed in their own homes; they report stories from friends; they confess to fears about violence in their own intimate relationships and confusion regarding how to handle such violence. They talk about the pressures not to talk about the violence.

Making the Connection: Reframing the Violence

For me recounting these experiences is a testament to the power of narrative. Through them I relive the intensity of experiences in which I am both an insider and an outsider; through them I offer the reader a context for my analysis. In the act of telling I try to maintain an awareness of the complexities and tensions inherent in my own perspective position. I am any and all of the many aspects of my "identity." I am woman, Euro-American, professional, feminist, and a target of such violence in the past. All these aspects may be salient; they make the enterprise a complex and daunting one.

"To what extent do these accounts of your experiences in China, India, Pakistan, and Poland turn those women into the exotic 'other'?" a dear friend asks. At first I am non-plussed; then, in turn, irritated by, resentful of, and angry with the question—a certain sign that it is a good one. "I have always tried to be mindful of an 'imperial' or 'colonial' mentality and the temptation and trap of instant expertise which foreign travel encourages," I sputter.

But I know she is reminding me of two of the most serious and significant problems which recur in "Western" feminist analysis. The first problem is the construction of a category "woman." "Woman" is presented as a universal and homogenized category, but its referent is an ethnocentric one—the experience and representations generated by "Western, white, middle-class" culture. To the extent that "other" women are acknowledged as "woman," they are produced and represented as a composite, reductive, a historical singular "Third-World woman"—the "exotic" other. This construction of the category "woman," with its implicit exoticized and objectified counterpart, ignores or denies the complexity and diversity of women's lived material experience (Mohanty 1991). Not only is it a source of tension among women of different classes, cultures, and races in the United States, it also is a significant barrier between middle-class Euro-American women speaking as feminists and women in other countries. Of no less importance is the second problem. Travelogue narratives often assume a neocolonial posture: the Euro-American writer rediscovers herself in the mirror of the "other."

I recognize that it is at best, foolish and naive, and at worst, insensitive to believe that I am immunized from the temptation to ignore or minimize the specifics of context. Yet I am propelled by my response to the pain and denial I have encountered to find the appropriate inclusionary categories for these experiences. When I argue for a reframing of violence against women within a universalistic human rights framework, my goal is to utilize such categories.

My argument for adoption of an analysis of violence against women within a human rights framework does not rest solely upon the experiences I have detailed in the Prologue. I believe there are other, even more persuasive reasons which speak to the desirability of reframing the issue. Violence against women, especially in the home, may not be identified in many societies as a significant problem. Even if it is even recognized as a problem, all too often it is distinguished from other forms of punishable violence in a society; this distinction confines it to the category of "discipline" or response to "provocation"; it is minimized, or denied, or viewed as individual and aberrant rather than a culturally justified and endorsed systemic practice designed to silence and to coerce a clearly identifiable population. These outcomes are the most important and compelling reasons for removing the analysis of the violence from the realm of the private, from the confining reach of the culturally specific, and from the arbitrary and limiting boundary of the nation-state. The absence of a broad, transnational, and transcultural indictment of the violence constitutes a telling statement about women as citizens; they are the targets of unpunishable and, therefore, implicitly endorsed violence.

There are two segments to my reframing endeavor. The first step, in the next section, reconsiders the implications of the American common-law doctrine of coverture, which structured marital property arrangements in the United States from colonial times to the end of the nineteenth century; the second step, in the final section, moves from coverture in the United States to the international human rights arena to develop the argument that violence against women is a form of terrorism.

Reading many of the reported nineteenth-century divorce cases, one is struck by wives' allegations of extensive, recurring, physical violence. It becomes apparent that underpinning and reinforcing the common-law doctrine of a husband's control over marital property was the unpublished infliction of violence upon his wife. In other words, violence against women in the home was the readily available and normatively endorsed accompaniment of coverture.

By the late nineteenth century many of the formal incidents of coverture had been abolished, and married women were able to claim a separate legal identity. Nevertheless, the threat and actual occurrence of violence in their homes did not disappear; nor were efforts made by the state to deter it through punishment.

What are we to make of a situation in which specific formal structures of subordination and control articulated in legal doctrine are eliminated by legislative enactment and/or judicial construction, but the coercive practices of violence, or the threat of it, which support and maintain such subordination and control, are tacitly endorsed? Surely the coercion is critical to the maintenance of the subordination; surely the practitioners of that coercion are aware of the utility of their strategy. Can it be said that contemporary practitioners of such coercion actually reenact coverture by denying a separate identity to their spouse or partner? I am prepared to say that we can make such a connection and, thereby, explore the possibility that coverture has not yet been abolished in the United States.

I argue that such contemporary violence and the response of our legal system to it does constitute a current manifestation of what we conventionally consider the discarded and archaic American domestic relations common-law doctrine and practice, coverture, or the erasure of a separate legal identity for married women. More specifically, I suggest that a legal system which "naturalizes" violence against women in the home, by allowing perpetrators to act without fear of punishment by the state, is a legal system devoted·to maintaining control over women. For violence against women in the home was and is premised on beliefs regarding the "rightness" of male power and the "entitlement" of men to exercise control over women's behavior and actions.

Clearly this reexamination of old common-law doctrine is far more than a mere exhumation. It is an analysis designed to reconnect what scholars often sever by periodization.

Beyond the enterprise for its own sake there is another significant reason for such an inquiry. It is designed to connect women in the United States with women in other parts of the world where coverture clearly exists as a formal legal practice. I suggest that openness or responsiveness to the possibility that a version of coverture exists in our society requires us to revise our assessment of the assumed location of our "stage of development"; it is an antidote to self-serving proclamations about the "advanced" or "enlightened" (read "superior") status of American women.

The second step of the reframing is developed in the final section of this chapter. There I argue that the term "domestic violence" is burdened with undesirable cultural implications and limitations; this leads to an exploration of a more expansive international human rights framework.

Within that wider framework, however, there are several options. I elect to ground my analysis in the category of "terrorism," which I maintain has the greatest potential for accurately identifying the psychological, sociological, and political situation of women who are the targets of "naturalized" violence against them in the one place where they are most likely to be situated—their homes.

Coverture and Violence: The Construction of Legal Identity in Marriage

Ask any teacher of family law or property law about the shift in the status of married women in the United States and you will, in all likelihood, be referred to the Married Women's Property Act of 1848 in New York. The impact of this pioneering reform was the abolition of coverture in New York and other common-law jurisdictions by the end of the nineteenth century. Under the common-law doctrine of coverture, the legal identity of a married woman was merged with her husband; she was protected or sheltered—a *feme covert*. "By marriage, the husband and wife are one person in law; that is, the very being or legal existence of the woman is suspended during the marriage, or at least is incorporated and consolidated into that of the husband" (Blackstone 1765, p. 442). Under the New York reforms, married women were granted a separate legal identity which endowed them with the capacity and competence as a matter of law to participate in the commercial economy as separate legal persons.

Unpacking the logic of the doctrine of coverture is an instructive exercise; it reveals the relationship among gender, identity, and law. According to the logic of coverture, women must be (or need to be) supported; in order to ensure that support, women marry and engage in household services for their husbands. "Marriage obligates a wife to perform household services in return for benefit of her husband's duty of support, thus absorbing the wife's entire worth into the marital unit while requiring the husband's economic participation in that unit only to the extent of support" (Johnston, Jr. 1972, p. 103). These services constitute the entirety of women's *legally* cognizable contributions to a marriage; since contribution is the measure of worth, and women's contribution is nonmonetized service, their worth is easily and readily absorbed into the marriage relationship; absent any independent value attributable to their services and, therefore, to them, married women have no basis for a claim to a separate legal identity; as their worth is absorbed in an all-consuming relationship with their husbands, so, too, their identity is incorporated.

In a patriarchal world, all women are connected to men and derive their identity from their connection with men who are fathers, guardians, or husbands. In fact, the legal category *feme sole* for an adult woman was a residual one. It signalled the absence of a status relationship to a male as father, guardian, or spouse.

In contrast, men have legal identities as men, regardless of marital status, which "after marriage remain *sui juris* as fully as before the marriage" (*Burdine v. Amperse*, 1866); their adult "selves" are never totally absorbed, incorporated, or suspended in a marriage relationship. Under the common law, there appears to have been no comparable well-developed designation of *homme sole*,[1] since all men who were not slaves possessed an independent self and, therefore, full legal identity.

Coverture was not simply an isolated set of formal legal principles with handicapping consequences for women in the commercial economy of the colonies and the United States. It was a crucial component of a historically situated sex/gender system whose prevailing ideology provided a particular construction for the status relationships of both slave and nonslave women.

Coverture was a designation of limitation and exclusion. It encoded beliefs regarding women's capacity and competence to act in the world. It confirmed and validated a sex-based locus of virtually unaccountable power and control[2] in a marital relationship. It was a manifestation of cultural consciousness and a statement about the condition of citizenship.

To reinforce this identification of a sex-based locus of power and control, a wide range of culturally salient justifications were marshalled. The selective use of theology, political theory, and economics reinforced the claim that a family must have a clear, ascriptive locus of power—one that was sex-based. Theology connected family to God's kingdom, which was unquestionably hierarchical. An earthly manifestation of God's will and command, family must be structured like that kingdom; there must be a designated head of each family. And since, though God transcended the sex/gender system, the cultural referents for the Deity were male, hence the designated heads of His earthly will—*the family*—must also be male.[3]

Both political and economic theory reinforced the theologically ordained structure of family. Political theory identified the family as the building block or basis of society and the state, though women, even as family members, are virtually absent from the works of Western political theorists. Like a polity, a family must possess a hierarchical structure. Logically, there must be one designated head for a family whose will prevails by virtue of an assigned place in the structure.[4] The absence of a clear rule designating a head would create disharmony and strife in the family and, consequently, both in the polity and in the market which were best served by *a priori* clear—that is, sex-based—designations of competence in civic matters and in commercial transactions.

Separately, or in combination, these beliefs spoke to the self-evident "naturalness" of the family structure of coverture. Even a skeptic might be convinced by the array of theology, political theory, and economics which proffered dire predictions of societal disorder and chaos in the wake of any proposed separate legal identity for married women. No wonder that contesting this seemingly closed belief system was the first important task of nineteenth-century American feminism.

While the most economically disempowering aspects of the doctrine of coverture were officially abolished by the end of the nineteenth century, it was not until the final quarter of the twentieth century that the last formal vestiges of the doctrine in a commercial setting were eliminated. The enactment of the Equal Credit Opportunity Act[5] recognized the competence of all women, regardless of status, to establish creditworthiness on their own account.

Underscoring and ensuring the "naturalness" of a coverture regime's designation of sex-based power relationships were a set of enforcement rules. Under the English common law, the "rule of thumb" specified a "limitation" (using a rod no thicker than a thumb) upon the violence allowed to be inflicted on a wife. This doctrine and its American modification, which distinguished correction from abuse causing permanent injury, granted permission to a husband to inflict violence, characterized as "discipline" or "correction," upon his wife. In some cases, American judges appear to have distinguished such behavior from a "beating,"[6] for which an abused woman could initiate a peace warrant requiring the accused to post a bond assuring a stipulated period of peaceful behavior toward her. However, for all practical purposes the American version of the common-law doctrine served to "naturalize" violence against all nonslave women in that sphere to which they were assigned—the home. It upheld the principle that sex-based power and control in the home was desirable as a matter of law and public policy.[7]

Evidence for the frequency and pervasiveness of violence against women in the home is available from a wide array of sources, including writings and speeches of nineteenth-century marriage reformers, the arguments of supporters of prohibition, the reports of social workers in urban slums, and divorce cases in which wives accused their husbands of extreme cruelty (Pleck 1987). As a wife was expected to provide services to her husband, so, too, was she expected to obey him under threat of physical sanction, unless it became "unsafe for her to cohabit with him and be under his dominion and control" (*Palmer v. Palmer,* 1828).

Women seeking divorce had to meet threshold standards of danger to themselves, and had to reassure the court that their behavior demonstrated the womanly virtues of patience and forbearance (Perkins 1809; Lawrence 1832; Burr 1842) rather than the unworthy behaviors associated with "provocation" (Barrere 1819). Threats of violence without actual assault were not grounds for divorce (Hill 1806; Mason 1831; Kennedy 1878). Depending on the "character and condition of the parties" (a judicial politesse for class), even physical violence might not suffice (Bailey 1867). At least one court, in granting a divorce, relied on the dramatically articulated criterion of "the impossibility of her fulfilling the duties of matrimony in a state of dread" (Bailey 1867, p. 380). While several state statutes required persistent violent conduct to establish cruelty, others balanced continuity in the acts of violence against their severity, or denied divorces when "moderate force" was used (Schoulder 1944, pp. 90–94).

Though several states (Maryland, Delaware, and Oregon) were marginally responsive to the late nineteenth-century reformers' campaigns, and enacted legislation authorizing the whipping of abusive husbands, it was not until 1920 (two years after the passage of the women's suffrage amendment) that the beating of a wife had become illegal in all states (Pleck 1987, pp. 108–121). Despite the outlawing of such violence, the gap between law on the books and lived experience was a pronounced one. In fact, new "progressive" institutions such as Family Court, to which family abuse cases were routinely referred, focused on reconciliation rather than punishment, thereby sidestepping the issue of the violence. For the first six decades of the twentieth century, the battered woman's situation remained largely unchanged and unnoticed.

The demise of the formal doctrine of coverture did not signal the eradication of beliefs regarding the "naturalness" or appropriateness of sex-based power in marital relationships and the use of coercive means, including violence and abuse (Schuler 1992, p. 11), for securing or maintaining that power. In the interval between the formal elimination of coverture and the present, there is no reason to believe that the violence abated.

When the second wave of feminism began to interrogate the status of women (especially middle-class Euro-American women), emphasis was placed initially on pay equity, sexuality, and personal freedom. With the emergence in the seventies of rape and pornography as issues, contemporary feminists rediscovered battered women, and the, at times, lethal level of resistance on the part of men to efforts to divest them of privilege. I argue that the continuation of the violence, and the widespread failure of the state to address and punish it, are contemporary manifestations of the practice of coverture in the United States; the men who abuse or batter their spouse or partner practice that domination and control which is the *sine qua non* of coverture. I recognize that this claim is open to several challenges: ahistoricism, or at least the blurring or conflating of historical boundaries, or, worse yet, engagement in a mere semantic dispute. My answer is that this response is shortsighted and parochial. In no other relationship established and "privileged" by law or contract is such physical violence condoned; in no other relationship enjoying the protection of the state is such physical violence minimized or denied. Simply put, coverture cannot be said to have disappeared when its essential enforcement mechanism is available and widely used to maintain power and control in a marriage. That the structures of subordination persist in reshaped form is not unique to women's subordination in families. Critical race theorists understand well the premise that "contemporary inequalities and social institutional practices are linked to earlier periods in which the intent and cultural meaning of such practices were clear" (Matsuda et al. 1993, p. 6).

As a cofacilitator of court-mandated educational groups for batterers, I have repeatedly heard revealing statements of deeply held beliefs made by batterers which speak to the daily life practices of coverture—the muting or denying of a separate and separable identity for a partner or spouse. Men are "in charge" of a relationship; it must be structured to their liking or comfort; abuse and violence are among the means to "ensure" these outcomes and to control a partner or spouse who challenges the ordering of domestic life. "She provokes me because she knows what I like and what I don't like"; "she just needs to be smacked around once in a while to keep her in line"; "she needs to be reminded who is in charge"; "a little violence clears the air between us." These statements speak to well developed notions of sex-based power, control, and hierarchy. These men rely on strong gender-based differences in a clear, hierarchically ordered relationship which are supportive of and essential to coverture. As I listen to them, I envision a chorus of men at any point in history chanting a version of this litany.

Many of these men report surprise when they are arrested or brought before a judge. They often assert either that they had no idea that "there was a problem" or that their partner has distorted or exaggerated what transpired between them. They express contradictory reasons for their behavior: either they were deliberate and justified in their infliction of violence and abuse because they were provoked or attacked by their partner, or they were "out of control" because they were provoked and, therefore, are simultaneously not culpable and justified in their infliction of violence and abuse.

I have focused on personal statements made by batterers to suggest a new direction for evidence-gathering regarding the continuation of a belief system. I believe it would be a category mistake to identify these beliefs as individual pathologies, or the men who articulate them simply as desperately needy individuals. These attitudes and beliefs, and the practices they justify, are affirmations of shared social norms and conventions. These men, as they are quick to tell you, have acted upon their beliefs and "unfortunately" were "caught" by a legal system which is "unfair to men." Each of them has stories about friends or family members who also were or are abusive, but whose actions went or go unpunished.

Identifying and understanding contemporary manifestations of coverture provide an expanded perspective for the analysis of sex-based power relations and hierarchy in marriage and partnering. Such a perspective suggests additional interpretations for the coercing and silencing of women, and connects the coercion to a well-developed historic tradition. It creates opportunities for an additional meaningful level of connection and understanding among different women in the U.S., as well as with women in other parts of the world where coverture exists. It provides a context for developing an international response to the violence—one based on legal doctrines which transcend the boundaries and practices of any nation or state.

During the 1970s in the U.S., feminists identified painful and, at times, life-threatening conditions under which many women led their lives. Insisting on public discussion of these conditions, feminists argued that activities hitherto unrecognized or marginalized issues be placed on the nation's political agenda (Loseke 1992). "Wife abuse" was resurrected as a "public" not a "private" problem.

In their campaign to change ideology and reform practice, these feminists constructed a compelling reconfiguration of "wife abuse": the "battered woman." Men were identified as offenders whose violence was intended to maintain their power and control by any and all means available to them; women were the victims who do not create their victimization; the law enforcement and legal systems, through their failure to protect, were the source of battered women's revictimization. Abusive behaviors were identified as morally, socially, legally, and politically intolerable; battered women required and deserved public sympathy and support. By 1979, two new common classification categories, "battered spouse" and "battered woman," were added to the International Classification of Diseases Clinical Modification Scheme compiled by the U.S. National Center for Health Statistics. It was estimated that up to one half of all American women and approximately two thirds of women who are separated or divorced have been the targets of violence and abuse (Mahoney 1991, pp. 2, 10, 11).

As political and cultural activists, feminists are well aware that reframing, recasting, or recontextualizing issues such as abuse in the home is an exercise in unpacking ideology and interrogating consciousness, though the enterprise is sometimes dismissed as the stuff and substance of armchair scholarship. For example, in the pressing immediate world of law practice, where an order of protection for a battered woman or the disposition of the charge against the batterer may be the paramount issue, reframing may seem to be a marginal beneficial activity. Naming and categorizing is not a neutral activity; it is a deeply political one. For language exposes as well as masks. Recasting the "harmless" activity of "flirting" or being asked to provide "sexual favors" as sexual harassment exposed a dimension of the gendered power hierarchy in the workplace outside the home, and in the academy. Grappling with the development of adequate and sufficient terms to identify the relationships among the parties involved in various new reproductive technologies reveals the deep convictions we possess and the stereotypes we rely upon when reproduction and family life are at issue. The act of reframing has been and can continue to be important in changing legal outcomes.

Often recasting takes what is designated as a "personal situation" and identifies it as a social and political issue. Often, recasting provides a foundation for a re-viewing of an issue in new ways. In turn, this re-viewing may result in the emergence of new and different assessments and evaluations of a problem. Finally, this re-viewing may lead to the development of innovative strategies for the future.

What Do Terms Have to Do with It? International Human Rights and Terrorism in the Home

What terms and categories do we use when talking about the violence? What name do we assign to it and what cultural baggage does the particular designation carry?

I believe that there is a clear need to continue the reframing process for "violence" as a category in women's lives which was initiated by the "battered women's" movement of the 1970s. The process must be marked by searching, inspired, and informed scrutiny. It must not only be mindful of and sensitive to the difficulties and complexities generated by the use of violence against women to maintain power and control, but also attentive to the cumulative impact on women's lives of the denial of the existence of such violence (Mahoney 1991, pp. 10–18; Schneider 1992, pp. 520, 529–42).

If my claim that reframing begins with the exploration of language is persuasive, then the starting point for this portion of my analysis should be a focus on the use of language in identifying and detailing the violence. First, we must underscore the significance of not having explicit parallel language structures for different types of violence. Second, we must recognize that characterizing some violence as both "domestic" and "private" explicitly diminishes or minimizes its seriousness for women both in theory and practice (Nicholson 1988, pp. 220–21). Third, we must acknowledge the fact that retention of the modifying term "domestic" handicaps and narrows further inquiry.

When we talk about violence, we do not utilize the terms "stranger violence" and "domestic violence" as parallel terms. We separate out from "violence" abuse which occurs between partners or in a family by modifying and characterizing it with a term connoting a status relationship—"domestic." The unmodified term "violence" which is applied to situations not involving intimates is "real" and, therefore, clearly punishable. By its linguistic location, the category "domestic," which modifies and specifically locates violence, is residual and, perhaps, less clearly subject to disapproval or punishment. While we recognize the unmodified term "violence" as a strategy for asserting control and domination and creating terror, we may fail to make the same connection for the modified term, even though violence during a partnering relationship or at the time of separation is a strategy designed to achieve the same results.

Like the modifiers "marital" or "date" for rape, the term "domestic" modifying violence contextualizes and locates the activity or act in the "private" sphere—one governed by relationships of sexual intimacy and emotion. In such a complex and murky location, there is enormous, often unrecognized, cultural investment in minimizing the significance attached to the violence. Perhaps one of the most poignant examples is found in police practice. Calls to the emergency number 911 which are labeled as "domestics" may be treated as less important or serious than others;[8] law enforcement officers as well as judges may identify the incident as a "tiff," "spat," or "lover's quarrel."

Both critical legal theory and feminist theory underscore the salient message that there are no essential properties for the public/private dyad. Rather, the dyad provides justifications for particular political and economic practices and the legal doctrines which buttress them. Despite the designation of "domestic" as private, family and state are not unrelated institutions. Family socializes its members to accept a pattern of hierarchical gender relations; social, economic, religious, and cultural institutions assist in perpetuating male control over women's sexuality, mobility, and labor, inside and outside the home; the state provides the legal basis for family and other institutions to perpetuate these relations.

"Domestic" is not merely a physical or spatial locale. It encompasses status relationships which have both political and legal boundaries and consequences. Invoking the term "domestic" signals the segregation and delimitation of inquiry and critique in the United States, in other societies, and in the international law context. In the United States, the attribution of the term "domestic relations" to an issue tends to remove it from a national civil rights agenda. Such a move denies or severs connection to one of the most enlightened dimensions in contemporary American jurisprudence. In this instance, the term "domestic" trumps and, thereby, narrows the focus of inquiry. In societies subject to colonization or imperial penetration, the term "domestic" is often an integral part of nationalist ideology. It signals the locus for the preservation of tradition, and usually designates women as responsible for maintaining it—albeit under male guidance and control. This designation of women as "preservers of tradition" is paradoxical. Often it is the rationale for a concomitant denial of women's capacity outside the home; in turn, it may serve to shield the violence in the home from public scrutiny. The violence remains part of tradition.

In an international law context, "domestic" signals that the subject matter is internal to the nation-state, rather than a matter subject to scrutiny and review by the international community. When challenged by international human rights advocates, the formulaic defensive response of classifying the violence as "domestic," especially when the issue is, more accurately, a "domestic" issue embedded within a "domestic" issue, is extremely appealing. These disparate and politically counterproductive connotations of the term "domestic" should suffice to give one pause prior to adopting the term "domestic violence" as a legal category. To avoid the burden of undesirable cultural, political, and legal implications, I suggest that we replace it.

One possible replacement option is a category which has significant cultural purchase in the United States—civil rights. Using this approach, crimes inside and outside the home which are motivated by the victim's gender are bias crimes that violate the victim's right to be free from discrimination on the basis of gender. Like race-targeted violence, gender-targeted violence is understood as silencing a victim. This reduction to a subservient status is, presumably, the antithesis of our shared beliefs regarding human dignity. One commentator expands the boundaries of the civil rights analysis by suggesting the similarities between the situations of battered women and involuntary servitude, since outbreaks of violence are often triggered when the batterer believes that the target has failed to serve him in the way he deserves and desires (McConnell 1992).

Undoubtedly eliminating the scope and purview of civil rights for women by incorporating gender-based conditions which deny or seriously hamper the exercise of such rights does invigorate and enhance the protections of citizenship for women. In fact, advocates in the U.S.

Congress[9] have introduced a legislative package which relies on this approach. They recognize its specific cultural resonance in the United States. Nevertheless, a civil rights perspective is limited in its appeal for other societies whose historic and political experience differs markedly from our own, even if the violence against women in the home is a common denominator. I believe that we are better served by relying on an international human rights framework. I am persuaded that the value of this broader perspective lies in its inclusive "bottom line." As international human rights theory and practice move beyond the limitations and constraints of traditional, Western, liberal, political theory, they articulate an expansive vision which substitutes a global "our" for a narrower "my" rights. We know that family violence, especially wife abuse, is a widespread phenomenon (Levinson 1989, pp. 7, 33–36); the global "our" is clearly applicable to it, despite the fact that "some acts of violation are not crimes in law, other are legitimized in custom or court opinion, and most are blamed on the victims themselves."[10]

For Euro-American feminists, there is an additional benefit in using the international human rights approach. We can resituate ourselves in the international community; we can confront and address the privilege of white skin and middle-classness in most of our outlook and analysis. As we interrogate the violence we can connect violence against women as a major issue in human rights and, therefore, in development theory and in practice for *all* parts of the world, including our own.

The attractiveness of the discourse of international human rights resides in its reliance on legal principles which will realize human dignity. International human rights *naturally* inhere in the human person and are inalienable;[11] they are neither granted by the state, nor are they the result of one's actions in the performance of duties or obligations (Donnelly 1982, p. 305). Rather, they "logically and morally take precedence over the rights of the state and the society, which are viewed as major contributors to the realization of these rights and also the greatest potential violators of basic human rights" (Donnelly 1982, p. 306). These rights are challenges both to the averted gaze of society and to the official indifference of the state.

> Having a right places someone in a protected position. To violate someone's right is not merely to fail to do what is right but also to commit a special and important personal offense against the rightholder by failing to give him [sic] his [sic] due, that to which he [sic] is entitled. To violate a right goes well beyond merely falling short of some high moral standard. (Donnelly 1982, p. 304)

At times, human rights principles are posited as conflicting with particular cultural practices. Cultural relativists, those who stress the importance of regarding social and cultural practices from the standpoint of members of the community of practitioners, are quick to point out that there is a definitive set of beliefs and customs which can or ought to establish criteria for a moral or legal evaluation of a practice. Yet it is important to emphasize that despite their announced relativist perspective, at least some cultural relativists become cultural absolutists, especially when practices involving women as the keepers of tradition are the focus of controversy (Bunch and Carrillo 1991, p. 2). An excellent example of such a colloquy is the response to culturally external critical judgments regarding female genital excision. Practitioners claim that it underpins their community social structure and *must* be retained, despite the danger it poses to women's health and lives. Such a claim not only presumes that culture is fixed and static, but also that it is brittle and incapable of creative adaptation. It is reminiscent of the formulaic justifications for coverture in nineteenth-century America.

Staking out an international human rights claim for the issue of violence against women is by no means coterminus with an uncritical acceptance of or satisfaction with the language and interpretation of existing international covenants, declarations, and conventions.[11] Many of these documents have been written with a male referent, even when gender-neutral language is employed; they have been interpreted through the lens of a widely shared sex/gender system which privileges the power and authority of men. Not surprisingly, women's rights discourse occupies the unenviable position of being generally positioned at the periphery of human rights discourse, both challenging and defending the dominant human rights model as it attempts to fit its causes into that model" (Engle 1992, p. 519).[12]

The Universal Declaration of Human Rights, for example, entitles all to "the rights and freedoms set forth in this Declaration, without distinction of any kind, such as race, color, sex, language, religion, political opinion, national or social property, birth or other status" (UDHR, Article 2). Those women who fought for the inclusion of "sex" in the declaration intended the provision to address the problems of women's subordination. Nevertheless, the "universal human rights" identified in the declaration may not be applied to practices affecting women. The most telling oversight or omission for purposes of this essay can be found in the fact that although the declaration states "No one shall be subjected to torture or to inhuman or degrading treatment or punishment" (UDHR, Article 5), the provision has not been interpreted to apply to the battering or the raping of a wife by her husband.

In addition to general universal declarations, there are international instruments containing specific enumerations of rights designed for particular categories of persons. The Convention on the Elimination of All

Forms of Discrimination Against Women (CEDAW), proposed in 1979, is the most salient one for this inquiry. Article 15 of the convention provides that State Parties "shall" (not merely "take all appropriate measures") accord the rights of legal personhood to women. This commitment and directive for women's full legal capacity is based on the premise that women's essential human rights require recognition of women's legal and *de facto* capacity to conduct themselves as responsible adults (Freeman 1993). While this provision of the convention challenges the doctrine of coverture, the convention makes no mention of violence against women, which underpins and supports coverture.

In 1989, this lacuna was noted by the Committee on the Elimination of Discrimination Against Women, which monitors CEDAW (*CEDAW Newsletter* 1989, p. 2). That same year the commonwealth countries relied upon an interpretation of Article 5 of the convention which calls for the modification of social and cultural patterns, sex roles, and stereotyping that are based on the idea of the inferiority or the superiority of either sex as applying to violence against women.[13] At the March, 1992, meeting of the U.N. Commission on the Status of Women, a document which defined violence against women as "any act, omission, controlling behavior or threat, in any sphere, which results in or is likely to result in physical, sexual or psychological injury to women" (*Women News* 1991, p. 1) was issued by the commission. This definition includes wife battering, nonspousal violence, and marital rape.

That same year CEDAW issued General Recommendation No. 19 which moved beyond the traditional parameters of analyzing violence perpetuated or condoned by the state. That recommendation identifies gender-based violence as discrimination which violates women's human rights, and notes the close connection between discrimination, violence, and violations of human rights and fundamental freedoms. It specifies that the Convention on the Elimination of Discrimination Against Women covers both public and private acts by stating that no woman is free or enjoys human rights when violence against women is tolerated by her country, community, employer, or family. It interprets the convention so that gender-based violence is contrary to numerous specific articles. Additionally it urges governments to take legal and other measures to prevent such violence (International Women's Rights Action Watch, 1992, p. 28).

Some scholars voice concerns that "special" conventions such as the Convention on the Elimination of Discrimination Against Women may marginalize groups outside the human rights mainstream. They argue that "it seems strange that 53% of the world's population should require 'special' treatment under a particular treaty. This would seem to imply that 'human' rights do not incorporate 'women's rights', leading to the further conclusion that 'human' rights are indeed 'mens' rights, inapplicable to many women" (Chinken and Wright 1992, p. 103). While acknowledging the timeliness of this concern and critique, it must be recalled that the greatest impetus for addressing the issue of violence against women has been generated by interpretation and expansion of the provisions of CEDAW, rather than by reliance on other international human rights documents which are not population-specific and which, either as written or as interpreted, have not been fully responsive to the scale and scope of the issue of violence against women.

In the spirit and tenor of expanded and revisionist interpretation of the issue of violence against women in their homes, for the term "domestic violence" I propose substitution of the term "terrorism." I have adopted the term only after much careful consideration. Initially, when I considered reframing the term "domestic violence," I hesitated. Why? Acknowledgment of the term "terrorism" was *frightening,* even as I recognized that it encoded unarticulated dimensions of women's experiences with violence. Conceptually and psychologically, the terms "sex-based discrimination" and "violence" seem easier to manage than "terrorism." But, as I have allowed myself to work through the implications of this reframing, I am increasingly persuaded of the usefulness of the term.

We all share some derivative knowledge about "terrorism"—even if only through powerful television images and sound bites. We may not wish to fly on certain airlines or visit certain places because we have been informed of terrorist threats or have seen actual incidents; we may have traveled in countries where we are warned not to pick up seemingly innocuous unopened packages or bags left unattended. In its conventional usage, "terrorism" refers to a political stance and a strategy of governance or opposition to a government. Terrorism relies on well-developed tactics of intimidation and coercion, buttressed by physical violence. Whether it is used to defend privileges or to threaten and challenge them, the underlying premise is the destabilization of a civilian population (Taussig 1989).

Regimes or groups seeking to terrorize populations utilize three tactics to enhance their credibility: unannounced and seemingly random but actually calculated attacks of violence; psychological as well as physical warfare aimed at silencing protests and minimizing retaliatory responses from the targets of violence; and the creation of an atmosphere of intimidation in which there is no safe place of escape. Whether terrorist intimidation relies on tactics in which the identity of the particular target is incidental to the overall objective, or whether it is directed toward a particular identified individual or category of persons, the results may be similar. People may not be able to judge when and whether they are safe or at risk. Personal identity and human connection are deeply compromised; they are replaced by a widespread sense of insecurity, passivity, and defeatism.

"Terror works through an inner voice quoting the outer madness . . . like other systems (it) possesses an underlying structure, its own grammar as it were" (Suarez-Orozco 1990, p. 366) which includes: shared denial, followed by defensive rationalizations, and, eventually, by internalization/ elaboration of the terror. The denial consists of "knowing what not to know" or "percepticide" (Suarez-Orozco 1990, p. 367).[14] The ensuing rationalization involves the substitution of a plausible, at times formulaic reason for some self-serving motive. The third stage, internalization/ elaboration of the terror, is only possible when the imminent danger subsides. It consists of the terror returning in the form of a new conscious-ness of events and images previously denied, forbidden, and only half-known—a compulsion to speak the unspeakable (Suarez-Orozco 1990, pp. 366, 369–70).

Not all persons who also become targets of terrorism respond in similar ways or even in a consistent manner over time. Characterizing the targets of terrorism as either only victims or only resisters of the terror risks overstructuring or overdefining them. Some targets may respond by acts directed against the perpetrators of the violence; other targets may consider their very survival as a challenge to the terrorism; yet others may succumb to understandable feelings of defeat and denial. Conventional general categories of class, race, or ethnicity are not accurate predictors of individual responses to the violence.

There are strong and striking parallels and similarities between terror-ism as a strategy used to destabilize a community or society consisting both of women and men, and the abuse and violence perpetrated against women in intimate or partnering situations. Like terror directed at a community, violence against women is designed to maintain domination and control, to enhance or reinforce advantages, and to defend privi-leges. Like other individuals or communities who experience politically motivated terrorism, women whose partnering and intimate relationships are marked by violence directed against them live in a world similarly punctuated by traumatic and/or catastrophic events, such as threats and humiliation, stalking and surveillance, coercion and physical violence. Within a family structure, women are likely to be the targets of violence, and men are likely to be the perpetrators. Whether the violence is identi-fied as the imposition of discipline, as a strategy of family governance, or as an act of masculinity, the consequences are the same. Women learn that they can be kept in their culturally and socially designated "place" by the threat or imposition of physical injury.

The threat of violence which is paradoxically both predictable and unpredictable, the seeming omnipotence and omniscience of the perpetrator, the fear of possible harm to other loved ones, the threatened or actual loss of social attachments all serve to construct an often unescapably violent world for the woman who is the target of the violence. These "traumatic events overwhelm the ordinary systems of care that give people a sense of control, connection and meaning ... (they) generally involve threats to life or bodily integrity, or a close personal encounter with violence and death" (Herman 1992, p. 33). The reaction to such traumatic or catastrophic events experienced by many targeted women is more than fear for their immediate safety or the safety of their children; they may be immobilized; the trauma of the violence governs, guides, or influences their actions and decisions (Loseke 1992, pp. 20, 36; Kelly 1988, p. 120). In such situations survival becomes a form of resistance to the terrorism.

"Traumatic events may sever normally integrated functions (such as physiological arousal, action, cognition and memory) from one another" (Herman 1992, p. 34). Over time, numbing or constrictive symptoms may replace alternating feelings of unpredictability and helplessness. For example, in order to cope with the coercion and physical violence, the targeted woman may experience "disowning" her own body.[15] To the observer, "the traumatized person may no longer seem frightened and may resume the outward forms of her previous life. But the severing of events from their ordinary meanings and the distortion in the sense of reality persist" (Hoff 1990, p. 48).

Just as persons caught in situations of politically inspired terrorism display a range of responses to the fear and tragedy it generates, so too, women whose experience in partnering situations is marked by violence demonstrate a variety of behaviors and coping mechanisms for their situation.[16] Unlike targets of conventionally defined terrorism, however, women in violent partnering relationships who are the targets of terror often do not elicit sympathy or respect for the oppression they face. All too often the inquiry reverts to the nature and extent of their "provoking" the violence and abuse inflicted upon them. In this conceptual shift they and their experiences are disconnected from the social, cultural, economic, and political context of domination and subordination. Instead they become the incarnation of stereotypes such as "nagging bitch," woman with a "bad attitude," or a castrating female. Their responses to the violence are critically evaluated according to culturally endorsed images of individuals as autonomous, mobile, and able to take charge of their lives.

In this exercise of connecting "terrorism" to domestic violence and of folding this reframed issue of domestic violence into human rights discourse in a more compelling and challenging manner, I am aware of the pitfalls attendant on the enterprise. I have relied on outlining the profoundly similar disruptive psychological and social consequences of terrorist violence in different contexts to establish the grounds for re-framing the issue of violence against women as a form of "terrorism." In so doing, I hope I have moved beyond a simplistically reductionist psychological explanation for the violence, to the political and cultural context of gender-based power and control. In situations of politically inspired terrorism directed against civilian populations, the governing questions are not: Why didn't people flee? or: What is the particular incident which forms the basis for the claim of terror? or: What is the reasonable response in such a situation—all queries that mask the struc-ture of domination by focusing on the targets alone. Similarly, the issue in situations of violence and abuse in the home is not: Why didn't she leave? or: What particular incident is the basis for her claim? or: What would constitute a reasonable response in her situation? Rather the que-ries should be: Who benefits from allowing the violence to continue often unabated? What structures does violence in the home against women reinforce? What explains the ferocity of the denial of the violence? The answers to these questions might also shed some light on our hesitancy to label "domestic" violence a form of terrorism.

Notes

I thank my research assistant Debbie Gottschalk and acknowledge the ongoing generous support and encouragement of Professors Martha Fineman, Martha Chamellas, Judy Scales-Trent, Liz Schneider, Linda Kerber, and the ongoing strict scrutiny of Professors Betsy Cromley, Hester Eisenstein, Claire Kahane, Carolyn Korsmeyer, Liz Kennedy, and Carol Zemel.

1. For a rather unusual contemporary situation in which an *homme sole* category has been constructed by a court, see Dill 1984. The Virginia court avoided an equal protection challenge by construing two provisions of the Virginia statute allowing for a *feme sole* equitable estate (thereby barring a surviving husband from exercising his curtesy) to create by implication an *homme sole* estate (which would permit a husband to bar his widow from exercising her dower rights).

2. See Grossberg 1985, pp. 5–6, for a discussion of the seeming inconsistency and incompatibility between early republican characterizations of men in the polity and men as governors of the home. See, also, Hartog (1991).

3. See Genesis 3:16 (man is woman's master as a result of Eve's temptation); 1 Cor. 11:3 (man is to woman as Jesus Christ is to man).

4. Tyler 1868, p. 313–14, relies on arguments of men's physical strength and their worldliness, aptitude for business, and, therefore, "more judgment" as compared with women. He acknowledges that there "are exceptions . . . but the law designs to keep in view the ordinary course of things."

5. Equal Credit Opportunity Act, 15 USCA ss 1691–9(e).

6. See *People v. Winters*, Decisions in Criminal Cases, Clinton Oyer and Terminer, 10 July, 1823. Husband has no right to beat his wife or inflict punishment on her, but

he may defend himself against her and may restrain her from acts of violence towards himself or towards others, for he is accountable for her acts which injure others (wife interfered with husband's disciplining of their child and "made such noise as to alarm the neighborhood"); William Brook's Case, The New York City Hall Recorder, 66, 1821. Man has a right to govern his family but not to beat his wife.

7. "The common law has given the husband sufficient power over the wife, to render the interference of a court unnecessary in all ordinary cases." *Perry v. Perry*, 501–502 (1831) (defendant wife's cruel and violent behavior constitutes grounds for divorce).

8. Empirical research regarding Buffalo Police Department compliance with a court-approved settlement by a SUNY Buffalo law student, Ruth Yashpan (on file with Isabel Marcus).

9. At this writing a proposed federal Violence Against Women Act, which focuses on rape and domestic violence, is being considered by the U.S. Senate (S. 11) and the House of Representatives (H.R. 1133).

10. Bunch and Carrillo 1991, p. 7, citing G. A. Shwarth, "Of Violence and Violation: Women and Human Rights" (1986).

11. "One cannot fully renounce, transfer or otherwise alienate one's human rights. To do so would be to destroy one's humanity, to de-nature oneself, to become other (less) than a human being and thus is viewed as a moral impossibility." (Donnelly 1982).

12. Engle (1992) identifies three approaches taken by women's rights advocates: doctrinalist, institutionalist, and external critique. She considers the first two approaches consistent with liberal feminism and the third approach identified with radical or cultural feminists.

13. Bunch and Carrillo 1991, citing "CEDAW: The Reporting Process—A Manual for Commonwealth Jurisdictions" (1989).

14. The term "percepticide" was coined by a psychoanalyst, Juan Carlos Kusnetzoff.

15. See Hoff 1990, pp. 34–37, for first-person narratives from women in the U.S. For accounts by women from different countries, see Schuler 1992, pp. 49–256. For a discussion of the relationship between victim and torturer, see Timerman 1981. Timerman identifies his passivity as a mechanism for preserving his energy and strength to withstand torture (p. 34–35).

16. See Schneider 1992, p. 548–67, for a discussion of the new dilemmas posed by the continuing tension between notions of victim and agency.

The Violence of Privacy

by Elizabeth M. Schneider

Marriage is a coming together for better or for worse, hopefully enduring and intimate to the degree of being sacred. It is an association that
promotes a way of life, not causes; a harmony in living, not political
faiths; a bilateral loyalty, not commercial or social projects. Yet it is an
association for as noble a purpose as any involved in our prior decisions.
Griswold v. Connecticut, 1965

Introduction

Griswold v. Connecticut, from which the text above is taken, has been
heralded for introducing a new era of possibility for the right to privacy.
In the years since *Griswold* was decided, protection of a sphere of family
privacy from state interference has been viewed as "good." Yet, understood through a lens of gender, and more particularly shaped by the
experiences of battered women, the concept of privacy is more complex
and ambiguous.

The notion of the family as a sphere of privacy, immune from state
interference, is central to *Griswold.* But *Griswold* involved a state law
that prohibited contraception and is premised on an idealized vision of
marriage as "enduring and intimate," promoting "harmony in living."
For women in the United States, intimacy with men, in and out of marriage, too often results in violence. The concept of freedom from state
intrusion into the marital bedroom takes on a different meaning when
it is violence that goes on in that space. The concept of marital privacy,
established as a constitutional principle in *Griswold,* historically has been
the key ideological rationale for state refusal to intervene to protect
battered women[1] within ongoing intimate relationships.

This chapter explores the ways in which concepts of privacy permit,
encourage, and reinforce violence against women, focusing on the complex interrelationship between notions of "public" and "private" in our
social understandings of woman abuse.[2] Historically, male battering of
women was untouched by law, protected as part of the private sphere of
family life. Over the last twenty years, however, as the battered women's
movement in this country has made issues of battering visible, battering
is no longer perceived as a purely "private" problem, and has taken on

dimensions of a "public" issue. There has been an explosion of legal reform and social service efforts: the development of battered women's shelters and hotlines, many state and federal governmental reports, and much state legislation. New legal remedies for battered women have been developed which have been premised on the idea of battering as a "public" harm. However, at the same time, there is widespread resistance to acknowledgment of battering as a "public" issue. The ideological tenacity of conceptions of battering as "private" is revealed in the United States Supreme Court's decision in *DeShaney v. Winnebago County Department of Social Services* (1989), in the inadequacy of legal reform efforts to date, and in tensions that exist within the battered women's movement.

The concept of privacy poses a dilemma and a challenge to theoretical and practical work on woman abuse. The notion of marital privacy has been a source of oppression of battered women and has helped to maintain women's subordination within the family. However, a more affirmative concept of privacy, one that encompasses liberty, equality, freedom of bodily integrity, autonomy, and self-determination, is important to women who have been battered. The challenge is not simply to reject privacy for battered women and opt for state intervention, but to develop both a more nuanced theory of where to draw the boundaries between public and private, and a theory of privacy that is empowering.

This work is an effort to begin a conversation about the complex role that concepts of privacy do play and might play in work on woman abuse. It builds on earlier work on the role of law and concepts of public and private (Taub and Schneider 1982), particularly in the area of woman abuse (Schneider 1986b, pp. 644–48; Schneider 1986a), and the affirmative potential of privacy (Schneider 1991, pp. 179). I begin with a brief overview of the meanings of "public" and "private" in American family life. I then move to a discussion of three different dimensions of the way in which notions of privacy affect both theory and practice in this area. First, I explore current legal reform efforts on behalf of battered women, and examine the persistence of denial of battering as a "public" issue. Second, I identify shifting parameters of "public" and "private" in reform efforts on woman abuse. Finally, I return to *Griswold* and argue for the development of affirmative conceptions of privacy linked to autonomy to enhance battered women's empowerment.

Privacy: The Meanings of Public and Private

Historically, the dichotomy of "public" and "private" has been viewed as an important construct for understanding gender. The traditional notion of "separate spheres" is premised on a dichotomy between the "private" world of family and domestic life (the "women's" sphere), and the "public" world of marketplace (the "men's" sphere) (Olsen 1983, pp. 1499–1501). Nadine Taub and I have discussed elsewhere the difference between the role of law in the public and private spheres (Taub and Schneider 1982, p. 117). In the public sphere, sex-based exclusionary laws join with other institutional and ideological constraints to directly limit women's participation (Taub and Schneider 1982, p. 121). In the private sphere, the legal system operates more subtly. The law claims to be absent in the private sphere, and has historically refused to intervene in ongoing family relations (Taub and Schneider 1982, p. 121).

> Tort law, which is generally concerned with injuries inflicted on individuals, has traditionally been held inapplicable to injuries inflicted by one family member on another. Under the doctrines of interspousal and parent-child immunity, courts have consistently refused to allow recoveries for injuries that would be compensable but for the fact that they occurred in the private realm. In the same way, criminal law fails to punish intentional injuries to family members. Common law and statutory definitions of rape in most states continue to carve out a special exception for a husband's forced intercourse with his wife. Wife beating was initially omitted from the definition of criminal assault on the ground that a husband had the right to chastise his wife. Even today, after courts have explicitly rejected the definitional exception and its rationale, judges, prosecutors, and police officers decline to enforce assault laws in the family context. (Taub and Schneider 1982, pp. 121–22)

Although a dichotomous view of the public sphere and the private sphere has some heuristic value, and considerable rhetorical power, the dichotomy is overdrawn (Kerber 1988, p. 17). The notion of a sharp demarcation between public and private has been widely rejected by feminist and critical legal studies scholars (Freeman and Mensch 1987; Minow 1990a, pp. 156–60; Symposium 1982). There is no realm of personal and family life that exists totally separate from the research of the state. The state defines both the family, the so-called private sphere, and the market, the so-called public sphere. "Private" and "public" exist on a continuum.

Thus, in the so-called private sphere of domestic and family life, which is purportedly immune from law, there is always the selective application of law. Significantly, this selective application of law invokes "privacy" as a rationale for immunity in order to protect male domination. For example, when the police do not respond to a battered woman's call for assistance, or when a civil court refuses to evict her assailant, the woman is relegated to self-help, while the man who beats her receives the law's tacit encouragement and support (Olsen 1983, pp. 1507, n. 39, 1537).

Indeed, we can see this pattern in recent legislative and prosecutorial efforts to control women's conduct during pregnancy, in the form of "fetal" protection laws. These laws are premised on the notion that women's childbearing capacity, and pregnancy itself, subject women to public regulation and control. Thus, pregnant battered women may find themselves facing criminal prosecution for drinking liquor, but the man who battered them is not prosecuted.[3]

The rhetoric of privacy that has insulated the female world from the legal order sends an important ideological message to the rest of society. It devalues women and their functions, and says that women are not important enough to merit legal regulation (Taub and Schneider 1982, p. 122).

> This message is clearly communicated when particular relief is withheld. By declining to punish a man for inflicting injuries on his wife, for example, the law implies she is his property and he is free to control her as he sees fit. Women's work is discredited when the law refuses to enforce the man's obligation to support his wife, since it implies she makes no contribution worthy of support. Similarly, when courts decline to enforce contracts that seek to limit or specify the extent of the wife's services, the law implies that household work is not real work in the way that the type of work subject to contract in the public sphere is real work. These are important messages, for denying woman's humanity and the value of her traditional work are key ideological components in maintaining woman's subordinate status. The message of women's inferiority is compounded by the totality of the law's absence from the private realm. In our society, law is for business and other important things. The fact that the law in general claims to have so little bearing on women's day-to-day concerns reflects and underscores their insignificance. Thus, the legal order's overall contribution to the devaluation of women is greater than the sum of the negative messages conveyed by individual legal doctrines. (Taub and Schneider 1982, pp. 122–23)

Definitions of "private" and "public" in any particular legal context can and do constantly shift. Meanings of "private" and "public" are based on social and cultural assumptions of what is valued and important, and these assumptions are deeply gender-based. Thus, the interrelationship between what is understood and experienced as "private" and "public" is particularly complex in the area of gender, where the rhetoric of privacy has masked inequality and subordination. The decision about what we protect as "private" is a political decision that always has important "public" ramifications (Michelman 1990, p. 1794).

In general, privacy has been viewed as problematic by feminist theorists (MacKinnon 1989; Copelon 1988, p. 303; Minow 1990a). Privacy has seemed to rest on a division of public and private that has been oppressive to women and has supported male dominance in the family. Privacy reinforces the idea that the personal is separate from the political; privacy also implies something that should be kept secret. Privacy inures to the benefit of the individual, not the community. The right of privacy has been viewed as a passive right, one which says that the state cannot intervene (Copelon 1988).

However, some feminist theorists have also explored the affirmative role that privacy can play for women (Allen 1988). Privacy is important to women in many ways. It provides an opportunity for individual self-development, for individual decision-making, and for protection against endless caretaking (Allen 1988, pp. 70–72). In addition, there are other related aspects of privacy, such as notions of autonomy, equality, liberty, and freedom of bodily integrity, that are central to women's independence and well-being. For women who have been battered, these aspects of privacy are particularly important. In the following sections, I explore three dimensions of privacy in work on battered women that are aspects of this broader feminist critique. First, I examine how the legacy of viewing male battering of women as a "private" problem leads to denial of the seriousness of the problem. Second, I explore ways in which views of battering as "private" persist despite growing recognition of battering as a "public" problem. Finally, I speculate on ways that concepts of privacy might be used affirmatively to empower battered women, rather than to support abuse.

Dimensions of Privacy

The Denial of Power and the Power of Denial

The battered women's movement grew out of the rebirth of the women's movement in the 1960s, and it is one of the areas in which the women's movement has made an enduring contribution to law. Like sexual harassment, the "problem" of battering and the social and legal construct of a "battered woman" did not exist in this country until the women's movement named it.[4] The battered women's movement revealed to the public hidden and private violence. Over the last twenty years, the battered women's movement has been involved in efforts to provide services for battered women, to create legal remedies to end abuse, and to develop public education efforts to change consciousness about battering. The battered women's movement saw battering as an aspect of fundamental gender relations, as a reflection of male power and female subordination.[5]

As a result of the battered women's movement during the last two decades, the general problem of domestic violence and the more specific problems of battered women have entered public consciousness in the United States. The severe problems that battered women face have been documented by government reports,[6] legal and social science literature,[7] and media reports, including front-page headlines, coverage of trials and television programs.[8] State[9] and federal[10] legislative reforms have focused on improving the legal remedies available to battered women, and support services for battered women have been developed (Schneider 1990b, pp. 59–64).

Domestic violence is the leading cause of injury to women in the United States (U.S. House, 100th Congress, 1987). According to FBI statistics, one woman in the United States is beaten every eighteen seconds (*Report of the Gender Bias Study of the Supreme Judicial Court*, 1989, p. 584). Between two thousand and four thousand women die every year from abuse (Federal Bureau of Investigation, U.S. Department of Justice, 1984). Thirty percent of all women killed every year are slain by their partners (*Report of the Gender Bias Study of the Supreme Judicial Court*, 1989, p. 584). Battering of women by their husbands or men with whom they are in intimate relationships cuts across racial, class, ethnic, and economic lines.[11] Police involvement, nationally, in cases of domestic violence exceeds involvement in murder, rape, and all forms of aggravated assault.

Woman abuse is an aspect of the basic gender inequality built into the very fabric of American family law. Myths concerning battered women, for example, that they provoke and like the violence, are widespread (Gordon 1988, pp. 281–88). The police and the courts have historically failed to intervene to protect battered women because battering is perceived as a "private" problem, neither serious nor criminal. When the battered women's movement began, battered women had, effectively, no legal remedies.[12]

Over the last twenty years, there has been considerable change. There is now a wide range of groups and organizations that have emerged around the country to assist battered women. These groups have developed a range of approaches. They have focused their efforts on providing services to battered women, by founding shelters for battered women, setting up telephone hotlines, challenging police practices that fail to intervene effectively to protect battered women, and working to advance legislation that offers legal remedies for battered women. Some groups also have developed programs to work with battering men.[13]

Today there is greater public familiarity with these problems. Federal and state task forces have recommended reforms of legal, social welfare, and health care systems (Schneider 1990b, pp. 20–24). Some lawsuits against the police have compelled police departments to arrest batterers (*Thurman v. Torrington*, 1984; *Bruno v. Codd*, 1977; *Nearing v. Weaver*,

1983). Almost all states now have domestic violence legislation providing for orders of protection for women, and legal sanctions for their violation and/or criminal remedies for battering.[14] In short, there has been an explosion of law reform efforts to assist battered women.

Work on issues of battered women is now at a turning point. Some reforms have been institutionalized, and problems of battered women have achieved credibility and visibility. To some degree, a public dimension to the problem is now recognized. However, federal, state, and private funding resources put into these reform efforts have been small. There has been little change in the culture of female subordination that supports and maintains abuse. At the same time, there is a serious backlash to these reform efforts, and many of the reforms that have been accomplished are in serious jeopardy. For the last several years, while writing a report on national legal reform efforts for battered women for The Ford Foundation (Schneider 1990b), I have been amazed at the enormous accomplishments of the battered women's movement over the last twenty years. Indeed, I can think of few recent social movements that have accomplished so much in such a short time.

However, I have also been stunned by the depth of social resistance to change. Although battering has evolved from a "private" to a more "public" issue, it has not become a serious political issue, precisely because it has profound implications for all of our lives (Bunch 1989, p. 74). Battering is deeply threatening. It goes to our most fundamental assumptions about the nature of intimate relations and the safety of family life. The concept of male battering of women as a "private" issue exerts a powerful ideological pull on our consciousness because, in some sense, it is something that we would like to believe.[15] By seeing woman abuse as "private," we affirm it as a problem that is individual, that only involves a particular male-female relationship, and for which there is no social responsibility to remedy. Each of us needs to deny the seriousness and pervasiveness of battering, but more significantly, the interconnectedness of battering with so many other aspects of family life and gender relations. Instead of focusing on the batterer, we—as a society—focus on the battered woman, scrutinize her conduct, examine her pathology and blame her for leaving the relationship, in order to maintain that denial and refuse to confront the issues of power. Focusing on the woman, not the man, perpetuates the power of patriarchy. Denial supports and legitimates this power; the concept of privacy is a key aspect of this denial.

Denial takes many forms and operates on many levels.[16] Men deny battering in order to protect their own privilege. Women need to deny the pervasiveness of the problem so as not to link it to their own life situations. Individual women who are battered tend to minimize the violence in order to distance themselves from some internalized negative concept of "battered woman." I see denial in the attitudes of jurors, who try to remove themselves and say: It could never happen to me; if it did, I would handle it differently (Bochnak, et al. 1981; Koonan and Waller 1989 p. 18; Note 1988, p. 598). I see denial in the public engagement in the Hedda Nussbaum/Joel Steinberg case, which focused on Hedda Nussbaum's complicity, and involved feminists in active controversy over the boundaries of victimization.[17] The findings of the many state task force reports on gender bias in the courts have painstakingly recorded judicial attitudes of denial.[18] Clearly, there is serious denial on the part of state legislators, members of Congress, and the Executive Branch, who never mention battering as an important public issue. In battering, we see both the power of denial and the denial of power. The concept of privacy is an ideological rationale for this denial and serves to maintain it.

The concept of privacy encourages, reinforces, and supports violence against women. Privacy says that violence against women is immune from sanction, that it is permitted, acceptable and part of the basic fabric of American family life. Privacy says that what goes on in the violent relationship should not be the subject of state or community intervention. Privacy says that it is an individual and not a systemic problem. Privacy operates as a mask for inequality, protecting male violence against women.

The Shifting Parameters of Private and Public

As work on battered women has evolved, social meanings of what is private and public, and the relationship between them, have become more complex, Traditionally, battering has been viewed as within the private sphere of the family, and therefore unprotected by law. Yet, as Martha Minow has suggested, this social failure to intervene in male battering of women on grounds of privacy should not be seen as separate from the violence, but as part of the violence.

> When clerks in a local court harass a woman who applies for a restraining order against the violence in her home, they are part of the violence. Society is organized to permit violence in the home; it is organized through images in mass media and through broadly based social attitudes that condone violence. Society permits such violence to go unchallenged through the isolation of families and the failures of police to respond. Public, rather than private patterns of conduct and morals are implicated. Some police officers refuse to respond to domestic violence;

some officers themselves abuse their spouses. Some clerks and judges think domestic violence matters do not belong in court. These failures to respond to domestic violence are public, not private, actions. (Minow 1990b, pp. 1671–72)

Although social failure to respond to problems of battered women has been justified on grounds of privacy, this failure to respond is an affirmative political decision that has serious public consequences. The rationale of privacy masks the political nature of the decision. Privacy thus plays a particularly subtle and pernicious ideological role in supporting, encouraging, and legitimating violence against women. The state plays an affirmative role in permitting violence against battered women by protecting the privileges and prerogatives of battering men and failing to protect battered women, and by prosecuting battered women for homicide when they protect themselves. These failures to respond, or selective responses, are part of "public patterns of conduct and morals" (Minow 1990b, pp. 1671–72).

Over the last several years, the meaning of what has been traditionally viewed as public and private, concerning issues of battered women, has shifted. In some sense, a public dimension of the problem has increased. There are now legal decisions that have held police forces liable for money damages for failure to intervene to protect battered women, an explosion of state legal remedies to protect battered women, and federal legislation to assist battered women in implementing remedies. All of these approaches suggest a more public dimension to the problem, or at least a recognition by governmental bodies, speaking with a public voice, that they must acknowledge and deal with the problem. Some of the rhetoric surrounding issues of violence against women has shifted from the language of private to the language of public.

However, at the same time, the notion of family violence as within the private sphere has been given additional support by the Supreme Court's decision in *DeShaney v. Winnebago County Department of Social Services* (1989). In *DeShaney,* the Court held that the state had no affirmative responsibility to protect a child who had been permanently injured as a result of abuse committed by his custodial father, even when the state had been investigating the child abuse for several years (*DeShaney v. Winnebago,* 1989, pp. 200–202). The majority opinion reflects a crabbed view of the world that reasserts a bright-line distinction between public and private. Family violence is private and therefore immune from state scrutiny because, implicitly, the state had no business to be there in the first place and no responsibility to intervene at all. *DeShaney* revives the notion that family violence is private and the distinction between public and private action places this violence beyond public control (Minow

1990b, pp. 1666–76). *DeShaney* is already being interpreted by courts around the country to limit police liability in suits brought by battered women.[19]

The tension between public and private is also seen in the issue of what legal processes are available to battered women, and the social meaning of those processes to battered women in particular, and to society at large (Schneider 1986b, pp. 623–48). Over the last several years, the range of legal remedies has expanded, and there has been an explosion of statutory reforms. For example, there are civil remedies, known as restraining orders or orders of protection. These are court orders with flexible provisions that a battered woman can obtain to stop a man from beating her, prevent him from coming to the house, or evict him from the house (Finn 1989, pp. 43–44). There are also criminal statutes that provide for the arrest of batterers, either for beating or for violation of protective orders (Buel 1988, pp. 214–215). Although there remain serious problems in the enforcement and implementation of these orders, the fact that such formal legal processes exist is evidence of a developing understanding of the public dimension of the problem. By giving battered women remedies in court there is, at least theoretically, public scrutiny, public control, and the possibility of public sanction. In addition, some states impose marriage license fees to generate funds to be used for battered women's services, thus making an important statement about the public impact of purportedly private conduct, as well as implying an important ideological link between marriage and violence.[20] On the other hand, some of these extensive state statutory provisions have been challenged by battering men on constitutional grounds, including invasion of rights to marital privacy.[21]

At the same time that these remedies have been developing, there has been a move towards more private and informal processes, notably mediation. Most battered women's advocates are critical of mediation, because they believe that informal modes of dispute resolution substantially hurt battered women who are disadvantaged with respect to power, money, and resources (Sun and Woods 1989; Hart 1990; Lerman 1984; Grillo 1991). Mediation is viewed as signaling that battering is the women's individual and private "problem" that should be "worked out," and that the state has no role (Lerman 1984, pp. 84–89). A general mood in legal circles, in favor of alternative dispute resolution and less adversarial forms of problem solving, has helped to legitimate mediation and obscure its problematic implications in this circumstance (Lerman 1984, pp. 88–89). However, it is more accurate to see the move to mediation and more informal processes as a reflection of the low priority accorded family law issues, generally, and battered women's problems, in particular, by the law (Lerman 1984, pp. 88–89).

Recently, the importance of criminal remedies for battering, particularly mandatory arrest provisions, has been increasingly recognized (Buel 1988, pp. 215–16). Activists have argued that criminal remedies, generally, and mandatory arrest, in particular, are important remedies that send a clear social message that battering is impermissible, and, because criminal remedies are prosecuted by the state, give more public force to the sanction. However, even civil remedies, such as orders of protection and tort suits against batterers, initiated by individual women against individual men, can send a social message. These lawsuits use formal court process, are subject to public scrutiny, and the legal decisions arrived at in those cases also make a public statement. In particular, the tort action may carry a greater social meaning in light of the demise of the historic bar of interspousal immunity, the social dimension of the claimed harm, and affirmative nature of the claim for damages.[22] Other examples of alternative procedural frameworks that carry more public meaning include the articulation of battering as a civil rights violation,[23] an international human rights violation (Thomas and Beasley 1994), and as involuntary servitude (McConnell 1992).

Indeed, the development of these more formal processes has several important ramifications in promoting public education and helping to redefine violence as a public issue. First, because of the availability of these legal remedies, there are more proceedings in court, and the participants, judiciary, court personnel, and public are educated about the problem of domestic violence. Public participation in these disputes may well have contributed to changing attitudes concerning the acceptability of violence against women (Resnik 1987, p. 419). The media frequently focus on court cases, so there are many articles in newspapers and programs on television about these cases.[24] Analysis of the actual implementation of these legal remedies, and the failure of the courts to enforce these provisions, has been widely publicized in the many state gender-bias reports, and has further expanded an educational process within the states.

The development of more formal processes has also been important to battered women. An empirical study of battered women's experiences in obtaining restraining orders in New Haven, Connecticut, concluded that temporary restraining orders can help battered women in ways other than increasing police responsiveness or deterring violent men; "the process is (or can be) the empowerment" (Chaudhuri and Daly 1992, p. 246). The authors emphasize that "[t]his occurs when attorneys listen to battered women, giving them time and attention, and when judges understand their situation, giving them support and courage" (Chaudhuri and Daly 1992, p. 246). However, they observe that:

> as important, although unfortunately less frequent, women's empowerment can occur when men admit to what they have done in a public

> forum. Such conversations and admissions can transform the violence
> from a private familial matter, for which many women blame themselves,
> to a public setting where some men are made accountable for their acts.
> (Chaudhuri and Daly 1992, p. 246)

This study underscores the importance of legal representation, another issue that reveals the tension between public and private. Although
battered women now have remedies that are available to them "on the
books," they have no assured access to lawyers to represent them. Many
battered women have limited resources and cannot afford to hire a
lawyer. Moreover, there are few lawyers who are sensitive to their issues
and problems. State statutory schemes do not provide for counsel; indeed
many of the protective order statutes specifically provide the option for
battered women to represent themselves.[25] Battered women's advocates,
formerly battered women or shelter workers, usually without formal
legal training, are now the crucial link between battered women and the
legal system, and also frequently the child welfare and social service
systems. Battered women's advocates help battered women to navigate
the legal system, and assist them in every facet of the process (Schneider
1990b, pp. 56–59). Although battered women's advocacy has played a
critical role for battered women, and has contributed a woman-centered
form of representation, it is necessarily limited. Even the simplest litigation concerning restraining orders may involve complex issues of divorce,
support, and custody, and the lack of skilled legal representation effectively discriminates against battered women.

These examples illustrate the contradictions posed by more informal
processes. The problem of lack of legal representation highlights the
dilemma that a more formal process would pose. Because counsel is not
provided, and has not been required by any of these statutes, battered
women's advocates have been able to assist many battered women who
would not otherwise have been represented. If counsel were required,
but not provided by the state, those battered women who cannot pay
for representation would be severely disadvantaged. Only the provision
of free counsel, knowledgeable about these issues, would make a substantial difference. Thus, although in theory we might prefer a more formal
legal process for battered women, in practice, under present conditions
of scarce legal resources, it may not be realistic.

Finally, the complex interrelationship between private and public can
be seen within the battered women's movement itself. Until about fifteen
years ago, the terms "woman abuse" and "battered woman" did not
exist. "Linguistically, it was classed with the disciplining of children and
servants as a 'domestic', as opposed to a 'political' matter" (Fraser 1990,
p. 213). Feminist activists in the battered women's movement named the
problem in a different way; they claimed that battery was not a personal,

domestic problem but a systemic, political problem. Battering was not the result of a particular man or woman's difficulties, but part of a larger problem of male domination and female subordination.

Nancy Fraser describes the meaning of this redefinition in the following way:

> Feminist activists contested established discursive boundaries and politicized a previously depoliticized phenomenon. In addition, they reinterpreted the experience of battery and posited a set of associated needs. Here they situated battered women's needs in a long chain of in-order-to relations that spilled across conventional separations of "spheres"; they claimed that in order to be free from dependence on batterers, battered women needed not just temporary shelter but also jobs paying a "family wage," day care and affordable permanent housing (Fraser 1990, pp. 213–14).

The battered women's movement began with a clearly political and public agenda. Battered women were not viewed primarily as individual victims but as potential feminist activists. Activists organized battered women's shelters, which were woman-centered refuges and sites of consciousness-raising. The organization of shelters was nonhierarchical and egalitarian; many formerly battered women went on to become counselors or advocates. Many battered women who had blamed themselves developed a more political perspective, and began to identify more with other women rather than with the men who battered them (Fraser 1990, p. 214).

However, as the issue of woman abuse became a more legitimate political issue, and battered women's organizations and shelters began to receive government funding, "a variety of new, administrative constraints ranging from accounting procedures to regulation, accreditation and professionalization requirements were imposed" (Fraser 1990, p. 214). Many organizations began to develop a service, rather than activist, perspective.

> As a consequence, publicly funded shelters underwent a transformation. Increasingly, they were staffed by professional social workers, many of whom had not themselves experienced battery. Thus, a division between professional and client supplanted the more fluid continuum of relations that characterized the earlier shelters. Moreover, many social work staff have been trained to frame problems in a quasi-psychiatric perspective. This perspective structures the practices of many publicly funded shelters even despite the intentions of individual staff, many of who are politically committed feminists. Consequently, the practices of such shelters have become more individualizing and less politicized. Battered

women tend now to be positioned as clients. They are only rarely addressed as potential feminist activists. Increasingly, the language game
of therapy has supplanted that of consciousness raising. And the neutral
scientific language of "spouse abuse" has supplanted more political talk
of "male violence against women." Finally, the needs of battered women
have been substantially reinterpreted. The very far-reaching earlier
claims for the social and economic prerequisites of independence have
tended to give way to a narrower focus on the individual woman's
problems of "low self-esteem." (Fraser 1990, pp. 214–15)

Thus, the battered women's movement itself has experienced the tension between a more systemic "public" definition of the problem and an
individualistic "privatized" vision. Even within the movement, we see
internal tensions and pressures to move to a more privatized definition
and experience of battering. Privacy encourages a focus on the individual, and avoidance of collective definition, systemic analysis, and social
responsibility.

I have described elsewhere how the articulation of rights claims by the
battered women's movement in both civil and criminal contexts raised
important questions for feminists about how to view the state, and sharpened debate over the role of law in modifying the public/private dichotomy (Schneider 1986b, pp. 642–48). These debates have centered
around the ideological importance of criminalization in defining battering as a public harm, and heightened the movement's analysis of
reforms. These issues have become more complex as more legal reforms
have become available. However, the tensions of privatization within the
movement emphasize the need for recommitment to an analysis that
links battering to the broader problems of women and identifies the
need for social and economic resources, education, jobs, child care, and
housing. Without access to these resources, violence against women will
endure.

As work on battered women moves forward, the meanings of public
and private shift, but each new development reveals the ideological constraints of privacy in a different form. This brings us full circle.

The Affirmative Potential of Privacy for Battered Women

To this point, it may seem that *Griswold* has little potential for battered
women. The right of marital privacy protected in *Griswold* seems to justify
the argument for marital privacy that permits male battering of women.
Is *Griswold* significant only as the constitutional articulation of the cloak
of privacy that has historically maintained woman abuse?

It is important to remember that the litigation in *Griswold* emerged from a struggle for women's rights.[26] The articulation of a right to privacy in *Griswold* resulted from "the patent suffering imposed by restrictive reproductive laws" (Copelon 1990–1991, p. 38). I want to suggest that the problematic doctrine of privacy should be redrawn under the shaping influences of the battered women's movement. Influenced by a sensitivity to gender, and informed by experience of woman abuse, privacy can be reconstructed and reformulated.

The evolution of Justice Douglas's own privacy jurisprudence from *Griswold* suggests the affirmative possibilities of privacy (Schneider 1991, pp. 642–48). In *Griswold,* the Court confronted a constitutional challenge to Connecticut's birth control statute, which prohibited the use of contraceptives and counseling concerning the use of contraceptives, by doctors who had been convicted under the statute. Douglas identified the harm resulting from this statute as intrusion into the privacy and intimacy of the marital relationship (Schneider 1991, p. 179). He developed the right of privacy based on the associational aspects of marriage as an important relationship that requires protection, and grounded it in a recognition of human intimacy and connection as an important value (Schneider 1991, p. 179). However, it is in his concurring opinion in *Roe v. Wade* and *Doe v. Bolton* (1973) that Justice Douglas developed his most expansive articulation of the right to privacy.

In *Roe,* Douglas developed three separate dimensions of these rights of privacy and liberty. First, he described the "autonomous control over the development and expression of one's intellect, interests, tastes and personality" (*Roe v. Wade* 1973, p. 211), which he saw as absolutely protected by the First Amendment against government interference. Second, he saw "freedom of choice in the basic decisions of one's life respecting marriage, divorce, procreation, contraception, and the education and upbringing of children" (*Roe v. Wade* 1973, p. 211). Third, Douglas described "the freedom to care for one's health and person, freedom from bodily restraint or compulsion, freedom to walk, stroll or loaf" (*Roe v. Wade* 1973, p. 213). These rights, although fundamental, are subject to some control by police power, and are subject to regulation on a showing of a compelling state interest.

Douglas then applied these dimensions of privacy and liberty to the situation of a woman who faces state prohibitions on abortion. He concluded that a woman is free to make the basic decision whether to bear an unwanted child, for "childbirth may deprive a woman of her preferred lifestyle and force upon her a radically different and undesired future" (*Roe v. Wade* 1973, p. 214). He described in moving detail the harm that women face:

> [F]or example, rejected applicants under the Georgia statute are required to endure the discomforts of pregnancy; to incur the pain, higher

mortality rate, and aftereffects of childbirth; to abandon educational
plans; to sustain loss of income; to forgo the satisfactions of careers; to
tax further mental and physical health in providing child care; and, in
some cases, to bear the lifelong stigma of unwed motherhood, a badge
which may haunt, if not deter, later legitimate family relationships. (*Roe
v. Wade* 1973, pp. 214–215)

It is significant that Douglas developed these aspects of privacy and
liberty in the context of women's rights to reproductive control. In *Roe*,
Douglas expressed a vision of a privacy right as something far more tied
to an affirmative concept of liberty than a right to be left alone, or than
protection from intrusion into the marital bedroom as in *Griswold*. This
view of privacy, as an aspect of liberty, is an expansive concept that
has a number of different dimensions. First, there is the dimension
of autonomy over the development and expression of one's "intellect,
interest, tastes and personality." Then there is the decisional dimension—
"freedom of choice in the basic decisions of one's life respecting marriage,
divorce, procreation, [and] contraception." There is also freedom from
intrusion, restraint, and compulsion, and freedom to care for oneself
and express oneself. We see the interrelated dimensions of privacy:
autonomy, decisional privacy, what some have called restricted access
privacy, and affirmative self-expression as aspects of the liberty that
Douglas describes as part of the Fourteenth Amendment. Liberty/free-
dom is the larger concept, within which these aspects of privacy are
subsumed.

Justice Douglas' affirmative view of privacy and liberty in his concurring opinion in *Roe* was a product of the massive educational process
concerning a woman's right to abortion that had gone on around the
country for several years with the growth of the women's movement.
In many cities around the country, women were coming forward in
courtrooms and meeting places to tell their stories. Women forced the
courts to confront the fact that every year women had abortions at
enormous physical and psychic cost. Justice Douglas's opinion directly
responded to the range of arguments presented in feminist briefs in
Roe. Feminist briefs in *Roe* argued broadly that reproductive choice was
central to women's equality, both in allowing women to become full
persons, and in achieving full participation in society (Copelon 1988,
pp. 314–15). The briefs also linked the rights to reproductive control
with women's autonomy and ability to be sexual, and emphasized the
disproportionate impact of criminalization on the poor. They presented
to the Court a full factual and legal picture of the range of harms that
women suffered as a result of abortion restrictions. For example, the
amicus curiae brief submitted by Nancy Stearns of the Center for Constitutional Rights for New Women Lawyers presented arguments concerning

the prohibition of abortion as an affirmative infringement of women's liberty, as sex discrimination, and as cruel and unusual punishment under the Eighth Amendment.[27] This brief especially focused on the practical impact of criminalizing abortion on women's lives, and was filled with rich, textured descriptions of the harms that women suffered as a result of prohibitions on abortion, and the central role that reproductive choice had for women's lives. Douglas's opinion, more specifically than the majority opinion in *Roe*, echoed these themes, in particular, the harms to women's liberty and freedom.

Justice Douglas's concurring opinion goes further than the majority opinion in making an explicit link to liberty, and in developing the more affirmative dimensions of autonomy, self-determination, and self-expression. It also presages concern with privacy as too narrow a grounding for the right to abortion that feminist legal theorists have subsequently expressed. Douglas's affirmative view of privacy as a dimension of liberty and his grounding of the abortion right on liberty in his opinion in *Roe* resonates with critiques developed by feminist legal scholars of the privacy right as the doctrinal basis for the abortion decision.

Feminist theorists have viewed as problematic the articulation of a right to privacy, as opposed to liberty, as the doctrinal basis for the abortion decision in *Roe* (Copelon 1988, pp. 314–16). Feminists have argued that the abortion right should have been founded upon the concept of liberty, rather than privacy, as it is women's freedom and autonomy that are at stake. Although feminist theorists have understood that there are many dimensions to privacy, such as decision-making, autonomy, self-determination, and human and sexual self-expression, privacy has been viewed as problematic for the reasons previously discussed. The right of privacy, a passive right that said the state could not intervene was viewed in contrast with the right to liberty, that emphasized the harms women suffered if they could not get abortions and seemed to imply that the state had an affirmative obligation to ensure that women can exercise their freedom. Douglas's concurring opinion suggests the radical potential of the concept of privacy—articulating it as not only the right to be let alone, but as affirmatively linked to liberty and the right to autonomy, self-expression, and self-determination. The notion of women as agents of their own lives is an important and powerful concept that transcends the common experience of the concept of privacy. Unfortunately, the radical potential of the concept of privacy has not been actualized by more recent decisions of the Court, such as *Bowers v. Hardwick* (1986), where the right to sexual autonomy and personal and emotional self-realization was directly implicated (Copelon 1988, pp. 319–20).

The importance of this more affirmative dimension of privacy is underscored by the problem of woman abuse. The rationale of privacy legitimates and supports violence against women; woman abuse reveals the violence of privacy. Privacy justifies the refusal of the state to intervene, of judges to issue restraining orders, of neighbors and friends to intervene or to call the police, of communities to confront the problem, and of social workers to act. Yet when we look at the more affirmative dimensions that Douglas articulates in *Roe,* we can see the importance of these perspectives in thinking about woman abuse. Battered women seek autonomy, freedom of choice with respect to the basic decisions of life concerning intimate association, freedom from battering and coercion, and freedom to be themselves. They seek the freedom to survive free from violence. We need to begin to articulate these affirmative claims as abortion activists did in *Roe.*

Conclusion

The challenge is to develop a right to privacy which is not synonymous with the right to state noninterference with actions within the family (Eisler 1987, pp. 292–93), but which recognizes the affirmative role that privacy can play for battered women. Feminist reconstruction of privacy should seek to break down the dichotomy of public and private that has disabled legal discourse and public policy in this area. Male battering of women is a serious public problem for which we need to accept collective responsibility; it requires a dramatic program of mass public reeducation similar to the drunk driving campaigns over the last several years. At the same time, while claiming woman abuse as a public problem, we do not want to suggest that state intervention is always the answer. Frank Michelman has observed that, even if we understand that the personal is political, this insight does not answer the question of the appropriate boundaries of state intervention (Michelman 1990, p. 1794). Others have detailed the ways in which state intervention will always be problematic for women (Olsen 1985, pp. 858–61), and we can see this in the limitations of legal reforms and the child welfare investigations of battered women on failure-to-protect grounds.

However, we also do not want to reject the genuine values and benefits of privacy for battered women. Thinking about privacy as something that women who have been battered might want makes us think about it differently. Battered women seek the material and social conditions of equality and self-determination that make privacy possible (Copelon 1990–1991, pp. 44–50). Privacy that is grounded on equality, and is viewed as an aspect of autonomy that protects bodily integrity and makes abuse impermissible, is based on a genuine recognition of the importance of personhood more true to the vision of privacy that Douglas evolved from *Griswold* (Radin 1982; Michelman 1990). Such a notion of privacy could challenge the vision of individual solution rather than social responsibility for abuse. Conceived differently, privacy could help keep women safe, not battered.

Notes

This chapter was previously published as an essay in the symposium honoring the 25th anniversary of *Griswold v. Connecticut* in the Connecticut Law Review 23: 973–999, and has been revised for this book.

1. This essay uses the terms "battered women," "woman abuse," and "male battering of women" interchangeably, although they have different meanings. I have criticized the term "battered women" as problematic both because it focuses the problem on the woman who is abused, rather than the battering man, and because it is a static term that defines the woman in a totalizing and stereotypical way, and connotes helplessness. See, generally, Schneider 1990a. In contrast, many activists now use the term "survivor" to emphasize the strength and resources of women who have been battered. The term "woman abuse" is very general but focuses attention on a continuum of physical and verbal abuse. The phrase "male battering of women" is useful because it describes the problem more accurately, but is unwieldy.

    Although the problem of gay and lesbian violence is serious and important, this essay focuses on male battering of women. Much of what I discuss is applicable to women who are battered by other women, but lesbians who have been battered face additional problems which make the question of privacy more complex. See, generally, Lobel 1986; Robson 1990.

2. I use the words "private" and "public" in quotes in order to emphasize that there is no single natural meaning to the terms, but several socially constructed meanings.

3. The dichotomy of women as private/men as public changes when women are viewed as childbearers. In *Muller v. Oregon,* 208 U.S. 412, 421 (1908), the Supreme Court emphasized that "as healthy mothers are essential to vigorous offspring, the physical well-being of women becomes an object of public interest and care in order to preserve the strength and vigor of the race."

    Several recent cases involving battered pregnant women dramatize the contrast between the treatment of pregnant women and battering men. A pregnant woman in Wisconsin who sought medical care for injuries she sustained as a result of a beating by her partner was subsequently arrested and charged with criminal child abuse for drinking during pregnancy. *Reproductive Rights Update,* 2 February, 1990: 3–4. Diane Pfannensteil of Laramie, Wyoming was arrested for drinking while pregnant and charged with felony child abuse when she went to the hospital to be treated for bruises suffered from her husband choking and beating her. *Boston Globe,* February 11, 1991: 12. In Massachusetts, Josephine Pellegrini was prosecuted for allegedly taking cocaine while she was pregnant. Ms. Pellegrini was described in news reports as "a battered woman who was terrified of [her live-in boyfriend]," who was also the father of her three children and a suspect in the abuse of her infant son. *Boston Globe,* August 23, 1989: 1.

4. For a discussion of the history and development of the battered women's movement, see Schechter 1982.

5. Schecter 1982, pp. 43–52. According to feminist analysis of women battering, violence has traditionally been a means of maintaining control over women as a class by men

as a class: "When a husband uses violence against his wife, people often view this as a random, irrational act. In contrast, feminists define wife abuse as a pattern that becomes understandable only through examination of the social context. Our society is structured along the dimensions of gender: Men as a class wield power over women." (Bograd 1988).

6. See, generally, Attorney General of the U.S. Dep't of Justice 1984; United States Comm'n of Civil Rights 1982; National Inst. of Justice, Dep't of Justice 1986; The Family Violence Prevention and Services Act: A Report to Congress 1988; Finn and Colson 1990.

7. Examples of recent books on woman abuse include Blackmun 1989; Bograd 1988; Sonkin 1987; Gondolf and Fisher 1988; Gordon 1988; Hoff 1990; Pleck 1987; Walker 1989.

8. For a discussion of popular media images of woman abuse, see Minow 1990b.

9. For discussion of the range of state legislation that has been developed to assist battered women, see Schneider 1990b. For an analysis of state legislation regarding restraining orders, see Finn 1989.

10. Major federal legislation on domestic violence includes The Victims of Crime Act of 1989 (VOCA), 42 U.S.C. §10601 (1989), that offers compensation to victims of domestic violence, and The Family Violence Prevention Services Act, 42 U.S.C. §10410 (1989) (now The Child Abuse Protection Adoption and Family Services Act of 1988), that assists states in providing services to prevent family violence, and coordinates research, training, and clearinghouse activities. Senator Biden has proposed federal legislation on rape and domestic violence in the Violence Against Women Act of 1991. See S. 15, 101st Cong., 1st Sess. (1991).

11. Attorney Gen. of the U.S., Dep't of Justice 1986, 11. For a discussion of problems faced by women of color who have been battered, see Allard 1991; Crenshaw 1991; Rasche 1986; and Richie 1985.

12. For an overview of the development of the battered women's movement, see Schechter 1982, pp. 53–112. For an overview of model advocacy groups across the country, see Schneider 1990b, pp. 102–08.

13. For a discussion of batterer's programs and the reasons why men batter, see Ptacek 1988, pp. 133–56; Adams 1988, pp. 176–96.

14. See Finn 1989, pp. 60–73, for an overview of civil restraining legislation enacted across the country.

15. For an exploration of the phenomenon of denial and the importance of naming violence generally, see Kelly 1988, pp. 114–31.

16. Martha Mahoney's discussion of the problem of denial, in Mahoney 1991, was very helpful to me in writing this section.

17. The Joel Steinberg/Hedda Nussbaum case involved the murder of their adopted daughter, Lisa Steinberg, who was beaten to death by Joel Steinberg. This case focused on the examination of Hedda Nussbaum as both a victim of abuse and a neglectful mother. See Sullivan, "Defense Tries to Show Nussbaum Liked Pain," *New York Times,* December 9, 1988: B2. Some feminist response to the case centered on Hedda Nussbaum's "complicity," and not upon Joel Steinberg's terrorization of the family:

Systemic battering combined with misguided, though culturally inculcated, notions of love is not a sufficient excuse to exonerate Hedda Nussbaum from her share of culpability in Lisa Steinberg's death. . . . When decent, honorable women insist that a piece of Hedda Nussbaum resides in us all, they give the Joel Stein-bergs of this world far too much credit and far too much power. More insidiously, they perpetuate the specious notion that women are doomed to be victims of the abnormal psychology of love at all cost. (Susan Brownmiller, "Hedda Nussbaum, Hardly a Heroine," *New York Times*, 2 February 1989: A25).

18. See, e.g., Unified Court System of the State of New York 1986; Loftus 1986; Massachusetts Supreme Court 1990.

19. *DeShaney* has made it difficult for victims of woman abuse to bring Section 1983 claims against the state for failure to protect them from battering. Courts are rejecting substantive due process claims, which are typically based on the alleged existence of a "special relationship" between the victims and the state (whether as a result of previous knowledge of the harm they faced at the hands of their abusers or because the state had issued a protective order), as incompatible with *DeShaney*. See, e.g., *Balistreri v. Pacifica Police Dep't*, 901 F.2d 696, 700 (9th Cir. 1990); *Luster v. Price*, No. 90–0115–CV–W–8, at 10, (W.D. Mo. July 5, 1990) (LEXIS, Genfed library, Dist. file); *Hynson v. City of Chester*, 731 F. Supp. 1236, 1239 (E.D. Pa. 1990); *Dudosh v. City of Allentown*, 722 F. Supp. 1233, 1235 (E.D. Pa. 1989). Only in two cases involving battering men who were arguably more "public" actors, where batterers were either close friends of the police chief, *Freeman v. Ferguson*, 911 F.2d 52, 53 (8th Cir. 1990) (plaintiff alleged that the husband was a close friend of the police chief and the chief in fact directed other police officers not to intervene on behalf of the wife), or a member of the police force himself, *Muhammed v. City of Chicago*, No. 89–C–6903 (N.D. Ill. Jan. 15, 1991) (LEXIS, Genfed library, Dist. file) have district courts held that plaintiffs should be given the opportunity to prove a duty-to-protect claim. But see Borgmann 1990, pp. 1314–17 (arguing that issuance of protective orders should overcome *DeShaney*). One court has held, post-*DeShaney*, that a court's protective order issued pursuant to Pennsylvania's Protection from Abuse Act might create a property interest in police protection. *Coffman v. Wilson Police Dep't*, 739 F. Supp. 257, 264 (E.D. Pa. 1990).

As a result of the diminishing availability, after *DeShaney*, of Section 1983 due process claims based on the notion of a special relationship, battered women may have to turn to alternative theories to sue the state for its failure to protect them. Such theories include equal protection violations, claims that the state has failed adequately to train its agents in domestic violence situations, or claims based on state tort law. Some courts dismissing section 1983 special relationship claims at least have been willing to permit plaintiffs the opportunity to bring such claims. See, e.g., *Balistreri*, 901 F.2d at 701–702; *Freeman*, 911 F.2d at 55 (permitting plaintiff to pursue an equal protection claim); *Hynson*, 731 F. Supp. at 1240–41; *Dudosh*, 722 F. Supp. at 1236 (permitting plaintiff to pursue an equal protection claim based on city's failure to train adequately its police force). See generally, Note 1990 (arguing that, post-*DeShaney*, battered women's best chances of suing state actors for failure to intervene lie with due process suits not dependent on a special relationship theory, such as a state failure to train, equal protection challenges, and state tort theories).

20. Mo. Stat. Ann. § 455.205 (1986) authorizes a surcharge of ten dollars in each marriage dissolution case for domestic violence shelters. Ariz. Rev. Stat. Ann. §12-284 provides that eighty percent of monies gathered for marriage licenses shall be deposited (Supp. 1993) in a domestic violence shelter fund. Minn. Stat. Ann. § 357.021 (1991) provides that a portion of the marriage dissolution fee shall be used for emergency shelter and support services to battered women.

21. For constitutional challenges to some of the marriage license fee provisions, see *Browning v. Corbett,* 153 Ariz. 74, 734 P.2d 1030 (1987); *Boynton v. Kusper,* 112 Ill.2d 356, 494 N.E.2d 135 (1986); *Crocker v. Finley,* 99 Ill.2d 444, 459 N.E.2d 1346 (1984); *Villars v. Provo,* 440 N.W.2d 160 (Minn. Ct. App. 1989).

    Griswold has been raised as a defense by men to marital rape on the ground that it protects marital privacy. These challenges have been rejected by courts. In *Commonwealth v. Shoemaker,* 359 Pa. Super. 111, 518 A.2d 591 (1986), the court rejected the defendant's privacy challenge on the ground that the right to privacy should be overridden by the compelling state interest protecting the "fundamental rights of all individuals to control the integrity of his or her body." *Id.* at 116, 518 A.2d at 594. Other cases involving privacy challenges to marital rape have taken a stronger position, suggesting that marital privacy was never intended to cover nonconsensual acts. *Williams v. State,* 494 So.2d 819, 828–29 (Ala. Crim. App. 1986); *People v. Liberta,* 64 N.Y.2d 152, 165, 474 N.E.2d 567, 574, 485 N.Y.S.2d 207, 214 (1984), cert. denied, 471 U.S. 1020 (1985). Significantly, in rejecting this argument, some courts drew analogies to woman abuse, with one court suggesting that "[j]ust as a husband cannot invoke a right of marital privacy to escape liability for beating his wife, he cannot justifiably rape his wife under the guise of a right to privacy." *Liberta,* 64 N.Y.2d at 165, 474 N.E.2d at 574, 485 N.Y.S.2d at 214. See, also, *Merton v. State,* 500 So. 2d 1301, 1304 (Ala. Crim. App. 1986); *State v. Rider,* 449 So. 2d 903, 906 n.6 (Fla. Dist. Ct. App. 1984). But see *People v. Forman,* 145 Misc. 2d 115, 121, 546 N.Y.S.2d 755, 760 (N.Y. Crim. Ct. 1989), where the defendant argued that his associational liberty interests protected by *Griswold* were violated by the issuance of a temporary order of protection.

22. For analysis of the developing area of domestic violence and torts, see L. Karp and C. Karp (1989); "D.C. Court Declines to Recognize Independent Tort of 'Spouse Abuse'" (1989); "Victim of Battered Woman's Syndrome Recovers in a Civil Action for Battery and Emotional Distress" (1990).

23. Lawyers in some states are exploring whether their civil rights statutes can be interpreted to cover domestic violence. See Mass. Gen. L. Ann. ch. 265, § 37 (West 1990); N.J. Stat. Ann. § 10:5–1–10:5–42 (West 1976 & Supp. 1991) (the New Jersey Law Against Discrimination). The pending Violence Against Women Act of 1991 also defines gender bias as a civil rights violation in Title III of the Act.

24. However, more media have focused on cases involving battered women who have killed their assailants than the "ordinary" case of a battered woman who cannot get into a shelter, cannot get a restraining order, and may risk losing custody of her children for failing to protect them from the batterer. Emphasis on the latter types of situations would squarely focus public attention on the battering man and the failure of social responsibility.

25. Most civil restraining order statutes have no provisions for counsel and are designed for *pro se* applicants. Though legal advocates are bridging the representational gap in new and creative ways, battered women are still in desperate need of adequate legal representation because civil restraining order litigation inevitably involves issues of custody, support, and visitation. Schneider 1990b, pp. 51–52, 56–59. For a discussion of the problem of legal representation in restraining order litigation, see Finn and Colson 1990, p. 19.

26. Catherine Roraback, one of the plaintiff's lawyers in *Griswold,* underscored this concept in introductory remarks at the symposium honoring the 25th anniversary of

Griswold v. Connecticut at the University of Connecticut Law School in 1991, for which this essay was written. Much of the discussion of Justice Douglas' jurisprudence in *Griswold* that follows is from Schneider, Commentary: The Affirmative Dimensions of Douglas's Privacy, in *He Shall Not Pass This Way Again: The Legacy of Justice William A. Douglas* 179 (S. Wasby ed. 1991).

27. Brief *Amicus Curiae* on behalf of New Women Lawyers, Women's Health and Abortion Project, Inc., National Abortion Action Coalition 14–24, *Roe v. Wade,* 410 U.S. 113 (1973) and *Doe v. Bolton,* 410 U.S. 179 (1973). I worked on this brief as a law student intern with Nancy Stearns at the Center for Constitutional Rights.

Victimization or Oppression? Women's Lives, Violence, and Agency

by Martha R. Mahoney

All work with subordinated people confronts, at least to some extent, the challenge of analyzing structures of oppression while including an account of the resistance, struggles, and achievements of the oppressed. Much recent social commentary has criticized overly describing women as victims. Some of these voices come from the right: in these accounts, feminists harm our own cause and our own gender by constructing women as victims, by "whining," and by exaggerating the incidence of rape, abuse, and other violations of women. Feminists have also expressed concerns about the ways in which stereotypes of women's helplessness and dependency can be exacerbated in the course of fighting against the abuse of women. These arguments have quite different emphases and implications, but both point toward avoiding overemphasis on victimization.

Fighting oppression requires describing and confronting it. Describing harm has been a particularly important project for feminism, because many aspects of women's oppression were previously hidden (as in woman battering and incest) or naturalized (as when date rape is called promiscuity, or the economic needs of those who care for the young are defined as innate dependency). The emphasis on the dangers of victim-talk can therefore be misleading. Rather, the problem is twofold: first, the abuse of women and its consequences must be explained without defining the woman herself by the experience of abuse; second, the woman's perceptions and the context of her life must be explained—defending the reality of *this woman's* experience—in a way that locates her experience within patterns of systemic power and oppression.

Several factors in law and in popular culture combine to make it difficult to portray both oppression and struggle in women's experience of domestic violence. Agency—acting for oneself—is generally seen as an individual matter, the functioning of an atomistic, mobile individual.

Agency and victimization are understood in relation to each other: agency is exercised by a self-determining individual, one who is not victimized by others. Social and legal inquiry focuses on the experience of individuals, stripping away the societal context of oppression and hiding the ways in which a relationship between individuals in a particular case is similar to other abusive relationships. Law especially emphasizes acts of physical violence, and this emphasis in turn hides broader patterns of social power, patterns of power within a given relationship, and complexity in the woman's life, needs, and struggles.

Women live under conditions of unequal personal and systemic power that affect all aspects of our lives. On this uneven terrain, we find whatever we achieve of love, productivity, and resources to care for ourselves and our dependents. The experience of structural inequality is, for each woman, the experience of her life: race and culture, sexuality, work and family are aspects of her life, struggles, and consciousness. When women work for wages, our lives as workers are shaped not only by the workplace but by the needs of our children, the social assignment of household care to women, and the power structures of our intimate relationships. The unremarked backdrop at work and at home is an absence of rights to either shelter or employment.

Violence at the hands of intimate partners, a relatively common event for women, is experienced in this context of love and responsibility, work and obligation, commitment and uncertainty. "Violence is a way of 'doing power' in a relationship." (Stets 1988, p. 109). The batterer seeks power and control through patterns of coercive and violent behavior (Dobash and Dobash 1979; Hart 1986). Women's responses to battering are shaped by the needs, struggles, and commitments of our lives. Our previous experiences, the batterers' quest for control, and the inevitable social context of power are all crucial factors in our decisions about relationships.

Social stereotypes and cultural expectations about the behavior of battered women help to hide women's acts of resistance and struggle. Both law and popular culture tend to equate agency in battered women with separation from the relationship. Women who seek love and survival for ourselves and our families are treated as if our only choices are to "stay" or "leave." "Staying" is a socially suspect choice—often perceived as acceptance of violence—though "leaving" is often unsafe. In fact, women often assert ourselves by attempting to work out relationships without battering. Separation assault, the violent and sometimes lethal attack on a woman's attempt to leave a relationship, proves that the power and control quest of the batterer often continues after the woman's decision to leave. The prevalent social focus on leaving conceals the nature of domestic violence as a struggle for control, pretends away the extreme dangers of separation, and hides the interaction of social structures that oppress women.

Law is an interactive part of political struggle and cultural perception, shaped by culture and in turn affecting it. Rather than reconsidering general questions of structure and agency, this essay examines what makes it difficult in law and in feminism to present a complex account of women as both oppressed and struggling. A focus on victimization can be misleading: images of women as victims are the *result* of many social and legal pressures. Feminists need to identify the structures and stereotypes that cause even complex accounts of women's lives to be understood as accounts of victimization. Instead of focusing on avoiding or promoting excessive victim-talk, we need to seek tactics, issues, and descriptions of women's experience that reveal the systemic nature of oppression *and* the phases of our experience as we live them.

The first section of this essay criticizes the notion of agency that under-lies the dichotomy between agency and victimization. I discuss many ways in which law and litigation reinforce this concept and affect feminist struggle. The second section discusses the problems with equating agency in battered women with exit from violent relationships. Finally, I describe current work in several areas of law, including torts, family law, and criminal law, that translates an understanding of battering as a pattern of power and control into particular work on legal issues faced by women.

Acting Under Conditions of Oppression: Agency and Victimization

Feminist analysis grows out of the articulation of women's experience. The battered woman's movement—including advocates, feminist theo-rists, battered women themselves—brought battering to light and defined it as a social problem (Schecter 1982). A great deal of progress has been made, none of it sufficient to the need: the proliferation of restraining order statutes and recent enactment of stalking laws, the establishment of shelters, development of judicial and police training, and treatment programs for batterers, are all examples of progress in response to this movement.

Much recent social commentary has argued that feminists harm the interests of women by portraying them as victims. Feminist activism around rape and sexual harassment, particularly, has been criticized for treating women as frail and vulnerable in ways that are detrimental to our own interests.[1] Popular writing about battered women who kill their abusers reflects the fear that women will evade responsibility for their actions by claiming weakness. The hidden premise of these arguments is that women are already unproblematically independent actors today, or, if we are not, the main obstacle is our own consciousness.

These denials of the oppression of women have real cultural resonance, because in our society most people have a strong sense of agency in their own lives. As bell hooks has pointed out, oppressed people often cannot afford to feel powerless. Women who face exploitation daily "cannot afford to relinquish the belief that they exercise some measure of control, however relative, over their lives" (hooks 1984, p. 45). This sense of agency often represents both sound self-knowledge and also denial of the impact on the person of oppression and suffering; it may be both "true" and "false" consciousness at once. A battered woman may know her own strength in survival and care for her children, valuing her own keen decision-making under pressure, yet continue to deny the cumulative harm to her self-esteem and her safety wrought by the betrayal of trust and incidents of violence in her relationship. Aware women attempting to act in the interests of themselves and their children often respond to oppression with resistance, survival, and partial victories, like women who seek to stop violence without leaving their marriages (Mahoney 1992). These tensions in work with battered women reflect the ways agency and victimization are socially defined in relation to each other. Victimization implies the one-way exercise of power, harm without strength; agency implies freedom from victimization.

A woman's belief in herself as an actor in her life can prevent her from identifying her experience as similar to that of other women who experience oppression. This problem is exacerbated when the definition of "victim" is so stigmatizing that it is impossible to reconcile with perceiving agency in oneself or in others. The fact that a sense of agency can defeat awareness about subordination is crucially important *whether or not this consciousness of agency is "false,"* because the result reinforces the societal denial of the very existence of oppression (Mahoney 1992).

Denial is a particular problem in domestic violence, because the social stigma attached to being a battered woman is great. bell hooks tells of giving Lenore Walker's first book, *The Battered Woman,* to a young black woman who had been severely beaten by her partner. The woman's family threw the book out—they did not want her to feel less self-esteem, and they perceived the label "battered woman" as inevitably implying victimization (hooks 1989). Women are often reluctant to identify themselves as battered women, even when approaching shelters and hotlines for help (Schecter 1982; Mahoney 1991). Women who know their own strength therefore do not recognize their experience as battering, and some are deterred from seeking assistance. "Strong women do not get involved in abusive relationships. I am a strong woman, therefore I was never involved in an abusive relationship. ... My experience was not that experience." (Lesemann 1991). Many women describe physical threats and even violent assaults as "emotional abuse" or keep silent about them entirely.

The fiction that violence is exceptional is fundamental to stereotypes that portray battered women as helpless, dependent, and pathological. If it were understood that violence is really everywhere, then it would not be difficult to accept that violence happens to ordinary women. Individual women could then begin to overcome their own denial of painful experience, a particularly dangerous component of broader social denial of the prevalence and seriousness of domestic violence.

Feminists have also pointed out the dangers of overemphasizing victimization. In general, feminists have sought to reveal and analyze overarching structure of oppression, and to show many ways in which oppression defines the experience of being female, without defining women by the experience of being harmed. bell hooks (1984) and Angela Harris (1991) argue that the creativity and strength under conditions of oppression shown by many women of color add a complex vision of women's experience to accounts of the exploitation of women. In work with battered women, Susan Schecter pointed out that individualized concepts of victimization hid the link between the oppression of women and the fight against domestic violence (Schecter 1982, p. 252). Catharine MacKinnon, in contrast, emphasizes women's suffering under comprehensive, interrelated, brutal systems of inequality: "Stereotypes that see [women] as victims are overtaken by the reality in which they are victimized." (MacKinnon 1991b, p. 1293).

As expert testimony on battered woman syndrome first won acceptance in courts, Elizabeth Schneider cautioned against emphasis on helplessness and victimization in battered women (Schneider 1986a). Schneider pointed to a tension between victimization and agency in work on domestic violence. Emphasizing victimization might make it difficult for juries to reconcile lack of agency with the women's violent acts of self-defense against her abuser (Schneider 1986a, 1992). Neither concepts of agency nor of victimization fully take account of women's experiences of oppression and resistance in relationships (Mahoney 1992; Schneider 1992). Schneider called for rejecting the all-victim or all-agent approach to women's experience and for fuller exploration of the meaning of agency in the lives of battered women (Schneider 1986a).

I agree with Schneider's concern, and this essay is part of that exploration. Even when feminists do not emphasize helplessness and passivity in battered women, courts have imposed the cultural stereotypes held by judges, social workers, and other legal actors to recreate concepts of battered women as victims without agency (Schneider 1986a; Mahoney 1991). Even when battered women energetically seek to protect themselves and their children, their actions are often misinterpreted as pathological or incompetent. We cannot get past the dichotomy between agency and victimization without understanding the structural and cultural pressures that insistently construct victimization out of women's experiences.

Why is it so difficult to see both agency and oppression in the lives of women? Why did society and law respond to a movement against battering with a concept of "battered woman" that defined the woman by the harm that had been done to her? I have come to believe that the problem lies in part in prevailing social and legal concepts of agency. In our society, agency and victimization are each known by the absence of the other: you are an agent if you are not a victim, and you are a victim if you are in no way an agent. In this concept, agency does not mean acting for oneself under conditions of oppression; it means *being without oppression*, either having ended oppression or never having experienced it at all. This all-agent or all-victim conceptual dichotomy will not be easy to escape or transform.

Social historians and advocates focus their research on women seeking help and attempting to change their lives; not surprisingly, they have been quicker than psychologists and legal scholars at identifying agency and struggle among battered women. In Linda Gordon's history of family violence (1988), women who were attacked in their homes sought solutions in many ways. These women tried to reform their partners, tried to leave them, and sought protection against the attacks. The women approached social workers at agencies with claims of entitlement to assistance. Battered women advanced whatever claims the workers were capable of hearing at that historical moment, basing their claims variously on economic need, their own physical safety, and their children's safety. They tried to care for themselves and their children. And gradually, cumulatively, these women shaped an "entitlement not to be beaten," and forced social workers to begin helping them end the violence.

Advocates working with battered women today also often emphasize women's struggles and resourcefulness. Battered women are described as "survivors" rather than victims (Gondolf and Fisher 1988; Hoff 1990). In ironic contrast to theories of "learned helplessness" in battered women (Walker 1979, 1984), Gondolf describes "learned helplessness" among the helping professions as a phenomenon which occurs when a systemic lack of resources gives rise to the inability of professionals to meet the needs of battered women, resulting in the erosion of hope and initiative among professionals (1988, pp. 22–23, 99).

In law, however, the focus of legal inquiry (and therefore the focus of legal scholarship) did not often recognize these diverse methods of self-assertion. The insistently individualized construction of our lives in law denied the multifaceted experience of much of our existence as women (West 1988; Cornell 1991a). Both the individualized construction of women's lives and the focus on sexual relationships as central to women's oppression tend to hide the crucial importance of motherhood in particular, and the care of dependents in general, in the lives of many women (Fineman 1991a, 1991c, 1992).

Law misses the duality and resistance described by social historians and advocates in part because most litigation about domestic violence takes place in an individualized context rather than a socialized one. The early days of the modern women's movement placed accounts of abuse in social and political context, not only through consciousness-raising and the sharing of experience (frequently discussed in feminist theory today) but also through speakouts, art, poetry, political demonstrations, and scholarly research—many of which involved some form of social testimony to the reality of women's experiences of abuse. In litigation regarding domestic violence, however, class action lawsuits are extremely rare; battered women seldom come to court in ways that show them as one of many like themselves. Political efforts, such as the recent movement for clemency for women who killed their abusers and had limited opportunity to describe the battering at trial, have the potential to increase social awareness of the number of battered women imprisoned. The original trials of women now seeking clemency, in contrast, took place in individualized contexts. Even if battering was the subject of testimony at those trials, an incident-focused approach to battering misses patterns of power and control in abusive relationships. The woman's responses seem unique and problematic because there is no context demonstrating the commonality of her experience.

Cultural stereotypes of women are imported into law through standards of reasonableness and "objective" intuitions about what behavior is appropriate in women who are hurt by our partners (Mahoney 1991). The cultural preoccupation with exit from violent relationships is reinscribed in law through the preconceptions and expectations of legal actors, including judges, juries, social workers, and attorneys. To date, the best answer the legal system has achieved is to explain battered women's behavior psychologically, through battered woman syndrome, which is offered to explain failure to separate as well as other aspects of the woman's perceptions and behavior. There is an ironic circularity here: battered woman syndrome itself is often understood to describe helplessness and pathological dependency in women, even when experts include sociological factors such as lack of safety or societal support for battered women in their discussion. Explanations for failure to leave are understood as focusing on victimization—in part because they explain "failure."

Law and legal argument contain ideological assumptions about agency that make it difficult to show both oppression and resistance in the lives of battered women. Most fundamentally, the fiction of formal equality hurts all subordinated people. In labor law, for example, the notion that employers and employees are equally free to leave the work relationship is a fundamental underlying tenet of American capitalism. In family law, as Martha Fineman's work has shown, concepts of formal equality incorporated into divorce reform efforts have created a legal regime that devalues caregiving and hurts the interests of single mothers and children (Fineman 1988, 1991a). The structure of much legal argument incorporates this concept of formal equality. If you prove that you lack effective agency, the law may protect you from the harshest results of enforcing your contracts; otherwise, you are an equally powerful free actor whose contracts will be enforced. The notion of people as actors on a playing field permeates legal argument: if you prove your status as a victim wrongfully placed behind obstacles or off the field, you get to be helped back on so that you too can "play." This view of agency as the functioning of an autonomous, mobile, individual actor has a flip side of victimization, with important consequences for battered women.

It is difficult—it may be impossible—to represent agency and struggle in women's lives in relation to a negative-state, libertarian approach to law. One telling example is the direction of struggle over women's rights in the areas of pregnancy, motherhood, and abortion. Contemporary feminist organizations have put more energy into abortion rights than they have into rights to subsistence. The privacy approach to abortion, which casts reproductive choice as a balancing of interests about decision-making, has been contrasted with an "affirmative right to choose" which allows a woman to exercise control over her own body and life decisions (Schneider 1986b). But the feminist emphasis on a right to choice about childbearing, rather than a right to sufficient income to actually bear and *raise* a child, does not fundamentally challenge a negative-rights regime. This is not only an idea about legal rights—it also contains a concept of agency which implicitly asserts that a woman's decisions would be unconstrained if the state kept its power off her body. Under any legal theory, abortion rights are still rights *against interference,* consistent with a concept of woman as a free actor jeopardized only by interference with her ability to choose. The battle over Medicaid funding of abortions, while it posed some question of state responsibility to protect woman's choices, still would not have guaranteed to any woman the right to bear a child and have enough money to actually raise that child. Negative rights protect choice only against intervention by the state, leaving in place the set of assumptions that treat people as formally equal. When faced with the actions of Operation Rescue, and other groups that blockaded abortion clinics and kept women from getting abortions, the Supreme Court recently held that the right to choose abortion was protected only against interference by the state, a holding clearly incompatible with a positive right to choose to have an abortion.[2]

The most facile explanation for feminism's focus on rights against *interference* with regard to the decision to terminate a pregnancy, rather than rights to choose whether or not to bear *and raise* children, is that the majority of women deciding the path of feminism were white and middle-class, and therefore felt less acutely the difficulty of rearing children. While negative rights are more resonant for people with middle-class resources, this is an inadequate answer, given the many strands of feminist thought and action over time. In part, this is because work *in law* tended to track liberal, rather than radical ideas (Fineman 1983, pp. 813–14). Recent struggles over leadership within the National Organization for Women illustrate the debates among feminists over the primacy of abortion rights in the work of that organization. The defense of abortion rights remains critically important for women—and critically difficult—yet this emphasis continues to allow feminist dialogues to be slanted toward a vision of agency and choice that ultimately misrepresents the experience of most women.

The direction of legal struggles for women was channeled by what we won (the partial and temporary successes of negative rights) as well as what we lost. At the same historical moment that the women's movement of the 1970s developed, all legal battles for positive rights failed. There is no affirmative right to housing[3] or even temporary shelter; to child care; to welfare support and subsistence adequate to the size of the family;[4] nor any positive right to employment outside of procedural rights against arbitrary terminations from government jobs. For a time, however, some negative rights could be won, such an abortion rights under a privacy theory, or the right not to be treated in impermissibly discriminatory ways. These negative rights had to be defended in law even more energetically because no positive rights had been won. However, negative rights presume a world of autonomous free actors operating in a hollow social shell—an "empty state" (Casebeer 1989). America lacked either a labor party or a broad political movement that could create a bridge between these feminist demands, and help develop a broader vision of agency and choice in decisions about bearing or raising children. Also, the fact that gender is a constitutionally suspect classification, while poverty is *not* a suspect classification, tends to encourage a focus on sexualized aspects of oppression rather than the economic hardship that often accompanies childbearing in this society.

Some strands of feminist theory have fought against this tendency to emphasize negative rights (Cornell 1991b). Issues of women's reproduc-

tive health, repeatedly raised by black feminists over time, remain important in feminist organizing among women of color (Avery 1991). bell
hooks treats racism as part of violence against women and has described
a "cycle of violence" in intimate relationships that starts in the workplace
and includes economic oppression and insecurity (hooks 1984). The
concept of substantive, positive rights is important to transforming the
construction of women as either helpless victims or fully autonomous
agents. But this will not be easy to change, because the forces that channeled the feminist movement toward struggles to defend negative rights
have not disappeared.

The atomistic assumptions that sustain this view of agency have been
repeatedly challenged in feminist theory. Feminists have explored the
ways women seek fulfillment in ways that are sometimes individual and
sometimes interdependent (West 1988; Cornell 1991a). Theoretical work
on motherhood can help reveal the ways agency is not merely either
individual or collective in the traditional, political sense, but also shared.
Martha Fineman describes the social necessity of caregiving and the
inevitable "derivative dependency" experienced by those who provide
care to others (Fineman 1991c). Fineman's work on motherhood seeks
to reorient family law around this dependency and caregiving and away
from sexual ties between adults, showing the need to reallocate society's
resources to recognize and protect the work women really do. This
approach to families poses profound challenges to the ways law currently
treats women and families (Fineman 1992b).

Law's narrow view of agency also represses accounts of complexity in
women's experience through its blunt power over our relationships with
our children. Admissions of maternal weakness, or discussion of guilt
about the ways in which we are not good mothers, can result in the loss
of children to a former partner in a custody action, or to the state of
actions alleging child neglect or terminating parental rights. Feelings of
uncertainty or inadequacy as mothers, deep and painful emotions shared
only with closest friends and family, were never elaborated publicly in
the ways that accounts of harms to women, such as rape and battering,
were developed. There were no speakouts on maternal guilt.

In legal feminism, more attention has been paid to pregnancy (especially in relation to work for wages) and to rights against continuing
unwanted pregnancy than to the years of emotional commitment and
physical work that are involved in motherhood. In the areas of child
custody and property division at divorce, concepts of formal equality
supported "gender-neutral" standards that inherently devalued women's
nurturing and the activities of caregiving (Fineman 1991a). The very
attempt to develop gender-neutral standards required *devaluing* every-

thing attached to women's gender, inherently valuing work men did more highly (Fineman 1988).

Linda Gordon has argued that feminists fear we will lose women's status as deserving "victims" if we acknowledge aggression in women: "These complexities are at their greatest in the situation of mothers because they are simultaneously victims and victimizers, dependent and depended on, weak and powerful" (Gordon 1990a, p. 82). Elizabeth Schneider criticizes the good mother/bad mother dichotomy as an example of the "dichotomous characterizations of victim and agent" (Schneider 1992, p. 555). This victim/victimizer paradigm, while it recognizes the differentiated relations of inequality in women's lives, reflects and reproduces individualistic concepts of agency. In this society, the experience of motherhood is both creative and oppressed *whether or not violence is present*. The struggles of women with children are not comprehensible within any idea of agency that looks only to any woman's atomistic needs and actions.

Law stands ready to punish admissions of weakness—even when no "victimizing" was done by the woman—when custody is disputed by ex-husbands or by the state in actions regarding parental rights. No-fault divorce tends to make abusive behavior invisible. Battered women face the danger of losing custody of their children to abusive ex-partners for a number of reasons: because violence against the mother was often not considered relevant to custody decisions, although this legal regime is changing; because custody evaluators saw allegations about domestic violence as suspiciously manipulative actions by the mother; and because stigma regarding battered women tainted the evaluation of maternal fitness in custody disputes (Cahn 1991; Mahoney 1991). Many women lacked economic resources necessary to wage prolonged custody battles or to defend themselves against allegations that they failed to properly care for their children.

Two recent cases exemplify some of the difficulties faced by battered women with children. Lorraine Smith, a member of the Chippewa tribe, suffered a brain hematoma while she had a newborn baby and another child under two. She was left with visual impairment, a limp, and limited use of her left hand.[5] She moved back to Michigan and separated from her husband. She stayed with her parents for several days. She then sought shelter at a domestic violence shelter and at another institution, neither of which could accommodate her children. One week after her arrival in the state, unable to find a residence where she could care for them, she contacted the Department of Social Services for assistance. The department petitioned the court to take jurisdiction over the children, based on Lorraine's disabilities and her temporary lack of adequate shelter arrangements for the children. After seven weeks, at the formal hearing, she had visited the children regularly, saved money, and arranged to rent a trailer later that day; she had found a young woman volunteer from the domestic violence shelter to live with her and help with physical care of the children.

The court held that "neglect" could be found to support taking jurisdiction over the children without any finding of parental blameworthiness. Her temporary lack of shelter and the limitations of her disability were identified as "neglect" because the children could not at that moment receive "proper care." Admonishing the father to accept more responsibility for the care of his children, the court adopted a plan to keep the children in a foster home for one month and then place them with their father and their maternal grandmother (currently unable to take them because of the grandmother's health). The father and his mother would then receive additional services from DSS to help care for the children. The Michigan Supreme Court affirmed, asserting that this outcome would not chill the willingness of disabled parents to seek help because the purpose of the juvenile code was to keep families together and this plan would "reunite [the children] with their parents [sic]." The dissent argued that there was no evidence that the children had ever been neglected, that many good parents experience unemployment or other hardships, and that neither temporary disability nor inadequate resources could constitute grounds for removing children from the care of a parent.

The indications that battering was involved—the shelter contact and possibly also the nature of Lorraine Smith's injury—were not explored in either the majority opinion or the dissent. In this case, the "admission" of disability and the requirement of a few weeks to save money and secure housing and necessary assistance were a sufficient basis for taking children from their mother. The extraordinary challenges for a woman with two babies in separating from a relationship were unnoticed, even though Smith was surmounting those hardships. For this court, this woman's agency was invisible. Her struggles were redefined as inadequacy.

A more recent case shows even more dramatically the dangers of stigmatizing battered women as helpless and victimized. Sharon Benn had three children under the age of ten. Her violent husband had been repeatedly ill with diabetes and renal failure.[6] The state took custody of the children because of their father's physical violence. No harm by the mother was alleged. Although the court later justified its decision by stating that she had failed to protect them, no failure to protect was alleged when they were taken by the state, and Sharon had no further opportunity to protect them because they were not again in danger from their father. Apparently, violence had usually occurred when she was absent, and the children were told not to tell her about it.

Sharon's court-appointed therapist was the chief clinical psychologist at a men's prison. He diagnosed Sharon as suffering from depression, "battered wife syndrome," and some other problems. He found her too involved with her own problems to empathize with her children's needs, but she was intelligent, insightful, and resourceful enough to benefit from psychotherapy. She proceeded in counseling, and the doctor found on later testing that she had improved. Sharon separated from her husband at the time the children were taken, went back to seeing him when the psychologist said it would be good to do so because he had been making progress, and separated from him finally a year later after he was charged with having sexually abused the youngest child.

In 1989, at a hearing on termination of her parental rights, Sharon testified without contradiction that she had fully carried out her contract with the Department of Social Services. She took parenting classes and visited her children regularly. She took stress management classes, participated in groups for battered women, and was currently a volunteer at the Child and Parent Center. She admitted to having spanked her children in the past but said she had learned that this was not only abusive but also unnecessary and ineffective. She had almost completely paid for her neat and clean two-bedroom mobile home, which was large enough for the children. She paid her own bills and had enrolled in a community college, working toward an associate's degree. She had begun divorce proceedings as soon as she could afford to do so and had not lived with Robert in almost a year. Her divorce in fact became final two months after the termination proceeding.

Termination of parental rights is a drastic legal measure that has been called "a death sentence on the relationship."[7] The court terminated Sharon's parental rights to her children, clearing the way for adoption by another family, because of testimony by the psychologist that Sharon *might* enter another abusive relationship at some time in the future. The only other evidence presented to show Sharon had any potential to continue an abusive relationship was a social worker's statement that Sharon had held hands with her husband *once* during an interview at the Family Assessment Clinic in 1988, after they separated but before divorce proceedings began. The Michigan Supreme Court declined permission for a late appeal, finalizing this decision, because it was "not persuaded that the questions presented should be reviewed by [the] Court." Justice Levin, dissenting, drew on scholarship by many domestic violence experts refuting the myth that battered women have a tendency to reenter abusive relationships.

Once women like Sharon Benn and Lorraine Jacobs have been hurt by their partners, there is real danger that no act of agency—including separation—will be sufficient to win understanding in the courts. It is humbling and frightening for a woman to admit that she is probably no stronger than Sharon Benn, because Sharon Benn lost her children. But I can muster no belief that, with her resources, I could have done better.

In our society, descriptions of hardship and pain are understood as showing personal weakness *because* of our concepts of agency. Popular cultural forums such as TV talk shows have heightened awareness of the prevalence of abuse, but these media presentations often lose the context of shared experience of struggle that was present at speakouts against violence and is essential to make sense of both agency and oppression. The ideology that pushed feminist legal argument away from positive substantive rights is apparent in Lorraine Smith's case: the court treated a disabled young woman, newly separated, with two very young children, as if she should have been able to secure a stable housing situation more quickly than she did. The concept of formal equality in which caregiving is made gender-neutral is also reflected in the Smith case. These gender-neutral standards reward men by overlooking women's work and energy (Fineman 1988). Lorraine's children were taken from their mother, who had found a way to care for them despite adversity, and awarded to a disinterested father—all under the rubric of reuniting children with their "parents."

Some commentators would argue that feminists have brought these horrors upon themselves by promoting a view of women as victims that undermines perceptions of women's strengths.[8] While feminist choices about legal and social strategies do matter, I do not believe feminists can be held responsible for the tensions between agency and victimization that reflect deep social prejudices and preconceptions. Battered woman syndrome and the concept of learned helplessness have been criticized for "psychologizing" women (Gondolf and Fisher 1988) and thereby promoting stereotypes of helplessness and dysfunctionality. Possibly such concepts could have indirectly influenced the legal treatment of Sharon Benn through promoting such stereotypes, despite the clear lack of support for the idea that abused women tend to get back into abusive relationships. But surely stereotypes of battered women could not account for the court's failure to perceive agency in Lorraine Smith, when the question of violence was essentially ignored. The legal system refused to recognize these women as exercising agency even as they worked to separate from violent relationships, did many things to regain the ability to care for their children, and solved difficult problems with limited resources.

In law and popular culture, to challenge the current ideology in which agency and victimization are each the flip side of the other and each known by the absence of the other, we need strategies that reveal both agency and oppression and facilitate resistance. Below, I offer two examples of such approaches. The popular concept that treats agency in women as synonymous with exit from violent relationships must be challenged to make comprehensible the many ways women assert ourselves in response to violence. Litigation strategies that treat battering as a pattern of power and control are essential to show both agency and oppression in the lives of women, making women's experiences and life choices comprehensible.

Agency and Exit: Redefining Separation from Violent Relationships

> I don't believe anything you['re] saying. . . . The reason I don't believe it is because I don't believe anything like this could happen to me. If I was you and someone had threatened me with a gun, there is no way that I could continue to stay with them. Therefore . . . I can't believe that it happened to you.
>
> A judge in Maryland, quoted in Maryland Gender Bias in the
> Courts Report (Murphy 1993).

> The test of whether clemency should be considered in cases where the request is based on [Battered Woman Syndrome] must be: Did the petitioner have the option to leave her abuser, or was the homicide realistically her only chance to escape? The test is a narrow one—and must be—to avoid the manipulation of BWS as a rationalization for cold-blooded murder.
>
> Governor Pete Wilson of California, in a press release discussing
> clemency decisions, May 28, 1993

When women experience violence in intimate relationships, we assert ourselves in a variety of ways. We attempt to change the situation and improve the relationship; we seek help formally or informally from friends, family, or organizations; we flee temporarily and make return conditional upon assurances of care and safety; we break off relationships. Continuing the relationship may therefore be part of a pattern of resistance to violence on the part of the woman.

On the other hand, a woman may continue the relationship because of uncertainty about other options or her ability to subsist or care for dependents, because of depression and dislocation that come with intimate loss and harm, or because she is afraid that leaving will trigger lethal danger—because, essentially, she is held captive. When a woman encounters the grave lethality that characterizes some batterers, survival is her primary concern; resistance becomes the project of staying alive, which will *only* involve flight when it seems either possible or safer than staying. The physical acts and relocations which are summarized in the concepts of "staying" or "leaving" therefore do not necessarily support conclusions about whether a woman is functioning as an agent in her life.

Discussions of domestic violence often treat "staying" as identical with victimization (Schneider 1992, pp. 557–58). The issue of exit colors almost every legal and social inquiry about battering. Social and legal emphasis on exit reflects a concept of agency as the functioning of an atomistic, mobile individual, and this concept of agency also reflects a binary opposition between agency and victimization. Emphasizing exit defines the discussion of violence in ways that ignore the woman's lived experience and the personal and societal context of power, focusing instead on whether her responsive actions conform with social expectation. The idea that women should leave—and that a woman acting in her own interest will always leave—is shaped by this atomistic view of agency.

Assumptions about staying and leaving, and the concepts of agency and victimization that underlie them, need to be challenged and transformed. But women's lives intersect the legal system at moments of great urgency, when remaking social expectation is too large a task. We therefore explain "failure" to leave rather than attempting to reckon with all the ways women struggle to protect themselves and assert themselves in abusive situations. This concedes a concept of agency that is doubly misleading: its individualism fails to describe the multiple responsibilities women face, and its pretense that women are free actors *after* separation is contradicted by frequent news reports of women attacked and killed by former partners.

Violence against women is relatively common in American society, although law and popular culture treat it as rare and exceptional.[9] The fiction of exceptionality which helps maintain denial of the prevalence of violence also supports the idea that battered women should leave but somehow fail to do so. If violence is everywhere—if it is in fact part of the story of marriage in this society—we need a different account of how women struggle with brutal control and coercion.

Violence usually begins after a woman has made a deep investment of her love, energy, and self into the relationship. Violence often begins after marriage, sometimes during pregnancy. The first incident of violence is *always* a surprise, a departure from what went before either absolutely (he never showed this kind of temper before) or at least qualitatively (he was angry before, but never angry in this way.) Violence and coercion are not committed by someone the woman calls a "batterer," but by her lover, husband, or partner—often, the father of her children.

Deciding whether a loved one must be redefined as a "batterer" raises questions about the deepest structures of the woman's intimate life, her safety, and needs of her children. This decision can be particularly difficult because society vests in women a great deal of responsibility for the relationship between children and their fathers. One woman who divorced a brutally abusive husband ten years ago recently commented that, although she did not regret leaving him, she believes that the loss of closeness with their father had proved to be bad for her children.

Many authors have treated violence in the context of power and control (Dobash and Dobash 1979; Schecter 1982). The long struggle to reveal the prevalence and harm of domestic violence often emphasized incidents of violence, however, rather than placing the woman's experience in the context of her life in an oppressive society, or emphasizing the abusive patterns of the batterer's quest for control. Inquiry focuses on particular incidents of violence and the woman's response to them. When battering is seen only as discrete episodes of physical assault, this facilitates the position that leaving the relationship is the sole appropriate form of self-assertion. But battering reflects a quest for control that goes beyond separate incidents of physical violence and that does not stop when the woman attempts to leave. A focus on control reveals the danger that violence will continue as part of the attempt to reassert power over the woman.

Relationships involve many incidents of betrayal of trust, negotiations of solutions, and attempts to rebuild and continue. Many (perhaps most) relationships also involve abuses of male power. Yet social expectations and many legal standards impose on the battered woman an obligation to leave that is not present in other abusive circumstances. If a woman's husband pushes her to the floor and tells her he just had an affair with her best friend, it is not clear which betrayal will be more painful to her or which will seem the greater danger to the relationship. If she tries to change his behavior—tells him to stop, seeks counseling, and extracts assurances from him—and later he is unfaithful again, friends and family will probably comfort her: Well, you tried to work it out. If he hits her again, however, and violates his promises to stop, people will ask: Why didn't you leave? Love is an acceptable reason for trying to work out infidelity, but women who love their partners and hope to get them to stop battering are treated as crazy or masochistic (Littleton 1989).

The requirement that battered women leave pretends away the work involved in forging a family and the love and commitment at stake in relationship (Littleton 1989; Mahoney 1991). The idea that women *should* leave relationships also hides real hardships for women and for the children they may be raising. Economic oppression becomes an issue that is raised defensively, to "explain" why a woman "failed" to leave, instead of being understood as always part of the matrix of her choices and decisions.

The question "why didn't you leave?" implies that exit is always the appropriate response to violence, and tends to hide all the things women actually do to cope with violence and to resist the batterer's quest for control. This "shopworn question" (Jones 1986, p. 296) implicitly asserts both that leaving is possible and that it will bring safety. In truth, either staying or leaving are often dangerous acts for women. When a woman tries to stop battering without leaving, or stays because she fears retaliation, she may find that failure to exit is used against her socially and legally.

The categories of "staying" and "leaving" collapse women's actions into categories that hide many acts of self-assertion. A woman might tell her partner to stop, seek counseling, make him promise not to do it again. But these acts of agency are subsumed into the category of "staying" and seen as a problematic failure to leave. A woman whose partner is violent may go stay with family or friends, or take formal or informal shelter, for a few days. Retrospectively, this will also be categorized as "staying" with a batterer because the separation was only temporary. Legal and social inquiry then turn to investigation of "staying" as a problem, rather than giving attention to the help and support a battered woman needs to effectuate her goals.

If the woman succeeds in continuing the relationship without further violence—if he does not hurt her again—no one will know it. She disappears from the radar screen: no shelter requests, no emergency calls, no police reports. This will be defined socially as a normal relationship, regardless of whether other forms of control and nonphysical abuse continue. There will seldom be inquiries about past histories of violence in any relationship that does not present itself as currently violent. If anyone does interview this woman, she will appear as a successful strategist. She will be seen as an agent in her life if his violence has stopped *even if these same acts in another woman would be called "staying" and treated as lack of agency.*

Women's successes at ending violence are virtually invisible, perpetuating the concept that "staying" is irrational. Barbara Hart recounts a story of a church community in Michigan that intervened to support a woman who was determined to end violence without losing her marriage. Women from the church community arranged housing for the woman and her children, helped pick up her children from school, and helped negotiate a requirement that the batterer work within a men's prayer group from the church and attend counseling. Men from the church supported this plan and added a requirement that the batterer take a sabbatical from his campus ministry. The couple reconciled after two years of extended work and counseling, and the woman reported no further violence. No contact with any formal help structures was made in this case, and, since the woman never sought divorce or other legal intervention, she will not be counted in any study.

Statistics offered to show the recurrence of violence indirectly offer evidence about temporary or permanent cessation of violence in some relationships. In various studies, twenty-seven percent of women who reunited with their batterers experienced violence within six weeks, and fifty-seven percent experienced violence within six months (Dutton 1992, p. 44). These figures do in fact show the dangers of recurrent violence, but they also reveal that more than forty percent of women reported no violence for six months after returning to a relationship. Of course, a woman faced with decisions about her relationship does not see herself as choosing a statistical category, but as facing a profoundly personal question of whether she can believe that *with this partner* she will be safe at this time.

In an original and thoughtful study, Lee Bowker interviewed women who had "solved the problem of violence" without leaving their relationships (Bowker 1983). He asked these women to describe their experience in detail and had them describe the strategies they used when their husbands became violent. The women had threatened divorce, sought formal and informal help, left temporarily, hidden, and fought back. Some had complied with the batterer's demands to avoid further confrontations, and some tried to persuade the men to change. Bowker found that certain strategies had been more effective than others at stopping violence. More than half the husbands had ended their violence either from fear of divorce or from desire to rebuild or regain a relationship.

The women in Bowker's study are the success stories that become invisible in studies of recurrent violence. Their actions tracked the actions of many battered women. Of course, at the moment those women decided to give their partners one more chance, they actually had no way to know whether they would eventually be praised for strategizing or treated as dysfunctional for "staying." Women who "succeed" in stopping violence without permanently leaving the relationship have made decisions that are not treated as legitimate or intelligent in women who "fail" to halt the violence of their lovers. Inside the framework imposed by the question "why didn't she leave," women become socially defined as strong or weak depending on what their batterers do next.

The social insistence that the woman should leave treats the actions women often take as illegitimate unless those actions succeed in stopping violence. This undermines a woman's effort to make the fundamental areas of life more her own. The requirement that women promptly and finally separate from their partners contain assumptions about mobility and autonomy in the lives of women that overlook emotional and economic interdependence. This view actually *increases inequality* by stripping legitimacy and social respect from the very things most women do.

The battered woman may find any actions on her part other than separation prove costly in a number of ways that go beyond the predictable dangers of further physical abuse. Failure to exit is often treated, in law and elsewhere in society, as evidence against the woman's account of the facts, her competence, even her honesty. Either the abuse never happened (if it really happened, she would have left), or it was not severe (if things were that bad, she would have left)—and in either instance, her veracity is subject to challenge. In custody evaluations, when a woman's account of violence is not believed, she may be regarded as manipulative or disruptive of the parental relationship of the children's father by the professional performing the assessment.

When it is clear that violence actually has occurred, but leaving is considered the appropriate act of agency by the woman, failure to exit becomes an indication that something is wrong with the battered woman. Battered women who killed their abusers have been required to account in court for their failure to leave. Expert testimony on battered woman syndrome is frequently admitted to explain this problem psychologically (Schneider 1986a). Battered woman syndrome has been criticized for psychologizing women and for its emphasis on "learned helplessness"— the idea that abused women develop a deficiency at perceiving exit when it is actually available. The emphasis on explaining *failure* to leave tends to highlight theories of "learned helplessness" and to downplay the range of psychological responses to violence in women. Rather than asserting the complex needs of a woman's life and her attempts to meet them, the emphasis on "leaving" also tends to shape sociological explanations of women's actions defensively. A woman's lack of resources becomes an explanation for "failure to leave," when in fact all her choices, including the relationship she forged, the compromises she has made in the past, and her decisions after physical abuse begins, have been affected by the lack of social rights to a job, income, child care, and housing.

Leaving could not become the focal question about battered women without this concept of agency as the functioning of a wholly mobile, autonomous, individual, free actor. Once leaving becomes the question, all of our answers accept and reinforce the constraints of this framework. Once we concede exit as the test of agency, we are forced to explain women's deficiencies at agency. This rhetorical trap is so profound that many aspects of work on battering are organized around this underlying concern, from shelter intake forms that ask why a woman failed to leave earlier, to practitioners, who warn that they will not work with her unless she leaves immediately, to the state governor, quoted above, who linked clemency for battered women to demonstrated inability to leave the relationship.

Violence does not end when a woman decides to leave a relationship. The recognition of danger is essential to challenging the equation of agency with exit from violent relationships. Separation assault is the violent attack on a woman's body and volition by which a batterer seeks to keep her from leaving, force her to return, or retaliate against her departure (Mahoney 1991). These attacks take place when the batterer feels his control eroding. The most dangerous moment may come when a woman makes a decision to leave, at the moment she actually walks out, or shortly after she has left. Because the key issue is control, flight might even create a temporarily enhanced sense of power in the batterer, which would turn to loss of control (and acts of violence to reassert control) later, when the woman refused to return and began building a new life.

Separation assault is an easy concept to grasp. Reports of women killed by ex-partners appear regularly in local newspapers all over the country. We recognize this attack instinctively: this is what most orders for protection seek to prevent, and the reason most shelters have secret addresses and telephone numbers. Naming this assault is one way to help show the relationship between control and coercion during and after relationships, and to help transform the cultural presumptions embodied in the question: Why do they stay? This concept should not be used to test whether women were justified in fearing assault after leaving, or to explain women's "failure" to leave, but to make the continuation of violence after separation part of our picture of battering.

Separation is often the moment when the batterer's quest for control becomes lethal. One study of interspousal homicide found that more than half of the men who killed their wives did so after the partners had separated. Men could not cope with feeling bonded with the women they loved. Unable to face dependence on women, the men struck out when they felt abandoned. Spousal homicide resulted from "individuals attempting to solve by their action the riddles of culture that the events of life force on them" (Bernard et al. 1982, pp. 274, 279). Close examination of police reports and supplementary records reveals that many more women are killed by former partners than are reported in police or FBI statistics (Campbell 1992, pp. 100–101). One author estimates that more than half of the women who leave abusive relationships are followed, harassed, or further attacked after separation (Browne 1987, p. 110).

Identifying separation assault helps reveal both the woman's action (separation) and the batterer's retaliation, demonstrating both oppression and resistance in battered women. Once attacks on separation are cognizable, it becomes obvious that not all domestic violence happens in the home. Domestic violence does not only happen to women who fit the stereotype of a battered woman as dependent, helpless, or homebound. Repeated separation assaults characterize many of the published cases in which battered women killed their abusers. In custody determinations, separation assault can help reveal the batterer's quest for control as part of the dynamics among the parties.

The workplace is often a locus of attacks by the batterer (Friedman and Couper, n.d.). Most women can change residences more easily than changing jobs or child-care arrangements, so separation assault is particularly likely to take place at work or on the way to work. Workplace attacks have received little social recognition, however, in part because of cultural myths regarding traditionalism and dependency in battered women, and in part because of the cultural certainty that domestic violence takes place within the private walls of the home. Also, women conceal harassment as much as they can, to protect their jobs and because they fear stigmatization if they disclose problems with abuse. Exploring the problem of separation assault helps to counteract stereotypes of dependency in battered women. Workplace attacks underline the feminist argument that violence is *not* truly a "private" problem.

Identifying the workplace as a locus of domestic abuse also helps demonstrate the interactive totality of oppression in the lives of women. One woman, interviewed because she was a plaintiff in an important labor case, had been threatened with death if she left her violent husband (Faludi 1991, p. 397). Betty Riggs, a plaintiff in a different labor case, had agreed to the company's demand that she accept sterilization in order to avoid losing her job at an American Cyanimid plant. Riggs wanted the job because it offered potential independence from a brutal marriage. Threatened by the mobility Betty gained from the income of a good industrial job, her husband got a job at the plant so that he could keep track of her. When he beat her at work, he received only a reprimand by the company (Faludi 1991, p. 444).

I have found no comprehensive statistics reporting attacks by intimate partners on women at work. Newspapers and television seem to report only cases in which women die. In Miami, where I follow the news, several women have been killed recently at their workplaces by ex-partners. A school cafeteria worker was slain by her ex-boyfriend. A woman who worked as a hairdresser at the airport was killed on the way to work by an ex-husband who had followed her to Florida from another state. A woman who worked in the deli department of a supermarket was shot in the parking lot. When her abuser arrived at her job and began harassing her, she attempted to leave, but she died before reaching her car. A computerized search of newspaper files reveals many similar stories around the country, each known only locally, and each making only brief mention of the fact that the assault happened at work.

Identifying domestic abuse as a phenomenon that happens at work makes many new legal questions appear. Was a woman "on the business of the employer" for the purpose of an employer's group life insurance policy when she was killed when coming to work along a route the employer required her to take?[10] Is abuse or harassment the sort of reason for leaving a job that should entitle a woman to collect unemployment insurance? Although many employers try to cooperate with women who are being harassed at work (Friedman and Couper, n.d.), can gender discrimination laws protect women who face job loss their because abusers harassed them at work?

Attention to these legal inquiries can help transform social understanding of battering. Complex issues may arise when both partners work at the same place—a circumstance that is not uncommon because of involvement between coworkers, or because batterers may follow women into employment as part of a pattern of harassment. Did the circumstances of a relationship between the employees make employment a contributing factor to the assault, to permit a finding of injury "arising out of employment" for purposes of workers' compensation? What should an employer do if one employee has a protective order against another? What about the employer's responsibilities to other employees who may be hurt in the event of a physical assault at the workplace? Answering these questions is essential to protecting women, and will inherently help show the social costs of domestic violence and the active involvement in the world of many women who experience abuse.

As a way to reveal both agency and oppression in battered women, the concept of separation assault has both strengths and weaknesses. Separation assault has cultural resonance in part because it does not completely challenge the social focus on leaving. The term may be understood to answer the question: Why didn't she leave? with a twist emphasizing the batterer's power and control. This could indirectly reinforce the social and legal focus on exit. When exit remains the test of agency, separation assault becomes an excuse for flunking the test. Perpetuating the focus on exit continues to hide agency in women's efforts to forge families, and it conceals the need to develop positive protection of motherhood and of minimal living standards as part of this effort. Work on separation assault is most useful as one component of ongoing work that treats battering as a pattern of power and control, an approach which makes sense of both harm and resistance in women's lives.

Litigating Battering as Power and Control

What does it mean in actual legal proceedings to treat battering as a pattern of violent and coercive behaviors through which the batterer seeks power and control over a woman? In each case, the specific methods will vary that best illustrate power and control, and explain and facilitate women's resistance. Translated into litigation, this perspective helps legal decision-makers to understand the battered woman's experience. When power and control are described in terms that make both agency and oppression visible, it is easier for women to maintain self-esteem while recognizing harm.

Approaching battering as power and control will take different particular forms in many areas. Jane Murphy, of the University of Baltimore Law School, brings this approach into judicial trainings and into hearings for temporary restraining orders. She also finds it helps explain women's acts of "staying" *or* "leaving" to prove constructive desertion—which is important to battered women in Maryland, where no-fault divorces take two years. Treatment programs for batterers also often approach battering as a matter of power and control. Judge Cindy Lederman, who founded the new Dade County domestic violence court in Florida, believes that the combination of court control over batterers, treatment programs, and optional support groups for women and children can together provide greater safety within which a woman can make decisions about continuing or ending the relationship.[11] However, Barbara Hart warns against relying on treatment programs rather than emphasizing support and empowerment for women. She also cautions against privileging the professional assessment of the dangers posed by batterers over the woman's perceptions about lethality (Hart 1988).

Stalking laws provide some legal protection against separation attacks, but they are of mixed utility in revealing both agency and oppression in the experience of battered women. The passage of the first law against stalking in California was impelled by cases of violent attacks reflecting obsession with celebrities, as well as many instances of separation assault. The swift passage of these laws in many states seems to be motivated mostly by a concern with stalking in the domestic violence context. The term "stalking" has itself helped to popularize understanding of some of the potential dangers of separation, and stalking laws help invoke police protection against some assaults by ex-partners.

The concept of stalking has only limited usefulness, however, in showing agency as well as oppression. It invokes the notion of the woman as the object of male obsession and the target of attack, but it does nothing to show her resistance to violence before and after separation. Revealing obsession is simply not the same as revealing control in the domestic violence context. The stalking paradigm links attacks on an ex-wife with obsession with celebrities, rather than making these attacks part of the picture of coercion and power within a relationship and in society.

Stalking also does not address the many times that a decision to leave or threat of separation triggers the batterer's attack. When a man kills his wife and then himself, neighbors often comment that "they had been talking about divorce." This usually means that the woman was thinking of leaving—not that the man's urge to leave resulted in his murderous and suicidal rage. This fear of abandonment and violent response to the sense of personal disintegration at the end of a relationship is common to assaults that occur before or after physical separation has taken place.

In expert testimony for battered women who kill or harm their abusers, the concept of battering as power and control helps make sense of the woman's acts of resistance as well as her experience of harm. Psychologist Mary Ann Dutton illustrates battering for the jury using an enlarged copy of the "Power and Control Wheel" developed by Ellen Pence and the Duluth Abuse Intervention Project (Appendix 1). The Power and Control Wheel groups abusive behaviors into three categories: physical, emotional, and sexual abuse. Specific behaviors associated with each form of abuse are listed within the wheel. Dutton uses this graphic image to show the jury where the many behaviors described by a battered woman fit within the battering process.

Dutton considers the concept of a "cycle of violence" in battering relationships to be descriptive of some relationships but not a prescriptive concept into which the woman's experience should be fitted (Dutton 1992, pp. 28–29). Therefore, she describes "phases of the woman's experience" in relation to this relationship, her previous life experience, and the batterer's quest for power and control. These phases emerge from constructing with the woman a time-line of her life, rather than from an external model based on other relationships or predictive patterns.

Dutton also explains the phenomenon of separation assault, and the ways in which leaving may trigger urgent control impulses in the batterer. She quotes Sue Osthoff, of the National Clearinghouse for the Defense of Battered Women, who describes a "state of siege" in battering relationships. Dutton explains that this creates the context of power and control within which isolated, more identifiable incidents take place. Because physical violence, threats, and other controlling and abusive behaviors punctuate the whole stage of siege, incidents that seem minor separately are brought together as part of the complete pattern of power and control. Meaning does not lie in separate incidents but in their context in the woman's life and this particular relationship. Toward the end, in domestic homicide cases, many things may happen at once. The concept of the "state of siege" helps explain why lethal violence can erupt even though not all these events involved physical abuse.

In prosecuting batterers, understanding coercive patterns of power and violence can be crucial to success. Kathy Strahm, a prosecuting attorney in rural Brown County, Indiana, was approached during her second week on the job by Martha Boroughs, a defendant charged with writing a bad check who sought a continuance to allow payment of the money involved. Martha Boroughs asked to see the check and commented quietly, "I didn't even write this." Upon questioning by Strahm, Martha explained that her husband John had written the check. She begged Strahm not to charge him with forgery but to allow her to pay off the check. She admitted to being extremely afraid of her husband. Strahm arranged the continuance to lull John Boroughs into believing that all was well. Strahm wrote a memo to the file, noting that the defendant appeared to have a defense to the charges but was afraid of her husband.

The following week, a state police detective approached Strahm about the same woman, who was in "real trouble" because Boroughs had begun choking her into unconsciousness and might soon kill her. The detective and the prosecutor worked together to develop a plan for intervention. They arranged that John Boroughs should begin serving a prison sentence on traffic charges then pending in another county. They then offered Martha Boroughs an opportunity to press charges. After John had been in jail over a month, Martha felt safe enough to talk. She revealed a story of grotesque and horrifying violence: she had been repeatedly beaten, raped, kicked, confined, and choked. Her face was scarred because of an abscess in the bone resulting from the battering. John had cut an electrical cord, plugged it into a socket, and tortured her repeatedly with electric shocks. During John's telephone calls from prison, Martha recorded his threats to apply electrical shocks to her eyes when he returned.

Strahm treated each separate incident as a separate serious crime. John Boroughs was charged with fifty-two criminal charges, including five counts of attempted murder, eight counts of battery, fourteen counts of intimidation, and several counts of rape and deviate sexual conduct, that had taken place during the two-year marriage. Every incident of violence, small and large, was part of the picture of controlling and abusive behavior. Strahm sought to keep together as many counts as possible to show the pattern of battering. Fearing that the jury could not properly evaluate so many charges, the judge split the case into several trials covering different time periods. While prosecutors often attempt to keep many criminal counts in one trial, Strahm's approach was innovative in her careful work to break the batterer's dangerous control, as well as in her determination to prosecute all his criminal acts. In the first trial, John Boroughs was convicted and sentenced to eighty-five years in prison. An Indiana appellate court recently affirmed his conviction.

During Strahm's work on the trial, she found that Martha Boroughs had repeatedly made complaints about John's violence. The old complaints in the files looked just like those made by many other women. Each complaint described a discrete incident in which she had been struck—the most recent act of abuse. Martha had never actively pursued prosecution because she feared what John would do when he got out of jail, as he always did. Martha feared not only for her own safety, but for the lives of her children and her ailing father. Boroughs had threatened to kill them all if she ever left, one after another, to punish her and force her to come back to him. Taking the wife's safety seriously was crucial to successful prosecution. Strahm believes that prosecutors too seldom attempt to build the thorough foundation that will reveal the entire abusive pattern and enable prosecution.

The paradigm of battering as a matter of power and control helped a jury understand the harm of battering in a tort suit for damages brought by a battered woman in Minnesota. Theresa Harvieux sued her ex-husband, Greg Tavernier, for damages arising from emotional and physical abuse during her marriage. Tavernier, a county attorney, had betrayed to Theresa's children confidences he had obtained as her divorce lawyer. He had pushed her, pulled her hair, shaken her in an incident that left a red mark on the back of her neck, and kicked her under her chin, creating a bruise. Although Tavernier had pled guilty to fifth-degree assault, the criminal record had been expunged by court order prior to the civil trial.

Tavernier's acts were not sensational examples of violence, but they were part of a pattern of abusive and controlling behavior in the relationship. Kim Hanson, Harvieux's attorney, linked these incidents together for the jury. Hanson based much of her closing argument on Greg Tavernier's testimony in his own defense, which had "in essence, continu[ed] verbal and emotional abuse that she was put through during her marriage." The attempt to portray Theresa as "a bad mother or a loose woman, or [from] a no-good family" was not only abusive but irrelevant to the points at issue in the trial.

Hanson emphasized Tavernier's attitude of "control and disdain" toward his ex-wife: he had stated that she was "allowed" to save money, that she could choose between smoking and marriage to him, and that he was justified in interrupting her telephone calls if he disagreed with what she was saying. "Those sorts of remarks are indicative of a man who is obsessed with controlling this other person, whether through verbal or physical abuse." Hanson also emphasized the consequences for Harvieux in straightforward terms that invited no stigma or stereotype: "You heard the testimony of [a friend] and of her sister that this violence during her marriage to Greg changed her from a happy, free-spirited, independent, carefree woman into a nervous wreck."

Hanson had gained experience through working with domestic abuse advocates handling *pro bono* cases for battered women. She knew Tavernier's testimony reflected the most common defensive comments made by batterers: "It didn't happen; I didn't do it; it was an accident; she did it herself; she deserved it?" Hanson used this paradigm of batterer's defenses to choose incidents that highlighted the ironies for the jury in Tavernier's own testimony. Hanson's approach allowed the jury to link Tavernier's control attempts, his comments from the stand about the plaintiff, and the testimony about violence abuse with the patterns of anxiety, sleeplessness, depression, incapacity to form trusts or relationships, and other intimate harm that her client had suffered. The jury awarded ninety thousand dollars in compensatory and two hundred thousand dollars in punitive damages. The judge reversed an evidentiary ruling regarding Tavernier's guilty plea to fifth-degree assault and ordered a new trial, stating that the damages were plainly excessive for "a few relatively minor incidents of physical abuse."[12] A new judge was subsequently assigned to the case, which reached a settlement just before the new trial was scheduled.

Finally, women's struggles and resistance to oppression can be protected and explained through creative efforts to mobilize support for battered women. One attorney countered a threat to her client's custody of her children through community action. Ann Quigley (a pseudonym), was a woman with five daughters who had repeatedly fled from an extremely violent battering husband. Ted Quigley attacked her repeatedly and violated a restraining order. He purchased a handgun and showed it to his daughters during visitation. The girls protected their mother by escorting her everywhere, sleeping in the same bed with her, and keeping baseball bats throughout the house to protect her if Ted broke in. After a siege in which Ted held Ann hostage to prevent a divorce, Ann finally succeeded in divorcing him. The court considered transferring sole custody of the girls to Ted because of the danger created by Ted's attacks on Ann, but finally awarded custody to Ann and ordered supervised visitation for Ted.

Thereafter, someone shot through the window of Ann's living room while her youngest daughter was watching television. The girl was not injured. The police filed a report with child protective services. When an investigation revealed that the girls often protected their mother, the agency concluded that the girls were at risk of abuse. No one could prove Ted had shot through the window, and he had not hurt the girls except during the times they defended their mother. The child protection agency decided not to proceed against Ted but to file neglect charges against Ann for failure to protect her children from the risk posed by Ted.

Ann's attorney argued that the problem was not Ann's failure but a failure of the legal system and its several components. The court, how-ever, feared that the girls would be injured or die if they were not placed in foster care. Ann's attorney mobilized a community solution to protect the children and Ann. Neighbors organized a neighborhood watch and an escort service for Ann. The police agreed to expedite responses to calls from anyone on Ann's behalf, and began monitoring Ted's movements throughout the city. The public school arranged for outreach and sup-port for Ann and her daughters, to facilitate their academic achievement and emotional well-being. Ann's employer adopted a security system to protect her and coworkers from Ted's harassment and potential violence. When all this was presented to the court, the failure-to-protect charges were dropped.

Ann's story proves that it is possible to reorient our work on domestic violence around the lives and struggles of women. The paradigm of power and control will have different particular meanings in different cases. Translated into legal action, this approach can help ensure the safety of women, link emotional and physical abuse with the batterer's quest for power, and gradually break down atomistic assumptions about agency and women's lives and relationships.

Appendix 1

Power and Control Wheel

Domestic Abuse Intervention Project, 206 West Fourth Street, Duluth, Minnesota 55806, 218-722-4134

Appendix 2

Excerpts from Plaintiff's Closing Argument
Tavernier v. Tavernier

Ms. HANSON: [I'm going to] just go through by order of the questions that you're going to be answering on this special verdict form. The first question is whether or not defendant's actions constitute assault and battery of the plaintiff. And then the second question is whether such actions were a direct cause of harm to the plaintiff. . . .

There's lots of evidence . . . that a battery occurred on January 14th, 1990. You have the photograph of the injuries showing the long red mark across the back of her neck. You have the medical records from her treatment at the hospital which also had a little drawing of it, and a description. You have the testimony of the officer . . . who stated that he observed her injuries at that time. . . . You have the issuance of an order for protection in this case. . . . And, finally, you have the criminal charges and his plea of guilty to those charges of assault.

With respect to the other battery and the assaults, you have the testimony of the plaintiff concerning his use of physical force throughout their marriage. And you also have the testimony of [an eyewitness] concerning him coming into the bar and pulling her off the chair, and [the] observations about the injury to her chin when he kicked her and [the witness] went to pick her up at the hotel. . . .

[T]he next two questions on the verdict form concern did defendant intentionally inflict emotional distress on plaintiff. And if so, was such distress a direct cause of harm to her? Again, you have to answer both of these questions yes based on the evidence in this case. Him yelling at her as she's vomiting, threatening her with the loss of her children if she tells anybody what's going on, revealing confidential information about her to her young daughter. And the judge will instruct you that . . . as an attorney, [the defendant] had a continual duty to preserve [the plaintiff's] secrets and if he violated that duty, that violation is considered to be an infliction of emotional distress upon her.

And, again, this has come in through stipulation, that if we called [her daughter] to the stand she would have said that he told her that now she was thirteen she would start having sex just like her mother did, and that her mother had done drugs and started smoking when she was thirteen. That testimony, by the way, is unrebutted, he does not deny it.

Ninety percent of the testimony offered by the defendant and by his parents and even by his expert witness has also been, in essence, continuing verbal and emotional abuse that she was put through during her marriage. The whole thing was centered on trying to prove to you that she's a bad mother or a loose woman or that she really does have a no-good family.

For the most part, aside from all of that information, which really has nothing to do with this case and is really prejudicial, he has tried to deny everything. And he has tried by his denial to force you to take one side or another in determining this case. . . .

There are lots of clues through which you can determine which testimony is accurate. The first is that where it was possible, his story was effectively impeached by written documentary evidence. . . .

There are also clues in his own testimony on the stand. And this is just little things or remarks that show he has an attitude of control and disdain towards the plaintiff. I personally recall him saying . . . that she was allowed to save money. She could choose between smoking and getting married to him. Somehow or another he was justified in interrupting her telephone calls because he didn't agree with what she was saying. Those sorts of remarks are indicative of a man who is obsessed with controlling this other person, whether through verbal or physical abuse.

Now, denial can be a very effective way to respond, especially in cases such as this where most of the stuff is not going to be witnessed because it's occurring within the privacy of the home. . . .

I submit to you that it's not a coincidence that he admits something happened on the only two occasions where there were visible injuries observed by other people outside of their home. Let's look at his explanation of these injuries, which are totally unconvincing. With respect to the February of 1989 incident, they're engaged in a heated argument, he says leave me alone, get out, and then he felt something and he just shook his leg. And because he shook his leg she went with her daughter to stay in a hotel. . . .

Now, the harder questions are going to be questions five and six, which require you to determine a sum of money to fairly and adequately compensate the plaintiff in this case. There was some claim made during [the defense attorney's] opening statement that this is just a case about a woman unhappy with her divorce settlement or somehow interested in getting a bunch of money, but that's not true. This is a case about responsibility and accountability for the injuries inflicted on another human being. And the way our system holds people responsible or accountable in a case like this is through an award of money damages. You're going to have to place a dollar value on the pain and disability and embarrassment and emotional distress up to the time of trial and then continuing on into the future.

The evidence . . . [shows] that . . . she still has had nightmares, she's fearful, she's anxious, she can't slow down, she has to stay busy all the time, she's fearful and crying, even at a public baseball game with her friends.

Now, just because Ms. Harvieux can't afford a high-paid expert to come in here and testify in this case, it doesn't mean she's not still suffering from this abuse. [The adverse psychological expert's] testimony is just an opinion. . . . You heard the testimony of both [the plaintiff's friend] and of her sister that this violence during her marriage to Greg changed her from a happy, free-spirited, independent, carefree woman into a nervous wreck.

Finally, you're going to be asked to decide whether or not to impose punitive damages in this case. And punitive damages are based on the amount necessary to punish the defendant for his intentional acts of abuse and to deter others from doing this in our wider community. The judge will instruct you on some factors that you should consider.

You should consider the effect of other punishment. Now, you've heard him testify that even though he pled guilty to those charges, because of his special deal with the prosecutor, he has no criminal record. If this happens again next week, it will be as if it were the first time.

You need to consider the seriousness of the hazards of domestic violence to the public at large, to the other children and spouses out there suffering under domestic abuse. You can read almost daily in the paper, people are dying because of violence of this sort, it's a very serious hazard.

And then, lastly, you're considering the financial condition of the defendant, and that's why you'll have these other exhibits in here concerning his earnings over the last couple of years and his current salary. I would suggest to you that you consider an award of approximately $100,000, which is about two years of his salary, and that that award will be sufficient to punish him and also to act as a warning and to deter others out there from engaging in the same sort of conduct.

I want to thank you for your patience and for listening to everything and I wish you good luck in your deliberations.

Notes

The author wishes to thank Sharon Keller, Lynn Henderson, Joan Mahoney, Donna Coker, and Ken Casebeer for their comments and insight, and Jacqueline Becerra for research assistance.

1. The cover of the *New York Times Magazine* recently announced that "Rape hype betrays feminism." Roiphe 1993, p. 26. See also Morgenson 1992, p. 152 (reviewing Susan Faludi, *Backlash: The Undeclared War Against American Women*); Hughes 1992, p. 44 (describing competition among Americans for "victimhood"); Leo 1992.

2. *Bray v. Alexandria Women's Health Clinic*, 113 S. Ct. 753 (1993). Ironically, this opinion also reflects the high value that an ideology of negative rights places on the mobility of atomistic individuals: the constitutionally guaranteed right to travel interstate *is* protected against private interference, but to invoke law's protection the interference must be "aimed at" that right, rather than incidentally interfering with the objectives of women who travelled interstate to get abortions.

3. *Lindsey v. Normet*, 405 U.S. 56 (1972).

4. *Dandridge v. Williams*, 279 U.S. 471 (1970).

5. *In re Jacobs*, 444 N.W. 2d 789 (Mich. 1989). All facts are taken from the case. The opinion refers to this injury at one point as the result of a "stroke." Intracranial bleeding is also a common domestic violence injury.

6. *Matter of Farley,* 469 N.W.2d 295 (Mich. 1991). The published opinion is by Justice Levin, dissenting from the order denying Sharon Benn the opportunity to go forward with a late appeal.

7. Professor Robert Rosen uses this term, quoting Grand Master Marshall Farkas of Dade County, Florida.

8. See, e.g., Sally Quinn, "Who Killed Feminism? Hypocritical Movement Leaders Betrayed Their Own Cause." *Washington Post,* January 19, 1992, p. C1.

9. Statistics on the commonality of domestic violence vary widely. The question is obviously highly charged, and there are obvious difficulties with gathering reliable data. Lenore Walker and others have used an estimate that violence occurs in fifty percent of relationships, which has seemed reasonable to myself and other scholars (Walker 1979, 1984; Littleton 1989; Mahoney 1991).

   No-fault divorce tends to hide domestic violence. Two separate studies done in legal services offices found extremely high rates of domestic violence among women seeking divorces. In Brooklyn, out of six hundred female clients seen at legal services during a fifteen-month period, sixty percent admitted having been beaten during their marriage (Bowker 1983, p. 3). In Baltimore, out of fifty women seeking divorces over the course of five days, twenty had been battered sufficiently to be described as battered wives and thirteen more had experienced violence in their relationships at least once, making a total of sixty six percent who had encountered violence in their marriages (Mahoney 1992, p. 1288). Violence may be more likely to have occurred among couples who are now separating; violence can either reflect or cause a desire to end the relationship, or it may occur in retaliation for separation. Many women underreport their experiences of violence even when questioned directly (for example, calling threats made with loaded guns "emotional abuse" and failing to count marital rape as a form of "violence").

10. *McMillan v. State Mutual Life Assurance Co. of Am.,* 922 F.2d 1073 (3d Cir. 1990).

11. Lee Bowker's study in Milwaukee revealed that the cessation of violence did not guarantee success for the relationship, and many women went on to end the relationships later for reasons other than their partner's violence (Bowker 1983, p. 29).

12. Martha Irvine, "Battered Women File Civil Suits," *Minnesota Free Press* October 21–November 3, 1992).

Mapping the Margins: Intersectionality, Identity Politics, and Violence Against Women of Color

by Kimberlé Williams Crenshaw

Introduction

Over the last two decades, women have organized against the almost routine violence that shapes their lives. Drawing from the strength of shared experience, women have recognized that the political demands of millions speak more powerfully than the pleas of a few isolated voices. This politicization in turn has transformed the way we understand violence against women. For example, battering and rape, once seen as private (family matters) and aberrational (errant sexual aggression), are now largely recognized as part of a broad-scale system of domination that affects women as a class. This process of recognizing as social and systemic what was formerly perceived as isolated and individual has also characterized the identity politics of people of color and gays and lesbians, among others. For all these groups, identity-based politics has been a source of strength, community, and intellectual development.

The embrace of identity politics, however, has been in tension with dominant conceptions of social justice. Race, gender, and other identity categories are most often treated in mainstream liberal discourse as vestiges of bias or domination—that is, as intrinsically negative frameworks in which social power works to exclude or marginalize those who are different. According to this understanding, our liberatory objective should be to empty such categories of any social significance. Yet implicit in certain strands of feminist and racial liberation movements, for example, is the view that the social power in delineating difference need not be the power of domination; it can instead be the source of political empowerment and social reconstruction.

The problem with identity politics is not that it fails to transcend difference, as some critics charge, but rather the opposite—that it frequently conflates or ignores intragroup differences. In the context of

violence against women, this elision of difference is problematic, fundamentally because the violence that many women experience is often
shaped by other dimensions of their identities, such as race and class.
Moreover, ignoring differences *within* groups frequently contributes to
tension *among* groups, another problem of identity politics that frustrates
efforts to politicize violence against women. Feminist efforts to politicize
experiences of women and antiracist efforts to politicize experiences of
people of color have frequently proceeded as though the issues and
experiences they each detail occur on mutually exclusive terrains. Although racism and sexism readily intersect in the lives of real people,
they seldom do in feminist and antiracist practices. And so, when the
practices expound identity as "woman" or "person of color" as an either/
or proposition, they relegate the identity of women of color to a location
that resists telling.

My objective here is to advance the telling of that location by exploring
the race and gender dimensions of violence against women of color.
Contemporary feminist and antiracist discourses have failed to consider
the intersections of racism and patriarchy. Focusing on two dimensions
of male violence against women—battering and rape—I consider how the
experiences of women of color are frequently the product of intersecting
patterns of racism and sexism, and how these experiences tend not to
be represented within the discourse of either feminism or antiracism.
Because of their intersectional identity as both women *and* people of
color within discourses that are shaped to respond to one *or* the other, the
interests and experiences of women of color are frequently marginalized
within both.

In an earlier article, I used the concept of intersectionality to denote
the various ways in which race and gender interact to shape the multiple
dimensions of Black[1] women's employment experiences (Crenshaw 1989,
p. 139). My objective there was to illustrate that many of the experiences
Black women face are not subsumed within the traditional boundaries
of race or gender discrimination as these boundaries are currently understood, and that the intersection of racism and sexism factors into Black
women's lives in ways that cannot be captured wholly by looking at the
race or gender dimensions of those experiences separately. I build on
those observations here by exploring the various ways in which race and
gender intersect in shaping structural and political aspects of violence
against women of color.[2]

I should say at the outset that intersectionality is not being offered
here as some new, totalizing theory of identity. Nor do I mean to suggest
that violence against women of color can be explained only through the
specific frameworks of race and gender considered here. Indeed, factors
I address only in part or not at all, such as class or sexuality, are often

as critical in shaping the experiences of women of color. My focus on the intersections of race and gender only highlights the need to account for multiple grounds of identity when considering how the social world is constructed.

I have divided the issues presented in this chapter into two categories. In the first part, I discuss structural intersectionality, the ways in which the location of women of color at the intersection of race and gender makes our actual experience of domestic violence, rape, and remedial reform qualitatively different from that of white women. I shift the focus in the second part to political intersectionality, where I analyze how both feminist and antiracist politics have functioned in tandem to marginalize the issue of violence against women of color. Finally, I address the implications of the intersectional approach within the broader scope of contemporary identity politics.

Structural Intersectionality

Structural Intersectionality and Battering

I observed the dynamics of structural intersectionality during a brief field study of battered women's shelters located in minority communities in Los Angeles.[3] In most cases, the physical assault that leads women to these shelters is merely the most immediate manifestation of the subordination they experience. Many women who seek protection are unemployed or underemployed, and a good number of them are poor. Shelters serving these women cannot afford to address only the violence inflicted by the batterer; they must also confront the other multilayered and routinized forms of domination that often converge in these women's lives, hindering their ability to create alternatives to the abusive relationships that brought them to shelters in the first place. Many women of color, for example, are burdened by poverty, child-care responsibilities, and the lack of job skills. These burdens, largely the consequence of gender and class oppression, are then compounded by the racially discriminatory employment and housing practices women of color often face.[4] Women of color are burdened as well by the disproportionately high unemployment among people of color that make battered women of color less able to depend on the support of friends and relatives for temporary shelter.

These observations reveal how intersectionality shapes the experiences of many women of color. Economic considerations—access to employment, housing, and wealth—confirm that class structures play an important part in defining the experience of women of color *vis-à-vis* battering. But it would be a mistake to conclude from these observations that it is simply the fact of poverty that is at issue here. Rather, their experiences reveal how diverse structures intersect, since even the class dimension is not independent from race and gender.

At the simplest level, race, gender, and class are implicated together because the fact the fact of being a women of color correlates strongly with poverty. Moreover, the disparate access to housing and jobs—that is, the phenomenon of discrimination—is reproduced through their race and gender identity. Race and gender are two of the primary sites for the particular distribution of social resources that ends up with observable class differences. And finally, once in a lower economic class, race and gender structures continue to shape the particular ways that women of color experience poverty, relative to other groups.

These converging systems structure the experiences of battered women of color in ways that require intervention strategies to be responsive to these intersections. Strategies based solely on the experiences of women who do not share the same class or race backgrounds will be of limited utility for those whose lives are shaped by a different set of obstacles. For example, shelter policies are often shaped by an image that locates women's subordination primarily in the psychological effects of male domination, and thus overlooks the socioeconomic factors that often disempower women of color.[5] Because the disempowerment of many battered women of color is arguably less a function of what is in their minds and more a reflection of the obstacles that exist in their lives, these interventions are likely to reproduce rather than effectively challenge their domination.

While the intersection of race, gender, and class constitute the primary structural elements of the experience of many Black and Latina women in battering shelters, it is important to understand that there are other sites where structures of power intersect. For immigrant women, for example, their status as immigrants can render them vulnerable in ways that are similarly coercive, yet not easily reducible to economic class. For example, take the Marriage Fraud Amendments to the 1986 Immigration Act. Under the marriage fraud provisions of the Act, a person who immigrated to the United States to marry a United States citizen or permanent resident had to remain "properly" married for two years before applying for permanent resident status,[6] at which time applications for the immigrant's permanent status were required by both spouses.[7] Predictably, under these circumstances, many immigrant women were reluctant to leave even the most abusive of partners for fear of being deported. When faced with the choice between protection from their batterers and protection against deportation, many immigrant women chose the latter (Walt 1990, p. 8). Reports of the tragic consequences of this double subordination put pressure on Congress to include in the Immigration Act of 1990 a provision amending the marriage fraud rules to allow for an explicit waiver for hardship caused by domestic violence.[8]

Yet many immigrant women, particularly women of color, have remained vulnerable to battering because they are unable to meet the conditions established for a waiver. The evidence required to support a waiver "can include, but is not limited to, reports and affidavits from police, medical personnel, psychologists, school officials, and social service agencies."[9] For many immigrant women, limited access to these resources can make it difficult for them to obtain the evidence needed for a waiver. Often cultural barriers further discourage immigrant women from reporting or escaping battering situations. Tina Shum, a family counselor at a social service agency, points out that "[t]his law sounds so easy to apply, but there are cultural complications in the Asian community that make even these requirements difficult. . . . Just to find the opportunity and courage to call us is an accomplishment for many." (Hodgin 1991, p. E1). The typical immigrant spouse, she suggests, may live "[i]n an extended family where several generations live together, there may be no privacy on the telephone, no opportunity to leave the house and no understanding of public phones." As a consequence, many immigrant women may be wholly dependent on their husbands as their link to the world outside their homes.[10]

Immigrant women may also be vulnerable to spousal violence because many of them depend on their husbands for information regarding their legal status. More than likely, many women who are now permanent residents continue to suffer abuse under threats of deportation by their husbands. Even if the threats are unfounded, women who have no independent access to information will still be intimidated by such threats. And even though the domestic violence waiver focuses on immigrant women whose husbands are United States citizens or permanent residents, there are countless women married to undocumented workers (or who are themselves undocumented) who suffer in silence for fear that the security of their entire families will be jeopardized should they seek help or otherwise call attention to themselves.

Language barriers present another structural problem that often limits opportunities of non-English-speaking women to take advantage of existing support services (Banales 1990, p. E5). Such barriers not only limit access to information about shelters, but also limit access to the security shelters provide. Some shelters turn non-English-speaking women away for lack of bilingual personnel and resources.[11]

These examples illustrate how patterns of subordination intersect in women's experience of domestic violence. Intersectional subordination need not be intentionally produced; in fact, it is frequently the consequence of the imposition of one burden that interacts with preexisting vulnerabilities to create yet another dimension of disempowerment. In the case of the marriage fraud provisions of the Immigration and Nationality Act, the imposition of a policy specifically designed to burden one class—immigrant spouses seeking permanent resident status—exacerbated the disempowerment of those already subordinated by other structures of domination. By failing to take into account the vulnerability of immigrant spouses to domestic violence, Congress positioned these women to absorb the simultaneous impact of its anti-immigration policy and their spouses' abuse.

The enactment of the domestic violence waiver of the marriage fraud provisions similarly illustrates how modest attempts to respond to certain problems can be ineffective when the intersectional location of women of color is not considered in fashioning the remedy. Cultural identity and class affect the likelihood that a battered spouse could take advantage of the waiver. Although the waiver is formally available to all women, the terms of the waiver make it inaccessible to some. Immigrant women who are socially, culturally, or economically privileged are more likely to be able to marshall the resources needed to satisfy the waiver requirements. Those immigrant women least able to take advantage of the waiver—women who are socially or economically the most marginal— are the ones most likely to be women of color.

Structural Intersectionality and Rape

Women of color are differently situated in the economic, social, and political worlds. When reform efforts undertaken on behalf of women neglect this fact, women of color are less likely to have their needs met than women who are racially privileged. For example, counselors who provide rape crisis services to women of color report that a significant proportion of the resources allocated to them must be spent handling problems other than rape itself. Meeting these needs often places these counselors at odds with their funding agencies, which allocate funds according to standards of need that are largely white and middle-class.[12] These uniform standards of support ignore the fact that different needs often demand different priorities in terms of resource allocation, and consequently, these standards hinder the ability of counselors to address the needs of nonwhite and poor women.

As noted earlier, counselors in minority communities report spending hours locating resources and contacts to meet the housing and other immediate needs of women who have been assaulted. Yet this work is only considered "information and referral" by funding agencies and as such, is typically underfunded, notwithstanding the magnitude of need for these services in minority communities (Matthews 1989, pp. 287–88). The problem is compounded by expectations that rape crisis centers will use a significant portion of resources allocated to them on counselors to accompany victims to court,[13] even though there is some evidence to suggest that women of color are less likely to have their cases pursued in the criminal justice system (Collins 1990; Field & Bienen 1980). The resources expected to be set aside for court services are misdirected in these communities.

The fact that minority women suffer from the effects of multiple subordination, coupled with institutional expectations based on inappropriate nonintersectional contexts, shapes and ultimately limits the opportunities for meaningful intervention on their behalf. Understanding the intersectional dynamics of crisis intervention may go far toward explaining the high levels of frustration and burnout experienced by counselors who attempt to meet the needs of minority women victims.

Political Intersectionality

The concept of political intersectionality highlights the fact that women of color are situated within at least two subordinated groups that frequently pursue conflicting political agendas. The need to split one's political energies between two sometimes opposing political agendas is a dimension of intersectional disempowerment that men of color and white women seldom confront. Indeed, their specific raced *and* gendered experiences, although intersectional, often define as well as confine the interests of the entire group. For example, racism as experienced by people of color who are of a particular gender—male—tends to determine the parameters of antiracist strategies, just as sexism as experienced by women who are of a particular race—white—tends to ground the women's movement. The problem is not simply that both discourses fail women of color by not acknowledging the "additional" burden of patriarchy or of racism, but that the discourses are often inadequate even to the discrete tasks of articulating the full dimensions of racism and sexism. Because women of color experience racism in ways not always the same as those experienced by men of color, and sexism in ways not always parallel to experiences of white women, dominant conceptions of antiracism and feminism are limited, even on their own terms.

Among the most troubling political consequences of the failure of antiracist and feminist discourses to address the intersections of racism and patriarchy is the fact that, to the extent they forward the interest of "people of color" and "women," respectively, one analysis often implicitly denies the validity of the other. The failure of feminism to interrogate race means that the resistance strategies of feminism will often replicate and reinforce the subordination of people of color, and the failure of antiracism to interrogate patriarchy means that antiracism will frequently reproduce the subordination of women. These mutual elisions present a particularly difficult political dilemma for women of color. Adopting either analysis constitutes a denial of a fundamental dimension of our subordination and works to precludes the development of a political discourse that more fully empowers women of color.

The Politicization of Domestic Violence

That the political interests of women of color are obscured and sometimes jeopardized by political strategies that ignore or suppress intersectional issues is illustrated by my experiences in gathering information for this essay. I attempted to review Los Angeles Police Department statistics reflecting the rate of domestic violence interventions by district, because such statistics can provide a rough picture of arrests by racial group, given the degree of racial segregation in Los Angeles.[14] The L.A.P.D., however, would not release the information. A representative explained that one reason the information was not released was that domestic violence activists, both within and outside the department, feared that statistics reflecting the extent of domestic violence in minority communities might be selectively interpreted and publicized so as to undermine long-term efforts to force the department to address domestic violence as a serious problem. Apparently activists were worried that the statistics might permit opponents to dismiss domestic violence as a minority problem and, therefore, not deserving of aggressive action.

The informant also claimed that representatives from various minority communities opposed the release of these statistics. They were concerned, apparently, that the data would unfairly represent African-American and Latino communities as unusually violent, potentially reinforcing stereotypes that might be used to justify oppressive police tactics and other discriminatory practices. These misgivings are based on the familiar and not unfounded premise that certain minorities—particularly Black men—have already been stereotyped as pathologically violent. Some worry that attempts to make domestic violence an object of political action may only serve to confirm such stereotypes and undermine efforts to combat negative beliefs about the African-American community.

Concerns about the misuse of statistics are, of course, well-founded; however, suppressing the information appears to be an easy answer to the problem only so long as the interests of women of color subject to domestic violence are not directly assessed. The effects of this political "gag order" are particularly disturbing in light of the feminist imperative to "break the silence," a value grounded in the recognition that knowledge about the extent and nature of domestic violence is an important precondition to successful efforts to mobilize against it. This suppression is also troubling given the improbability that women of color would benefit significantly from the trickle-down effects of either the feminist mobilization against domestic violence or the more community-based mobilizations against intraracial crime in general. Thus, the mutual suppression of critical information rendered the possibility of a broad mobilization against domestic violence within communities of color less likely.

This story, although anecdotal, serves as a useful illustration to frame the more conventional ways that women of color have been sometimes erased within the political contestations between antiracism and racial hierarchy, and between feminism and patriarchy. As the discussion below suggests, these erasures are not always the direct or intended consequences of antiracism or feminism, but frequently the product of rhetorical and political strategies that fail to challenge race and gender hierarchies simultaneously.

Domestic Violence and Antiracist Politics

Within communities of color, efforts to stem the politicization of domestic violence are often grounded in attempts to maintain the integrity of the community. The articulation of this perspective takes different forms. Some critics allege that feminism has no place within communities of color, that gender issues are internally divisive, and that raising such issues within nonwhite communities represents the migration of white women's concerns into a context in which they are not only irrelevant but also harmful. At their most extreme, critics who seek to defend their communities against this feminist assault deny that gender violence is a problem in their community, and characterize any effort to politicize gender subordination as itself a community problem. This is the position taken by Shahrazad Ali in her controversial book, *The Blackman's Guide to Understanding the Blackwoman*. In this stridently antifeminist tract, Ali draws a positive correlation between domestic violence and the liberation of African-Americans. Ali blames the deteriorating conditions within the African-American community on the insubordination of Black women and on the failure of Black men to control them (Ali 1989, pp. viii, 76). Ali goes so far as to advise Black men to physically chastise Black women when they are "disrespectful" (p. 169). While she cautions that Black men must use moderation in disciplining "their" women, she argues that Black men must sometimes resort to physical force to reestablish the authority over Black women that racism has disrupted (pp. 174, 172).

Ali's premise is that patriarchy is beneficial for the African-American community (p. 67), and that it must be strengthened through coercive means if necessary.[15] Yet the violence that accompanies this will-to-control is devastating, not only for the Black women who are victimized, but also for the entire African-American community. The recourse to violence to resolve conflicts establishes a dangerous pattern for children raised in such environments, and contributes to other pressing problems. For example, it has been estimated that nearly forty percent of all homeless women and children have fled violence in their homes, and an estimated sixty-three percent of young men between the ages of eleven and twenty who are imprisoned for homicide have killed their mothers' batterers (Women and Violence Hearings, 1991, pt 2, p. 142). And yet, while gang violence, homicide, and other forms of Black-on-Black crime have increasingly been discussed within African-American politics, patriarchal ideas about gender and power preclude the recognition of domestic violence as yet another compelling incidence of Black-on-Black crime.

Efforts such as Ali's to justify violence against women in the name of Black liberation are indeed extreme. The more common problem is that the political or cultural interests of the community are interpreted in a way that precludes full public recognition of the problem of domestic violence. While it would be misleading to suggest that white Americans have been any more successful in coming to terms with the degree of violence in their own homes, it is nonetheless the case that race adds yet another dimension to why the problem of domestic violence is suppressed within nonwhite communities. People of color often must weigh their interests in avoiding issues that might reinforce distorted public perceptions of their communities against the need to acknowledge and address intracommunity problems. Yet the cost of suppression is seldom recognized, in part because the failure to discuss the issue mishapes perceptions of how serious the problem is in the first place.

The controversy over Alice Walker's novel, *The Color Purple,* can be understood as an intracommunity debate about the political costs of exposing gender violence within the Black community. Some critics chastised Walker for portraying Black men as violent brutes (Early 1988, p. 9; Pinckney 1987, p. 17). Others lambasted Walker for the portrayal of Celie, the emotionally and physically abused protagonist who triumphs in the end. Walker, one critic contended, had created in Celie a Black woman whom the critic could not imagine existing in any Black community she knew or could conceive of (Harris 1984, p. 155).

The claim that Celie was somehow an unauthentic character might be read as a consequence of silencing discussion of intracommunity violence. Celie may be unlike any Black woman we know because the real terror experienced daily by minority women is routinely concealed in a misguided (though perhaps understandable) attempt to forestall racial stereotyping. Of course, it is true that representations of Black violence—

whether statistical or fictional—are often written into a larger script that consistently portrays the African-American community as pathologically violent. The problem, however, is not so much the portrayal of violence itself as it is the absence of other narratives and images portraying a fuller range of Black experience. Suppression of some of these issues in the name of antiracism imposes real costs. Where information about violence in minority communities is not available, domestic violence is unlikely to be addressed as a serious issue.

The political imperatives of a narrowly focused antiracist strategy support other practices that isolate women of color. For example, activists who have attempted to provide support services to Asian- and African-American women occasionally report intense resistance from some of the leaders and institutions within those communities.[16] At other times, cultural and social factors contribute to suppression. Nilda Rimonte, director of Everywoman's Shelter in Los Angeles, contends that in the Asian community, saving the honor of the family from shame is a priority (Rimonte 1991; Rimonte 1989, p. 327). Unfortunately, this priority tends to be more readily interpreted as obliging women not to scream rather than obliging men not to hit.

Race and culture contribute to the suppression of domestic violence in other ways as well. Women of color are often reluctant to call the police, a hesitancy likely due to a general unwillingness among people of color to subject their private lives to the scrutiny and control of a police force that is frequently hostile. There is also a more generalized community ethic against public intervention, the product of a desire to create a private world free from the diverse assaults on the public lives of racially subordinated people. In this sense the home is not simply a man's castle in patriarchal terms, but it is also a safe haven from the indignities of life in a racist society. In many cases, the desire to protect the home as a safe haven against assaults outside the home may make it more difficult for women of color to seek protection against assaults from within the home.

There is also a general tendency within antiracist discourse to regard the problem of violence against women of color as just another manifestation of racism. In this sense, gender domination within the community is reconfigured as a consequence of racial discrimination against men. Of course, it is probably true that racism contributes to the cycle of violence, given the stress that men of color experience in dominant society. It is therefore more than reasonable to explore the links between racism and domestic violence. But the chain of violence is more complex and extends beyond this single link. Moreover, arguments that characterize domestic violence in communities of color as the acting out of frustrations over denial of male power in other spheres tend to be tied to claims that eradicating the power differentials between men of color and white men will solve the problem. Yet, as a solution to violence, this approach seems counterproductive, first, because men of power and prestige also abuse women, but most importantly, because it buys into dominant images of male power that are socially damaging. A more productive approach—one more likely to benefit women and children as well as other men—is to resist the seductive images of male power that rely on the ultimate threat of violence as a legitimate measure of male agency. The legitimacy of such power expectations can be challenged by exposing their dysfunctional and debilitating effects on families and communities of color. Moreover, while understanding links between racism and domestic violence is an important component of any effective intervention strategy, it is also clear that women of color need not await the ultimate triumph over racism before they can expect to live violence-free lives.

Race and the Domestic Violence Lobby

Not only do race-based priorities function to obscure the problem of violence suffered by women of color; certain rhetorical strategies directed at politicizing violence against women may also reproduce the political marginalization of women of color. Strategies for increasing awareness of domestic violence tend to begin by citing the commonly shared assumption that battering is a problem located in the family of the "other"—namely, poor and/or minority families. The strategy then focuses on demolishing the straw man, stressing that spousal abuse also occurs in white elite communities. Some authorities are explicit in renouncing the "stereotypical myths about battered women" (Women and Violence Hearings, 1991, pt 2, p. 139). A few commentators have even transformed the message that battering is not *exclusively* a problem of the poor or minority communities into a claim that it *equally* affects all races and classes (Borgmann 1990). That battering occurs in families of all races and all classes seems to be an ever-present theme of antiabuse campaigns. (Women and Violence Hearings, 1991 pt. 1, p. 101; pt 2, pp. 89, 139). First-person anecdotes and studies, for example, consistently assert that battering cuts across racial, ethnic, economic, education, and religious lines. (Walker 1989, pp. 101–2; Straus, Gelles and Steinmetz 1980, p. 31; Clark 1987, p. 182 n. 74). Countless first-person stories begin with a statement like, "I was not supposed to be a battered wife." The inference, of course, is that there *is* a more likely vision of a battered spouse, one whose race or class background contrasts with the identity of the speaker to produce the irony. Playing on the contrast between myths about and realities of violence functions effectively to challenge beliefs about the occurrence of domestic violence in American society.

Yet this tactic is tricky business, one that may simultaneously reify and erase "othered" women as victims of domestic abuse. It is clear, on one hand, that attacking the stereotypes underlying dominant conceptions of domestic violence is both a feminist and antiracist strategy. By pointing out that violence is a universal problem, elites are deprived of their false security, while nonelite families are given reason not to be unduly defensive. Moreover, all battered women may well benefit from knowing that they are far from alone. But there is, nonetheless, a thin line between debunking the stereotypical beliefs that only poor or minority women are battered, and pushing them aside to focus on victims for whom mainstream politicians and media are more likely to express concern. While it is unlikely that advocates intend to play into such sensibilities— and it is even less clear whether favorable responses reflect these sensibilities—the rhetoric about and representations of battered women produced by power elites provide some grounds for concern.

An illustration of this troubling possibility is found in the remarks of Senator David Cohen in support of the Violence Against Women Act of 1991.[17] Senator Cohen stated:

> [Rapes and domestic assaults] are not limited to the streets of our inner cities or to those few highly publicized cases that we read about in the newspapers or see on the evening news. . . . It is *our* mothers, wives, daughters, sisters, friends, neighbors, and coworkers who are being victimized.[18]

Senator Cohen and his colleagues who support the Act no doubt believe that they are directing attention and resources to all women victimized by domestic violence. Despite their universalizing rhetoric of "all" women, they were able to empathize with female victims of domestic violence only by looking past the plight of "other" women, and by recognizing the familiar faces of their own. The strength of the appeal to protect "our" mothers, wives, daughters, and sisters must, on some level, be its race and class specificity. After all, it has always been someone's mother, wife, daughter, or sister who has been abused, even when the victim was imagined to be Black, Latina or poor. The point here is not that the Violence Against Women Act is particularistic on its own terms, but that, unless the senators and other policymakers consciously examine why violence remained insignificant as long as it was understood as a minority problem, it is unlikely that women of color will share equally in the distribution of resources and concern. It is even more unlikely, however, that those in power will be forced to confront this issue. As long as attempts to politicize domestic violence focus on convincing elites that this is not a "minority" problem but *their* problem, any authentic and sensitive attention to the experiences of minority women will probably continue to be regarded as jeopardizing the movement.

While Senator Cohen's statement reflects a self-consciously political presentation of domestic violence, an episode of the CBS News program *48 Hours*[19] shows how similar patterns of "othering" nonwhite women are also apparent in journalistic accounts of domestic violence. The program presented seven women who were victims of abuse. Six were interviewed at some length, along with their family members, friends, supporters, and even detractors. The viewer got to know something about these women as each was humanized through the telling of their stories. Yet the seventh woman, the only nonwhite one, never came into focus. She remained literally unrecognizable throughout the segment, first introduced by photographs showing her face badly beaten, and later shown with her face electronically altered in the videotape of a hearing at which she was forced to testify. Other images associated with this woman included shots of a bloodstained room and blood-soaked pillows. Her boyfriend was pictured handcuffed, while the camera zoomed in for a close-up of his bloodied sneakers. Of all the presentations in the episode, hers was the most graphic and impersonal. The overall point of the segment "featuring" this woman was that battering might not escalate into homicide if battered women would only cooperate with prosecutors. In focusing on its own agenda and failing to explore why this woman did not cooperate with prosecutors, the program diminished this woman, communicating, however subtly, that she was responsible for her own victimization.

Unlike the other women, all of whom, again, were white, this Black woman had no name, no family, no context. The viewer sees her only as victimized and uncooperative. She cries when shown pictures. She pleads not to be forced to view the bloodstained room and her disfigured face. The program does not help the viewer to understand her predicament. The possible reasons she did not want to testify—fear, love, or possibly both—are never suggested. Most unfortunately, she, unlike the other six women, is given no epilogue. While the fates of the other women are revealed at the end of the episode, we discover nothing about the Black woman. She, like the "others" she represents, is simply left to herself and soon forgotten. This episode presents the classic view of the pathological "other": the viewers peer through the dimly lit window into her life; they see the violence she experiences, but they cannot and do not understand why she stays. Communication—indeed, rationality itself—seems virtually impossible. The life of the "other" continues along as a predictably unfathomable script and thus serves as the symbolic backdrop against which more accessible and familiar voices speak.

I offer this description to suggest that tokenistic, objectifying, voyeuristic inclusion of women of color is at least as disempowering as complete exclusion. The effort to politicize violence against women will do little to address Black and other minority women if their images are retained simply to magnify the problem rather than to humanize their experiences. Similarly, the antiracist agenda will not be advanced significantly by forcibly suppressing the reality of battering in minority communities. As the *48 Hours* episode makes clear, the images and stereotypes we fear are readily available and are frequently deployed in ways that do not generate sensitive understanding of the nature of domestic violence in minority communities.

Race and Domestic Violence Support Services

Women working in the field of domestic violence have sometimes reproduced the subordination and marginalization of women of color by adopting policies, priorities, or strategies of empowerment that either elide or wholly disregard the particular intersectional needs of women of color. While gender, race, and class intersect to create the particular context in which women of color experience violence, certain choices made by "allies" can reproduce intersectional subordination within the very resistance strategies designed to respond to the problem.

Feminists, of course, cannot be held solely responsible for the various ways in which their political efforts are received. Usually, much more is demanded of power than is given. Nonetheless there are sites in which feminist interventions can be directly criticized as marginalizing women of color.

This problem is starkly illustrated by the inaccessibility of domestic violence support services to many non-English-speaking women. In a letter written to the Deputy Commissioner of the New York State Department of Social Services, Diana Campos, Director of Human Services for Programas de Ocupaciones y Desarrollo Economico Real, Inc. (PODER), detailed the case of a Latina in crisis who was repeatedly denied accommodation at a shelter because she could not prove that she was English-proficient. The woman had fled her home with her teenage son, believing her husband's threats to kill them both. She called the domestic violence hotline administered by PODER, seeking shelter for herself and her son. Because most shelters would not accommodate the woman with her son, they were forced to live on the streets for two days. The hotline counselor was finally able to find an agency that would take both the mother and the son, but when the counselor told the intake coordinator at the shelter that the woman spoke limited English, the coordinator told her that they could not take anyone who was not English-proficient. When the woman in crisis called back and was told of the shelter's "rule," she replied that she could understand English if spoken to her slowly. As Campos explains:

> Mildred, the hotline counselor, told Wendy, the intake coordinator, that the woman said that she could communicate a little in English. Wendy told Mildred that they could not provide services to this woman because they have house rules that the woman must agree to follow. Mildred asked her, "What if the woman agrees to follow your rules? Will you still not take her?" Wendy responded that all of the women at the shelter are required to attend [a] support group and they would not be able to have her in the group if she could not communicate. Mildred mentioned the severity of this woman's case. She told Wendy that the woman had been wandering the streets at night while her husband is home, and she had been mugged twice. She also reiterated the fact that this woman was in danger of being killed by either her husband or a mugger. Mildred expressed that the woman's safety was a priority at this point, and that once in a safe place, receiving counseling in a support group could be dealt with.[20]

The intake coordinator restated the shelter's policy of taking only English-speaking women, and stated further that the woman would have to call the shelter herself for screening. If the woman could communicate with them in English, she might be accepted. When the woman called the PODER hotline later that day, she was in such a state of fear that the hotline counselor who had been working with her had difficulty understanding her in Spanish. Campos directly intervened at this point, calling the executive director of the shelter. A counselor called back from the shelter. As Campos reports,

> Marie [the counselor] told me that they did not want to take the woman in the shelter because they felt that the woman would feel isolated. I explained that the son agreed to translate for his mother during the intake process. Furthermore, that we would assist them in locating a Spanish-speaking battered women's advocate to assist in counseling her. Marie stated that utilizing the son was not an acceptable means of communication for them, since it further victimized the victim. In addition, she stated that they had similar experiences with women who were non-English-speaking, and that the women eventually just left because they were not able to communicate with anyone. I expressed my extreme concern for her safety and reiterated that we would assist them in providing her with the necessary services until we could get her placed someplace where they had bilingual staff.

After several more calls, the shelter finally agreed to take the woman. The woman called once more during the negotiation; however, after a plan was in place, the woman never called back. Said Campos, "After so many calls, we are now left to wonder if she is alive and well, and if she will ever have enough faith in our ability to help her to call us again the next time she is in crisis."

Despite this woman's desperate need, she was unable to receive the protection afforded English-speaking women, due to the shelter's rigid commitment to exclusionary policies. Perhaps even more troubling than the shelter's lack of bilingual resources was its refusal to allow a friend or relative to translate for the woman. This story illustrates the absurdity of a feminist approach that would make the ability to attend a support group without a translator a more significant consideration in the distribution of resources than the risk of physical harm on the street. The point is not that the shelter's image of empowerment is empty, but rather that it was imposed without regard to the disempowering consequences for women who did not match the kind of client the shelter's administrators imagined. And thus they failed to accomplish the basic priority of the shelter movement—to get the woman out of danger.

Here the woman in crisis was made to bear the burden of the shelter's refusal to anticipate and provide for the needs of non-English-speaking women. Said Campos, "It is unfair to impose more stress on victims by placing them in the position of having to demonstrate their proficiency in English in order to receive services that are readily available to other battered women." The problem is not easily dismissed as one of well-intentioned ignorance. The specific issue of monolingualism and the monistic view of women's experience that set the stage for this tragedy were not new issues in New York. Indeed, several women of color reported that they had repeatedly struggled with the New York State Coalition Against Domestic Violence over language exclusion and other practices that marginalized the interests of women of color.[21] Yet despite repeated lobbying, the coalition did not act to incorporate the specific needs of nonwhite women into their central organizing vision.

Some critics have linked the coalition's failure to address these issues to the narrow vision of coalition that animated its interaction with women of color in the first place. Efforts to include women of color came, it seems, as something of an afterthought. Many were invited to participate only after the coalition was awarded a grant by the state to recruit women of color. However, as one "recruit" said, "they were not really prepared to deal with us or our issues. They thought that they could simply incorporate us into their organization without rethinking any of their beliefs or priorities and that we would be happy." Even the most formal gestures of inclusion were not to be taken for granted. On one occasion when several women of color attended a meeting to discuss a special task force on women of color, the group debated all day over including the issue on the agenda.

The relationship between the white women and the women of color on the board was a rocky one from beginning to end. Other conflicts developed over differing definitions of feminism. For example, the board decided to hire a Latina staffperson to manage outreach programs to the Latino community, but the white members of the hiring committee rejected candidates who did not have recognized feminist credentials even though they were favored by Latina committee members. As Campos pointed out, by measuring Latinas against their own biographies, the white members of the board failed to recognize the different circumstances under which feminist consciousness develops and manifests itself within minority communities. Many of the women who interviewed for the position were established activists and leaders within their own community, a fact that suggests that these women were probably familiar with the specific gender dynamics in their communities, and were accordingly better qualified to handle outreach than other candidates with more conventional feminist credentials.

The coalition ended a few months later when the women of color walked out. Many of these women returned to community-based organizations, preferring to struggle over women's issues within their communities rather than struggle over race and class issues with white, middle-class women. Yet as illustrated by the case of the Latina who could find no shelter, the dominance of a particular perspective and set of priorities within the shelter community continues to marginalize the needs of women of color.

The struggle over which differences matter and which do not is neither an abstract nor an insignificant debate among women. Indeed, these conflicts are about more than difference as such; they raise critical issues of power. The problem is not simply that women who dominate the antiviolence movement are different from women of color, but that they frequently have power to determine, either through material or rhetorical resources, whether the intersectional differences of women of color will be incorporated at all into the basic formulation of policy. Thus, the struggle over incorporating these differences is not a petty or superficial conflict about who gets to sit at the head of the table. In the context of violence, it is sometimes a deadly serious matter of who will survive—and who will not.

Conclusion

This article has presented intersectionality as a way of framing the various interactions of race and gender in the context of violence against women of color. I have used intersectionality as a way to articulate the interaction of racism and patriarchy generally. I have also used intersectionality to describe the location of women of color both within overlapping systems of subordination and at the margins of feminism and antiracism. The effort to politicize violence against women will do little to address the experiences of nonwhite women until the ramifications of racial stratification among women are acknowledged. At the same time, the antiracist agenda will not be furthered by suppressing the reality of intraracial violence against women of color. The effect of both these marginalizations is that women of color have no ready means to link their experiences with those of other women. This sense of isolation compounds efforts to politicize gender violence within communities of color, and permits the deadly silence surrounding these issues to continue.

I want to suggest that intersectionality offers a way of mediating the tension between assertions of multiple identity and the ongoing necessity of group politics. It is helpful in this regard to distinguish intersectionality from the closely related perspective of antiessentialism, from which women of color have critically engaged white feminism for the absence of women of color on the one hand, and for speaking for women of color on the other. One rendition of this antiessentialist critique—that feminism essentializes the category "woman"—owes a great deal to the postmodernist idea that categories we consider natural or merely representational are actually socially constructed in a linguistic economy of difference.[22] While the descriptive project of postmodernism of questioning the ways in which meaning is socially constructed is generally sound, this critique sometimes misreads the meaning of social construction and distorts its political relevance.

One version of antiessentialism, embodying what might be called the vulgarized social construction thesis, is that since all categories are socially constructed, there is no such thing as, say, "Blacks" or "women," and thus it makes little sense to continue reproducing those categories by organizing around them.[23] Even the Supreme Court has gotten into this act. In *Metro Broadcasting, Inc. v. FCC*, (110 S. Ct. 2997 (1990)) the Court conservatives, in rhetoric that oozes vulgar constructionist smugness, proclaimed that any set-aside designed to increase the voices of minorities on the air waves was itself based on a racist assumption that skin color is in some way connected to the likely content of one's broadcast. The Court said:

> The FCC's choice to employ a racial criterion embodies the related notions that a particular and distinct viewpoint inheres in certain racial groups and that a particular applicant, by virtue of race or ethnicity

alone, is more valued than other applicants because "likely to provide [that] distinct perspective." The policies directly equate race with belief and behavior, for they establish race as a necessary and sufficient condition of securing the preference. . . . The policies impermissibly value individuals because they presume that persons think in a manner associated with their race. (p. 3037, internal citations omitted)

But to say that a category such as race or gender is socially constructed is not to say that that category has no significance in our world. On the contrary, a large and continuing project for subordinated people—and indeed, one of the projects for which postmodern theories have been very helpful—is thinking about the way power has clustered around certain categories and is exercised against others. This project attempts to unveil the processes of subordination and the various ways those processes are experienced by people who are subordinated and people who are privileged. It is, then, a project that presumes that categories have meaning and consequences. This project's most pressing problem, in many if not most cases, is not the existence of the categories, but rather the particular values attached to them, and the way those values foster and create social hierarchies.

This is not to deny that the process of categorization is itself an exercise of power, but the story is much more complicated and nuanced than that. First, the process of categorizing—or, in identity terms, naming—is not unilateral. Subordinated people can and do participate, sometimes even subverting the naming process in empowering ways. One need only think about the historical subversion of the category "Black," or the current transformation of "queer," to understand that categorization is not a one-way street. Clearly, there is unequal power, but there is nonetheless some degree of agency that people can and do exert in the politics of naming. And it is important to note that identity continues to be a site of resistance for members of different subordinated groups. We all can recognize the distinction between the claims "I am Black" and the claim "I am a person who happens to be Black." "I am Black" takes the socially imposed identity and empowers it as an anchor of subjectivity. "I am Black" becomes not simply a statement of resistance, but also a positive discourse of self-identification, intimately linked to celebratory statements like the Black nationalist "Black is beautiful." "I am a person who happens to be Black," on the other hand, achieves self-identification by straining for a certain universality (in effect, "I am first a person") and for a concomitant dismissal of the imposed category ("Black") as contingent, circumstantial, nondeterminant. There is truth in both characterizations, of course, but they function quite differently depending on the political context. At this point in history, a strong case can be made that the most critical resistance strategy for disempowered groups is to occupy and defend a politics of social location rather than to vacate and destroy it.

Vulgar constructionism thus distorts the possibilites for meaningful identity politics by conflating at least two separate but closely linked manifestations of power. One is the power exercised simply through the process of categorization; the other, the power to cause that categorization to have social and material consequences. While the former power facilitates the latter, the political implications of challenging one over the other matter greatly. We can look at debates over racial subordination throughout history and see that, in each instance, there was a possibility of challenging either the construction of identity or the system of subordination based on that identity. Consider, for example, the segregation system in *Plessy v. Ferguson* (163 U.S. 537, 1896). At issue were multiple dimensions of dominance, including categorization, the sign of race, and the subordination of those so labeled. There were at least two targets for Plessy to challenge: the construction of identity ("What is a Black?"), and the system of subordination based on that identity ("Can Blacks and whites sit together on a train?"). Plessy actually raised both issues, challenging both the coherence of race as a category, and challenging the subordination of those deemed to be Black. In his attack on the former, Plessy argued that the application of the segregation statute to him, given his mixed-race status, was inappropriate. The Court refused to see this as an attack on the coherence of the race system, and instead responded by simply reproducing the Black/white dichotomy that Plessy was challenging. Because Plessy was not, by virtue of his nonwhite ancestry, white, he had suffered no injury by not being treated like a white man. As we know, Plessy's challenge to the practice of segregating those who were nonwhite was not successful either. In evaluating various resistance strategies today, it may be useful to ask which of Plessy's challenges would have been best for him to have won—the challenge against the coherence of the racial categorization system, or the challenge to the practice of segregation?

The same question can be posed for *Brown v. Board of Education* (397 U.S. 483, 1954). Which of two possible arguments was politically more empowering—that segregation was unconstitutional because the racial categorization system on which it was based was incoherent, or that segregation was unconstitutional because it was injurious to children categorized as Black and thus oppressive to their communities? While it might strike some as a difficult question, for the most part, the dimension of racial domination that has been most vexing to African-Americans has not been the racial categorization as such, but the myriad ways in which those of us so defined have been systematically subordinated. With particular regard to problems confronting women of color, when identity politics fail us, as they frequently do, it is not primarily because those politics take as natural certain categories that are socially constructed, but rather because the descriptive content of those categories and the narratives on which they are based have privileged some experiences and excluded others.

Along these lines, consider the Clarence Thomas/Anita Hill scandal. During the Senate hearings for the confirmation of Clarence Thomas to the Supreme Court, Anita Hill, in bringing allegations of sexual harassment against Thomas, was rhetorically disempowered in part because she fell between the dominant interpretations of feminism and antiracism. Caught between the competing narrative tropes of rape (advanced by feminists), on the one hand, and lynching (advanced by Thomas and his antiracist supporters), on the other, the raced and gendered dimensions of her position could not be told. This dilemma could be described as the consequence of antiracism's essentializing Blackness and feminism's essentializing womanhood. But recognizing as much does not take us far enough, for the problem is not simply linguistic or philosophical in nature. It is specifically political: the narratives of gender are based on the experience of white, middle-class women, and the narratives of race are based on the experience of Black men. The solution does not merely entail arguing for the multiplicity of identities or challenging essentialism generally. Instead, in Hill's case, for example, it would have been necessary to assert those crucial aspects of her location that were erased, even by many of her advocates—that is, to state what difference her difference made.

If, as this analysis asserts, history and context determine the utility of identity politics, how, then, do we understand identity politics today, especially in light of our recognition of multiple dimensions of identity? More specifically, what does it mean to argue that gendered identities have been obscured in antiracist discourses, just as race identities have been obscured in feminist discourses? Does that mean we cannot talk about identity? Or instead, that any discourse about identity has to acknowledge how our identities are constructed through the intersection of multiple dimensions? A beginning response to these questions requires that we first recognize that the organized identity groups in which we find ourselves are in fact coalitions, or at least potential coalitions waiting to be formed.

In the context of antiracism, recognizing the ways in which the intersectional experiences of women of color are marginalized in prevailing conceptions of identity politics does not require that we give up attempts to organize as communities of color. Rather, intersectionality provides a basis for reconceptualizing race as a coalition between men and women of color. For example, in the area of rape, intersectionality provides a way of explaining why women of color have to abandon the general argument that the interests of the community require the suppression of any confrontation around intraracial rape. Intersectionality may provide the means for dealing with other marginalizations as well. For example, race can also be a coalition of straight and gay people of color, and thus serve as a basis for critique of churches and other cultural institutions that reproduce heterosexism.

With identity thus reconceptualized, it may be easier to understand the need for, and to summon the courage to challenge, groups that are after all, in one sense, "home" to us, in the name of the parts of us that are not made at home. This takes a great deal of energy, and arouses intense anxiety. The most one could expect is that we will dare to speak against internal exclusions and marginalizations, that we might call attention to how the identity of "the group" has been centered on the intersectional identities of a few. Recognizing that identity politics takes place at the site where categories intersect thus seems more fruitful than challenging the possibility of talking about categories at all. Through an awareness of intersectionality, we can better acknowledge and ground the differences among us and negotiate the means by which these differences will find expression in constructing group politics.

Notes

I am indebted to a great many people who have pushed this project along. For their kind assistance in facilitating my field research for this article, I wish to thank Maria Blanco, Margaret Cambrick, Joan Creer, Estelle Cheung, Nilda Rimonte, and Fred Smith. I benefitted from the comments of Taunya Banks, Mark Barenberg, Darcy Calkins, Adrienne Davis, Gina Dent, Brent Edwards, Paul Gewirtz, Lani Guinier, Neil Gotanda, Joel Handler, Duncan Kennedy, Henry Monaghan, Elizabeth Schneider, and Kendall Thomas. A very special thanks goes to Gary Peller and Richard Yarborough. Jayne Lee, Paula Puryear, Yancy Garrido, Eugenia Gifford, and Leti Volpp provided valuable research assistance. I gratefully acknowledge the support of the Academic Senate of UCLA, Center for Afro-American Studies at UCLA, the Reed Foundation, and Columbia Law School. Earlier versions of this article were presented to the Critical Race Theory Workshop and the Yale Legal Theory Workshop.

1. I use "Black" and "African-American" interchangeably throughout this article. I capitalize "Black" because "Blacks, like Asians, Latinos, and other 'minorities', constitute a specific cultural group and, as such, require denotation as a proper noun." (Crenshaw 1988, p. 1332 n. 2, citing MacKinnon 1982, p. 516). By the same token, I do not capitalize "white," which is not a proper noun, since whites do not constitute a specific cultural group. For the same reason I do not capitalize "women of color."

2. It is important to name the perspective from which one constructs one's analysis; and for me, that is as a Black feminist. Moreover, it is important to acknowledge that the materials that I incorporate in my analysis are drawn heavily from research on Black women. On the other hand, I see my own work as part of a broader collective effort among feminists of color to expand feminism to include analyses of race and

other factors such as class, sexual orientation, and age. I have attempted therefore to offer my sense of the tentative connections between my analysis of the intersectional experiences of Black women and the intersectional experiences of other women of color. I stress that this analysis is not intended to include falsely, nor to exclude unnecessarily, other women of color.

3. During my research in Los Angeles, California, I visited Jenessee Battered Women's Shelter, the only shelter in the Western states primarily serving Black women, and Everywoman's Shelter, which primarily serves Asian women. I also visited Estelle Chueng at the Asian Pacific Law Foundation, and I spoke with a representative of La Casa, a shelter in the predominantly Latino community of East L.A.

4. Indeed one shelter provider reported that nearly eighty-five percent of her clients returned to the battering relationships, largely because of difficulties in finding employment and housing. African-Americans are more segregated than any other racial group, and this segregation exists across class lines. Recent studies in Washington, D.C., and its suburbs show that sixty-four percent of Blacks trying to rent apartments in white neighborhoods encountered discrimination. (Thompson 1991, D1). Had these studies factored gender and family status into the equation, the statistics might have been worse.

5. Racial differences marked an interesting contrast between Jenessee's policies and those of other shelters situated outside the Black community. Unlike some other shelters in Los Angeles, Jenessee welcomed the assistance of men. According to the director, the shelter's policy was premised on a belief that given African-American's need to maintain healthy relations to pursue a common struggle against racism, antiviolence programs within the African-American community cannot afford to be antagonistic to men. For a discussion of the different needs of Black women who are battered, see Richie 1985, p. 40.

6. 8 U.S.C. +s 1186a (1988).

7. The Marriage Fraud Amendments provided that, for the conditional resident status to be removed, "the alien spouse and the petitioning spouse (if not deceased) jointly must submit to the Attorney General . . . a petition which requests the removal of such conditional basis and which states, under penalty of perjury, the facts and information." 8 U.S.C. +s 1186a(b)(1)(A). The amendments provided for a waiver, at the attorney general's discretion, if the alien spouse was able to demonstrate that deportation would result in extreme hardship, or that the qualifying marriage was terminated for good cause. (+s 1186a(c)(4)). However, the terms of this hardship waiver have not adequately protected battered spouses.

8. Immigration Act of 1990, Pub. L. No. 101–649, 104 Stat. 4978. H.R. Rep. No. 723(I), 101st Cong., 2d Sess. 78 (1990), reprinted in 1990 U.S.C.C.A.N. 6710, 6758.

9. H.R. Rep. No. 723(I), 101st Cong., 2d Sess. 79, (1990) reprinted in 1990 U.S.C.C.A.N. 6710, 6759.

10. One survey conducted of battered women "hypothesized that if a person is a member of a discriminated minority group, the fewer the opportunities for socioeconomic status above the poverty level and the weaker the English language skills, the greater the disadvantage." (Pagelow 1981, p. 96). The seventy minority women in the study "had a double disadvantage in this society that serves to tie them more strongly to their spouses."

11. There can be little question that women unable to communicate in English are severely handicapped in seeking independence. Some women thus excluded were even further

disadvantaged because they were not U.S. citizens and some were in this country illegally. For a few of these, the only assistance shelter staff could render was to help reunite them with their families of origin (Pagelow 1981, pp. 96–97). Non-English-speaking women are often excluded even from studies of battered women because of their language and other difficulties. A researcher qualified the statistics of one survey by pointing out that "an unknown number of minority group women were excluded from this survey sample because of language difficulties" (Pagelow 1981, p. 96). To combat this lack of appropriate services for women of color at many shelters, special programs have been created specifically for women from particular communities. A few examples of such programs include the Victim Intervention Project in East Harlem for Latina women, Jenesee Shelter for African-American women in Los Angeles, Apna Gar in Chicago for South Asian women, and, for Asian women generally, the Asian Women's Shelter in San Francisco, the New York Asian Women's Center, and the Center for the Pacific Asian Family in Los Angeles. Programs with hotlines include Sakhi for South Asian Women in New York, and Manavi in Jersey City, also for South Asian women, as well as programs for Korean women in Philadelphia and Chicago.

12. For example, the Rosa Parks Shelter and the Compton Rape Crisis Hotline, two shelters that serve the African-American community, are in constant conflict with funding sources over the ratio of dollars and hours to women served. Interview with Joan Greer, Executive Director of Rosa Parks Shelter, in Los Angeles, California (April 1990).

13. Interview with Joan Greer, Executive Director of Rosa Parks Shelter, in Los Angeles, California (April 1990).

14. Most crime statistics are classified by sex or race, but none are classified by sex *and* race. Because we know that most rape victims are women, the racial breakdown reveals, at best, rape rates for Black women. Yet, even given this head start, rates for other nonwhite women are difficult to collect. While there are some statistics for Latinas, statistics for Asian and Native American women are virtually nonexistent.

15. In this regard, Ali's arguments bear much in common with those of neoconservatives who attribute many of the social ills plaguing Black America to the breakdown of patriarchal family values (see Raspberry 1989, p. C15; Will 1986a, p. A23; Will 1986b, p. 9). Ali's argument shares remarkable similarities with the controversial "Moynihan Report" on the Black family, so called because its principal author was now-Senator Daniel P. Moynihan (D-N.Y.). In the infamous chapter entitled "The Tangle of Pathology," Moynihan argued that:

> The Negro community has been forced into a matriarchal structure which, because it is so out of line with the rest of American society, seriously retards the progress of the group as a whole, and imposes a crushing burden on the Negro male and, in consequence, on a great many Negro women as well. (p. 29)

16. The source of the resistance reveals an interesting difference between the Asian-American and African-American communities. In the African-American community, the resistance is usually grounded in efforts to avoid confirming negative stereotypes of African-Americans as violent; the concern of members in some Asian-American communities is to avoid tarnishing the model minority myth. Interview with Nilda Rimonte, Director of the Everywoman Shelter, in Los Angeles, California (April 19, 1991).

17. On January 14, 1991, Senator Joseph Biden (D.-Del.) introduced Senate Bill 15, the Violence Against Women Act of 1991, comprehensive legislation addressing violent

crime confronting women. S. 15, 102d Cong., 1st Sess. (1991). The bill consists of
several measures designed to create safe streets, safe homes, and safe campuses for
women. More specifically, Title III of the bill creates a civil rights remedy for crimes
of violence motivated by the victim's gender (+52 301). Among the findings supporting the bill were "(1) crimes motivated by the victim's gender constitute bias crimes
in violation of the victim's right to be free from discrimination on the basis of gender"
and "(2) current law [does not provide a civil rights remedy] for gender crimes
committed on the street or in the home." S. Rep. No. 197, 102d Cong., 1st Sess. 27
(1991).

18. 137 Cong. Rec. S611 (daily ed. Jan 14, 1991), statement of Sen. Cohen.

19. *48 Hours: Till Death Do Us Part* (CBS television broadcast, February 6, 1991).

20. Letter of Diana M. Campos, Director of Human Services, PODER, to Joseph Semidei,
Deputy Commissioner, New York State Department of Social Services, March 26,
1992 (hereinafter *PODER Letter*).

21. Roundtable Discussion on Racism and the Domestic Violence Movement, April 2,
1992 (transcript on file with the *Stanford Law Review*). The participants in the discussion—Diana Campos, Director, Bilingual Outreach Project of the New York State
Coalition Against Domestic Violence; Elsa A. Rios, Project Director, Victim Intervention Project (a community-based project in East Harlem, New York, serving battered
women); and Haydee Rosario, a social worker with the East Harlem Council for
Human Services and a Victim Intervention Project volunteer—recounted conflicts
relating to race and culture during their association with the New York State Coalition
Against Domestic Violence, a state oversight group that distributed resources to
battered women's shelters throughout the state and generally set policy priorities for
the shelters that were part of the coalition.

22. I follow the practice of others in linking antiessentialism to postmodernism. (See,
generally, Nicholson, 1990.)

23. I do not mean to imply that all theorists who have made antiessentialist critiques
have lapsed into vulgar constructionism. Indeed, antiessentialists avoid making these
troubling moves, and would no doubt be receptive to much of the critique set forth
herein. I use the term vulgar constructionism to distinguish between those antiessentialist critiques that leave room for identity politics and those that do not.

Section II

Feminist Theory and Legal Norms

Introduction

by Joan Meier

Feminist legal thought has at its heart the goal of articulating the peculiarly male character of "traditional" or "mainstream" legal norms, and recasting those norms in light of women's experiences, realities, and values.[1] In the field of domestic violence, these legal norms have historically been a direct reflection of social and cultural norms which for centuries expressly approved the use of violence by male heads of household against women and children as a means of upholding the patriarchal family system.[2] Current American legal and social norms are more ambiguous: while family violence is nominally illegal and even criminal, most legal and social institutions still extend little if any recognition or help to victims of such violence, preferring to treat it as a private family dispute rather than a crime. Perhaps because the problems are more apparent in the implementation rather than the definition of the law, domestic violence has been a priority for American feminist activists for close to two decades, but has only recently begun to receive sustained legal analysis by feminist theorists.

The five papers in this section are indicative of the growing sophistication of feminist legal theory in this area. Each examines the assumptions underlying legal images and norms pertaining to domestic violence, and seeks to develop new theoretical frameworks and alternative vantage points from which to view the problem. Two of the papers—those by Rapaport and Van Praagh—analyze and question existing substantive legal standards regulating violence in the family. Eaton, Ashe and Cahn, Van Praagh, and Sells also challenge traditional legal modes of thought, rejecting the "all-or-nothing" approach to defining the "rights" of individuals in the family, and urging a more contextual, nuanced approach to intimate violence by the government and legal system. In their emphasis on the subject of family violence, on the need for "context," and on the voices of outsiders to the sociopolitical power structure, these papers are

121

archetypes of feminist legal thought which support and complement one another.

However, these papers also push the boundaries, not only of traditional legal discourse, but, to some extent, of "traditionally feminist" assumptions and analyses. Feminist legal thought has historically looked at women as the outsiders to society's norms and positions of power.[3] However, in feminism's "third phase,"[4] the feminist critique has begun to be applied to feminist thought itself, identifying those who have been left outside the *feminist* analysis—such as African-American women and lesbians—and examining the implications of these new outsiders' experiences for feminist thinking. Thus Marcia Sells and Shauna Van Praagh demand that the voices of children be heard in child welfare decisions; Marie Ashe and Naomi Cahn urge us to listen to the stories of abusive mothers as well as "good mothers" and children; and Mary Eaton confronts feminists with the troubling reality of intralesbian violence.

Perhaps not coincidentally, this broadening of the scope of feminist analysis necessitates an expansion of the feminist archetype—in which women are victims of male oppression and inequity—to encompass women as sometimes victimizers of other outsiders. However, opening up the feminist project to the reality of women's complicity in the suffering of others has the potential for challenging the fundamental *raison d'être* of feminism. Most of the authors in this Section are optimistic that abandoning the paradigm in which women are innocent victims of male power in favor of a more multifaceted and real depiction of women as simultaneous agents and victims of oppression can be accommodated by and is consistent with feminist thinking. However, these essays raise the question of whether the concept of "feminism," insofar as it treats gender as the fundamental construct, is still useful.

Woman as Perpetrator and Victim: Intralesbian Violence and Maternal Child Abuse

In "Abuse by Any Other Name: Feminism, Power and Intralesbian Violence," Mary Eaton attempts to do for sexual orientation what Kim Crenshaw and others have done for race.[5] Eaton challenges the "essentialism" of much of feminist theory as inadequate to account for lesbian oppression generally, and intralesbian violence in particular. At the same time, Eaton notes that intralesbian violence in particular poses a profound challenge for feminist analyses. The common thread in most feminist understandings of heterosexual domestic violence is the view that it is fundamentally a product of society's gender norms, an exercise of male power over women. The existence of intralesbian violence potentially either confirms or destroys this fundamental premise: if we look only at biology, intralesbian violence, by its mere existence, contradicts the gendered hypothesis for heterosexual domestic violence. If, on the other hand, intralesbian violence is seen as mimicking the gender roles of heterosexual society, a gendered explanation for domestic violence may still be valid.

In attempting to reach a tentative understanding of the dynamic of and reasons for intralesbian violence, Eaton notes several potential parallels between lesbian battering and what is known about heterosexual battering, including comparable rates of incidence and types of abuse. More importantly, same-sex battering appears similar to heterosexual battering in that in both contexts, typically one partner is the "batterer" and the other the "victim," rather than both being participants in a mutually violent relationship. Concomitantly, some aspects of "battered woman syndrome"—a phrase coined to describe the responses of female victims of male intimate violence—are also seen in the lesbian community.

Despite these possible parallels, Eaton argues that, at root, intralesbian violence may be quite different from heterosexual battering in some important respects. For example, the role of sexualization in domestic violence may differ greatly among lesbians and among heterosexuals. Other psychodynamics particular to lesbian relationships may well play a role in intralesbian battering. Most fundamentally, Eaton rejects the rigid projection of "male" and "female" roles on lesbians in battering relationships (as "butch" and "femme") as both inaccurately stereotypical, and subject to the same problems as stereotyped assumptions about the nature of abusers and victims in heterosexual relationships have been.[6]

As a result of the lack of easily defined pigeonholes in which to put intralesbian violence, victims of such violence are silenced even more than female victims of heterosexual battering. Intralesbian violence is denied by the dominant culture (through the legal system), the feminist subculture (represented by shelters), and the lesbian community, because it does not fit the stereotypes prevalent in any of these. The lesbian community's reluctance to "air its dirty laundry" in public may be shared by the black community, but the utter denial of lesbian battering by both the feminist and dominant cultures sets it apart fundamentally from the problems faced by both black and white heterosexual battered women.

In the end, Eaton calls for a "lesbian-specific model of intralesbian violence" which is separate from but coexists with feminist accounts of domestic violence. In-depth study of this phenomenon and development of a clarifying model are vital for lesbian victims of battering. But any such construct will have to incorporate the reality that, ultimately, both heterosexual and lesbian victims of intimate violence are victims of male power—because both are denied full self-determination in a culture which relies on male domination of women as the primary social determinant.

In "Child Abuse: A Problem for Feminist Theory" Marie Ashe and Naomi Cahn similarly challenge feminism to address another context in which women abuse others: maternal child abuse. The authors point out that child abuse by mothers is far more prevalent than has been generally acknowledged in feminist circles. Like intralesbian battering, maternal child abuse has been largely ignored by feminist thinkers, in part because this phenomenon is problematic for feminist theories, which have focused on ways women are victimized by men. Most existing feminist theories have either neglected the issue entirely, or dismissed maternal child abusers as either unnatural or as themselves pure victims of male or societal oppression.

Feminists' dismissal of abusing mothers has until now been partly a failure to counter patriarchal society's tendency to either idealize women as mothers or demonize women who violate the idealized image of the mother. These tendencies are apparent both in psychological theory, where the perspective of the child has dominated, and in governmental and legal policies regarding child abuse, where white male norms defining the proper role of women have traditionally reigned.

Ashe and Cahn urge us to abandon the pointless debate over whether abusing mothers are really agents of harm to children or victims forced by their oppression to do harm to children, that is, either "bad" or "good." Drawing on a recent development in feminist legal thought, postmodernist feminism, which calls for abandonment of essentialist categories and attention to the narratives of the excluded, the authors urge us to listen to the voices of abusing mothers to gain a more realistic and multifaceted understanding of them. Experience and psychological theory suggest that all mothers have ambivalent feelings toward their children; that no mother is all good or all bad; and that the reasons for abusing mothers' behavior have yet to be understood. To do justice to women (and children), feminism must find ways to give "bad mothers" a voice, and bring these outsiders too under the feminist umbrella.

Other Subcultures: Children and Religious Community

In "The Youngest Members—Harm to Children and the Role of Religious Communities," Shauna Van Praagh expands the focus to include the role of religious communities, as subcultures which both nurture and harm children. Like Eaton and Ashe and Cahn, Van Praagh calls for abandonment of a dichotomy embedded in traditional legal norms:

in this case, the conflict between parents' rights and the right of the state to intervene on behalf of children. Unlike Ashe and Cahn, however, she calls for a more child-centered analysis on which to base the proper scope of state interventions. Such an analysis, she suggests, must include understanding and recognition of the profound role religious communities can play in the life and well-being of children.

Recognition of the role of religious communities in the life and development of children cuts across the traditional "parent/state" dichotomy from two perspectives. On one hand, acknowledgement of the power of religious communities in cultivating children's identities and values necessarily tempers the traditional definition of the parents as the sole parties with rights and responsibilities toward children. On the other hand, Van Praagh argues that religious communities also serve children's interests in "developing a unique identity through membership." Moreover, religious communities can comprise an alternative normative culture, a kind of competing public or social authority to that of the state. Recognition of this subsidiary normative universe, along with society's established commitment to religious pluralism, should give rise to a more complex assessment of the costs and benefits of state intervention to protect children. Thus, rather than framing state interventions to protect children as a conflict between the state and parental rights to religious freedom, the analysis should also include the *child's* interests in membership in her religious community and the harm to the community from state intervention.

Expansion of the child's "domestic sphere" to include her religious community necessitates that we be sensitive to possible harms to children stemming from such communities. Justifications for physical beatings and even killing of children are found in more than one religion. Religious communities can create insularity, which reduces the opportunity for larger society to intervene to protect children. And, of course, religious creeds can lead to childrens' injuries or death when medical intervention is refused in favor of faith healing.

In calling for a more explicit and honest recognition of the positive and negative contributions of religious communities to children's development and well-being, Van Praagh does not purport to "resolve" the difficulties of particular cases or provide a single formula for deciding cases concerning children. Fundamental normative clashes between religious tenets and society's assessment of harm to children will still occur. However, a more cooperative and respectful interaction may be the very means necessary for resolving some of the most difficult value clashes and slowly developing some shared definitions of unacceptable abuse.

The Voice of the Child

In "Child That's Got Her Own" Marcia Sells brings us back down to earth with an examination of how feminist theory interacts with existing legal norms regarding child abuse in the real world of a prosecutor's office. Invoking the stories of several abused children, Sells questions the value of criminal prosecution for this most difficult of crimes. While feminist analyses and theories have given prosecutors tools for assessing child abuse, the impact of abuse, how to question children, and a conviction that it is cathartic for victims of abuse to "tell their story," Sells emphasizes the trauma to children who must testify against someone they love, and whose genuine voices cannot really be heard in court, because of the artificial constraints of legal questioning and cross-examination of witnesses. The priority of criminal prosecution is not to help children, but to win convictions. Whether or not convictions ultimately benefit the child victims, a far more delicate and sensitive process is necessary to work with and heal abused children.

Sells' paper is a plea for more active and effective involvement of Child Protection Services agencies. In her view, a noncriminal, "helping" response should at least be attempted before the harsh and inflexible hand of the criminal law is applied. However, too many agencies have ceded too much of their responsibility for intervention and assistance to the criminal prosecutors' offices, which often possess superior investigative resources. This trend is unlikely to be reversed anytime soon, particularly in light of the Supreme Court's decision in *DeShaney v. Winnebago County Department of Social Services*,[7] which foreclosed a constitutional cause of action against agencies for failure to protect children against abuse, on the ground that the state has no "affirmative" duty to protect private citizens from privately inflicted violence. Sells challenges *DeShaney*, arguing that agencies should be constitutionally required to follow through an intervention once it is begun, and to protect children's liberty interest in "bodily integrity."

The sterility of the *DeShaney* analysis epitomizes the inadequacy of our current legal system for dealing with harm to children. If society can move even part of the way to Sells' goal, it will be a better place for children.

Sexism in the Criminal Law: Of Hell, Fury, and Scorned Men

In "The Death Penalty and the Domestic Discount," Elizabeth Rapaport also examines the operation of legal norms pertaining to domestic violence in practice. However, she does so from the more global perspective of an empirical overview, and from the somewhat unusual vantage point of a study of capital punishment. Rapaport examines capital sentencing law and practice as an embodiment of society's moral values, with respect to the relative heinousness of different types of murderous violence. Her analysis is both quantitative and qualitative, and demonstrates the hypocrisy of the claim that our law protects and values the family.

Rapaport's qualitative analysis indicates that the law of capital sentencing is rooted in profoundly sexist norms. Whereas virtually every state treats killing of individuals for "predatory" (that is, financial) reasons as an "aggravating factor" meriting capital punishment, "[p]rotection of the hearth" does not appear to warrant treating domestic murders as similarly maximally reprehensible. To the contrary, Rapaport makes a compelling case that the legal system has adopted a "domestic discount," pursuant to which domestic murders of women who share the "hearth" of a man are virtually *immune* from the ultimate penalty.

Domestic homicide is seen as "mitigating" against the death penalty because it is typically seen as a "hot-blooded" killing, stemming from the perpetrator's loss of control and excessive emotion, rather than a "cold-blooded"—premeditated or deliberated—killing. Rapaport points out that the paradigm of the "crime of passion" centers around a man's killing of his wife when she is caught by him in the act of adultery, and stems from the sexist definition of male prerogatives over females in the family. Moreover, the "crime of passion" paradigm was not historically equally available to women who caught adulterous husbands in the act. That the rage of the rejected is not a gender-neutral emotion, but rather is a product of the sexist value system of male prerogatives over women, helps to explain why so few women commit "separation murders" comparable to those of men. Rapaport's analysis thus casts grave doubt on the gender-neutrality of the criminal law's time-honored distinction between "hot blood" and "cold blood" in ranking the relative heinousness of murder.

Professor Rapaport's empirical study appears to at least indirectly support her qualitative analysis. First, the male and female death row populations differ dramatically: while very few women are on death row, of those who killed a domestic partner, the vast majority killed for predatory gain, and only a tiny fraction killed to retaliate against the rejection of a male partner. The proportions are roughly reversed among the larger population of men. These data seem consistent with an intuitive sense that women do not often feel they have the right to "own" their men, and hence do not often kill in retaliation for their loss. Second, it is striking that approximately half the male domestic killers on death row were retaliating for their female victims' attempts to separate. On the one hand, the fact that some "separation killers" received death sentences may surprise feminists who believe that such murders are *not* usually recognized as maximally brutal by society. However, Rapaport points out that although many men kill female partners with whom they live, all of the male capital separation killers in the study had killed female partners who had already left; in other words, the heinousness of the killing of a partner is "discounted" when the victim lives with the killer. Moreover, the retaliatory separation murders which were capitally punished tended to involve aggravating factors, such as a history of felonious violence, or multiple murders including children or other family members. Thus, on balance, the data do support the old adage that a marriage license is a "license to beat," indeed, to kill, at least so long as the relationship has not been physically severed.

Conclusion

The papers in this Section all deal with an aspect of intimate violence which is either ignored or distorted by both established legal norms and established feminist legal theories. The authors call for an expansion of feminist analyses to account for these silenced voices, and a change in both legal and social processes to allow them to be heard. Ultimately, they call for a more compassionate legal culture. For only in such a climate can the needs of children and women be met and the causes of abuse be addressed once and for all.

Notes

1. Most feminist theorists are careful to emphasize the diversity and contradictions among feminist legal thinkers. However, for an analysis to be characterized as "feminist," some reductionism is unavoidable. Thus, Katharine Bartlett notes that feminist theory is defined in part by its "critical stance" toward the ways the existing order "affects different 'women as women'." (1990, p. 833). Christine Littleton defines the essence of "feminist jurisprudence" as taking "women's experience, as the starting point" for legal rules and norms. (1989, p. 25).

2. A classic statement of the patriarchal theory of the causes of domestic violence is contained in Dobash and Dobash, *Violence Against Wives* (1979). Elizabeth Pleck has also contributed a more nuanced examination of the history of American legal and social norms with respect to domestic violence (Pleck 1987).

3. Bartlett 1990; Littleton 1989. See note 1, *supra*.

4. Feminists' early advocacy for "equal treatment" in employment and elsewhere has been characterized as the "first generation." (Williams 1989, p. 99) (describing the landscape of the "first generation" as marked by laws which explicitly sorted the world by gender and concomitantly valuated those sharply defined spheres). The "second phase" of feminist advocacy focused on the legal and political significance of "traditionally female" concerns, and the male value system underlying seemingly neutral norms. (Fineman 1991; Dworkin and MacKinnon 1988; Resnick 1988.) The "third phase"

describes the recent and growing recognition of other outsiders to the feminist project, exemplified by the work of Kimberle Crenshaw (1989, p. 139) (criticizing the "marginalization of multiply-burdened" Black women in anti-discrimination law which results from feminism's single-axis gender analysis); Angela Harris (in Bartlett and Kennedy 1991, p. 235) (advocating a "post-essential feminism" that abandons the fallacy of a unitary self by recognizing that "difference—and therefore identity—is always relational, not inherent"); and Elizabeth Spelman 1988. For a profile of the practical and jurisprudential objectives of legal feminists in each of the three "stages," see Minow 1989, pp. 2–3.

5. Crenshaw 1989; Harris in Bartlett and Kennedy 1991, p. 235. See note 4, *supra*.

6. Mahoney 1991 (critiguing society's tendency to view the battered women as weak, passive, irrational, and abnormal).

7. 489 U.S. 189 (1989).

Child That's Got Her Own

by Marcia Sells

Charting the course for a child through the criminal justice system is like trying to explain the placement of the stars to someone who has never been able to see. But that is the responsibility of a prosecutor who handles child abuse cases. The questions a prosecutor asks or should ask herself are many: How do you use a child as a witness to prosecute her father, uncle, brother, mother, aunt, sister, cousin, or family friend? Who do we bring these cases into the criminal justice system? Are we really protecting the children? Or do we cause these children more harm?

The answers to each of these questions may lead us away from prosecuting these cases as criminal matters. Let me state at the outset that I am not an advocate of the idea that all criminal prosecution of child abuse is wrong, nor do I believe that we should abandon the process of having prosecutors investigate and prosecute child abuse. Prosecutors, a body of lawyers of which I am a former member, and others looking at how society responds to child abuse must look at the issues concerning child abuse and the law without our "objective" filters, and must try to analyze from a child's perspective to see whether other ways are available to handle both child physical and sexual abuse cases.

Children against their parents; child against family friend; daughter against father; these are the scenarios of prosecution in child abuses cases. But the usual legal parlance requires that a prosection is only "the state" against the perpetrator or defendant. A person working in the district attorney's office stands before the court and states "I represent the People of the State of" (fill in the blank—in my case New York). A prosecutor then must prove her case by presenting her witnesses before the judge and jury to prove "beyond a reasonable doubt" that the perpetrator committed the crime for which he or she is charged. The prosecutor's proof of the defendant's guilt usually requires witnesses. This is particularly true in a child abuse case or a crime of sexual or physical violence against a person. These witnesses/victims are supposed to be viewed as just "evidence" needed to prove the case. Not every prosecutor (or even most prosecutors) view her witnesses as just evidence, but the structure of the criminal process lays this particular boundary on criminal cases, unlike civil cases, where an individual can directly accuse her "perpetrator" of the civil wrong. Removing the person who was more affected by—harmed by—the crime is what criminal prosecutions achieve. This is the basis of our "civilized" criminal prosecution. We rationalize that an individual victim should not act as the prosecutor of his or her attackers because we—society—are attempting to remove direct retribution from the equation. My plea is not for personalized prosecutions, where people stimulate the Old West in 1993 fashion, and take each other to court for all our "criminal" wrongs or violations of society's moral codes. But there should be some recognition that the criminal justice system may not have all the answers for handling particular types of criminal cases, particularly those involving child abuse.

The nature of "legal advocacy" has traditionally required that there appear to be two very distinct sides: right versus wrong; good versus evil; villains versus innocent victims. This paradigm of criminal prosecution is often not appropriate for prosecuting child abuse cases. The difficulty with a system that requires a prosecutor in a child abuse case to regard the child as just a witness whose sworn testimony will help prove the guilt of a "terrible criminal" is that the child may love—often does love the perpetrator. This is particularly the case if the child is related to the person committing the abuse. The child witness has more than just a passing interest in the outcome. Not that other victims do not care whether their attackers go to jail or are punished in some other way. Children in abuse cases against a family member care because their whole world can change. They can wind up in foster care removed from their home, a relative or loved one can end up in jail, and other family members can be affected. These changes can often cause just as much, sometimes more, harm to children who have been abused. The level of anguish that these situations can cause also depends on the child's age and developmental state, and family and/or community resources available to assist the child. Unfortunately, in most of the cases I have handled as a prosecutor, the family and community resources were extremely limited. These factors have to be addressed if we are to develop better responses to handling child abuse cases and finding alternatives to criminal prosecution. Let's face it: if all we have to rely on is criminal prosecution, we have already lost the battle. The child has already been abused, and unlike doctors, we—prosecutors—cannot prescribe a medicinal remedy to soothe the pain or correct the injury. In order to achieve some success, not just as prevention but as healing, we have to look at other alternatives.

A focused review of how a prosecutor tries child abuse cases—informed by concepts from feminist legal theory—help us to rethink how child abuse cases are handled; the possible alternatives to criminal prosecution may be approached through looking at the actual handling of criminal cases and how the legal system can insure that children's "bodily integrity" remains intact (Thomas 1992).

Not until I left the full-time practice of law and began working at Columbia Law School, where I met Martha Fineman, did I spend my newfound freedom from legal practice to think about the ways that feminist theory and methodology had played a major role in my work as a prosecutor. Through my interaction with Martha, I began to realize that many of the methods that we used in such cases came from, even directly derive from, feminist theory and feminist legal theory. As prosecutors, we learned how to question a child witness based on the seven prime indicators of the "child abuse accommodation syndrome" (Summit 1983). The genealogical roots of this "syndrome" reach back to the rape trauma syndrome and further back to post-traumatic stress disorder (Burgess and Holstram 1974). The work of feminist legal theorists in the late 1970s and early 1980s, which shaped the way prosecutors tried rape cases, eventually filtered down to inform how prosecutors handled child abuse cases. The trauma of child abuse was slowly understood and incorporated into how prosecutors thought about trying these cases, and this added to other methodologies that were culled from theories about child development.

Listening to the voices of rape victims and their stories informed prosecutors about how they could represent rape cases to juries. The strong emphasis on listening to the voices of the victims that was be constructed in feminist legal theory did shape how child abuse victims were heard and their cases were tried. However, it is often difficult for a child's voice—as opposed to an adult woman's voice—to be heard in criminal cases. This does not just refer to the child's voice literally not being loud enough to be heard in a large courtroom. It also refers to the legal barriers that can prevent a child's voice or story from being heard in a criminal prosecution.

One example of the limiting effect that a criminal prosecution has on a child's "voice" is the determination of whether a child's testimony can be considered evidence or not. If a child is considered "too young" under the law to present testimonial evidence in a child abuse prosecution, then the case will end before any courtroom doors are ever opened. In New York State, a child under twelve years of age must be presented before a judge—prior to a trial or the presentation of evidence in a grand jury—to determine whether she understands the nature of an "oath." Does she understand what it means to "swear an oath" in court to tell the "truth."[1] A child must answer questions about what happens to her if she tells a lie, and, in some courts, must respond to questions about her beliefs and even about God.[2] If the judge is satisfied that the child understands "the nature of an oath" she may then be presented in a trial as a sworn witness, whose testimony can be considered as possibly credible evidence.[3] This is just one of the hurdles a child witness, together with the prosecutor, must clear to bring a child abuse case to trial through the criminal justice system.

When a case does go to trial, there are the rules of evidence that define not only what facts, but also how those facts can come before a judge or a jury. A child does not just tell a story. She must learn how to listen to questions and give appropriate answers. The prosecutor does all of the speaking for the state and the child—makes the opening statement, offers closing arguments, questions all witnesses and sometimes the defendant. During the trial we do not have children telling a narrative about the events that happened to them. In our criminal justice system, we must also allow the defendant the right to confront her or his accuser and allow his or her attorney to question the child through leading—and for a child at times—confusing questions that she must answer. In many of my cases a child would want to just tell "her story," not always presenting the facts in a chronological order or even in what may be considered "traditional" narrative format: a beginning, a middle, and an end.

A child's ideas about what should happen in a case are often silenced by the requirements of the criminal court. Witnesses in court must answer questions about what date the crime occurred; many children do not always remember exact dates. You learn when you prosecute child abuse cases that you have to ask whether an incident of abuse occurred near her birthday; a family member's birthday; a special holiday like Easter, Halloween, thanksgiving, Hannukah; or on a school day. This method of questioning a child witness works during direct examination—or while you are preparing a case, but when a child is asked questions during the defense attorney's cross-examination, she may get confused about the dates. There is no requirement that the defense attorney structure her or his cross-examination in the same way as the prosecutor structured the direct examination. Some would say it is probably antithetical to the idea of cross-examination and being an effective advocate for the defendant for a defense attorney to question a child witness in the same way as a prosecutor would for a direct examination. Therefore, since children (mainly children under the age of ten) usually have a difficult time discussing their abuse in chronological order, cross-examination can be extremely traumatic as well as confusing. A child may talk about an event that is uppermost in her mind, and that could mean she is discussing the third or fourth incident of abuse in a scenario of eight different abusive episodes.

One case involved Amelia (not her real name), an eight-year-old girl who had been sexually abused by her uncle. Amelia would see her uncle when she went to visit her father, who was separated from Amelia's mother and lived with his sister and her husband. She could only remember that the incidents of abuse occurred on weekends, and never knew an exact date, like March 3, 1986. So in court Amelia would say, "On the first weekend I went to visit my uncle did . . . and on the second weekend my uncle did. . . . " The defense attorney would question Amelia about incidents she said occurred on weekend two, and inquire how she could be sure that these incidents did not occur on weekend one, or even weekend visit four or five of that year. Amelia could not just "tell" what happened to her. Each incident had to be categorized by a specific data, time, and place in order to allow the defendant his opportunity to formulate a defense—an alibi—that he was not present in the house on weekend visit number four, so no abuse could have occurred at that time. This is just one example of the type of problems a child faces when she is subjected to testifying in a criminal proceeding. These types of concerns also challenge a prosecutor of child abuse cases.

As a prosecutor in the Kings County District Attorney's Sex Crimes/ Special Victims Bureau, I underwent a fairly thorough training program concerning the way to try child abuse—physical and sexual—cases. We not only learned how to try a case, involving opening statements, direct and cross-examinations, the introduction of medical evidence from a gynecological exam or pediatric exam by an emergency room doctor, the interpretation of serology evidence—tests for sperm, saliva, or other bodily fluids—and closing arguments; we were also well versed in the child abuse accommodation syndrome, the way that acondoloma acumenata (a sexually transmitted disease seen in some child sex abuse cases) can affect a child physically, or how to prepare a child witness for the courtroom and the questions (Summit 1983). It was important to the bureau that we learn how to question a child witness, know how to use the anatomically correct dolls, and learn how a child remembers dates or the time when an abuse occurred.

All of these "how-tos," though important and admirable, were taught to us much more in the spirit of winning a case than in making sure that the child victim felt better abut the process. In their view, the untraumatized child is a better witness than the one who falls out crying and screaming the moment she walks into the courtroom and faces all the people—jury, judge, defendant, and defense attorney. This is not meant as a slight against the office, my training, or all prosecutors. To a large extent, it is the nature of the system. We must win in order to remove the perpetrator from the home, school, neighborhood, or vicinity of the child victim. We prosecutors do not participate in the direct healing process of a child victim, except—as my office often did—to send a child to a clinical social worker, psychologist, or psychiatrist. This was often done when we were not able to obtain information from a child, and tried to ease it out of her by sending her to therapy (sometimes at the expense of the office).[4] However, the bottom line was that by learning these skills you could win cases, and that ultimately would help the victims because the defendants would be punished.

As child abuse prosecutors, we also considered or convinced ourselves that the process of testifying in court was cathartic for children. This is the same theory that is used to encourage adult female rape victims to testify; we think it is important for the children to tell their "story" to the jury. If the jury convicts, this is proof that someone "heard" them and believed their "story." However, it is hard for a child victim to tell her "own" story in a criminal courtroom for reasons discussed earlier. The American Heritage Dictionary of the English Language defines "own" as "a word used to intensify the fact of possession . . . or to maintain one's place in spite of attack." A reality about the court system—namely the criminal court system—is that a witness does not "own" her story— possess it, control it— in the courtroom; the lawyers do. A prosecutor— a good one—has to appropriate her witness' story in order to ensure that it is presented to the jury in a manner that they—the jury—can hear, identify with, and ultimately decide to believe in order to convict. A reliance on criminal prosecution as the only real remedy for abused children does not allow or fully explore other avenues that can lead to helping and possibly really assisting in the healing of abused children or their families.

The social agencies that are supposed to assist in the protection of children and aid in the healing of families by providing services for parents unable to care for their children, or training them in parenting skills in order to impede the spread of the cycle of violence or sexual abuse, have in some ways abdicated their responsibility to the child abuse units that have developed in district attorneys' offices. The statistics that reflect some of the intentional abuse children have suffered (for reasons that will be discussed later) are found in articles around the country. Some state "[i]n a typical year, more children are killed by their parents in California than die in accidental fires or falls or poisoning. . . ."[5] "Nationally 1000–2000 youngsters each year are murdered by their mothers or fathers. . . ."[6] In Florida, the *St. Petersburg Times* recorded that in 1992, sixty-eight children died due to abuse or neglect: forty-one were due to abuse and twenty-seven were due to parental neglect.[7] The *Chicago Tribune* reported that 2.9 million cases of suspected child maltreatment were reported in the United States in 1992.[8] Add this to the statement made by the National Committee for Prevention of Child Abuse that they have documented a fifty percent increase in child abuse deaths since 1985, and we realize that somehow the agencies assigned by various state and city governments to protect children are not completing the task.[9]

Child abuse units within district attorneys' offices have served to call more attention to child abuse—through the new training of prosecutors to handle such cases and the sensationalization of high-publicity child abuse cases. However, as the statistics stated earlier suggest, we need more preventive or earlier corrective measures to prevent the deaths or severe injuries resulting from parental or guardian abuse. These units have become the major investigative force in child abuse cases, rather than the bureaus of child welfare or departments of social services that had been assigned the original task to investigate these cases *before* turning to criminal prosecution.

In 1986, New York State established a child abuse hotline to handle calls from across the state concerning the sexual and physical abuse of children.[10] A case called into the hotline was then sent to the respective child welfare agency in the county where the abuse was alleged to have occurred. The particular county or city child welfare department was then required to investigate the case and make recommendations: to remove the child from the home; to file abuse and neglect charges against the parents in family court; or to allow the child to remain in the home, and assist the parent or guardian if necessary. Unfortunately, during my time as the head of the child abuse unit and as a prosecutor, many of these cases in Brooklyn were sent to our unit for investigation; therefore skipping the investigation by a child welfare bureau agent and the possible development of a family plan to assist in the prevention of further abuse and neglect, as opposed to the immediate criminal investigation and possible prosecution. In the time since I have left that office, this practice has not changed.

While working as a prosecutor, it was the stories of the children that were compelling. The time I have spent since then, reflecting on domestic violence and the effect of this violence on children in families, has sent me back to re-listen to these stories and what they say about a child's voice, her protection, the work of the child welfare bureau, and the appropriate responses toward these cases. Among the voices that I reviewed in my memory were those of four children who were raped and sodomized by their father. The Kronish family (not the real name) is a Hasidic Jewish family from Brooklyn. The children's case came to my attention through a child abuse hotline report. Mr. Kronish's therapist, a mandatory reporter under the New York State Social Service Law, reported the abuse to the hotline.[11] The report noted that the father confessed to his psychologist that he had digitally penetrated all his children—three boys and one girl—and that he had also raped and sodomized all children independently and in each others' presence. Of course, when I read the report I wondered if the bureau of child welfare in New York City (BCW) had investigated this case, especially since the hotline report was two months old when I had an opportunity to review it.

Part of the requirements the New York State legislature established for responding to hotline reports is that a case should be investigated within forty-eight hours of the report being made. Unfortunately, some cases are not investigated immediately by BCW, and some clearly requiring criminal prosecution are left on a desk uninvestigated. The result of all of this is that children in abusive situations—sexual or physical—may continue to live in unsafe conditions in their homes. Just such a situation existed for the Kronish children, who remained at home. In addition, the difficulty in placing children from Hasidic families in foster care (mainly because there are not many foster homes that will meet the religious needs of these children) may have also caused the BCW caseworkers problems with this case. This may also explain why, when they finally had an opportunity to review the report, it was sent to the district attorney's office.[12] BCW was allowed to send cases it believed would probably lead to a criminal investigation to our offices for us to follow up. This procedure was never intended as a substitute for BCW's own investigation. It is important to note that then, as now, there are more cases for BCW and district attorneys' offices to investigate than there are people to conduct the investigations. However, bypassing the BCW investigation and allowing an immediate criminal investigation forces children to enter into a system where their voice will be distilled and, as described earlier, possibly not heard.

The Kronish children were not happy, and neither was their mother, to see their case in the DA's office. However, once I had seen the report, I was required to follow up, and bring the children to my office to investigate the validity of the hotline report. Ranging in ages from seven to twelve, the Kronish children were each able to tell me about the incest that had been occurring in their home for almost four years. Each child offered details about a harrowing number of sexual abuse incidents that in all likelihood might not have come to light after four years had their father not confessed to the abuse during his therapy session. The father in some way recognized that he needed help, but did not stop the incest even after he was in therapy. Mr. Kronish's psychologist was required to report the confession of the abuse to the hotline; therefore, someone would be able to step in to protect the children.[13]

When the children came to my office, before we discussed their abuse, I explained to them who I was: "an assistant district attorney"; and what a prosecutor does: "tries to help people or children who have been in trouble because someone may have hurt them or taken something from them. Sometimes people who do things wrong are punished for what they do and it is my job to make sure that people who have done something wrong do not keep doing things to hurt another person." I am sure it was not in those exact words, and it probably took at least half of the first hour to discuss who I am and what I do. Still, this unnerved the children. Even when you soften the explanation about a prosecutor's job, children have watched enough television or heard their parents or other adults talk about crime and jail. The immediate fear of each of the Kronish children was that their father would leave their home and go to jail.

When I first began working as a prosecutor in these cases, I naively thought: Why should children care about their father (or any other family member who is an accused pedophile) going to jail or being punished after the individual had harmed them in such heinous ways either physically or sexually? However, an important concern of many children is that this will cause a disruption in their life, and although there is abuse they also have some love or affection for this family member (Goldstein, Freud and Solnit 1973). Children also fear that they are responsible for what is to them a sudden and disconcerting change in their family. Part of the training I described earlier did include ways to reassure children that they are not responsible for what is happening to the adult, but that the adult who inflicted this abuse on them is the culprit. Sometimes telling a child that her father, uncle, family friend was not necessarily going to jail, but that I was going to insure that he was helped for his problem, would assuage her. But many children react like Maria, a six-year-old girl who was being sexually abused by a family friend, telling me the story of the abuse and then saying they will not go to court to tell the story; they do not want to see their family member or friend go to jail. All my promises about trying to prevent jail and discussing plea bargaining process in a child's vernacular did not help. Maria still had the best line for me about how she felt about my trying to prosecute her family's friend for his abuse towards her. She said: "He just needs help." To which I responded: "I can get him help, but I have to make sure he does not do this again and knows that you do not want this to happen."

Maria, nonplussed, answered me, "Life is Life." Not much more I could say. Maria had essentially decided that telling someone about the abuse was enough. In her particular case, this was actually true; her family decided to keep the "friend" away from the house. It is the children whose abuser lives with them that have considerably more difficulty, and just telling about the abuse generally will not protect them.

In the Kronish case, the children were even more disheartened because, despite the abuse of the familial relationship, they were "an intact family." Of course, this intact family was internally corroding. The father was making the children swear not to reveal their "games" to anyone, not even their mother. Indeed the mother claimed she had no knowledge about these events and was concerned that I may have encouraged them to make these statements. Skepticism such as that expressed by Mrs. Kronish is expressed a great deal in these cases, because no one wants to believe that a family member would violate family trust to such a degree, and if a child claims that such a trust was indeed destroyed, the whole state of the family is questioned. At this stage, my concern focused on the possible outcome if the mother would not force the father to leave the house or honor the order of protection that I was going to file. How would he retaliate against the children for confirming his revelation to his therapist? How would I ensure the children's safety? Why did BCW not ensure the children's safety? A 1989 decision in the Supreme Court case of *DeShaney v. Winnebago County Department of Social Services* ensures that this practice could continue, entrenching a permanent abdication of responsibility by child welfare agencies.[14] The resulting lack of responsibility that agencies such as the Bureau of Child Welfare are legally allowed is part of the concern that has sparked my discussion concerning the need to include the child's own voice in the solution to child abuse problems. The *DeShaney* case does have some answers to these questions. This Supreme Court case essentially deprives the children of protection from their father's retaliatory abuse for disclosing his "indiscretions." The only manner in which to protect the children from further abuse would be to force his removal from the home, either by threatening to remove the children to foster care, and thus away from their mother, or by obtaining an order of protection requiring that he stay away from the home and the children. It is also possible, if the father remained in the home and I did not want to send the children to foster care, that I could have issued an order of protection. This would require the BCW to act quickly if necessary, and would also allow for quick action by the police.[15]

In another case, also reflecting, as the Kronish case does, some of the problems for abused children that the Supreme Court's decision in *DeShaney* has created, two children, Luther and June Williams (not their real names), were brought to the early complaint assessment bureau in the Brooklyn district attorney's office because they had run away from home. June and Luther had jumped out of the bathroom window of their apartment and over fences, and had walked about two and half miles to a police precinct with all their belongings in plastic grocery bags. At the precinct, the children stressed that they stayed with their father because if they told someone about the beatings their father would be angry. At the time that June and Luther found themselves in my office, they were about nine and seven years old. For a number of years they had endured physical abuse from their father, Mr. Williams. Their mother's whereabouts were not known, and it seemed that she had not lived with them for quite some time. It seemed to me and the young female police office who brought both Williams children to our office that June was the decision-maker concerning the children's choice to leave home. The police officer and I believed that June may have been sexually abused— as she was reaching puberty—but June never made a complaint about such abuse—no matter how many different ways we asked her. She and her brother only discussed the physical beatings.

If the bureau of child welfare had been involved in this case, they could have decided after hearing the children's story to send both these children back to their father. BCW could have arranged for the father to attend parenting classes, go into treatment for abusive parents and submit to having a home care attendant—all actions within the purview of child protective agencies. Though the agencies have this authority to require parents suspected of abuse to discontinue their abusive behavior, the agencies are not mandated to follow up and insure compliance with their prescribed plans. Luther and June apparently believed their only safe haven was the police precinct. They were fortunate that the police officer was willing to take a complaint, and that they live in Brooklyn where the district attorney's office takes responsibility to investigate child abuse cases.

The result in this case was that in the end we prosecuted Mr. Williams; the children went into foster care, and as far as I know are still in foster care. Again it was left to the criminal justice agency to rescue June and Luther. Now it is quite clear that June and Luther needed to leave their father's attacks, but under the Supreme Court's decision only children who are able to be independent actors can find sanctuary from abuse. If the children cannot leave, because they are too young or not emotionally or mentally capable of formulating a leaving plan, they are at the mercy of their abusers unless a child welfare agency rescues them.

Protecting children from abuse in their home is the intended role of the New York State Bureau of Child Welfare.[16] However, the Supreme Court, in its 1989 decision in *DeShaney*, decided that the Constitution does not confer protection on children for abuse suffered at the hands of their parents or any other private citizen that is not acting as an agent of the state.[17] The sad facts of this case are harrowing, and demonstrate how the court has allowed state child welfare agencies to abandon their protective role.

A little boy named Joshua DeShaney remains in a home for retarded children after the final beating by his father. Joshua was placed with his father after a divorce and custody battle was lost by the former Mrs. DeShaney. While Joshua was in his father's custody, there were reports filed by hospitals and even by Mr. DeShaney's former girlfriend against him for beating his son. At one point, the Winnebago County Department of Social Services ("DSS") in Wisconsin took Joshua out of his father's home briefly to investigate the possibility of abuse. Unfortunately, they returned Joshua to his father, and more abuse occurred, as noted by an emergency room doctor. However, the DSS never removed Joshua from the home again. The DSS worker noted the injuries, ordered the father's then-girlfriend to leave the DeShaney home, and recommended that Joshua attend a special after-school program. None of the recommended or ordered prescriptions were honored by Mr. DeShaney. When the final call came to the DSS office in Winnebago County, the worker is quoted as saying that she "knew that one day the phone would ring and say that Joshua was dead."[18] Considering the current state of poor Joshua's life, death might have been better. He was discovered with severe bruises and scars to his head, which resulted in his lapsing into a coma from which he recovered, but he suffered severe brain damage.

Despite this harrowing tale, and the very real abdication and abandonment by DSS of their role as protector of children from abuse, the Supreme Court of the Unites States, in its decision, decided that neither the DSS nor the state of Wisconsin had any duty to protect Joshua DeShaney from the abuse that his father inflicted.[19] The court believed that "when it [DSS] returned [Joshua] to his father's custody, it placed him in no worse position than that in which he would have been in had the state not acted at all."[20] The above comment unfortunately displays the Court's ignorance about the reality of child abuse cases, where retaliation after the abuse has been uncovered is often the next abuse.[21] Why would an adult, whose child has either told someone about the abuse she is suffering or "let the abuse be discovered in a hospital emergency room," be free to go home and inflict the child with further abuse?[22] It is mainly because states are too afraid to act. Retaliation or "separation assault" becomes just one more way for an abuser to continue to exercise control over the victim. If this is true for women in violent domestic relationships, why would the U.S. Supreme Court not recognize this to be exactly the situation that Joshua DeShaney was placed in when he was returned to his home after the abuse had been uncovered? Unfortunately, appellants in the *DeShaney* case do not appear to have addressed this sociological aspect of child abuse when discussing their arguments.

The Supreme Court justified its decision that Winnebago DSS did not have an obligation to protect Joshua because it found that the state is not required to "affirmatively protect citizens from the private actions of a third party."[23] The Court approached this case as only an argument of affirmative rights versus negative rights. The majority based its decision on its interpretation of the *Youngberg v. Romeo* and *Estelle v. Gamble* cases.[24] This negative rights view assumes that children are in some way "agents" or independent actors in an abuse situation. This same assumption has often been made in domestic violence cases involving adult female victims. However, the same assumption in child abuse cases is obscene. It makes a mockery of child abuse protection laws and the need to establish child welfare agencies. Somehow the Supreme Court, in its analysis in the *DeShaney* case, has decided that children who are placed in foster care are deserving of more protection than children who are known by the state to be in abusive situations in their own home.

It is my contention that the *DeShaney* case could have been decided in a manner more consistent with the reality of child abuse cases. Such a standard would focus on protecting children's "bodily integrity," and would force the state child welfare agencies to perform their duties. (Note 1990; Strauss 1989; Areen 1975). Under this standard the necessity for conjecture as to the casual connection of a private citizen not acting to protect a child is eliminated (Strauss 1989, p. 63). A change from *DeShaney* would allow children to bring a civil action against state child welfare agencies for not insuring the child's safety once they have stepped into a case. Of course, this will require some balancing of the constitutional protection, now only afforded parents under Section 1983, to prevent unnecessary state intervention into the family but also the rights of children to be safe from abuse.[25]

The Supreme Court's decision in *DeShaney* "creates the possibility that the state is not responsible for the physical harm caused a child, if a child is placed in custodial arrangement that is not worse than placement with parents." (Note 1990, p. 813). It is imperative that the gap be closed between abuse in the home and a state's duty to protect, because we are willing our children to certain disaster, and surely not assisting families to stay intact. Child welfare agencies under the rubric in *DeShaney* do not carry any burden to insure a child's physical safety, but only to protect the "sanctity of the family."[26] A "family" is not really preserved if, in the end, a parent or parents are sent to jail, and the children sent to foster care. One should not assume though, that every parent who has committed a criminal offense is capable or even willing to care, nurture, and protect his or her children. However, pushing the responsibility onto the criminal justice system to protect children from abusive parents who commit criminal acts of abuse surely is not the best answer. But it has become the only "check" on the bodily integrity of the children, and this is a delayed check, because invariably, when a case has actually reached the hands of a prosecutor, the situation has either advanced to where a child has, in the "best" scenario, survived minor or grave harm—like the Kronish or the Williams children—or in the worst, is dead or left, like Joshua DeShaney, severely and permanently injured.

The lack of enforcement of responsibility on child welfare agencies under the present standards established by the Supreme Court makes it possible for a parent to tell a child welfare agency that he or she has an "uncontrollable urge to beat his or her child [and] there would be no duty to protect because state knowledge of the abuse is irrelevant under DeShaney" (Note 1990, p. 813).[27]

The argument that the Court simply had to recognize, as Justice Brennan points out, is that if the Court had looked at this case in a manner extremely similar to the way the Court has handled entitlement cases (housing, welfare, Medicaid) it would have easily been able to find for Joshua.[28] A review of these types of cases is not possible in this article, but briefly, in such cases the Supreme Court has stated that it is not looking at the right to receive welfare or the right to have housing supplied by the state, but the right to receive these benefits once the state has provided for such services.[29] Therefore, a family receiving welfare cannot have those benefits cut off without a hearing to review why these funds may be taken away from them, and a woman cannot be effectively prevented from going to a hospital for an abortion if the state and the federal government have provided for that service. "Whether the person established a constitutionally protected liberty interest in bodily integrity, not whether the person has a right to protection from private violence" was the question that the Supreme Court really had to concern itself with (Note 1990, p. 815). The state of Wisconsin, like many states that have child welfare agencies, does inflict itself on a child—and her family—when its agents come in the home to "investigate" any allegations of child abuse. If, as in *DeShaney*, a child welfare agency has actually, at one time, removed a child from her home it has done more than just investigate; it is also taking over for the child and placing itself in a very "affirmative" role as the child's safe haven, for however long.[30] But, particularly as in *DeShaney*, child welfare has also imposed some procedures that a parent must complete: send the child to special classes or school, attend parenting skills sessions, remove the boyfriend or girlfriend from the home, or allow frequent home visits by the agency.[31] What else can it be saying to a family, and even to the child, but that the agency is here to insure that your parent does not hurt you any more? If Wisconsin DSS is now not responsible for such actions, then why should any parent follow—and as is the *DeShaney* case many do not—any mandated procedures that any child welfare agency demands of a parent.[32] Essentially, these parent skills programs, after-school programs for abused children, and the like are only recommended to prevent abusive parents from continuing their abusive behavior. At least where there is evidence to warrant the agency "monitoring" the family situation, parents must be made to attend these "mandated" self-help programs or cooperate with the "monitoring plan." The Supreme Court's decision removes the voice of authority as well as responsibility that these agencies could have to effect real change in an abusive family situation.

Adjusting our thinking to look at the bodily integrity of an abused child can also have an additional impact on children's liberty interest from unjustified state intrusions (Note 1990, p. 815). This could require the state to leave a child in her home, but establish mechanisms to monitor the family situation in order to prevent further abuse, aid the reversal of the abusive behavior, and aim toward healing the family while allowing the child to remain with her family. This also shapes the argument in feminist theoretical terms, because it does not require the view that a child be removed from a parent based on a state acting as *parens patriae*—a continuation of a protectionist patriarchal view—but rather allows a child's unheard voice to be heard before decisions about services are altered. A child, like any other member of a community or state, should be given the right to have certain services continue, particularly when the state or its agent—a child welfare agency—has been providing services. An expectation of service has been established in this situation, and a discontinuation of such services, particularly one as important as protecting or monitoring an abused child, should not occur unless a procedural review allows the child some voice about whether it will be harmful or not to discontinue the services. Yes, this reframes the argument raised in *DeShaney* from a substantive due process concern to a procedural due process concern. However, the process may also require that child welfare agencies, in reviewing and/or investigating these cases, must include in their analysis a review of cultural or family models that are not contradictory to the safety and security of the child. This can lead to elevating the professional standards of child welfare agencies, and improve their methodology for reviewing, investigating, and handling child abuse cases. The procedural due process review will not necessarily "open the flood gates" of litigation against child welfare agencies.

Some may be concerned that this approach may create impossible problems, because of the current practices under the Civil Rights Act, statute 42 USC § 1983.[33] Parents may file a Section 1983 claim that the "family unit" has been violated due to improper investigation procedures used by the child welfare agency while investigating child abuse allegations.[34] Will we have child welfare agencies afraid to go into a family's home to investigate for fear that the parents will file claims? Possibly, yes. However, allowing children a procedural avenue from which to counteract later agency inaction after some earlier action would fairly and more effectively protect the children. As my earlier comments about the handling of child abuse cases at the criminal level should indicate, relying too heavily on the criminal justice system to protect children is not our most effective route. It is interesting to note that currently a child may file a Section 1983 claim only after a state child welfare agency has removed her from her home and placed her in foster care.[35] In some way, the state then may have a complete disincentive to remove children from abusive situations because it can have actions brought by parents claiming unnecessary intrusion and children claiming their foster care placement is not safe.

The realities of the courtroom distort, and in some cases silence, the child's reality about her abusive family circumstances. Some may argue that a possible three-way struggle under Section 1983—parent versus state child welfare agency and child versus state child welfare agency— will not be useful either. But if we really look closely at the criminal process, we have already created a kind of three-way litigant situation— even though the state and the defendant are the named parties in each of these cases. Children are now, as witnesses, forced to choose sides against a loved one.[36] The question is, which seems better for achieving the intended goals of an intact family—letting abusive situations escalate, or trying to make the child welfare agencies more responsive to the children? Inevitably this will raise some concern that the state will be monitoring every home to prevent a child from bringing an action. However, what really may happen is that if a parent does not improve his or her behavior the child may be removed.

Removing a child from her home does not achieve the intended goal of keeping families intact. This also does not necessarily protect children effectively, either. The important goal must be to return the child's voice to the "child welfare" system. We have to listen when they are in pain, and require agencies to respond, either by removing a child when necessary, balancing the concerns of the child with those of the parent, or by monitoring the home appropriately. We must ensure that agencies do not abdicate responsibility when choices become difficult. We cannot rely solely on the criminal justice system to correct child welfare agency mishaps. It is imperative that we require child welfare agencies to listen carefully to the child's voice, and allow her story to protect her, reinforcing a compassionate decision-making process that does not rely on the criminal justice system as a fail-safe measure.

Notes

1. New York State Criminal Procedure Law, sections 60.20 et seq.
2. *People v. Groff* 71 NY.2d 101, 104 (1987).

3. *People v. Groff* 71 NY2d at 104.

4. At the King's County District Attorney's Office we had a member of our own victim services staff counsel children. She was a certified clinical social worker who had many years experience working with abused children.

5. *Sacremento Bee*, September 12, 1993, p. 1A.

6. *Sacremento Bee*, September 12, 1993, p. 1A; the statistical data was provided by Michael Durfee, a child psychiatrist who studies death by child abuse for Los Angeles County Department of Health Services.

7. "Good Parenting: Life or Death Lesson," *St. Petersburg Times*, September 3, 1993, p. 1B.

8. *Chicago Tribune,* July 25, 1993, p. 1C.

9. *Sacremento Bee*, September 12, 1993, p. A1; see other articles citing similar national statistics as well as local information about child abuse and child deaths due to abuse: *Chicago Tribune,* June 27, 1993, p. 1C; *Houston Chronicle*, May 7, 1993, p. 30A; *Arizona Republic*, May 2, 1993, p. 2A; *Chicago Tribune*, May 2, 1993, p. 1C (reporting on Missouri's child fatality review project that found that child deaths in that area had risen from twenty-five cases in 1989 to forty-six cases in 1992, and eighty-four percent increase).

10. New York State Social Service Law, sections 413 and 415 et. seq.

11. Social Service Law, section 415.

12. The practice of sending child abuse hotline reports to the DA's office began in our office and two other New York City DA's offices on a voluntary basis. There was never a state mandate that BCW send cases that could result in criminal prosecution to the district attorney's office.

13. Under New York State Social Service Law, section 415 et seq., certain people, including psychologist, teachers, and doctors, are mandated to report child abuse allegations to the hotline.

14. 489 US 189 (1989).

15. "Battered women's Substantive Due Process Claim: Can Orders of Protection Deflect *DeShaney?*" 65 *New York University Law Review* 1280 (1990). This note raised the question of whether a woman issued a protective order could claim that she was placed in a position where only the state that issued the order could protect her, and whether the state could be held liable if the woman were not protected. It is quite possible that this same scenario could be played out in a child abuse case. It would then require every state child welfare agency to issue an order of protection when an abused child is left in the home. The order of protection could be issued by the family court, and would simply require that the parent not strike or beat the child. I am sure this could pose a problem for some if the child were old enough to call the police and claim that her parent is abusing her when she is simply being disciplined.

16. Social Services sections on Dept. of Social Services, NY Social Services Law sec. 411 at sequence.

17. 489 US at 196–97.

18. 489 US at 209.

19. 489 US at 201.

20. 489 US at 201.

21. Children are the recipients of an adult "doing power." Martha Mahoney discussed violence as "doing power" in connection with violence against women, but the same is true in the case of violent and sexual abuse inflicted on children. (Martha Mahoney, "Victimization or Oppression? Womens Lives, Violence, and Agency" in this volume.

22. Mahoney labels the retaliation that women suffer when they try to confront an attacker or leave the abusive home as "separation assault."

23. 489 US at 196–198.

24. 457 US 307(1982) and 429 US 97(1976).

25. *Santosky v. Kramer* 455 US at 753.

26. 489 US at 203; *Santosky v. Kramer* 455 US at 754.

27. 489 US at 201.

28. 489 US at 204 and 208.

29. 489 US at 208.

30. 489 US at 192.

31. 489 US at 192.

32. 489 US at 192–193.

33. "Every person who, under color of any statute, ordinance, regulation, custom or usage of any State, . . . subjects, or causes to be subjected, any citizen of the United States . . . to the deprivation of any rights, privileges, or immunities secured by the Constitution and laws, shall be liable to the party injured in an action at law, suit in equity, or other proper proceeding for redress. . . .

34. *Hodorowski et al. v. Ann Ray, Mary Ellen Burns & Texas Department of Human Resources*, 1988, 844 F2d 1210, 7th Circuit; *Duchesne v. Sugarman*, 1977, 566 F2d 817, 825, 2nd Circuit. ("Most essential and basic aspect of family privacy is the right of the family to remain together without the coercive interference of the awesome power of the state.")

35. *DeShaney v. Winnebago*, 489 US at 196.

36. There are a number of child abuse cases that are never brought to a criminal trial because there is no physical evidence, and the child is unable or unwilling to testify.

The Youngest Members: Harm to Children and the Role of Religious Communities

by Shauna Van Praagh

The Children of Communities

"It is probably because we have so many things in us that community is so important." So says Azaro, the spirit child who chooses to live in this world, in Ben Okri's *The Famished Road* (Okri 1991, p. 446). Different as he is from the other children around him, Azaro recognizes the significance of community, in his case that of his family and commune in an ever-changing Nigeria, and the multiplicity of factors—whether experiences, persons, spirits, gods—that shape each one of us. So many things, so many possibilities, and yet the connection to community remains crucial even when, as Azaro knows first-hand, it can result in hardship and pain, as well as love, warmth, and elation.

Far from Azaro's reality, we live in a place that rarely acknowledges the role of community, and does so even less in the context of discussing children's lives, development, and needs. We engage in rhetoric about children as our future, and we express horror at the reality of violent pain in children's lives, at the same time that we fail to find ways in which to reinforce the caretaking abilities of the individuals and communities which play substantial parts in those lives. Children are the youngest members, not only of families (whatever their makeup), but also of communities which are capable of exercising considerable influence, power, and responsibility. And they are significant members, both in the sense that they are affected by the norms, politics, and dynamics of each community to which they belong, but also in the sense that the communities themselves depend on children for their survival and continuance.

In the discussion to follow, I address domestic violence towards children by asking how our response and analysis might shift if we were to consider community as part of the domestic sphere that can be both nurturing and harmful for children. While not explicitly part of a femi-

nist analysis of domestic violence and privacy, the discussion raises connected issues with respect to boundaries and relationship, and asks related questions about power, responsibility, and remedies. That is, how
do we draw lines between the sphere of community in which parent-
child relations may flourish or falter, and the sphere of the state whose
interference may be experienced as aggressive intrusion? How do we
respond to a power structure in which children generally hold little
or no power, and depend on those around them? And who holds the
responsibility for defining and remedying serious harm to children?
While I do not promise to answer these questions in full, I hope to touch
on several aspects of them, uncover gaps in the available analysis, and put
forward some suggestions for thinking about domestic violence aimed at
children who have "so many things in [them]."

Shifting the Parent versus State Framework

Traditional legal analysis with respect to domestic violent harm to
children places the family, embodied in the individual parent or parents
whose privacy and liberty are at stake, against the state, armed with its
parens patriae power. In the United States especially, child-rearing has
commonly been understood as the responsibility of parents, and the
decisions associated with the upbringing of children have been relegated
to the private realm as a crucial component of the constitutional protection of individual autonomy. Further, the law's strong respect for "natural" parental rights with respect to child-rearing has extended to parental
control over the religious upbringing of their children (*Meyer v. Nebraska;
Pierce v. Society of Sisters; Prince v. Massachusetts; Wisconsin v. Yoder*). Thus,
a broad substantive due process or privacy right, in combination with the
individual right to free exercise of religious beliefs, results in considerable
parental power over children. That power is taken away, and those
individual rights thereby violated, only when the law intervenes based
on its compelling interest to protect children from serious violence, abuse,
or harm.

While a discussion of domestic violence aimed at children usually turns
on the concepts of parental or family privacy, and state intervention in
the form of child welfare and protection agencies, I will focus here on
the parental right to freedom of religion that acts as a parallel buffer
between child and state. The relationship between children and the
religious communities to which they may belong questions an analytical
model that casts parental power over religious upbringing against state
power to remedy harm caused by that upbringing. That is, religious
communities themselves may play a significant part in a child's development, and thereby act as one of many mediators between parent and

state. At the same time, they may be implicated in the infliction of harm upon children, and their role deserves to be explored as we engage in part of a larger inquiry about the appropriate response of law to domestic violence.

Religious communities are, of course, only one of many kinds of communities to which a child may belong, and which play a role in the life of a child. Education and recreation communities, communities based on the sharing of ethnicity, race, culture, or language, and neighborhood communities brought together by common experience and concerns may all be significant to a child's development, and the potential for overlap among various communities is easily apparent. I have chosen to focus on religion and religious communities in this discussion for a number of reasons. First, as already indicated, constitutional protection of the free exercise of religion, when paired with the protection of family privacy, results in a formidable barrier between the state and the parent who acts according to religious beliefs. Second, affiliation with religious communities is widespread in the United States (Wald 1992, pp. 7–15), with a large majority of Americans identifying themselves as "religious."[1] Third, religious doctrine is analogous to law in its authoritative structure and influence, and adherence to rules may be crucial in order to maintain membership (Cover 1983). Finally, the strong influence of religious beliefs upon child-rearing practices suggests the need for an exploration of both the beneficial and harmful effects of religious communities upon their child members. For example, the roots of child punishment can be located in religious texts and convictions, and links have been suggested between physical punishment and abusive violence (Thomas 1972; Greven 1991; Miller 1983).

The Dynamics of Religious Community as Mediator

Before exploring ways in which religious communities, the norms they articulate, and the ways of life they require may be harmful to children, an alternative framework for understanding the relationship among children, parents, religious communities, and the state needs to be sketched out. Instead of subsuming the claims of religious communities within parental freedom-of-religion arguments, a child's connection to community can be valued for the way in which it serves that child's interests in developing a unique identity through membership. That is, guarding a "domestic" sphere in which a child is cared for may include securing the child's relationship to a given religious community.

Full recognition of individual freedom of religion in the United States, guaranteed by the First Amendment, includes the long-established ability to pass on one's religious beliefs to one's children, and to enforce religious practices within the family (Friedman 1915–16; Galanter 1966, pp. 228–9). The landmark decision of *Wisconsin v. Yoder*, in which Amish children were allowed to leave school after eighth grade in accordance with the tenets of the Old Order Amish community, can be read as reinforcement of the "primary role of parents in the upbringing of their children . . . established beyond debate as an enduring American tradition."[2] That is, the religious beliefs and practices of Amish parents included the exercise of power over their children with respect to the question of education.

Wisconsin v. Yoder can be alternatively read, however, as support for the pluralist character of the United States (Minow 1989b, p. 968), a character in which religion plays a significant part. That is, by deferring to the norms of the Amish community on the issue of education, the Court seemed willing to recognize the diversity of modes of child-rearing and indeed, the diversity of children themselves. This way of reading *Yoder* forms the basis for appreciating the way in which religious communities interact with the family—traditionally seen as the locus of maximum constitutional protection for the individual (Brownstein 1990, p. 102)—by implementing a substantive system of laws and practices for subscribing group members. The actions of parents *vis-à-vis* their children may be protected by law on the basis of individual freedom, but they can be understood to stem from a commitment to a community of persons who share the same beliefs, and from a sense of obligation or accountability to that community (Tushnet 1986).

Usually then, the law may recognize the ability of parents to enrol their children in private religious schools, refuse to procure medical treatment for them, or enforce absolute separation whereby children are forbidden from involving themselves in social relationships or extracurricular activities—all in the name of parental religious conviction. We can translate that attitude to one of support for the flourishing of different religions in a pluralistic society, and we might go further by suggesting that children themselves have an interest in the strengthening of the communities to which they belong. In other words, instead of framing an argument against state intrusion in terms of parental privacy or freedom of religion, the argument could be based on the child's "membership interests" served by connection to a religious community.

Two concepts need clarification before moving to an investigation of how the religious community may serve as a source of harm in addition to one of positive identity. First, how do we envision religious communities and the way in which they interact with the "domestic" sphere in which most children live? Second, how does the power structure within religious communities inform their relationship with children?

For the purposes of this discussion, we can understand religious communities in a large, liberal society as self-perceived, small, normative universes coexisting with the larger normative structure of the state (Cover 1983). For members of these groups, the authoritative structures of the religious community address many details of internal family life (Weisbrod 1987–88), and the law's commitment to certain policies with respect to the family may be experienced as an attack on the self-defined jurisdiction of those communities. While this model is easier to apply with respect to orthodox, insulated communities, it can also be applied to more liberal, integrated communities, in the sense that the state may act to override the norms of either kind of group through legislation or court decisions.

An awareness of the self-conception of religious groups as parallel regulators of the family allows us to expand our definition of the "domestic" sphere. The teachings of a religious community with respect to children may be translated into parental practice, and therefore become central to a child's day-to-day life. And yet, while religions concern themselves with doctrine relating to the rearing of children, children do not choose to be members subject to that doctrine. Child membership in religious communities, in fact, is unique in that it is not based on any notion of the free choice to join or not join, otherwise fundamental to a liberal appreciation of religiosity. At the same time, child membership is crucial to the continuation of religious communities, and, as we have seen, it is generally enforced through the liberal mechanism of individual freedom of religion held by parents.

The power structure of the religious community and its relationship to children thus becomes clear: the membership level represented by children is one without power as compared to those levels represented by adults (of course, women and men usually represent different power levels). Indeed the community has a vested interest in exerting power over its child members. This observation takes nothing away from the notion that children may develop their identities partially within their religious community or communities; nor does it deny that the community may be nurturing and supportive, educational, and significant to a child's sense of self. Yet it does suggest that the considerable control that a religious community may exert over the life of a child, whether or not through parental practices, carries with it negative potential. The same connections that have just been sketched as worthy of protection in a child's life may need to be readjusted or indeed severed if they result in severe harm to that child.

Violence in an Expanded Domestic Sphere

Child abuse, or violent harm directed at children, can be connected to religious communities in three general ways. First, the insularity of the community, in protecting members from outside observance or scrutiny, may shield children from needed help. The case of Yaakov Riegler, widely reported in 1992, might be read as an example. Yaakov, an eight-year-old mentally retarded boy whose family belonged to an insular Orthodox Jewish community in Brooklyn, was beaten to death by his mother, four years after the New York City child welfare system had first learned about abuse in the Riegler family.[3] While the harm cannot be said to be directly correlated to religiosity or religious values in this type of case, the way of life of the community might indeed serve as a barrier to remedies available on the outside. In another much-publicized example, and one where the connection between child and religious community is even clearer, given the absence of parents, the cases of children sexually abused in Catholic orphanages focus on the possible insularity associated with domestic life.

Second, the community may require punishment for failure to conform to its norms or standards—or, at least, parent members of the community may understand their obligations to include punishment of children who do not obey the tenets of their religion. As an example, we need only turn to the *Child, Family and State* casebook widely used in law school courses dealing with children and law, to find the following problem (Mnookin and Weisberg 1989, p. 263):

> Eleanor Papillon is a 20-year-old single parent. She is a devoted member of a fundamentalist religious sect, one of the tenets of which is to strongly disapprove nonmarital sex. Eleanor's son Danny is four years old. When Eleanor took Danny in for an annual medical checkup, the pediatrician—Dr. Thomas Stein—noticed that Danny had bruise marks on his arms, stomach, back and buttocks. The doctor asked Eleanor what had happened. Eleanor said that during a visit to his aunt's house three days before, Danny had been discovered under a bed with his pants off with a little girl, also aged four, who had her pants off. Eleanor reported that she had beaten Danny that night at home, after she became enraged by his refusal to admit what he had done.

Introduced to provoke a discussion of the tension generated by the parental privilege to use corporal punishment, the social interest in child protection, and the value of family privacy, the problem also raises the difficult issue of the interaction between the norms of the group to which the mother belongs and the norms of the state. If we stretch the domestic sphere in the way suggested above, the religious community can also be seen to play a role in what looks like excessive physical punishment. In a more drastic example (and one where the community is understood as cultural rather than strictly religious), the parents of Tina Isa, a sixteen-year-old girl whose job at a fast-food restaurant and desire to take part in high school social events clashed with traditional Palestinian culture, were found guilty of murdering their daughter after attempts to control her activities failed.[4]

Third, and most difficult to confront, the teachings and practices of the religion itself may harm children. They may endorse severe physical or even sexual abuse, they might be understood to result in serious emotional or psychological harm, or they may prevent access to necessary care. As the reader will no doubt note, difficulties in definition immediately arise with respect to this assertion. Obviously, the state—including child welfare officials and courts—may invest in a concept of harm different from that held by the religious communities in question. In labeling *abusive* certain behavior, mandated or at least supported by religious norms, the law interferes dramatically with the community itself, and aggressively severs the bonds between child and religious community.

A particularly striking example in the realm of "strong discipline" crossing into physical abuse is that of a Montana case (*State v. Riley*) in which members of the River of Life Tabernacle acted according to their religious tenets in beating a young child with a fiberglass stick and forcing him to stand for long periods of time in cold mud. The child died as a result, and members of the community were convicted of homicide. Indeed, as argued recently by Philip Greven, contemporary fundamentalist Protestant doctrine on child-rearing in general is informed by the themes of submission and suffering, and in turn teaches that God requires spanking, discipline, the use of the rod, and the breaking of children's independent wills (Greven 1991, pp. 60–61):

> Anglo-American Protestants have always been among the most vocal public defenders of physical punishment for infants, children and adolescents. They have provided many generations of listeners and readers with a series of theological and moral justifications for painful blows inflicted by adults upon the bodies, spirits, and wills of children. These defenses remain crucial to any understanding of the earliest sources of suffering and violence in our lives and culture. It is no accident that the shelves of evangelical and fundamentalist Protestant bookstores throughout the land are filled with books advocating physical punishments as the "Christian" method of discipline, essential to the creation of morality, spirituality, and character, and vital, ultimately, to the salvation of souls.

From the religious community's point of view, of course, these actions are believed to serve the interests of the children involved, both in this world and in that to come. And yet, if we refer to the work and analysis of Alice Miller (Miller 1983), as does Greven, we might worry about the destructive consequences—including anxiety, fear, hate, depression, dissociation, sadomasochism, domestic violence, aggression, and delinquency—that have been attributed to the physical punishment of children (Greven 1991, Part IV).

In a context different from abusive punishment, but one in which the clash in child-rearing norms between specific religious communities and the state is particularly marked, adherence to the notion of faith healing can have a negative or even fatal impact on the life and health of children. Statutory exemptions from child abuse and neglect statutes for parents who rely solely upon spiritual healing are currently being questioned, and Christian Science parents whose children have died as a result of lack of medical care have been prosecuted in several states.[5] From the perspective of the community, the law's reaction to its principles constitutes a severe attack on its relationship with member children. Indeed, a recent case found the Christian Science Church liable for the wrongful death of a member's son who received no medical treatment for meningitis, and thus targeted the community *per se* rather than the individual parents of the child.[6]

Finally, it should be noted that the norms of religious communities need not be translated as domestic violence in order to be perceived as harmful by those outside the community. That is, religious values, teachings, and practice, usually transmitted through parents and therefore perceived as within the sphere of parental discretion, can have an appreciable impact on a child's education, social skills, sexual behavior, and options for adulthood. The response of the Catholic Church to New York City's decision to distribute condoms in public high schools provides a contemporary example.[7] To the religious community in question, this was illicit encouragement of sexual activity from outside the family sphere; to the school board (and, generally, from a secular perspective), the action was necessary to protect children from HIV infection should they engage in sexual relations. Calls by the Church for a parent-requested exemption of teenage children from the program might be characterized as potentially harmful for the children thereby affected.

Definition Difficulties and Public Clashes

The very suggestion that harm to children might be connected to the religious communities to which they belong requires a distancing from the perspective of the communities themselves. While the possibility of such harm does not weaken the notion that religious communities may play a significant role in the lives of children, it does raise substantive questions as to the nature of that role. Enlarging the "domestic sphere" through the addition of religious community, then, does not insulate the relationship between community and children from scrutiny. But it does mean that the law, in intervening to protect children's interests, needs to justify its readiness to cross into that sphere and disrupt the relationship.

The task is complicated by definitional difficulties. The three ways in which the religious community may be implicated in domestic violence, as I have sketched them above, all involve normative clashes. How does the law define appropriate discipline, excessive insularity, dangerous practice? And if the state has trouble with those definitions in general, how much more exaggerated does the problem become when the definitions conflict with those operating within separate subcommunities?

We might start to respond to the problem of definition by pointing to the worst kinds of violence aimed at children, including those resulting in death, and saying confidently that, at least here, we know harm when we see it. Indeed, it seems relatively easy to target physical and sexual abuse of children and to override any defenses for such behavior put forward on behalf of the community. It is much harder if we move into the fuzzy area of emotional or psychological harm, and ask whether the law has the responsibility of protecting children from what seem to be harmful consequences of religious teachings, practices, or ways of life. Not only do we open the door to an assessment of all modes of child-rearing, but we place children at risk of losing their caregivers based on inexact and, at worst, biased expert assessments (Fineman 1991a, pp. 109–126).

What might initially seem like a clean line between physical violence and psychological harm, however, looks more like a blurred spectrum on closer inspection. As the examples described above indicate, it is not easy to differentiate between physical discipline and religiously inspired unacceptable beating, nor between well-intentioned alternative healing methods and deadly refusal to procure medical help. Nor is it obvious that the law should be barred from concerning itself, for example, with restricted educational opportunities or access to information regarding health and sexuality. Rather than trying to differentiate between bodily and mental integrity of children in a search for a comprehensive definition of "harm," then, it may be more fruitful to investigate the nature of the normative conflict at stake and, from there, to suggest steps to be taken in resolving that conflict.

The model referred to until now for understanding the relationship between religious communities and their member children has been one in which the community enters the domestic sphere, otherwise understood to include the child and her family (whatever its form). In considering "domestic violence," then, the possibility that religious communities play a role was clear, given their interaction with the child's domestic life. The definitional difficulties over norms or principles that in turn might affect children thus took on the form of a clash between the law, operating in the nondomestic sphere of the state, and the religious community, as embodied in domestic or private practice.

Yet, if we remember the structure of the relations between the community and the state, as described earlier, we see that the religious community, even if understood as a player in the domestic world of family life, is not confined to that sphere. Rather, it takes on the role of conflicting *public* authority, in the sense that it provides a normative structure self-perceived in many ways as parallel to that of the state. We are confronted, then, not only with the question of when the law can and should intervene on behalf of children—in the sense that such intervention moves law explicitly into the private web of relationships within which children grow—but also the question of when the law, on behalf of the secular state, can confront and override competing normative structures in society.[8] This overlap with issues concerning the pluralist nature of the state signals the need for even more careful justification of legal remedies on behalf of children.

The difficulties in definition, then, can be characterized as public level clashes. A secular liberal society subscribes to ever-changing norms with respect to children, their needs and opportunities, and the dangers that confront them. Based on those norms, religious tenets and practices—deemed just as authoritative by the communities that adhere to them—can be violated by the law. The challenge in the realm of domestic violence or harm lies not only in recognizing the conflict and its consequences for a plurality of community structures and for the interests of both community and children in maintaining links with each other, but also in responding to the needs of children whose bodies and futures might be at stake.

The Implications of State Intervention

We can start to meet the challenge by realizing that what have been understood to be private spheres of family and religion have always been shaped and restricted by the notion of "harm." That is, the state has always intervened in order to protect children. By looking at the law's record of intervention, we can ask how the law has responded to the needs of children, whether it has done so effectively, and how it has acknowledged the relationship of religious communities to their youngest members.

Traditionally, the parental power embodied in the individual right of free exercise of religion has been subject to compelling interests on the part of the state, acting in accordance with its *parens patriae* power. In *Yoder*, Chief Justice Burger referred to *Pierce v. Society of Sisters* as a "charter of the rights of parents to direct the religious upbringing of their children," but hastened to add that this power of parents may be limited when their decisions place the health or safety of their children at risk or present heavy social burdens.[9] The model of analysis, then, for dealing with potential links between religious practice and danger to children is thus one in which parental power can only be replaced by state intervention in the form of remedial measure. Within this analytical framework, the meaning or degree of harm to children that would justify infringement of the constitutional rights of parents or the severing of parent-child relations has been left open by courts and commentators, who, realizing the impossibility of providing a clear definition, have preferred to defer to an equally indeterminate assessment of "best interests."

Given the significance of religious communities and children for each other, and the way in which that relationship can mediate the content of the domestic sphere, the traditional model just described seems severely limited. That is, it seems to assume that state intervention in response to domestic harm to children has serious implications only for the parents involved. It is the individual rights of those parents (understood by the Court in *Yoder* to be a monolithic unit within a nuclear family) that are on the line in the analysis, and the result of any balancing of those rights against the compelling interests of the state simply provides an indicator of their content. State interference with parental religious freedom has clear implications for the religious communities involved, however, and a traditional "state intervention with parental power" analysis not only excludes community from the domestic sphere, but leaves no space for the recognition that a legal response to harm to children may signal a clash between the normative authorities represented by religious communities and state.

Two connected problems arise from the fact that the legal model of analysis fails to convey significant aspects of the issues at stake. First, in the guise of targeting parental failure to care for children, the state may damage a religious community without any appreciation for the pluralistic nature of society and the diversity of families, communities, and indeed children. In a particularly stark example (*In re State ex rel. Black*), the Utah State Department of Public Welfare, in 1953, forcibly removed children from their fundamentalist Mormon parents, who had continued to practice polygamy according to their religious beliefs even after the United States Supreme Court, in the late nineteenth century, had deemed the practice to be an offence (*Reynolds v. United States*). The Utah court referred to legislation requiring parental provision of "the proper maintenance, care, training and education contemplated and required by both law and morals," in allowing the state to "protect" the Mormon children by taking them into custody.

Thus, behind a thin disguise of concern for the harmful impact of parental actions on children, the state issued an attack on the fundamentalist Mormon community and its normative authority with respect to its members. Ironically, by using the mechanism of taking children from their parents in order to target the Mormons, the state recognized (and targeted) the significance of children's membership to the continuation of a community. And yet, the failure of the court to offer substantial justification for its actions, beyond pointing to the immoral conduct of fundamentalist Mormon adults, highlights a serious gap in the legal model based on individual parental freedom against state intervention. We cannot begin to explore the connections between the law's definition of and response to domestic harm to children and its recognition of the claims of a diverse society while that gap remains.

The second, and connected, problem with the traditional analytical framework is the way in which it prevents us from investigating the perspective of the children involved. As long as the issue centers on the extent of individual freedom of religion as exercised by parents, it is difficult to appreciate the way in which religious communities themselves, albeit often modulated through the actions of parents, can be positive and enriching for children. In the case just referred to, for example, the court simply assumed that the interests of the children were in conflict with those of the fundamentalist Mormon community. At the same time, a framework of simple interaction between individual parent and child that does not assess the impact of religious community as mediator means that the law cannot easily probe the possibility of violence and harm in connection with that community. Earlier, I suggested that an enlargement of the "domestic sphere" to include religious communities and their norms uncovered three general ways in which those communities might be implicated in harm to children. A traditional freedom-of-religion framework cannot make room for those considerations. Yet neither can a framework that stems solely from the perspective of religious communities who want to maintain their normative power. Rather, even as we appreciate the perspectives of parent and community, the challenge of responding to the needs of children, and truly justifying state intervention on that basis, remains.

Room for Responding to Children?

What might it mean to justify state intervention from the perspective of children who grow and develop in the care of individuals and communities? One major response to observations of the power exercised over children, whether by individual parents or by communities, has been to create, argue for, and enforce children's "rights." As Martha Minow has pointed out, the traditional story told about the history of family law includes a move from traditional dependency of children to increasing autonomy as individual rights-bearers (Minow 1985, pp. 832–34). Children have been transformed from the objects of parental control to special charges of the state to individuals subject to state power. As Minow suggests, this is a deeply flawed picture. In the context of child abuse, the traditional constitutional guarantee of due process or privacy has not been adapted in a way that might meet children's needs (*DeShaney v. Winnebago County Dept. of Social Services*). And, while religious rights for minors have been suggested (Colby 1982; Note 1978; List 1963–64), the way in which a conflict among parent, child, and state might be resolved has not been articulated (Richards 1980; Woodhouse 1992). Thus, while the rhetoric of children's rights has increased, the meaning and substance of such "rights" have not always, nor yet, been defined in a way responsive to the realities of children's lives (Minow 1986; Fineman 1989; Olsen 1992).

In *Yoder*, the dissenting opinion by Justice Douglas tried to take seriously the viewpoint of the Amish children involved by demanding that they be heard on the question of leaving school after eighth grade. Thus, in addition to the two possible readings of the case alluded to above— as a strengthening of parental rights, and, alternatively, as a recognition of diversity within the state—*Yoder* can be referred to for the dissent's attempt to respond to the desires of the teenage members of the Amish community. Unlike the majority, Justice Douglas did not assume an identity of interest between parent and child, but rather envisaged parents and indeed community as entities against which children are entitled to assert their rights or freedom.

Justice Douglas's opinion raises crucial and extremely difficult questions with respect to the perspective of children in the resolution of issues affecting their lives, but the questions have largely been left unanswered. A large part of the reason lies in the fact that, if "rights" entail privacy, defined through a boundary between individual and others, then it is almost impossible to envisage "rights" for children. Children generally are never isolated as individuals; rather they rely on others for care, guidance, and development. A liberal notion of rights and autonomy, built on barriers between the child and caregiving parent or community, does not fit with that reality. Child advocates in general have to search for a better way to understand children as integrated with those around them, and to respond to their needs.

One way of resolving the uneasy application of rights and autonomy to the situation of children is to attempt to redefine those notions along feminist lines, such that they take dependency and connection into account (Nedelsky 1989, 1990; Minow 1987). Instead of outlining a different vision of children's autonomy here, however, I will describe the concerns to be confronted if we went to appreciate the relationship between children and their communities, and, at the same time, redress the destructive potential of that relationship. By articulating those concerns, and thinking about how the law should meet them, we can initiate responses to domestic violence and harm that meet the interests of child members of families and communities.

Overlapping Challenges: "So Many Things"

As sketched above, the traditional legal model for understanding state intervention on behalf of children seriously hurt in a way connected to religious principles or practice displays sufficient respect neither for the religious communities thereby implicated nor for the realities of the lives of the children thereby affected. By contrast, our search for an articulated justification for state intervention in such cases starts with an appreciation of the importance of community and the ways in which it influences and interacts with childhood. It includes the recognition that the negative potential of the community-child relationship, against a background in which the law perceives one of its roles as that of remedying harm to children, implies a clash on the public level of pluralism. And it incorporates the notion that, even given the significance of community to children and vice versa, the perspective of children might differ from that of a community which exercises considerable power *vis-à-vis* its youngest members.

Based on these elements, we can see that the religious community has a viable role to play in any case where a charge of domestic violence, abuse, or harm against a child's caregiver is met by a defense based on religious freedom. The norms of the community can have a legal impact in the sense that they provide specific reasons for defying state intervention. By referring to the community, the court may be reluctant to find as "abusive" religiously based behavior that would otherwise be seen as such. Yet I am not prepared to move from an acknowledgment of the role of religious communities to a call for deference to their norms. In finding a place for religious communities along a spectrum of attitudes that range from ignoring their perspective to deferring to it, the following concerns need to be articulated and met.

First, we have to confront the ease with which courts may approach different norms as strange, fanatical, or harmful. The majoritarian, secular bias of social workers and judges may make them all too quick to take children away from their communities in order to "save" them. We need to be wary of the fact that interventions against domestic violence have been in the past, and continue to be, discriminatory in their attempts to enforce state-derived notions of proper parenting (Gordon 1986, 1988). The consequences of this tendency seem, at first glance, especially bad for the religious communities at stake. Not only are they removed from the child's domestic sphere, but they are attacked on a public level and prohibited from promoting their teachings and authority. Further, without young members, the future of the communities in question is dealt a fatal blow. Finally, adults, too, find their membership in a given religious community questioned or destroyed, if their religiously based child-rearing practices are deemed abusive.

The consequences can be equally severe for the children whom the state's actions are meant to protect. Pulled from the families and communities in which they have flourished, children lose their sense of membership and support. Obviously, the risk of such drastic measures being taken in response to nonharmful difference must be minimized. That is, we need a guiding principle that encourages diversity and accepts the possibility of variation in norms, principles, and practices affecting children. In the different yet related context of motherhood, we need to move away from a monolithic notion that adversely affects mothers that do not fit the mold (Fineman 1991b; Kline, 1992). Here, we need to accept the "multiplicity of imaginative visions" (Duclos 1990, p. 380) provided by the many communities that make up a pluralistic society, and translate that into a multiplicity of child-rearing norms and behaviors.

Second, we need to confront a simplistic relativism that may be misplaced and, in some circumstances, dangerous. An "oversensitivity" to the specificity of a religious community might lead a court to accept too quickly that the norms of a certain religion or culture dictate what would otherwise be labeled unacceptable violence. The risk to be avoided here is one of falsely constructed defenses, whereby powerful members of a community manipulate relativism in a way that can hurt less powerful members, especially children (Gordon 1986, pp. 470–472; 1988, p. 295). If such defenses work as intended, a community member can try to excuse violent behavior by saying that religious norms dictate or at least contemplate his actions. Regardless of whether the court fully allows the defense in the sense that it refrains from intervention, the very willingness to accept that a religion mandates sexual abuse or the breaking of bones, for example, can stem from the same bias responsible for the first concern articulated above.

Children are clearly affected by this second, unwanted, yet possible approach. For example, a readiness to accept excessive and abusive discipline in response to a child's failure to abide by religious norms (one of the ways in which community may be implicated in harm), might have severe and even deadly consequences for that child. We need a second guiding principle, then, to coexist with the encouragement of diversity. That is, our response to this concern should be an awareness of the way in which power may be exploited when adult members refer to community practices as the reason for their actions toward children. These two principles coexist only uneasily, of course, and a working overlap between them may be extremely difficult to imagine, much less implement. We have to work out a way in which law respects diversity and, at the same time, avoids misplaced reliance on claims of difference.

The third and final concern is also the most complex, and it incorporates the task just described. We need to confront the continued avoidance of the issues surrounding a normative clash between the state and religious communities in cases relating to domestic violence directed at children. The choices to be made between preservation of religious traditions and the interests of community members may often be "excruciating" (Minow 1989b, p. 977), but, in situations of harm to children, they are also crucial. Unless the law appreciates the significance of its decision-making for the religious communities involved, and then takes the step of articulating its reasons for issuing what might well be experienced as an attack by those communities, the clash of norms remains silent and unresolved.

In response to this concern, the final guiding principle, as we move towards a meaningful response to harm to children, is one based on creativity and cooperation. A multifaceted principle, it invests in the possibility for normative change, both in secular society and within religious communities themselves. It also envisages a spectrum of remedies in response to children's pain, mirroring the spectrum of beliefs, practices, and relationships that affect children's lives.

I will sketch briefly what I mean by this last principle, and challenge the reader to continue where I leave off. The definitions of child abuse, domestic violence, and harm remain open-ended in our society, and differ across the many communities that constitute it (Gelles 1980, pp. 82–84). Norms that incorporate those terms are thus always changing. But this is not a phenomenon restricted to the state. Instead, the norms of religious communities can also change, and, in fact, may change over time, in response to external factors and to the demands of internal members. As we have seen, religious communities can be very influential with respect to the individuals who adhere to them: for many, religious community constitutes the most significant authority in their lives. Religious communities are thus extremely well-situated to address and stop the same harm that they might otherwise ignore or perhaps propagate. They already provide counselling, direction, and education, and some have acknowledged the existence of domestic violence among members, and are evolving into effective support systems.[10] Instead of relegating religious communities to the domestic sphere (based on their connection to family relations), we can focus on their public personae, and imagine a process of cross-jurisdictional cooperation, in which the definition of unacceptable harm to children can slowly be worked out.

By moving towards a definition of abuse to children through a process that includes the very communities that may be implicated in that harm, the law recognizes normative pluralism at the same time that it acknowledges the sometimes conflicting responsibility for providing remedies for harm. And here we find the final branch of a principle of creativity and cooperation. If we understand that relationships between children and their communities can be positive and identity-informing, at the same time that they can be negative and integrity-damaging, then we might be less willing to allow state intervention on behalf of children to destroy those relationships. That is, the law needs to be creative in its response to domestic violence, and needs to provide a spectrum of remedies from counseling, to ongoing partnership and supervision, to participation with community leaders, to, at the extreme, a rearrangement or severing of connections between the child and her community. The last option usually entails separating children from parents who are community members, and, although this discussion has not focused on the parent-child relationship *per se*, it is clear that its dissolution is usually the most severe way, from the perspective of the child, to end the connection to community.

In acknowledging some of the concerns surrounding an analysis that makes religious community an important reference point in redressing harm to children, I have merely highlighted the contours of general guiding principles that begin to respond to those concerns. By doing so, I hope to have somewhat furthered a search for a way to meet the challenge of, on the one hand, recognizing conflict and its consequences both for pluralism and for the links between communities and their youngest members, and, on the other, responding to the needs of children who may be hurt or damaged within the context of community membership. But the search does not end there. We have a long way to go, and a slow process to engage in, before we can articulate clearly what we mean by justified intervention with respect to domestic violence or harm aimed at children. And we have "so many things" to grapple with before we recognize how important—both in a positive and negative sense—community may be.

Notes

This chapter draws in part from Shauna Van Praagh, "Follow the Children: Laying the Foundation for a Renewed Understanding of the Individual, Religious Community and

State," LL.M. thesis, Columbia University School of Law, May 1992, unpublished. Thanks are due to Kent Greenawalt, Martha Fineman, and Jane Spinak—all members of my doctoral committee—for helpful comments on that earlier work, and to the participants in the Feminism and Legal Theory Workshop, April 1992. Thanks also to René Provost and Roxanne Mykitiuk for their suggestions and encouragement. My ongoing appreciation goes to the Canadian Social Sciences and Humanities Research Council, which makes my doctoral research and writing possible.

1. A 1991 survey of religious affiliation found that ninety percent of Americans identify themselves as religious. 86.5 percent are Christian and identify themselves with dozens of Christian denominations, with Roman Catholics making up the largest of these (twenty-six percent of Americans), followed by Baptists, Methodists, and Lutherans, respectively. 1.8 percent identify themselves religiously as Jews, Judaism being the largest non-Christian faith, and 0.5 percent as Muslims ("Portrait of Religion in U.S. Holds Dozens of Surprises," *New York Times*, April 10, 1992, p. A1).

2. 406 U.S. 205 at 232. The majority opinion by Chief Justice Burger rests not only upon the power of the Amish parents, a power which is recognized as subject to limitation, but also upon the nature of the Amish community.

3. "As Mother Killed Her Son, Protectors Observed Privacy," *New York Times*, February 10, 1992, p. A1.

4. "Terror and Death at Home Are Caught in F.B.I. Tape," *New York Times*, October 28, 1991, p. A14. This case emerged in a different light much later, when it was found that Tina had knowledge of her father's involvement in a bomb plot. The "cultural differences" explanation for the parents' action thus takes on the character of a "cover," but the fact that it was put forward and taken seriously remains significant.

5. See, among others, Paula A. Monopoli, "Allocating the Costs of Parental Free Exercise: Striking a New Balance Between Sincere Religious Belief and a Child's Right to Medical Treatment," 18 Pepperdine L. Rev. 319 (1991), Christine Clark, "Religious Accommodation and Criminal Liability," 17 *Florida State U.L. Rev.* 559 (1990), Note, "California's Prayer Healing Dilemma," 14 *Hastings Constitutional Law Quarterly* 395 (1987).

6. "Church Found Liable in Death of Boy, 11," *The Toronto Globe and Mail*, August 21, 1993, p. A7.

7. See "Judge Upholds Distribution of Condoms in High Schools," *New York Times*, April 24, 1992, p. B3, for the state court's rejection of the claims made in opposition to the program.

8. Of course, the nonneutral, majoritarian nature of state standards can and should be questioned in a way that falls beyond the scope of this discussion. That is, state norms can be understood to be co-opted, or at least infiltrated, by mainstream Christian values, and this understanding forms part of a complex background to the conflicts between state and nonmainstream religious communities.

9. 406 U.S. 205, 233–34 (1971). This limitation had been noted and enforced in *Prince v. Mass.*, 321 U.S. 158 (1944).

10. See Horton and Williamson 1988. The collection incorporates the perspectives of abuse experts, religious leaders, victims, and perpetrators of domestic violence. The traditional ideology that combines the sacred nature of the family and the subordinate position of women had contributed to a denial that abuse occurs in religious families. The religious community, seen as a support system in other areas, must evolve into an effective support system with respect to family violence as well, and, in some circumstances is slowly doing so.

Child Abuse: A Problem
for Feminist Theory

by Marie Ashe and Naomi R. Cahn

During the past two decades there has developed a broad professional and popular awareness of child abuse as a disturbing and not uncommon reality within American society.[1] This development has been accompanied by many accommodative responses in legislation and in legal process. Prosecution of child abuse has greatly accelerated; children's accounts of sexual abuse and other forms of abuse have come to be recognized as deserving credence;[2] and procedural accommodations have been instituted in many jurisdictions to enable child victims to tell their stories. Increased awareness of child abuse has been accompanied by popular reactions of outrage and horror and by widespread condemnation of perpetrators.

The accounts of child abuse delivered through both popular media and various types of professional literatures tend to tell the story of child abuse with a focus on the experience of the child victims, and devote only very limited attention to the realities and experiences of perpetrators of such abuse. While parents, and particularly mothers, are regularly brought under the jurisdiction of trial courts in child dependency proceedings, pursuant to which children are removed temporarily or permanently from their custody, there is a surprising dearth of literature about the complexities of such parents. The developing contemporary understanding of child abuse within and without the legal system, to the degree that it focuses on perpetrators of abuse, tends to reduce to a story of "bad mothers."

In this article we sketch an overview of prevailing cultural interpretations of "bad mothers" by considering the figure of the "bad mother" in various feminist and other accounts. We argue that "bad mothers" and their implication in child abuse have been largely ignored by feminist theory and have been reductively treated in other prevailing accounts.

We urge the commitment of feminist theory to intensive consideration of these realities.

Our writing has developed out of related, though not congruent, experiences that we have had in representing "bad mothers" in our legal practices.

NAOMI CAHN

In my first year after law school, I worked in a legal services office on a "Dependency Project" (so called because the legal proceedings concerned whether children were dependent on the state). With my colleagues, I represented parents (mothers, generally—fathers were rarely around) who had been accused by the city's child protective services office of abusing or neglecting their children.

I generally met my clients at the time of their first court appearance, which occurred after the city had removed their children and at a point when my clients were attempting to make some sense of what had happened to them and to the children—why the children had been taken away. I can remember few clients who admitted, at such a hearing, to having committed any of the alleged neglect or abuse. Typically, my clients consistently denied the allegations, in spite of the fact that they were frequently well documented by the city. The city often produced medical records showing burn marks or fractured bones to document children's injuries. On behalf of my clients I routinely asserted that the children's mothers had not committed the alleged abuse; that the abuse must have been committed by someone else who had access to the child (a relative, a boyfriend of the mother, or another child); and that the mother had not reported the abuse because she had not been aware of it.

For a long time, with perhaps my first fifty clients, I believed these mothers. I believed that they had not beaten, burned, struck, or kicked their children; that they were all good mothers who would never do such things; and that their children had been unfairly removed from them. These beliefs were important to me. I was not sure that I could continue to represent my clients unless I believed that they were innocent, that they were not bad mothers. There was a part of me that could not believe that a mother would really abuse her child. When friends asked me how I could represent abusive parents, I patiently explained that my clients were innocent.

After some time, after experiencing many clients who denied having done anything to hurt their children, I started to fight my own innocence, my own images of bad maternal behavior. Gradually, I realized that some of my clients had done none of the acts of which they were accused; but that others had indeed abused their children, that some of them had burned their children with cigarettes, and that some had watched while their husbands or boyfriends sexually abused their young daughters and sons.

I did not quit my job. To some degree, I invoked the justification that many criminal defense lawyers use. I justified my work by reminding myself that the city, with all of its power, had wrongfully interfered in my clients' families. I assured myself that, based on constitutional principles of due process, my clients were entitled to representation. To some degree, I also suspended my own judgment of my "bad mother" clients because I did not know how to understand what these women had done. It was hard for me to reconcile my image of a bad mother with the women whom I was representing, and, eventually, I stopped trying to do so.

Marie Ashe

I, too, began my law practice with a heavy caseload of child abuse and neglect matters. Practicing in a public defender's office, appointed sometimes to represent children and sometimes to represent parents (mostly mothers) in abuse and neglect cases, I found myself challenged to give some adequate account—to myself, to my nonlawyer friends and acquaintances, as well as to other lawyers—of the reasons why I chose to represent "those people."

My experience resembled Naomi's, in that the family situations I encountered most frequently were ones in which the biological fathers of children were absent and the parent charged with the alleged abuse or neglect was the children's mother. That work frequently brought me into contact with the novice prosecutors and inexperienced social workers often assigned to determine whether or not to bring family matters into court. It often seemed to me that social workers and prosecutors lacking experience with the lives of both children and mothers were prone to exaggerate the significance of certain parental acts or omissions in matters that they defined as constituting abuse. Their perceptions and assessments of the kinds of maternal behaviors that should be tolerated without the mandated intervention of courts or social service agencies often differed from mine. I was often distressed by prosecutors' readiness to file abuse and neglect charges against parents upon social workers' characterizations of certain parental behaviors as "inappropriate." I frequently bristled in frustration and anger at the degree to which that prissy-sounding, unexamined, and apparently foundationless epithet—"inappropriate"—was invoked to justify the temporary or permanent removal of children from their mothers. And I was often pained by the apparent failure of social workers and prosecutors to appreciate the violence perpetrated by the legal process upon a child when he or she is abruptly and forcibly wrenched away from parents who, however inadequate, are nonetheless familiar. At some point during those years of practice I reached the conclusion, from which I have not departed, that I had *never* seen a single case in which I believed that the *absolute* termination of parental rights had been justified.

With all these reservations and concerns about the law relating to child dependency—particularly as that law was applied in trial courts in the three sociologically and geographically distinct jurisdictions in which I have practiced—I have, nonetheless, had to recognize that sometimes mothers do behave abusively in ways that it is impossible for me to minimize, and in ways that it is difficult for me to understand or to interpret.

It has been troubling to see a client's baby lying in a hospital nursery, his groin burned, blistered and pustulated. It has been troubling to see a young boy who has suffered a fractured skull, whose arms and legs have been broken in the first year of his life, and whose face has lost all appearance of symmetry because of neurological damage. It has been troubling to see a four-year-old-girl behaving in the stylized sexual fashion which evidences that she has been a victim of sexual abuse and that she will likely continue to be such a victim. And it has been particularly troubling to know that in each of these cases, and in others, the harms and injuries appeared to have been tolerated or directly perpetrated by my "bad mother" clients.

Encountering these realities, I have had to ask myself about the moral meaning of the work of representing "bad mothers." I have felt that question of moral meaning raised frequently by my clinical law students who often, at the start of a semester of clinical work, articulate strong aversion to representing "bad mothers." I have come to expect to hear from at least one student each semester the statement: "The one thing I would never want to have to do is represent a parent who had abused a child." As awareness of child abuse increases, it seems particularly important to consider prevailing constructions of "bad mothers," and to examine popular and theoretical understandings of these women, in order to be able to address that question of moral meaning. For me, this article is an attempt to begin that inquiry.

The need to turn to theory in examining the "bad mother" is a need that arises out of pain—pain that both gives rise to and is supported by inquietude or even horror. Writing of theory as a "liberatory practice,"

bell hooks has identified theory as having its roots in pain and desperation, and as offering a "location for healing" (hooks 1991, pp. 1–12). In
these phrases, hooks echoes a notion of French feminist Julia Kristeva,
who has suggested that every question is rooted in pain (Kristeva 1987).

Interpretations of the "bad mother" can be found in literature; in
popular culture; in sociological, psychological, and psychoanalytic theory; as well as in law and legal practice. These interpretations raise issues
that have been variously addressed or ignored by feminist theories. In
this chapter, we will outline some of the dominant interpretations of the
"bad mother" that we have begun to consider. Our overview will attempt
to point out "where we have been," by exploring, some of the interpretations that have been constructed by prefeminist theory; "where we are,"—
by considering some recent specifically feminist explorations of the figure
of the "bad mother"; and "where we ought to go," by examining the
possibilities and the limitations that seem inherent in liberal feminist,
cultural feminist, radical feminist, and postmodernist approaches to "bad
mothers."

The "Bad Mother" in Literature

If we define the "bad mother" as the woman whose neglectful, abusive,
reckless, or murderous behaviors threaten or destroy her children, we
can locate her powerful figure throughout the literature of Western
culture. She is apparent in Ancient Greek literature, in the familiar
figures of Medea murdering her children to the horror of the chorus;
in Agave, in *The Bacchae*, murdering her son Pentheus, tearing apart his
limbs and bearing his head into her city; and in Jocasta, the fatefully
destructive mother of Oedipus (Warner 1955). In each of these literary
figures is manifested a powerfully destructive woman whose excessive
and transgressive violation of some law brings destruction upon herself,
her household, and her community.

The bad mother is prominent in Judeo-Christian mythology as well.
She appears in the disturbing figure of the infanticidal Lilith, defined
in Jewish apocrypha as the first wife of Adam. She also operates centrally
in the biblical account of the judgment of Solomon. That account, which
is often cited as a paradigm of wisdom and of good judgment, marks
the foundational importance that the definition of a "bad mother" has
had for Western culture and for Western law (Ashe 1991).

Anxiety about the distance properly to be maintained between mothers
and their children is apparent in the Biblical rule-codifications of Deuter-
onomy and of Leviticus, which prescribe ab-jection of the maternal body,
constructing it as an object for avoidance. The requirement and the
practice of separation from that maternal body, anthropologists have

suggested, is institutionalized and ritualized through bodily acts, through the practice of dietary avoidances that reflect that separation (Kristeva 1982; Douglas 1966).

The "bad mother" has been a common character in the most familiar of Western fairy tales, in which she often figures as a "step"-mother.[3] She has been central in both nineteenth- and twentieth-century English language fiction (Gilbert and Gubar 1979). In such literary representations, the "bad mother" is typically figured as horrifying, as excessive in some essential way, as greatly to be feared. She is so often depicted as split off from the normal reality of "good motherhood" that she is characterized as the bizarre and "crazy" persona—the "madwoman" consigned to "the attic" of deviance or marginality. The "bad mother" is depicted as the figure always threatening to exceed or to violate the norms that prescribe the boundaries and the scope of her duty. Her boundary violations have tragic consequences for her community, inviting destruction upon all its members.

From perhaps inaccessible beginnings, the "bad mother" operates archetypally and paradigmatically to construct its own "other"—the "good mother"—who becomes, by extension, the "good woman," a figure highly constrained and highly constraining. This "other" to the "bad mother" model is defined in our oldest literature. She appears, for example, in Biblical accounts that define with particularity the activities of her daily life (Proverbs 31:10–31 King James Version). She has continued to operate into the contemporary period. Alicia Ostriker has observed of that "good motherhood" that it is ". . . selfless, cheerful, and deodorized. It does not include resentment, anger, violence, alienation, disappointment, grief, fear, exhaustion—or erotic pleasure. It is ahistorical and apolitical. It excludes the possibility of abortion" (Ostriker 1986, p. 179). Clearly it does not include the reality of child abuse.

It can be argued that the "bad mother," in her literary appearances, operates as a character within a child's story. In her standard manifestations, she appears not in her own complexity and moral agency, but as an "other" defined from the perspective of a fearful and deprived child.

In recent years, women writing fiction and poetry, as well as other feminist work, have attempted new formulations of "motherhood" that escape the constraints imposed upon women by the power of competing prefeminist models of "bad" and "good" motherhood.[4] This work has relevance for lawyers and legal theorists, in that it weakens the foundations of the stereotype, and invites a new and different appreciation of the complexity of the bad mother/child abuser. Such writing attempts to figure the bad mother from her own situation, as the subject rather than the mere object of narrative. It may support the possibility of more complex characterizations of the bad mother as a moral agent in her own right, rather than as the simple projection of a threatened and mythifying childlike imagination.

Discussion of this project can be found in recent feminist literary theory (Du Plessis 1990). Illustrations of it have been apparent in the novels of Edna O'Brien (O'Brien 1992), Toni Morrison (Morrison 1987), Mary Gordon (Gordon 1985), Sue Miller (Miller 1986), and Marge Piercy (Piercy 1976)—each of whom has constructed critical and newly imagined figures of the neglectful or abusive mother, images attempting to "do justice" to the realities of women's lives. In these emergent figures there are mothers whose apparent destructiveness cannot be seen simply as "evil," "incomprehensible," or "crazy." It may be that the richness of these efforts—like the richness of abortion poetry analyzed by Barbara Johnson (Johnson 1987)—resides in their embodying at one and the same time the voices and stories of neglected children, of abused children, of murdered children, and of highly complex "bad mothers."[5]

The "Bad Mother" in Popular Culture

Joan Williams has written of a gender war between women that "pits 'mommy versus mommy' " in the context of the work/family conflict for working mothers.[6] Her concept of a gender war is useful to describe prevailing views of mothers in popular culture. On the one hand, as Williams points out, popular media have recently focused on the departure of women from the workplace to spend time with their children. These mothers are depicted as selfless, and as finding fulfillment in their role as caretakers. They are interpreted as acting in the ways that mothers are supposed to act. Williams contrasts this image with that of the "harried super-mom," who is expected to work, to take care of children, to act as housekeeper, and to perform as a wife. A third image—one that is central to this article (although beyond the scope of Professor Williams's examination of gender wars)—is of a woman who is neither the selfless mother, nor the supermother, but is the neglectful or abusive mother depicted either as utterly unnatural in her agency or as utterly victimized. This figure, too, becomes a focus of gender wars. She is either blamed for her individual, autonomous choice to abuse her child, or she is pitied for her victimization and her utter lack of choice. A war of interpretation thus surrounds the bad mother figure, and centers on the issue of "agency." This struggle involves competing understandings of such women, one which defines them as fully responsible moral agents and another which defines them as victims of individual men and of patriarchal society.[7]

Over the past five years, there have been two particularly troubling images of bad mothers in popular culture: the portrait of an individual woman, Hedda Nussbaum; and a picture of a class of women, namely pregnant, drug- (especially crack-) addicted women. Each has been controversial, and each has produced images of good mothers against images of bad mothers; of women as victims versus women as perpetrators of abuse. The story of Hedda Nussbaum has deeply divided feminists; the question of how to respond to pregnant women who abuse drugs has created similar division.

Popular accounts of the Nussbaum case are in general agreement concerning its facts. Hedda Nussbaum met Joel Steinberg in 1975. Throughout their relationship, Steinberg abused Nussbaum severely, frequently causing visible bruises as well as fractured bones. In 1981, Nussbaum and Steinberg illegally adopted a then-two-year-old child whom they called Lisa. Six years later, Lisa died as a result of severe physical abuse apparently perpetrated directly by Joel Steinberg. Although criminal charges were initially brought against Nussbaum on the basis of Lisa's death, those charges were eventually dropped, and she testified against Steinberg at his manslaughter trial, in which he was convicted.

Responses by feminists to the Nussbaum case fell into two categories. On the one hand, Nussbaum was canonized as the archetypal victim (Span 1989, p. B1). Three hundred prominent women signed a letter requesting that the public refocus its attention onto the men responsible for domestic violence, rather than blaming the victim who remained in an abusive relationship (Span 1989, p. B1). According to this view, Hedda Nussbaum was so victimized as to be incapable of moral agency. On the other hand, there were those who "blamed" Hedda Nussbaum and regarded her as a fully responsible, autonomous agent. Susan Brownmiller suggested, for example, "that Hedda Nussbaum, far from being a passive victim, was an active participant in her own—and Lisa's—destruction" (Brownmiller 1989, p. A25).

Similarly conflicting views have been expressed about pregnant, crack-addicted mothers who have been featured as important figures in various media. Throughout the country, many pregnant women who use crack have been charged with child abuse. One reporter has noted that "more and more judges and lawmakers have come to view these mothers as criminals who victimize children, rather than as victims themselves" (Hoffman 1990, Sec. 6, p. 34). The use of crack by pregnant women unquestionably endangers fetal health. However, the justification of he prosecution of pregnant women by reference to the state's interest in assuring the birth of healthy children erases any appreciation of the pregnant woman's motivations and of her liberty.

On the other hand, many writers have urged that the problem of crack-addicted, pregnant women must be placed in its social context to be properly understood. Many argue that these women should not be subject to criminal liability for their actions. This perspective reflects an understanding that, to the extent that these women have any moral culpability, it is highly diminished. Proponents of this view note that there are insufficient programs for pregnant women seeking drug treatment, and that prosecutions have a disproportionate impact on poor and on minority women (Roberts 1991).

Both the conflicting characterizations of "bad mothers" in popular cultural discussions of Hedda Nussbaum and in the depiction of pregnant, drug-addicted women seem inadequate. As perhaps most parents have reason to know, and as occasional feminist writings on motherhood have clearly stated (Rich 1976), the gap between purportedly "natural" feelings of intimacy and nurturance and "unnatural" feelings of aggression and rage has been enormously exaggerated. Popular simplistic and reductive interpretations of abusive mothers may constitute attempts by parents to drive away a recognition of their/our own tendencies toward verbal and physical violence against children. Both the model of the bad mother as autonomous, powerful, fully responsible evildoer, and the countervailing model of her as helpless victim create barriers to our respectful understanding of women whom we experience as disturbing and challenging.

"Bad Mothers" in Psychology and Sociology—Empirical Studies

Accounts of bad mothers appear not only in literature and in popular culture, but also in the stories told by the social sciences.[8] These include both theoretical and empirical accounts. In our review of current literature, we have been surprised to discover abusive mothers studied far less frequently than we had expected, and defined very tentatively by existing data.

Data show that approximately two and a half million children are abused each year in the United States (Daro and Mitchel 1990, p. 2). Some data suggest that there may be a bias among child protective service workers monitoring situations of abuse to believe that the abuse is the mother's fault (Stark and Flitcraft 1988, pp. 98–99). It is difficult, however, to find accurate data on how much of the domestic abuse of children is perpetrated by mothers as opposed to other family members. This is, presumably, because the organizations that collect data covering abuse have tended to focus on children rather than on the perpetrator—that is, they have tended to focus on reporting the abuse and its effect on children, rather than on identifying the perpetrator of particular abuse. These patterns of data collection are not adequately informative concerning the amount of abuse directly perpetrated by mothers. Data from the studies discussed below do indicate that rates of abuse by women may be comparable to rates of abuse perpetrated by men.

In her historical review of the records of the Massachusetts Society for the Protection of Cruelty to Children from 1880 to 1960, Linda Gordon found that mothers were reported as child abuse perpetrators in forty-six percent of cases, and fathers in the remaining fifty-four percent (Gordon 1988, p. 173). These raw figures are somewhat misleading because, as Gordon explains, "fathers were *much* more likely to abuse children in proportion to how much time they spend in child care" (Gordon 1988, p. 173). Gordon concluded that when the women whom she studied did abuse children, their violence had taken essentially the same form as had men's abuse (Gordon 1988, p. 175).

In its analysis of national reports on child abuse and neglect between 1976 and 1982, the American Humane Association similarly substantiated Gordon's claim that the caretaking parent (male or female) was more likely to abuse the child (Russell and Trainor 1984). But, contrary to Gordon, this study also found that men were more likely to be associated with major and minor abuse, while women were more likely to be associated with neglect.

In a study that used reports from battered women who were temporarily staying in shelters during the early 1980s, Jean Giles-Sims found that 92.7 percent of women and 88.9 percent of their male partners had used a violent tactic on the child in the household during the previous year,[9] and Giles-Sims also found that the men in question had used these tactics nearly twice as often as had the women.[10] Further, the men studied appeared to have been more likely to use more severe abusive tactics on their children than were women. Giles-Sims found that during the six-month period following their stays at battered women's shelters, all women used some form of violent tactic on their child; however, women's use of abuse tactics decreased during this follow-up period (Giles-Sims 1985, pp. 207–208).

Evan Stark and Anne Flitcraft have examined the relationship between child abuse and violence against women (Stark and Flitcraft 1988; Stark and Flitcraft 1985). In their study of 116 women at the Yale-New Haven Hospital whose children had been referred to a hospital committee for possible abuse or neglect, Stark and Flitcraft found that a father was three times more likely to have battered a child in families where he was also battering the mother than in families where women were not being abused (Stark and Flitcraft 1988, p. 106). They concluded that "battering is [probably] the single most important context of child abuse" (Stark and Flitcraft 1985, p. 165). In other studies of violence against women and abuse of children, researchers have concluded that battered women may be twice as likely to abuse their children as women who are not battered (Straus, Gelles, and Steinmetz 1980, pp. 216–217). Finally, when the parents abuse one another, this familial reality almost definitionally implicates abuse of the child or children resident in the family. Children who witness parental violence are affected cognitively, emotionally, and physically (Walker 1984). While research on the effect of domestic violence on children is still comparatively new, several themes have emerged. First, children suffer enormously simply by witnessing the violence between their parents (Wallerstein and Blakeslee 1989). One experimental study examined children who had witnessed violence perpetrated against their mother by her male partner, without themselves having been subject to abuse. This study compared those children to a control group of children who had neither witnessed, nor been subject to, abuse. The researchers found that, as compared to the control group, the children of the battering relationships showed more aggression, exhibited impaired cognitive and motor abilities, and were delayed in verbal development (Westra and Martin 1981). This and other studies have begun to define the negative behavioral and emotional effects experienced by children who witness parental violence (Cahn 1991).

Research also supports the conclusion that there is a "reproduction" of domestic violence which makes it likely that the suffering experienced by child witnesses of violence will be transmitted beyond the children themselves. Because children learn from their parents, they may eventually imitate the abusive behavior they have witnessed, replicating patterns of violence in their own relationships. One study has reported that almost half of the children from abusive families repeated the pattern they had learned in childhood, and were abusive in their own intimate relationships in their early adulthood (Wallerstein and Blakeslee 1989). Children learn that abusers have enormous power in the family, and they may conclude that sexual relationships are normally or necessarily accompanied by violence (National Center on Women and Family Law 1987).

Most of the studies discussed in this section have examined either the psychological and other impacts on children of their own experiences of abuse or the statistics that attempt to document the number of "bad mothers." They have not focused on sociological factors that may affect women who have committed child abuse. These accounts have not generally treated, in any depth, the politics and sociology of patriarchal society,[11] nor have they offered self-accounts that abused women might be able to offer. Thus they do little to displace the unexamined "bad mother" stereotype.

The "Bad Mother" in Psychological Theory

The bad or abusive mother is constructed not only in empirical sociological and psychological studies but also in the predominant strains of psychological theory of the twentieth century. The "bad mother" has been treated extensively by Freudian theory in its original and contemporary expressions. Bad mothering has also been the focus of theory, such as that of Alice Miller, that has attempted to distinguish itself very explicitly from Freudian approaches. It will be useful to consider how the "bad mother" has been represented in both theoretical accounts.

Freudian Theory

It is striking that, while abusive mothers have just begun to be cautiously described in empirical literature, they have been at the center of psychoanalytic theory for a long time. They appear as highly and very confidently defined figures within Freudian doctrine, in its traditional formulations as drive theory and in its updated variations as object-relations theory. "Drive theory" argues that psychic life is *determined* by fundamental unconscious drives, and that cultural life requires the painful repression of these drives (Freud 1930). Drive theory is a biologically deterministic theory. "Object-relations" theory refers to expressions within psychoanalytic and developmental psychological theory that emphasize the importance of primary emotional relationships in constituting human personality. Object relations theory is not necessarily deterministic to the same degree as drive theory. In each of these versions, the figure of the mother is marked by designations that resonate with moral associations. Within traditional Freudian theory the mother is cast, with her sisters, as inevitably lacking (castrated) and as incapable of full moral development. According to Winnicott, in object relations theory, she is partially—if somewhat begrudgingly—redeemed by her possibilities as the "good-enough" mother (Winnicott 1965).

The Freudian view of motherhood is necessarily implicated with a general Freudian orthodoxy concerning the development of "normal" women and of "normal" female sexual experience. The Freudian account tells the story of a developmental process through which little girls become reconciled to their castrated natures, and define their sexuality by turning in the direction of passivity and masochism. Good motherhood demands of women a suppression of aggressive and sexual sensuality and of other-than-specifically-maternal creativity.

In the derivative object-relations school of psychoanalytic theory, even the marginally good-enough mother is characterized by her "masochistic-feminine willingness to sacrifice" (Winnicott 1960) as well as by her total and exclusive involvement with her child. Susan Sulieman has suggested that psychoanalytic theory is essentially a "theory of childhood" (Sulieman 1985, pp. 352–377), and that the account of motherhood offered by psychoanalytic theory is always a drama of the child. Within psychoanalytic theory, the "good mother" will always and inevitably—in spite of her accomplishing the sublimations that make her a "good mother"— be a "bad mother" too. She will be experienced by the fantasizing child as castrating as well as castrated, as a phallic mother, all-powerful and threatening, whom the child, male or female, will, in the Oedipal process, come to devalue, and from whom the child will have to make a profound separation in order to construct a self.

Feminist contributions to psychoanalytic or developmental psychological theory of the last several years have attempted to reformulate that "child's story" by stressing the cultural constructedness of motherhood and its reproductions. Dorothy Dinnerstein and Nancy Chodorow, for example, have sought to deliver psychological theory from its simplistic tendencies to blame individual "bad mothers" for the ills of the larger culture (Dinnerstein 1976; Chodorow 1978). Dinnerstein has stressed the destructive impact that the institution of exclusively maternal child care has had upon society as a whole. She has proposed that alteration of that institution might reduce the misogyny of the culture to the degree that it would direct against powerful fathers as well as powerful mothers the rage inevitably evoked in children passing through ordinary developmental processes.

While the stories proposed by both Dinnerstein and Chodorow constitute powerful critiques of the relegation of child care to the institution of motherhood, it remains the case that each gives an account that is, like the tales of traditional psychoanalytic thought, much more fully a "child's story" than a "mother's story." Both accounts, while attempting to introduce critical perspectives on gender into psychoanalytic thought, fail to take account of the intricate context of the lives of mothers, and to some degree express the experiences of some ahistorical and essential "child." Like Freud, Dinnerstein and Chodorow appear to take as given the necessity that the developmental process will be painful, and will occasion profound discontent. In this respect, the theories of Dinnerstein and Chodorow seem to accept as inevitable that children will experience "bad mothering," whether that "mothering" be delivered by women or by "mothering" fathers.

Alice Miller

A very significant development in psychological literature has occurred with the publication in English in the last several years of a number of writings by Swiss psychologist Alice Miller (Miller 1981; Miller 1983; Miller 1990a; Miller 1990b). These works represent perhaps the strongest theoretical treatments focusing very directly upon child abuse and its implications for human development and for human history. Alice

Miller's work, which has become well known by psychologists and by a popular readership, clearly warrants examination by feminist theorists because of its new and explicit focus on child abuse, and because of its unequivocal emphasis on parental responsibility. Both these emphases raise particular challenges to feminist theory.

Miller's work can be distinguished from both traditional and feminist developmental and psychoanalytic theory in various ways. Indeed, Miller takes pains to disassociate herself from traditional psychoanalytic theory. She is critical of feminism to the degree that feminism has ignored or denied the reality of child abuse. Miller explicitly and purposively defines her work as a telling of children's stories. In this work, which makes the experiences of children absolutely central, Miller accomplishes explicitly what psychoanalytic theory does implicitly. Miller's writing is replete with accounts of the woundings of children's souls as well as of their bodies. She identifies as abusive the acts and omissions by which parents and other adults both injure children, and persuade children that the injuries were "for their own good." The basis of Miller's criticism of psychoanalytic theory is that it is insufficiently child-centered, and that it in fact operates as an *apologia* on behalf of abusive parents.

Alice Miller indicts traditional psychoanalytic theory with her insistence that it has concealed and denied the realities of child abuse and of children's sufferings. She emphasizes that psychoanalytic theory has encouraged us to consider children's accounts of *real* abuse (including sexual abuse) to be childish fantasies. She argues, further, that psychoanalytic theory encourages a hopeless resignation to the inevitability of children's being required to submit, as a part of the acculturation process, to experiences of mistreatment. Psychoanalytic approaches have these effects, in part, by virtue of their very nature as "analysis." In Miller's view, to the degree that the psychoanalytic approach valorizes an intellectual and analytic attitude, it discourages the reexperiencing of feelings that could provide powerful knowledge of the meaning of suffering. She argues that psychoanalytic theory works to distance or distract adults from awareness of the traumas they suffered in their childhoods. For Miller, this distancing implicated in psychoanalytic theory has caused that theory to impede the determined, resolute, and conscious confrontations with the reality of child abuse that might lead to meaningful change, and that, in Miller's view, are necessary for the very survival of our planet.

Miller defines the mistreatment of children as "the greatest crime that one human being can commit against another—causing psychological deformation in the next generation. . . ." (Miller p. 51). She emphasizes that *all* children are victimized by *most* adults. In order to address that harmful reality, she urges an emotional—rather than an intellectual—

discovery by adults of our own unique childhood histories. She urges that adults become consciously aware of the humiliations and losses of our own childhoods, so that we will be able to avoid reproducing those injuries in the experiences of our children.

Miller emphasizes that our understanding of the suffering of children will depend upon our listening to and heeding children. She urges our attention to the body language of children, which clearly manifests the reality of their sufferings. She defines a standard of child care that is *ever* attentive to the realities and the importance of children's feelings, and that refuses ever to erase that reality or to justify it in the name of any abstraction. Miller can be seen as expressing a "return to the body" of a kind often remarked in feminist writings—but the bodily experiences to which she would have us re-turn are the experiences of all children.

Miller articulates a critique of feminism based on what she sees as its ideologically based failure to acknowledge the reality of women's perpetrations of child abuse. She argues with reference to mothers' failures to protect their daughters against sexual abuse, for example:

> [T]he feminist movement . . . comes up against its ideological limits. It sees the problem as being rooted exclusively in the patriarchy, in the male exertion of power. This simplification leaves many questions unasked. Perhaps it is too early to ask these questions since they would threaten the image of the idealized mother. Yet we must wonder: What causes a man to rape women and children? Who made him so evil? In my experience it is not always the fathers alone. . . .
>
> I have noticed that some feminists don't care to listen to such questions, yet they are at a loss when they constantly hear of mothers who, instead of protecting their sexually abused daughters, leave them to their fate or even punish them. . . .
>
> These considerations are not intended to detract from the merits of the feminist movement in its approach to child abuse but rather to encourage the breaking down of old boundaries. The process of exposing lies must not be brought to a standstill by new ideological untruths, by illusions and idealizations. (Miller 1990a, pp. 76–77)

Miller's account of child abuse from the child's perspective is in some senses grandly historical, and in others ahistorical. On the one hand she sees the abuse of children as the mechanism for the perpetuation of evil and destruction throughout history; on the other she has no particular interest in exploring the cultural contexts within which what she defines as "abuse" occurs. Indeed, Miller seems impatient of accounts that might seem to explain, to rationalize, or to define the occurrence of child abuse as inevitable. She observes:

The situation of an adult woman confronted by a brutal man is not the same as that of a small child. Although, because of her childhood, the woman can see herself as equally helpless and thus may overlook her chances of defense, she is in fact no longer helpless. Even when her rights are inadequate, even when the courts are on the side of the man, an adult woman can speak up, report, look for allies, and she can scream (assuming she hasn't, as a child, learned not to). (Miller 1990a, p. 77)

Alice Miller's message is not one likely to be easily or readily received and assimilated by feminism. Miller's reminders of children's suffering can be resisted by feminists for various reasons. In some of its expressions, feminism has not been exempt from the ideological error that threatens every "ism," and feminism can fall into the error of so exclusively addressing the oppression of *woman as women* that it becomes exclusive of or intolerant of the accounts of others' pain. Thus, some strains of feminist theory might tend to ignore Miller's work precisely because it is not clearly gender-specific in its focus. It is also true that Miller's writing can have the effect of evoking feelings of something like guilt in adult women (and men, too, presumably) who read it and measure their care for their own children against its standards. Feminists are understandably resistant to being drawn into experiencing this kind of "parent guilt" that often readily reduces to "mother guilt." This is particularly the case for feminists who are struggling to their utmost to make the best choices they can for themselves and for their children in a culture that offers few satisfactory options. Many mothers struggle to make do with "private" solutions to the problem of nurturing children, in the absence of adequate "public" ones. Understandably, they do not welcome reminders of the inadequacies of those private arrangements. Often they prefer to deny those inadequacies and the degree to which they occasion pain and suffering for children.

But whatever difficulties Alice Miller's work poses for feminism will have to be faced. Miller's story of child abuse is so powerful that it becomes impossible for her readers to forget. Feminist readers are reminded by Miller that feminist theory *must* address the realities of child abuse perpetrated by women, and that feminist theory must somehow include those realities.

"Bad Mothers" in Dependency Proceedings

This section briefly explores the prosecution of mothers for child abuse and neglect. It focuses on cases where the mother has been battered as well. In this discussion another definition of "bad mothers" emerges through a consideration of the state structures which regulate them.

One of us was told about a city attorney who represented a battered woman seeking an emergency protection order against her husband to prevent further violence. The day before the court hearing, the battered woman's sworn testimony asserted, he had:

> punched her in the head and face and body, bruising her throat. He then hit her in the back with a chair, smashed her head into some paintings on the wall, stomped on her head with his foot, and swung at her with the legs from a table he had just broken. He told her that wherever she was, he would hunt her down and kill her. . . . The Petitioner is very afraid and the children are visibly upset. . . .
>
> Respondent has a hstory [sic] of hitting and threatening the petitioner. . . . On her birthday last year he beat her so bad [sic] she could not walk.

After waiting in a large public room for several hours to see an attorney, and then waiting several more hours in the courthouse to see the judge, the petitioner began arguing with her two children. The children, who were four and six years old, had been making a lot of noise, and fighting with each other while they waited. Their mother took off her shoe, and threatened to hit the children (she may actually have hit them); the children became quiet, and the mother put her shoe back on. The mother then went in to see the judge, and was granted an emergency protection order. Her lawyer, whose office also represents the city in child abuse prosecutions, reprimanded the mother, and may have subsequently reported her to the local child abuse authorities on the basis of his observation of her threat to the child.

This sequence of events, culminating in the lawyer's report of child abuse, is an instance of the tendency, discussed above, to focus on the child's story without considering that of the mother. It also demonstrates a failure to contemplate the implications for the child of the possibility of being removed from his or her family. It is a common assumption that the function of the child protective services caseworkers is to obtain a fuller account of events through the process of investigation. However, it has been the authors' experience that, even when a contextualized story begins to be developed by an investigating social worker, that story tends not to include an account of the risks associated with the removal of children from maternal care to foster care. Legal commentary has begun to develop this part of the story. Indeed, many recent lawsuits against state agencies responsible for foster placements have alleged inadequate care and conditions, such that children who are removed from their homes may indeed be placed in more abusive situations.

All states, and the District of Columbia, have a variety of methods for dealing with parents who abuse or neglect their children. These range from prosecution for the underlying criminal offense to civil actions under abuse and neglect statutes. The civil abuse and neglect procedure is generally first triggered by a report to child abuse authorities. When such a report has been made, the state can remove the child from the home without a hearing, albeit only for a few days. Then the state must establish that it has met the statutory criteria for intervention; upon an adjudication that the state has met its burden of proof, the court can decide upon an appropriate disposition. The focus of the "child protector" system is, of course, to ensure that children are safe; almost invariably, this seems to require removing the child as soon as possible from her family.

The definition of bad mothering applied in the prosecution of child abuse and neglect is a broad one, and few explicit standards curb the discretion of prosecutors. For example, in the District of Columbia, an abused child is defined as:

> a child whose parent, guardian, or custodian inflicts or fails to make reasonable efforts to prevent the infliction of physical or mental injury upon the child, including excessive corporal punishment, an act of sexual abuse, molestation, or exploitation, or an injury that results from exposure to drug related activity in the child's home environment." (D.C. Code Ann. § 16–2301(23) (Supp. 1990))

Such a broad standard allows prosecutors to define appropriate parental behavior as they see fit. As a result, the system will reflect the race, class, and gender biases of prosecutors, who have tended to be white, middle-class, and male. Mothering is taken out of its context in abuse prosecution, and is judged by a judiciary that assumes middle-class, sexist, and racist norms.[12] Mothers—across classes and cultures—are expected to perform in ways that satisfy those norms.

Criticism of the limitations of prosecutorial and judicial judgment does not resolve the problematic of child abuse as a legal and moral issue. It does not by itself offer guidance concerning the distinctions of blameworthiness that might properly be made between and among parents who abuse their children. It does not answer the question of whether the civil or criminal law should, for example, treat battered women who abuse their children differently from male child abusers and differently from other abusive women. Various commentators have begun to struggle with these questions. Consider the thoughts of Albert Alschuler:

> Imagine that a brutal man (call him Joel Steinberg) and a lover whom he has physically abused for years (call her Hedda Nussbaum) have

participated in the same act of child abuse. Imagine further that the battered woman participant has no defense of insanity or duress but that she comes close. The seriousness of the crime (judged in the abstract) is the same for both offenders. Still, I think that their "desert" differs greatly and that imposing identical sentences would offend ordinary concepts of "proportionality."[13]

The question, of course, (which Alschuler does not address) is *why* he would hold the woman less culpable than the man.

Not everyone subscribes to the same "ordinary concepts" that Alschuler does. Indeed, his opinions differ from those of many judges and social service workers who, studies indicate, are likely to blame mothers for anything that happens to their children (Gordon 1988, pp. 262–263). This difference appears to be caused by conflicting images of women: on the one hand it seems to be proposed by commentators such as Alschuler that because they are victims of male patriarchy, battered women should not be blamed for hurting their children, when they themselves are being battered; on the other hand, it appears to be assumed by many workers in the field that because mothers are supposed to be nurturant, their culpability exceeds that of other adults when they are abusive.

Martha Minow has proposed a partial answer to this dilemma of determining responsibility and culpability. Minow has suggested that the context of bad mothers, which includes family dynamics and a society unresponsive to domestic violence, is perhaps to blame for family violence (Minow 1990, pp. 1682–1683). This proposition provides a context for understanding the mother's actions: why she did not leave the abusive situation; why she did not (or could not) prevent her partner from abusing a child; and why she may herself have abused her child. This interpretation allows us to move beyond mere blaming of the mother herself and permits us to focus on her embeddedness within systems that foster violence. This account is importantly suggestive. While it does not entirely resolve the issue of how to understand the bad mother as moral agent, it reminds us of the need for examination of context, a reality to which much feminist theory has reliably directed attention.

Feminist Theory

In order to explore the relevance of the accounts of good and bad mothering and of children's experiences for feminist theory, it will be useful to consider certain strands of feminist work that can be designated loosely as liberal feminism, cultural feminism, radical feminism, and postmodernist feminism. We use these categories mindful of the fact that many authors transcend them. Some may be regarded as "cultural feminist" for one line of inquiry and as postmodernist in another context or at a different stage of their thinking. Moreover, there are considerable differences among those who occupy the same categorical space. Nonetheless, because these categories have been frequently utilized by others, we use them here as a heuristic device for our own analysis. Each of these strains of feminist theory has found expression within legal theory in discussions of reproductive issues, and each has, to some extent, considered motherhood. The related issue of child abuse, however, has not yet received extensive treatment by any of them. This discussion explores how different strands may be able to contribute to a better understanding of abusive mothers.

Liberal Feminism

The strain of feminist theory often designated as "liberal feminism," which emerged in the 1960s, focused largely on supporting women's access to, and equality in, the workplace. Liberal feminism typically emphasized the value of individual and autonomous personal development for both men and women. It stressed that biology should not determine destiny (Tong 1989, p. 31). Because their goal was to demonstrate the ways in which sex- or gender-based classifications limit women, those employing liberal arguments deemphasized pregnancy and motherhood, viewing them as too "confining" in terms of gender ideology for women (Fineman 1992, p. 302). The "equal treatment" approach supports a conception of men and women that emphasizes their "sameness" rather than their "difference." Accordingly, pregnancy is treated as merely one of a multitude of physical disabilities that both women and men may experience, rather than as a defining experience for women (Williams 1984–85, p. 327). This analysis has led liberal feminists to support, for example, parental leave from work, rather than maternity leave, on the theory that parents should be treated equally and that mothers should not receive "special treatment" (Ross 1991). Legal treatment of women and men on the basis of their "differences," it has been argued, would likely result in the marginalization and stereotyping of women, and also in men's continuing failure to assume an appropriately equal share of parenting responsibility.

Liberal feminists argue that women's biology does not require that they stay out of the workplace in order to provide child care, any more than it limits women to "nurturing" occupations such as teaching or nursing (Tong 1989, p. 28). They assert that such stereotypes prevent women from achieving their potential (Ashe 1987, p. 1141). While liberal legal feminists acknowledge that there are differences between men and women, they believe that the appropriate focus is on differences among women and differences among men. Thus, while motherhood is not entirely ignored, the primary focus is on barriers to women's equality, such as assumptions based on stereotypes about women's abilities. But a focus on the importance of the inclusion of women in the workplace can minimize the difficulties—including child neglect, and perhaps abuse— occasioned by the inability of highly stressed and exhausted working parents to provide adequate attention and nurturance to children. The focus of liberal feminism—at least in its original formulation—on same- ness may have contributed to its failure to look beyond the issues raised by the inclusion of women in the workplace, and its failure to confront fully issues relating to women's reproductive experiences and the reality of child neglect or abuse.

Few, if any, feminists focusing on equality and sameness theory have addressed the issue of child abuse perpetrated by women, and this is not surprising. The deemphasis of the differences between women and men can erase or distract attention from significant contextual differ- ences that attach to the biological and cultural conditions that typically do differentiate the reproductive and child-caring experiences of women and men. Because the story of liberal feminism is, in general, a story of the sameness of women and men, and because the woman imagined by it is a separate, independent, autonomous individual, liberal feminism never considers the complexities of the moral agency of mothers in relationship to children, nor the legal treatment able to do justice to that reality. This limitation was highlighted as early as 1984 by Sylvia Law, in a critique of liberal feminism that focused specifically on women's reproductive differences (Law 1984). Current internal critiques of liberal feminism include Wendy Williams' recent work, in which she acknowl- edges the diversity of women and the need to challenge a world "con- structed on a male model" (Williams 1989, p. 108).

Cultural Feminism

The strand of feminist argument typically identified as cultural femi- nism has generally been distinguished by its focus upon the differences that exist between women and men, and by its support for the position that women and men should be treated differently by the law for some purposes. For example, many cultural feminists typically assert that women invoke an "ethic of care" in their moral reasoning, in contrast to men who are more oriented toward an ethic of rights. Cultural feminism delineates many strong distinctions between men and women. It defines women as more caring and more oriented towards relationships than are men. It characterizes women as tending to perceive morally troubling problems as situations in which people might be hurt (Jack and Jack 1989, p. 173), and as trying to resolve conflicts by strategies that maintain connection and relationship (Noddings 1984). Men, by contrast, are viewed as less connected to others, and instead oriented towards individual autonomy and impartial rules. It is asserted that men tend to see problems in terms of violations of abstract rights (Jack and Jack 1989, p. 173), rather than in terms of real and complex relationships between people.

The experience of mothering is central to this theorizing (West 1988). A number of cultural feminists suggest that it is because women are mothers that they are more connected to others. Their image of a mother is one who "naturally" recognizes and appreciates her interdependence with her children (West 1988, p. 27). Cultural feminists celebrate women's role as nurturer. Indeed, they often emphasize women's positive characteristics to a degree that erases certain negative aspects of women's experience and activity (Williams 1989).

In legal theory, the valorization of motherhood has led "difference" feminists to advocate special protections to accommodate women's particular experiences (Littleton 1987). Gender neutrality has been challenged as disadvantageous to women. Thus, for example, in discussions of pregnancy benefits, it has been argued that maternal leave policies should be supported even in the absence of gender-neutral parental leave, because such policies recognize women's special needs, and are appropriate to ensure women's equality within the workplace.

The willingness of cultural feminism to embrace the reality of difference between women and men, as well as its focus on motherhood, might suggest that theory's greater capacity for interpretation of "bad mothers." Indeed, the argument that it is important to understand the pain in women's lives as different from that which men experience (West 1987) could lead to an increased recognition of why women abuse their children. However, the celebration of motherhood does not—at least at this point—include "bad mothers." Indeed, it is not entirely clear what a coherent cultural feminist analysis of "bad mothers" could be.[14] The largely uncritical—and often essentialist—emphasis on "caring" as an attribute of women hardly leaves room for consideration of women who do not or cannot care for their children, and seems to offer no escape from the prevailing images of "bad mothers" as either utterly unnatural or utterly victimized.

Radical Feminism

Another strain of feminist inquiry, so-called radical feminism, has focused more intensively on the nature of gender relationships than on the nature of the motherhood *per se*. To the degree that it has treated motherhood, however, it has been characterized by a very marked devaluing of the self-sacrificing aspects of good motherhood supported by cultural feminism (and, as suggested above, by prevailing psychological theory). Thus, for example, there is apparent in Catharine MacKinnon's writing a strong impatience with cultural feminism's high valuation of nurturant behavior (MacKinnon 1987a, p. 39; MacKinnon 1985). According to MacKinnon's analysis, the "nurturance" touted by the cultural feminists is merely the learned behavior of victims (MacKinnon 1987a, p. 39; MacKinnon 1985). Further, she would characterize the positive valuation of such behaviors by cultural feminists as an instance of "false consciousness" (MacKinnon 1987a, p. 39; MacKinnon 1985).

The discourse of radical feminism, of MacKinnon's "feminism unmodified," expresses a refusal to recognize positive and empowering experiences that some women report even within the limits imposed by motherhood as a cultural institution. Thus, MacKinnon speaks disparagingly, in "Unthinking ERA Behavior," of mothers who failed to engage in effective political activity because they were at home "wiping their babies' asses" (MacKinnon 1987b, p. 759). This reductionist discourse denigrates the experiences of many women who read it as denying or erasing the significance of their central relationships with their children.

Radical feminism has been sharply criticized for its consignment of women-as-mothers to the category of the "falsely conscious." While MacKinnon and other radical feminists write powerfully about issues of sexuality in ways that emphasize that the category "women" cannot and must not be reduced to the category "mothers," it remains the case that radical feminism is inadequate in its treatment of motherhood. Recently, there has been an attempt to use radical feminism to understand pregnant, crack-addicted women as victims of patriarchy (Oberman 1992). This analysis continues, however, to treat women as victims, without control over their own lives, and as victims of false consciousness. It is thus a reductive analysis that fails to cover women's agency in any adequate manner. For this reason, it offers limited insights with regard to the problem of feminist theory's struggle with the reality of the "bad mother" as a perpetrator of child abuse. It suggests an account of the role of patriarchy in creating bad mothers, but denies the potential agency of women who abuse.

Postmodernist Feminism

In recent years, certain legal theory has come to be marked by features that can be identified as "postmodernist." These features include a characteristic awareness of the partiality and contingency of every claim to knowledge, an eschewing of "grand narrative" and "grand theory" in favor of smaller narratives, and, as expressed in feminist legal theory, have included, specifically, an avoidance of the claim to speak for all women. The critical efficacy of much of postmodernist feminist legal theory has thus often been accomplished by its introduction or reintroduction of subjectivities that had been obscured or denied by dominant accounts.

To the degree that postmodernist feminism is "postmodernist" it expresses profound and persisting skepticism; to the degree that it is "feminist," it expresses—within a world in which everything is "thrown into question"—conviction and certainty concerning the reality of the cultural oppression of women. Postmodernist feminist theory tells certain stories that have given rise to the belief in the oppression of women; stories that support this belief; and stories that begin to suggest possibilities of escape.

Within feminist legal theory, issues of "reproduction," of violence toward women, and of the intersections of gender and racial oppressions have begun to be treated in specifically postmodernist narratives. Accounts of "bad mothers" have, however, been absent from such analyses, just as they have been absent from or reductively defined in negative terms in most feminist theory. The reasons for this reality are both intellectual and political. As has been suggested, it has seemed impossible to provide an adequate account of "bad mothers" within the binaristic limits of traditional theory without reducing the discussion of motherhood to stereotyping essentialism. Further, feminists have not found it politically desirable to emphasize the "badness" of some mothers. Feminist theory has, however, been seriously limited by its failure to engage with the reality of the "bad mother."

Postmodernism has created a space within which new kinds of inquiry into the experiences and motivations of "bad mothers" can be undertaken. Postmodernist approaches support new directions for interpreting the intersections between violence against women and violence by women. Postmodernism legitimates stories of "bad mothers" as essential to theory. It both recognizes the difficulties of telling such stories, and invites their tellings as "local knowledge" (Ashe 1989). Postmodernism supports the possibility of new imaginings, not only by opening up the possibility of various "new narratives," but also through the creation of a space within which those narratives—including narratives of children as well as those of women, for example—can intersect. Thus a specifically and explicitly postmodernist feminism may offer the greatest possibility for engagement of feminist theory with the reality of child abuse by "bad mothers."

Postmodernist directions allow for enriching interactions among the various emphases of liberal, cultural, and radical feminisms. Jane Swigart's nonlegal writing concerning "bad mothering"—work not easily categorized as liberal, cultural, or radical in its feminism—is an instance of such an approach (Swigart 1991). Swigart's writing manifests some postmodernist characteristics in its intermingling of narrative and its interdisciplinary treatment of both literature and psychology. It provides a powerful critical account of the stereotype of "bad mothering." The book does not explicitly take up the question of when judicial intervention into families is justified and necessary, nor does it explicitly explore how the "bad mother" stereotype might be displaced within the existing legal system. Swigart's book does, however, provide a powerful commencement of the task of telling the "bad mother" story from the perspective of both mothers and children. The incorporation of such complex perspectives into feminist legal theory concerning motherhood—"good" and "bad"—remains to be accomplished.

New Directions

It is our belief that most feminist writers who have attended to the reality of child abuse perpetrated by mothers have minimized the extent of such abuse, have ignored its pervasiveness, or have attempted to define it away. As we have already suggested, we are not surprised that feminist theorists would attempt such simplified resolutions for political and intellectual reasons. It is promising that feminist work is beginning to acknowledge and struggle with the reality of child abuse committed by mothers.

Feminist theory has much to contribute to a fuller appreciation of the realities of the "bad mother." The attention paid to context that liberal, radical, and cultural feminism have all advocated and variously practiced is one significant contribution. In so-called "failure-to-protect" situations, for example, contextualized examination can often disclose fairly readily the reasons why a mother may not have intervened to prevent abuse of a child by her boyfriend or husband. Such an examination may disclose that the mother was being abused herself; that she feared further abuse; that she had a history of prior unsuccessful attempts to intervene; that she did not fully understand what was occurring; and so on. Some feminists have begun the work of examining the contexts of mothers, or pregnant women, who "fail" to protect.[15] The seemingly more difficult challenge to feminist theory presented by mothers who actively abuse their children is one that must be undertaken for both theoretical and practical reasons.[16]

Practically, it must be recognized that the sheer pervasiveness of the reality of abuse of children by mothers demands exploration and discussion. It is impossible for feminism to continue to ignore the numbers of women who are abusive to their children. They appear too frequently for us to label them as aberrational, or for us to claim that they do not represent "women." Many of us have represented these women as their lawyers and have had to struggle with feelings of frustration, horror, or denial outside of any framework that assists either our exploration of their experiences or our exploration of our own experiences in representing them.

The theoretical justification for feminism's need to encounter "bad mothers" relates to the lager feminist project of reconstructing images of women. Feminism is limited to the degree that it fails to give some account of aspects of women which seem ugly or undesirable. As many feminists have argued, the meaning of "woman" is not unitary; not only does it go beyond white, middle-class, heterosexual women, it also includes "bad" mothers. In its attempt to provide accounts of the multiplicity of women's realities, feminist theory must explore the different forms that those realities take. If feminist theory is "outsider" criticism,[17] "bad mothers" are an example of "outsiders" to feminist theory. A feminism that excludes or reduces any woman is clearly inadequate. What we are urging here is that feminism attempt to include these outsiders, and that it do so by attending to and by developing the kinds of narrative expressions that many writers have seen as most helpful to "outsiders."

Our overview of the image of the "bad mother" in literature, in the stories told by the social sciences, by the legal culture, and by popular culture, as well as by feminist theory in general, discloses only the slightest outlines of a counternarrative detailing the contextual realities of "bad mothers." The fuller development of new narratives will require the commitment of all storytellers to persistent inquiry and to persistent self-examination. It will require the willingness of all storytellers to recognize the partiality of every account, and will require the willingness of listeners and speakers to raise the political and intellectual questions: Who is speaking? and: What is the basis of the speaker's claim to knowledge?

Addressing those questions can open up the possibility of new formulations. For example, a recognition by social scientists, by judges, and by lawyers that the realities of the lives which social scientists purport to describe or to define always exceed the categories into which they are forced should support a shift away from the uncritical reliance of courts on the "expert" stories about women and their children typical in custody proceedings (Fineman 1988). The raising of the question: Who is speaking? might similarly operate to expose the class, racial, gender, and other biases that often enjoy free play in the adjudication of child abuse matters. Similarly, a recognition of the erasures accomplished by abstraction in psychological theory could open up the possibility of more direct, more contextualized, and more persuasive storytelling about women—storytelling such as Alice Miller, for example, has begun to accomplish in her writing about children's experiences, and such as Jane Swigart has begun in her study of the emotional realities of mothering.

We have suggested, above, that such new tellings have begun to emerge in literary fiction and in other relatively isolated instances.[18] Those examples can serve as indications of the kind of narrative that might begin to dislocate the emotional and moral binarisms that impair our understanding of abusive parents. At the same time, they point out the daunting difficulty attached to such a project. Their rarity suggests something that our contact with "bad mothers" as their advocates also supports, namely, that such women are rarely able to speak effectively for themselves and of themselves, at least within the legal system.

By this we mean not only that such women experience the violence of having to reshape the realities of their experiences to accommodate a legal discourse that demands narrowing and erasure. "Bad mothers" are as constrained as their judges and prosecutors by the ambivalences that underlie and give rise to binarisms defining "good" and "bad" motherhood. Thus, it has been our experience that women alleged to have abused or neglected their children are typically unable to self-define except by directly denying what has been alleged, by asserting its opposite. They often seem to see no alternative to reciting counterclaims: "I'm a good mother!" or "I would never hurt my child!"—and the counterclaims may be no more meaningful than the original claim of "badness."

The task of representing and interpreting "bad mothers" will necessarily be a joint project, involving people differently situated from the mothers themselves who can together begin an expansion of the relevant emotional and moral discourse, and a fuller examination of the mothers' agency, complicity, and victimization. Some of the writers discussed here have begun to demonstrate such beginnings. Within the strands of feminist thought discussed earlier, there are convergences which facilitate the exploration of these new narratives.

Gayatri Spivak argues the need to recognize the gap that exists between the experiences of oppressed people and the representation of those experiences by those who purport to understand them and to advocate on their behalf (Spivak 1988). It behooves us to be mindful of that reality as we struggle to represent both motherhood and childhood. It is essential that writers interpreting "bad mothers" be willing to recognize the limitations of our own perspectives. At the same time, feminist writers must recognize that if the representation of motherhood in some absolute sense exceeds our human limitations, that representational task nonetheless presents itself as perhaps our most compelling obligation.

Notes

A more complete version of this chapter appears in 2 Texas Journal of Women and the Law 75 (1993).

1. Popular awareness of child abuse has existed at other times in American history, too. For historical accounts of the incidence and the various perceptions of family violence, see Gordon 1988; Pleck 1987.

2. See Crnich and Crnich 1992 (case histories of child sexual abuse); Bass and Thornton eds. 1983.

    As is well known, Freudian-derived psychoanalytic theory and psychiatry have historically expressed skepticism regarding both children's and adults' stories of childhood abuse. For intensive discussion of this issue, see Crews, 1993; Schimek, et al. 1994.

3. Examples of such nearly universally known Western fairy tales include "Snow White," "Cinderella," and "Hansel and Gretel." For one analysis of the psychological significance of such stories, see Bettelheim 1976.

4. See Rich 1976; see also Lorde 1984 (exploring—from a lesbian mother's perspective— the experience of parenting a boy).

5. Toni Morrison's novel, *Beloved* (1986) is one of the most striking instances of this effort. In *Beloved*, Morrison accomplishes the separate and mingled utterances of a neglected child, a murdered child, and their haunted mother. For discussion of the theoretical implications of Morrison's work and other fictive narrative, see Ashe 1992.

6. Williams 1991b, pp. 1624–29, uses the concept of gender wars in an attempt to reorient discussion of the work/family conflict away from conflicts within and among women over their choices between selfless motherhood and self-fulfilled work and towards challenges to the power differential between men and women which structures women's choices.

7. See Scott 1990 (looking at the agency of mothers of battered children as constructed by social services institutions); Gordon 1990 (arguing that these mothers are "active agents" because they provided narratives that contested those of social workers).

8. For a powerful critique arguing the nonobjectivity and the masculinist bias of social-scientific accounts relied on by courts for their "expert" value in adjudications of child custody, see Fineman 1988; Fineman and Opie 1987.

9. Giles-Sims 1985, interviewed twenty-seven women for this study. Information on their male partners is based on the women's reports. To measure the forms and extent of violence, Giles-Sims used a modified "Conflict Tactics Scale." This scale included a "Violence Index," which measured: "grabbing or shoving, slapping, kicking, biting, hitting with a fist, hitting or trying to hit with something, beating up, threatening with a knife or gun and/or using a knife or gun. The severe violence index or Abuse Index is restricted to the more serious acts of violence which are most likely to result in injury: kicking, biting, punching, hitting with an object, beating up, threatening with a knife or gun, and/or using a knife or gun." (Giles-Sims 1985, p. 207)

10. Men used the tactics 36.6 times, while women only used them 19.6 times (Giles-Sims 1985, p. 208).

11. But see the work of Gordon 1988.

12. For an historical perspective, see Gordon 1990.

13. Alschuler 1991, pp. 909–910; see, also, Minow 1990 ("The debate over whether to blame battered woman for her neglect or abuse of a child has a long history").

14. Recently, there has been some attention given to pregnant crack-addicted mothers. With regard to such women, cultural feminists might be expected to condemn the criminal prosecution of these women as a male, rights-oriented solution that fails to recognize the connection between the mother and her fetus. See Higgins 1990. She proposes, instead of criminal prosecution, a rethinking of the entire debate, with a focus on mother-child connections as central. To this end, she suggests that intensive drug rehabilitation provides a solution to the dilemma of these women. While such a solution does provide another perspective on this issue, it still does not acknowledge the realities of mothers who abuse their children. A focus on mother-child connections reveals that mothers can abuse their children, a challenge to the cultural feminist celebration of caring motherhood.

15. Erickson 1991. She suggests that, in many "failure-to-protect" cases, the mother is being abused by the person who is also abusing the children. She questions whether the purposes of criminal law are being served when these mothers are prosecuted, because mothers have no reason either to report the child abuse or to seek medical care if they fear they will be prosecuted for failing to protect the child.

16. This also ties in with feminist debates over women's agency, women's control over their own actions in a patriarchal society. See Williams 1991b (discussing how "choices" for women are constructed); Czapanskiy 1991 (exploring how women are "drafted" into motherhood); Abrams 1990 (showing problems with ideological determination arguments that may obscure the possibility of choice).

17. See Matsuda 1989 (defining outsider jurisprudence as "derived from considering stories from the bottom").

18. O'Brien 1992; Morrison 1987; Rich 1976 (chapter titled "Violence: The Heart of Maternal Darkness").

Abuse by Any Other Name: Feminism, Difference, and Intralesbian Violence

by Mary Eaton

The Difference Difference Makes

It is now somewhat trite to observe that feminist theory, in the legal realm as elsewhere, suffers from a certain element of so-called "essentialism." What is meant by this, partly, is that feminism has mistakenly posited a "universalized" woman, for whom gender is her primary determinant, and whose experience "as a woman" is somehow untouched by other forces of systemic subordination, such a racism, classism, heterosexism, and ablism. Having not alerted itself to the potential differences that other systemic forces of subordination might make in women's lives, feminism has tended to draw its theoretical conclusions from the experience of the privileged few among the female class. In itself this would not necessarily be troublesome, were it not for the fact feminism tended not to notice that was what it was doing. The result, so goes the critique, has been the formulation of feminist theory which is partial, in the sense that its assumed but unarticulated position has been that of the white, heterosexual, middle-class, and able-bodied female, and which is consequently unresponsive to the "difference" made by differences of race, class, sexual orientation, and the like (Harris 1990; Spelman 1988; Crenshaw 1989; Kline 1989).

Critiques of gender essentialism have generated a variety of responses to the question of how to deal with "the difference issue." While essentialism has not, to my knowledge, ever been forthrightly defended on theoretical grounds, simply mentioning the string of oppressions apart form gender in the context of gender analyses is a widespread practice amongst feminist writers. To the extent that invoking the mantra of "racegenderclasssexualorientation" does have a theoretical foundation, it appears to be that the difference problem is only one of formal omission that can be rectified by explicitly naming the heretofore unmentioned.

Where the historical omissions of feminism have been engaged more substantively, some have suggested that the very notion of feminist thought should be problematized: since its methodology (listening to the experiences of women) and hence its politics (theorizing from that listened-to experience) are predicated upon an unfragmented identity within and between women—sites of serious contestation in these postmodern times—perhaps it is ultimately meaningless to be speaking in terms of "women" and therefore "feminism" at all. Less nihilistically, some very practical suggestions have been made to cure the solipsism of privilege in much feminist thinking, specifically, that we build feminist theory "from the bottom up" (Matsuda 1989; Crenshaw 1989).

Embedded within each proposed corrective are three critical assumptions about the nature of difference and its challenges.[1] The first, common to all, is that there are no meaningful differences between different differences. All treat difference, in other words, as if it were monolithic; as if differences of, say, race, posed no challenge discernably unique from differences of, for example, class. The second, likewise shared, is that there is no meaningful differences within feminism. The tendency has been to posit feminism as it if were a static and uniform entity against which difference can be measured. For example the debates over "hyphenated feminism" which occupied so much discursive space in the early 1980s barely figure at all in these new discussions of difference, as if those debates had been resolved and the controversy put to rest. And finally, context often appears as mere background in this discourse. Even assuming a singular difference and a homogenous feminism, difference seems to pose the same sort of challenge whether the issue is sexual violence, economic inequality, or reproductive self-determination. What distinguishes the various stances toward essentialism in feminism, of course, is that they regard the challenges posed by difference differently. If the problem posed by omission were simply a function of nominal discourtesy, then the practise of cataloguing oppressions might well emerge as a promising cure. Contrariwise, failure to theorize inclusively defies easy or formulaic rectification if difference matters in a more fundamental way. If the phenomenon of difference contradicts feminist principles at their core, then perhaps the time has come to recognize feminism as a movement and a politics once, but no longer necessary, and to embrace "postpatriarchy" as the sign of contemporary times. But the "difference difference makes," while still substantive, may not be quite so irreconcilable. There may be a way of dealing with difference, as by starting with the effect of the "bottom" that difference produces, that allows feminism to continue and to speak more fully to the panoply of gender experience that exists.

Choosing amongst these, or, for that matter, other theoretical alternatives becomes a very complex matter, then, once their assumptions about different differences, different feminisms, and different contexts are scrutinized. It may be, for instance, that in some contexts difference makes no difference (see, for example, cunningham 1991), and that feminism's exclusions could then be corrected by simply making mention of the erstwhile omitted. It may be that difference does make a difference, but one which strikes more at how we strategize than how we theorize (c.f. Spivak 1990). Perhaps the various systems of oppression operate in such fundamentally different ways and to such profoundly different effects, that it may be beyond our grasp to fashion a theory which truly does speak to the experience of all women in every context. but then again, perhaps there may be some way of reconceptualizing what otherwise are divergent experiences under some new umbrella concept (see, for example, Roberts 1993). If extant feminist analysis cannot fully capture the experience of those women whose lives are shaped by more than gender oppression, perhaps it should simply be limited in application to those women to whom it does speak, rather than be jettisoned entirely (see, for example, MacKinnon 1991). The 1990s may witness the end of "feminism unmodified,"[2] but not feminism as such. Consequently, asking what difference difference makes is complicated not only by problematizing what sort of difference exists if difference exists, but in relation to what, and to what effect. All of which is to say that including the obligatory list of oppressions (in the notes or the text, it matters not which) may be as distorting as suggesting that there is in fact a bottom up from which an inclusionary analytic could be constructed, but it depends.

My aim in this paper is both grand and limited. I hope to engage the problem of difference within feminist theorizing in a way which contemplates and embraces the prospect that the problem posed by difference is potentially very messy indeed. At the same time, space does not permit me to address the multiplicitous array of questions to which my proposed approach gives rise. I restrict my analysis, then, to lesbian difference and the challenges it raises for existing feminist accounts of domestic violence.[3]

There is no magic in my choice to examine abuse in the home as opposed to some other feminist problematic. My decision to discuss the difference of "sexual orientation" is, however, more substantive. In my view, of the differences amongst women that have been the subject of discussion in the difference debates to which I have referred, "sexual orientation" has received both scant and peculiar attention. Curiously, when sexual orientation is addressed at all, there appears to be a decided readiness to assume that it can be conceptualized completely within a gender framework, a readiness that appears mostly (albeit not entirely) absent in contemporary discussions of the differences posed by race, class, ethnicity, ability, and the like.[4] As I have argued elsewhere (Eaton 1994), the claim that lesbian oppression is coterminous with or is a subset of gender oppression may be theoretically convenient, but has yet to be subject to rigorous scrutiny. One of my aims here, then, is to test the broad theoretical proposition advanced elsewhere that the difference of sexual orientation, in effect, makes no difference.[5]

Although my concern is largely theoretical, the issue of feminism's ability to account for intralesbian violence is obviously not a question devoid of practical implications. For instance, shelter workers have had to grapple with the very difficult matter of whether shelter services, which were designed with the pressing problem of male-on-female violence in mind, ought to be made available to lesbians who claim to be battered by their lovers. The issue is a vexed one because the philosophy guiding the operation of shelters—taking the word of women who claim that they have been abused by their male partners—proves of very little use in single-sex domestic violence cases. The device of "believing the woman" simply does not assist when "the woman" can be either the victim or the abuser. The difficulty is especially acute in those cases where both members of a lesbian couple whose relationship has been scarred by violence claim to be battered and come seeking shelter.

Debate over the applicability to lesbians of feminist "remedies" which originated in heterosexual contexts has also arisen in the legal setting. For example, feminist lawyers struggled for the reform of the law of self-defense to make it more responsive to the pleas of women defendants who killed their abusive partners. As typically constituted, the defense of self-defense has required that a threat to one's bodily integrity be imminent, and that an accused's fear of their life be objectively "reasonable" before the use of lethal force could be legally justified. The twofold requisites of imminency and reasonableness were not necessarily problematic in and of themselves, but the way in which they were applied to battered women certainly was. Because many battered women kill their male violators in circumstances where, seemingly, they were not immediately threatened, and where there appeared to be ample opportunity to retreat from whatever threat of violence to themselves existed, self-defense was effectively unavailable to them as a defense to criminal charges. Feminist litigators struggled to convince courts to admit expert evidence of the "battered woman syndrome," the purpose of which was to assist juries in their determination of whether an accused's belief regarding the immediacy and the extent of the danger she perceived she was in was reasonable within the meaning of self-defense doctrine, and in many jurisdictions they succeeded.

The phenomenon of intralesbian violence posed a conundrum for feminist legal activists of an entirely different order from that confronting frontline workers. Whether shelters were equipped, philosophically speaking, to provide services for battered lesbians was a question of foundational dimensions. By contrast, no such rethinking of first principles, seemingly, was required of legal advocates who wished to extend a helping hand to lesbians in domestic crisis. Consequently, in the wake of courts' ceding to the admission of expert testimony on the effects of abuse, the feasibility of deploying the same defence in homosexual battering cases was clearly raised, and, in general, the response was sympathetic. The clear tendency within the legal literature is to make passing reference to the phenomenon of same-sex battery, and to suggest that extant legal remedies should be made equally available to homosexuals who find themselves in such situations (Cahn 1991; Bates 1991; Kinports 1988; Ensign 1990). Very few commentators performed the intellectual labor of articulating precisely why battered homosexuals should be placed on a equal legal footing with battered women (Dupps 1990; Harkavy 1982). Fewer still have traced the line of logic which the extension of heterosexual remedies to homosexual defendants seems to demand: that we should no longer refer to the cluster of traits associated with the impact of sustained abuse as "battered woman syndrome," but should speak instead of "battered person syndrome" (Anderson and Anderson 1992). At stake, then, was not so much the defence *per se*, but its status as a remedy reserved for women victims of male violation.[6]

The resolution of these and other such pragmatic dilemmas turns partly on how intralesbian violence is conceptualized within feminist theory and why. If intralesbian violence is "gendered" as is heterosexual violence, there is no clear reason why the mechanisms for dealing with or remedying domestic violence which emerged out of feminist analyses of "wife abuse" in the heterosexual context could not be made equally available to lesbians in domestic crisis. If, on the other hand, intralesbian violence cannot be theoretically articulated within gender paradigms, then perhaps lesbian-specific theories of and remedies for battering need to be developed. In what follows, I shall critically review the various ways in which intralesbian violence has been (or arguably could be) conceptualized by theoreticians of domestic abuse. Of all the questions respecting "difference" brought to the fore by the approach I am advocating, my primary concern here is with relationship of difference to different feminisms. I ask whether the reality of lesbian battering reveals that feminist thinking on intimate abuse is so fraught with error that it must be discarded as bad theory; whether it is simply (but irretrievably) heterosexually self-referential and should be confined to nonlesbians; whether, with some minor tinkering, it responds to lesbian reality very nicely; and, most importantly, whether the answers to these questions turn on the way in which the gender of domestic violence is theorized.[7] I argue that despite their variety, and hence the different ways they confront lesbian "difference," current theories of domestic abuse fail to account for lesbian battering in a satisfying way. My claim, in consequence, is that no single feminist theory of domestic violence can account for all women's experience of abuse in the home without doing its own kind of violence to the experiences of differently situated women with violence itself. One of the implications of an analysis like mine is that the partiality of feminist theories of domestic violence requires that they be abandoned as poor theory. I resist this implication. My call, instead, is for a lesbian-specific model of intralesbian violence which can coexist with heterosexual and perhaps other feminist accounts of abuse in the home.

The Body Politics of Abuse

Of those who have considered how the phenomenon of lesbian (and gay) battering should be theorized, two opposing views seem to have emerged out of the debates: one groups of theorists maintain that intralesbian violence is gendered while another insists that it is not.[8] Common to the analyses of both those who lay claim to the "gender" of intralesbian violence and those who deny that "gender" has much, if anything, to do with it, is their shared assertion that female-on-female batterings is, both phenomenologically and empirically, barely distinguishable from male-on-female violence.[9] This observed pattern of formal equality, if you like, between intralesbian violence and male-on-female battering supports both the position of gender proponents as well as gender detractors, since they adopt very different definitions of what "gender" is. Although it is not always made explicit, the point of contention between those who envision intralesbian violence as gendered and those who do not is, not surprisingly, over the significance of biology to understandings of gender and exercises of gender power.

Implicit in the argument of those who insist that the phenomenon of intralesbian violence irrefutably demonstrates that battering is not a gendered activity is the supposition that "gender" is synonymous with anatomical or biological sex. Only if "gendered" understandings of domestic violence are predicated on the facts that battery is mostly done by biological males, that they do it a lot, that they do it in particular ways and for particular reasons, and with identifiable effects on their victims, do the facts that biological females do it too, and do it with similar frequency, form and effect threaten gender-based accounts of domestic violence. For Island and Letellier (1991), for example, the fact of same-sex spousal abuse exposes feminist accounts to be the "antimale" theory they assert it to be. Their position, by contrast, is that batterers are basically sick people, who abuse simply because they can and because "we" let them get away with it. In a less caustic vein, Faulkner (1990) maintains that since present feminist frameworks do not adequately explain lesbian battering, they should be abandoned in favor of more subtle and complex analyses of "power." Because the epistemological stance she adopts is that of the lesbian, Robson's (1990) project is neither to extend nor to trash feminist theory. Nonetheless, she also suggests that the reality of intralesbian abuse "threatens the very gendered foundations of explanations for domestic violence." (p. 586)

For those for whom lesbian battering is but another illustration of gender power in action, "gender" is a social construct rather than an anatomical fact. Inequality between the sexes is fed by sex-role stereotypes, according to which men are encouraged to be aggressive, independent, and career-oriented, whereas women are conditioned to be accommodating, nurturing, and family-oriented. The differentiation of the sexes is also hierarchized, such that the traits associated with masculinity are more highly valued than those linked with femininity. These inequalities support individual men's sense of superiority and entitlement to the privileged positions they enjoy. Women who refuse to abide by sex-role norms threaten the system of male dominance premised upon them and the sense of security of its individual male beneficiaries, sparking men's need to control and suppress women, including by means of force. Homophobia and heterosexism also contribute to violence against women. They reinforce the system of sex-role differentiation on a general level in the following way. To be a lesbian is to "step out of line," to challenge the credo that women belong with men, want men, like men, and need men. A lesbian, in short, is perceived as a threat. Homophobia, "the irrational fear and hatred of homosexuals," and heterosexism, "the use of sexual identity for dominance and privilege," thus are integral parts of the system of sex inequality (Pharr 1990). Hence, lesbians challenge the established order between the sexes by virtue of the simple fact that they are lesbians. As individuals, when lesbians enter into battering relationships, they themselves behave in gendered ways. Certain traits or modes of behavior are socially understood as masculine or feminine, and although these are substantially correlated with the biological sexes, male and female respectively, they need not always be. To assert or maintain control over another human being through the use or threat of force or coercion is just such a masculine characteristic. When a lesbian abuses her lover, she is behaving in socially masculine ways; when a lesbian is victimized through her lover's violence, she is behaving in socially feminine ways; and therefore the battering is a gendered activity (Littleton 1989; Leonard 1990). Thus, sex-role theorists' explanation for why lesbians batter one another relies on a concept of internalized gender oppression: women batter other women because they have internalized the interconnected norms of heterosexism/homophobia and misogyny which lie at the core of the sex-role system (Benowitz 1986).

One could, of course, challenge both theoretical accounts of intralesbian violence for the suzerain status of empirical truths within them. But even making allowances for such suspect methods does not take one much further toward resolving whether lesbian battering is gendered or not. To put matters somewhat differently, even if the problems with scientism are put aside, and these theories are taken on their own terms, there remains the questionable assertion that there is in fact a certain uncanny symmetry between male-on-female and female-on-female violence.

Arguably, there are a great many parallels between intralesbian violence and heterosexual battery. For example, estimates of the rate of battering in heterosexual relationships run as high as eighty percent, or as small as twenty percent, disparities in statistics being primarily attributable to variations in the kind of behaviors categorized as abusive. When "battery" is broadly defined to include such things as psychologically or emotionally destructive behaviors, like demeaning one's partner in the company of others, insulting one's partner's character, appearance, or intellect, high-end estimates result. Smaller percentages are due to more restrictive definitions of abuse and/or other limitations on what constitutes a "battering relationship." Requirements that the abuse be physical, that it result in serious physical injury, that it be repetitive, or joined to an overall pattern of control or coercion, all have the obvious effect of reducing the numbers of relationships classified as "violent."

Estimates of intralesbian battering also differ, and their variance is similarly attributable to what is being counted, that is, how violence or abuse or battery is defined. In terms of real numbers, many more heterosexual women are bruised, beaten, maimed, and killed than their lesbian and gay counterparts. The important point, however, is that rates of incidence within the lesbian community are very comparable to projected rates for heterosexuals: they range from a low of seventeen percent to a high of 73.4 percent, figures which are not significantly different from those generated in studies of male-on-female intimate violence. Rates of abuse in gay male relationships are similar, if somewhat higher: The director of the Gay Men's Domestic Violence Project at the Community United Against Violence in San Francisco estimates that domestic violence occurs in fifty percent of gay male couples (cited in Island and Letellier 1991).

Not only would it appear that intralesbian violence occurs at a rate proportionate to the incidence of violence within the heterosexual community, it also seems that female-on-female violence is similar to male-on-female violence in form. In the late 1980s, a handful of male sociologists challenged feminist readings of domestic violence by emphasizing that women were not the only victims of abuse in the home: men, they insisted, were victims too. Feminists countered these degendered renditions of domestic violence by pointing out that the type of violence engaged in by women who were abusive toward their male intimates was different. Such women were, it was contended, acting in self-defense, a kind of violence of a qualitative order different from the sort exhibited by abusive men who, by contrast, were typically the initiators or aggressors. And, in fact, most researchers have discovered that in ninety-five percent of cases, the perpetrators were male, and the victims, their female intimates. In a sense, parallel problems have plagued battered lesbian advocates. In the absence of sex differentiation, female-on-female violence has been regarded as a shared affair, with both parties bearing equal responsibility for their abusive behavior. The notion of mutual battering has been challenged as founded more in myth than in fact, since, even within same-sex couples, reciprocal fighting is a rarity. In the vast majority of cases, there is a readily identifiable batterer and a batteree, a subject and an object, a doer and a done to. Advocates' success in arguing for the identification of an identifiable Victim and Perpetrator parallels the debate in the heterosexual context, making it exceedingly difficult to distinguish intralesbian violence as different in kind.

Nor, it would seem, can lesbian battering be set apart from heterosexual battering in terms of the specific types of violent behaviors indulged in by assaultive partners.[10] The majority of the respondents in Renzetti's 1992 study reported that they experienced both psychological and physical abuse (eighty-seven percent), very few being subjected to emotional abuse in isolation (eleven percent). Forms of physical abuse included pushing and shoving (seventy-five percent),[11] hitting with fists or open hands (sixty-five percent), scratching or hitting the face, breasts, or genitals (forty-eight percent) and throwing things (forty-four percent). Smaller, but as Renzetti notes, nonetheless "alarming" percentages were yielded for more serious types of physical abuse, such as carving numbers, figures, or words into the skin (one percent), putting guns or knives into the vagina (two percent), deliberately burning with a cigarette (one percent), and stabbing or shooting (four percent). Psychological abuse was on the whole more frequent, and included verbal threats (seventy percent), verbally demeaning in front of friends or family (sixty-four percent) or in front of strangers (fifty-nine percent), interrupting sleeping or eating habits (sixty-three percent), damaging or destroying property (fifty-one percent), abusing children (thirty percent) or pets (thirty-eight percent). The most frequent types of psychological abuse included being physically restrained, not being permitted to leave a room, being forced to sever ties or contacts with relatives or friends, having one's property stolen, and being confronted with suicide threats.

It would also seem that the psychological impact of systematic abuse is very much the same for lesbians as for their heterosexual sisters. In 1979 Lenore Walker published a book on domestic violence, in which she put forward her now renowned theory of the cycle of violence and learned helplessness. Violence between intimates, she maintained, follows a pattern whereby there is a tension-building phase culminating in an outbreak of explicit violence, followed by a period of contrition. Caught in the endless repetition of this pattern, simultaneously believing her mate's insistence that she deserves what she gets and his concomitant pleas for forgiveness and promises to change, the abused woman becomes incapable of conceiving of her ability to get help. Studies of lesbians who have been subjected to systematic violence and degradation by their lovers show that they exhibit the same psychological profile as their heterosexual counterparts. Self-identified lesbian victims similarly report that sustained abuse created in them feelings of low self-esteem, a belief that no one will take seriously their complaints, and a fear that they had nowhere to turn for help.

Although there are arguably a great many similarities between female-on-female and male-on-female abuse, it is probably premature to conclude unequivocally that the form and function of lesbian battering is the same as "wife abuse." For one thing, very little is known about intralesbian violence in comparison to heterosexual battering. The birth of the "battered lesbian's movement," if it may be called that, can probably safely be to traced to the early 1980s, not very many years after the first battered women's shelter was opened in 1977. In spite of this, and quite unlike heterosexual intimate violence, lesbian battering has been the subject of very little research and writing to date. Indeed, in making the claim of sameness, some commentators do not ground their arguments in any systematic study at all, but rather, in truly circular fashion, rest their case on a presumed equilibrium between same-sex and heterosexual violence. Some even state rather baldly that, since there is no sound reason to expect that lesbian battery is different from heterosexual battery, it must be the same. Island and Letellier (1991), for instance, base their estimates of the prevalence of gay male intimate abuse by extrapolating from figures gleaned from heterosexual studies. In consequence, their argument amounts to the tautological claim that the two phenomena are the same because they should be the same.

But even for those who do invoke the authority of scientific studies, problems remain. For instance, most who have cited high rates of violence amongst lesbians have drawn on samples which were minuscule. Renzetti's (1992) estimate of sixty-five percent, for example, was based on a sample of only one hundred respondents.[12] By contrast, Loulan (1987), who surveyed over 1400 lesbians, calculated that only seventeen percent of lesbians were involved in violent relationships. Further, the samples examined by these and other analysts were unrepresentative, in the sense that they were drawn from selected populations and not the lesbian "community" at large. Rather than seeking to canvas the gay community, Island and Letellier draw inferences from their own personal experience with gay intimate abuse, Island as a community volunteer, and Letellier as a survivor of his ex-lover's violence. Both authors hold graduate degrees, and, although they do not specifically indicate their race, there are indications that both men are white. Renzetti is more forthcoming about the limitations of her study, acknowledging that her sample was "nonrandom." Respondents consisted, for instance, almost entirely of white (ninety-five percent), and well-educated women (forty-seven percent had a college degree and forty-two percent had received graduate or professional education).

Given the stereotypes about race and class have long distorted understandings of violence in intimate settings—given, that is, that people of color and working-class people have been ascribed a greater propensity to be violent—there is ample reason to be cautious in making the charge of unrepresentativeness. My point in raising this issue is not, however, to challenge estimates of the prevalence of intralesbian violence, but rather to open up the possibility that, because the little we know about the form and function of lesbian battering is limited to privileged (relatively speaking) white folk, what we do know about lesbian battering may be partial. More specifically, the few accounts of intralesbian violence amongst mixed-race lesbian couples that exist indicate that racism may play some role in why and/or in what form violence between lesbians occurs. Kannuha (1990), for example, documents the claims of two lesbians of color who were abused by their white partners. One reported that her partner used racial epithets and stereotypes while violating her. Another recalled a sadomasochistic ritual based on master/slave scenarios which, while begun as a mutual erotic exchange, ultimately disintegrated into a nonconsensual exercise in sexual and physical abuse. What these and other such accounts suggest is that even if gender could account for some aspects of intralesbian violence, it certainly cannot account for them all, unless "lesbian" really means "white lesbian," or unless race, like lesbianism, is really just another function of gender domination.

Apart from these methodological difficulties,[13] and more damningly, both the biologistic and gender-as-sex-role accounts fail in large measure to explore some areas of difference between lesbian and heterosexual battery. The degree to which intralesbian violence is sexualized may, for instance, be one area in which lesbian battering is distinct. Connections between eroticism and violence have been well documented in heterosexual contexts. We know, for example, that abuse of women in the home often takes the form of rape, and that violent episodes often are precipitated by the woman becoming pregnant (MacKinnon 1989). These observations suggest that there is something more to domestic violence than the fact that it involves assaultive behaviors in private spaces, specifically, that male violence and heterosexual sex are intricately interwoven in dynamics of male subordination of women. For the most part, however, and quite curiously, researchers of intralesbian violence have not even probed whether this is also true of abuse between lesbians, because they neglect to ask participants in their studies the kinds of questions which would elicit such information. Those working within the battered women's movement have noted that sexual abuse may be part of the battering scenario. However, there has been some disagreement over what constitutes "sexual abuse." In its statement on lesbian battering, the National Coalition Against Domestic Violence urged lesbians who had been involved in sadomasochistic relationships to "carefully examine the nature of consent" since, in the experience of its members, "in any relationship that involves violent activity, the line between consent, compliance and coercion tends to blur" (NCADV 1990). The coalition's choice to be careful in the language it selected to address the possible links between battering and S/M was well received by members of the lesbian S/M community, who had at other times felt unfairly maligned by battered women's advocates. They charged that some within the shelter movement had inaccurately portrayed S/M sexuality as itself a form of abuse, for reasons which apparently have to do with the fact that, whether controlled or consented to or not, sadomasochism is still at its core a violent activity. My point here is not to resolve the disagreement over whether lesbian S/M is *per se* abusive or not, but rather to highlight that if it is only or even primarily through the vehicle of sadomasochism that violence is sexualized in lesbian battering contexts, this marks intralesbian violence as qualitatively different from male battery of women, in which context the sexual nature of abuse does not necessarily require or in fact rely upon the ruse of erotic rituals.[14]

Differences between heterosexual and lesbian battering are not all speculative: there are also respects in which differences between female-on-female and male-on-female violence have been well documented suggesting that neither biologistic nor sex-role theories of intimate abuse fully capture the specificity of intralesbian violence. Many lesbians, even if "out" in other aspects of their lives, may decide not to disclose their sexual orientation to friends, family, or employers, for fear of loss of emotional support or the ability to sustain themselves financially. Anecdotal accounts reveal that one way in which psychological abuse is manifested between lesbians is by exploiting the vulnerability of the closeted or semicloseted lesbian by threatening to "out" her, or fostering her isolation and dependency on the abuser by in fact following through with such threats. This particular kind of abusive treatment is without

heterosexual equivalent. The fact that heterosexual women are sometimes accused of being lesbians by their abusive male lovers (Pharr 1988)
might arguably parallel the violence of "outing," or the threat thereof,
but the homology is obviously less than perfect.

Gloria Melnitsky, a therapist at the Gay and Lesbian Counselling service of Boston, notes as well that there are other distinct causes of woman-
on-woman abuse which seem to stem from the particular psychodynamics
of lesbian relationships. She observes, for instance, that the phenomenon
of "lesbian fusion"—or the melding of personalities/identities of women
involved in emotional/erotic relationships with each other—may precipitate unusually intense feelings of rejection or betrayal when a member
of a couple asserts her independence or indicates a need for separation.
Such feelings may partly account for why some lesbians resort to violent
extremes. As reported in the Gay Community News, Melnitsky has also
noticed in her work that, like heterosexual women, lesbians labor under
diminished senses of their self-worth, but in a compounded way: "When
you have two women, the sense of powerlessness, or clinging to whatever
power you get, is more acute" (quoted in Irvine 1984).

The lack of empirical proof of formal equivalence between male-on-
female and female-on-female violence aside, then, the claim to sameness,
especially in the biologistic account of domestic violence, is largely, if not
completely, undermined by the reality of the specificity of abuse between
and amongst lesbians. The sex-role paradigm could construct a rendering of the uniqueness of outing and fusion in the intralesbian dynamic,
presumably by relegating these phenomena to the realm of manifestations of internalized oppression. Apart from the more general problem
concerning its use as a convenient device to elide the shortcomings of
theory, there are more precise and profound respects in which accounting for the causes and cadence of the behavior of battering lesbians and
their victims through the vehicle of "false consciousness" is troubling.
In order for the sex-role argument to hold, lesbianism must be refigured
as the practice of heterosexual mockery, a play in which one participant
fills the role of "the boy" and the other "the girl." In Robson's (1990)
terms, the theory "hetero-relationizes" lesbianism. In so doing, feminist
theory of this sort feeds general heterosexist stereotypes about lesbians
in which fulfilling sexual connection is deemed impossible in the absence
of gender alterity, at best a bad copy and unfulfillable attempt to simulate
the "real thing." This imposition of a heteronormative framework upon
lesbian relationships is not only insulting, it is especially dangerous as a
cognitive device for understanding lesbian battering, because it feeds
the common myth about abusive lesbian relationships that "butches" are
batterers and "femmes" their victims.[15]

Taking Power Seriously

Although they sometimes advert to the heterosexism/homophobia displayed by the courts, the police, legislatures, and even battered women's shelters, biologistic and sex-role accounts frequently fail to factor these social realities into their analyses. In part, these theorists neglect to notice or attach much critical significance to systemic discrimination against lesbians, not because they dispute its existence, but because it falls outside the terms of the discourse within which their debate has been framed. That is, because the predominant concerns of biologistic and sex-role theorists relate almost entirely to the characteristics of intralesbian violence at an interpersonal, rather than institutional or societal level, the relation between lesbian battering and the larger context within which it occurs remains largely unexamined.

Feminists have long struggled with and disagreed over how to best respond to the material conditions of women's inequality, and that process, while sometimes more strategically than theoretically oriented, did implicate more basic questions about the meaning of gender subordination. The question of how to conceptualize domestic violence has not proved to be an exception: there have long been contending accounts within feminism of why spousal abuse happens, what its effects are, and how best to mobilize against it. It seems worth saying, however, that "liberal" paradigms of domestic violence, amongst which I would include the biologistic and sex-role views already discussed, have gained in prominence in recent years. My speculation is that this is so as a result of two, interrelated things: the growing commitment by feminists to ensure that theories of intimate abuse translate into the provision of concrete relief to individual women and, concomitantly, the increasing willingness of some grass-roots feminist movements to collaborate with the state in that endeavor. Women need safe houses in which they can seek refuge from the violence in their own homes. Women need litigators to assist them in fighting criminal charges, so that they will not end up incarcerated for having defended themselves against their abusers. But as Walker (1990) has demonstrated, the cost of state support for such initiatives has been the transmogrification of feminist discourse on domestic violence. The decided shift in feminists' focus away from a conceptualization of gender subordination as the system of male power over women buttressed by a wider network of social structures and institutions (and hence a critique of domestic violence grounded in these notions) to one founded more in individual or atomistic, notions of sex discrimination (and consequently a political analysis of domestic violence characterized by more classically liberal notions of harm) has been wrought by state involvement in feminists' struggles for social transformation.

As Johnston (1984) puts it, the systemic model of domestic violence emphasizes:

> the historical-legal precedent of male supremacy and the subordination of women in marriage and in society. The reasons men have historically beaten their wives originates [*sic*] from the belief that man has property rights over his partner. In return for economic dependence, women are expected to obey their husbands' demands. Wife abuse then is an extension of the social permission to control women. (Quoted in Walker 1990, p. 84)

There is no question but that male power in general, and the prerogative to chastise wives through physical punishment in particular, has been enshrined in Western culture across time. Acknowledging that this history has not been uniform, Dobash and Dobash nonetheless make a compelling case that, in Anglo-America, the right of men to use violence against their wives has long enjoyed not only normative, but legal status. While claims to cross-cultural uniformity are suspect, within the context of the United States at least, the legal institutionalization of male physical right over their spouses is well documented. After the American Revolution, the status enacted in the early colonies did not specifically entitle men to beat their wives, but judges imported the then-extant British common-law rule that assault was a legitimate way for husbands to "correct" their errant partners, Mississippi courts being the first to do so in 1824. Even after the legality of reasonable punishment was formally eschewed, judicial sympathy with the notion that it was no crime to assault one's wife continued to permeate the jurisprudence. Supported by legislatures' and judges' refusal/reluctance to regard physical violence against wives as an assault in law, police and prosecutors were loath to respond substantively to women's requests for protection from their abusive partners.

Law's reticence to interfere in the "private" relation between "man and wife" was understood by some feminists to be but one facet of larger, interlocking systems of social control of women by men. Swept into the analysis were economic and social relations, including the institution of marriage itself, to which they were integrally connected.[16] Marriage ostensibly offered women male support and protection, in a variety of senses, in exchange for the provision of household, reproductive, and sexual services. The attractiveness of the "bargain" was ensured through an interconnected web of social norms, practices, and ideologies. For instance, public-sphere labor opportunities for women were circumscribed to such an extent that dependency on a male wage was, for some women although certainly not all, virtually inescapable. The outright denial of the right to engage in waged labor, or somewhat less severely, the low remuneration afforded the paid labor women were permitted to perform, were rationalized on the footing that women could, should, and in fact did depend on the superior wage earning power of their husbands. So too, the notion that virtuous women confined their sexual encounters to the matrimonial bed permitted the neglect if not abuse of single mothers and their children at the hands of state agencies. Marriage not only offered women the potential of material comfort, it also held out the promise of psychic satisfaction and sexual safety. The twin rewards of desirability and legitimacy were granted to those women who could "get a man," and keep him. Single women, by contrast, labored under the stigma of being deemed neither attractive nor respectable. Unattached females were especially vulnerable to sexual violence, since their status as single women brought their veracity into question in contests over the meaning of sexual encounters. Thus, the practice of exclusive heterosexual monogamy was espoused as a shield from sexual assault, at least outside the home. In addition to these rationalizing discourses and practices, the social relegation of women to the private sphere was premised on the different nature of the public and private worlds, and the different nature of women and men. Women, through the operation of forces beyond human agency, were regarded as particularly suited to the realm of home and hearth, where the values of nurturance, caring, and connectedness reigned supreme. Men, by contrast, who by nature were self-interested and competitive, were better equipped to survive and perhaps thrive in the rough-and-tumble world of (public) work and (public) politics. The private, in general, and marriage, in particular, provided men some respite from the vicissitudes of public life. They offered a secure means of ensuring their bloodline, and unrestricted satisfaction of their sexual and emotional needs and desires. The price women paid in the "deal" of course, was the loss of many of the incidents of citizenship, particularly the right to corporeal integrity.[17]

This systemic analysis of male domination offered a rationale for why men battered their wives, and why women who found themselves in marriages marred by violence did not simply pack their bags and leave. Married women's violation of the gender-role expectations their husbands had of them could spark violent censure, but roles themselves formed only part of the total picture. Men enjoyed a proprietary relationship with their wives which entitled them to do with "their women" what they would. That relationship, moveover, was reinforced by an interconnected system of sociolegal rules and norms which rendered that which happened in private between a man and "his" wife nobody's affair but theirs, and thus beyond state scrutiny or intervention. From within this framework, appreciating why a woman who had been battered by her male intimate did not leave the relationship for a less violent, more fulfilling connection with someone else or for a satisfying life on her own did not rest solely upon the observation that repeated abuse profoundly affects one's sense of alternatives, that attempting to leave would assuredly attract heightened and perhaps fatal violence, or that one may yet continue to love someone otherwise so destructive. The social organization and institutional enforcement of the respective rights and responsibilities of men and women made leaving profoundly difficult.

Misreadings of systemic theorizing of why women's freedom to exit abusive relationships was so restrictive stem, I think, from its being taken too literally. Though the sexual protection racket has been identified by feminists as a constitutive element of malestream ideology and practice, awareness of the prevalence of marital and acquaintance rape belies any claim that women actually believe marriage offers them relative respite from sexually violent culture, and that women remain within violent marriages for that reason. The notion that leaving a relationships might expose one to heightened vulnerability to sexual assault is, in other words, more of a rationalizing discourse than material reality. But this is less true of women's fear of losing their children and their concern about their ability to be financially self-sustaining. Women who leave abusive male partners and take their children with them do attract state scrutiny, usually at the instigation of their abandoned lovers. Indeed, in some recent decisions, women who removed themselves and their children from violent situations lost custody on the footing that by allowing the violence to take place at all, they demonstrated themselves "unfit" to raise their offspring (Cahn 1991). So too, it is indisputable that the sex-discriminatory structure of the labor market operates as an impediment to women's ability to be economically independent particularly for those women who have relied on the superior financial stature of their male spouses.

Whether because it has taken a political backseat to more liberal accounts, or for some other reason, the systemic model of domestic violence has never, to my knowledge, been applied to the phenomenon of intralesbian violence. One rather obvious reason for this is that such systemic accounts have been so utterly premised on heterosexual relations that their transposition to a lesbian context seems self-evidently destined to fail. And, of course, on a very formalistic level, any theoretical model which posits the institution of marriage as its key element plainly does not speak to lesbian experience, since lesbians have been denied access to this institution, its common-law analogues, and the benefits that flow therefrom. But formalist arguments aside, more substantive engagement with the potential of the systemic critique of the causes and effects of domestic violence to make sense of the phenomena and experience of violence between lesbian intimates yields disappointment. That is to say, the particular sociopolitical inequalities undergirding the marriage relationship, which constitute the core of the critique, simply do not apply homologously to the phenomenon of lesbian battery, and perforce cannot offer the kind of explanatory power which feminist theory seeks to provide.

Of course, as women, lesbians, along with their heterosexual sisters, are victims of a misogynist culture marked by an inordinately high level of sexual violence, a profound devaluation of women's abilities, capabilities, and contributions in the world of work and beyond, and a studied indifference toward the well-being of mothers and their children, particularly if those mothers are "single." However, to the extent that women's inability to leave violent relationships was understood to hinge in part on a male-centered social order which worked to dissuade them from doing precisely that, the analysis cannot account for battered lesbians' impulse to stay in destructive relationships. There is, for example, arguably little correlation between women's economic dependency on their batterers and their economic vulnerability in the public sphere in the lesbian context. Lesbians share with heterosexual women unequal access to valued jobs as well as the devaluation of the work they do perform. But because many lesbians do not expect to rely on a male breadwinner, they are more likely to have engaged in waged labor in the public sphere, more likely, that is, to be economically self-sufficient. In consequence, unlike the very difficult situation faced by women who have depended upon a male wage and who worked without pay in the home, most lesbians have job histories upon which they can rely in seeking paid employment should they determine to leave a violent relationship and fend for themselves.[18] Lesbians are subject to sexual violence outside the home, to discrimination in employment, and to heightened state scrutiny of their relations with their children, but not or not only, it bears underscoring, because lesbians are women. The longer one remains in a lesbian relationship, the more likely one's lesbianism can become a matter of public knowledge. So too, leaving a troubled relationship often precipitates public awareness of one's lesbianism. Once the "fact" of one's lesbianism enters the public domain, heightened exposure to these risks and sanctions follows, almost as a matter of course.

In terms of explaining why battery happens, the systemic model again reveals itself to be heterosexually self-referential. Though the ideological devices of property and privacy powerfully support and entrench the practice of male supremacy, they do not, metaphorically or otherwise, capture why some lesbians are sometimes violent with their intimates, or why the institutions of dominant society react to the deployment of such violence as they do. There has never been, for instance, any philosophical or legal support for the idea that lesbian lovers enjoy a proprietary interest in one another or in their relationship. The point is perhaps best illustrated by the tragic story of Sharon Kowalski. Karen Thompson and Sharon Kowalski had been lovers for several years, had exchanged rings, and had named each other as beneficiaries in their respective life insurance policies. In 1983, Sharon was injured in a car accident which left her with extensive injuries: she was unable to walk, her communication skills were limited to hand and face signals, and her intellectual abilities were severely damaged. Karen Thompson petitioned for guardianship in order that she might make decisions concerning her lover's care. Kowalski's parents, or more accurately, Kowalski's father, immediately filed a counterpetition. In the interests of resolving the difficulties between them, and in order to further Sharon's best interests, Karen initially consented to the appointment of Donald Kowalski as guardian, but on the following conditions. She declined to recognize that Sharon's father was the most qualified or best suited to discharge the trust, and more importantly, secured for herself the right to equal access to relevant records, equal ability to consult with appropriate personnel, and equal right to visitation. Relations between Donald Kowalski and Karen Thompson continued to deteriorate, culminating in Mr. Kowalski's petitioning for termination of Thompson's rights. His motion was successful. Although the trial court directed Donald Kowalski to consider the best interests of the ward and any of her expressed wishes in making visitation decisions on Sharon's behalf, Kowalski immediately terminated Karen Thompson's visitation rights and moved Sharon to a different institution closer to her parent's home.

This turn of events prompted Karen Thompson to contest the fitness of Donald Kowalski as his daughter's guardian. The Minnesota courts rejected Thompson's challenge, crediting Mr. Kowalski's claim, in spite of his actions, that he loved his daughter "unconditionally." Mr. Kowalski's professed devotion to the well-being of his offspring proved superficial indeed. Sharon's expressed preference that Karen remain in her life was completely disregarded by her father, who not only denied that his daughter had maintained a long-standing lesbian relationship with Thompson, but asserted that even if such a relationship between Karen and Sharon had existed, the relationship was detrimental one, in that it would expose Sharon to the risk of sexual abuse. Seemingly, moreover, he was prepared to permit his child to decline in an institution rather than have any kind of connection with Sharon Thompson (*In re Guardianship of Kowalski*, 1986a and 1986b). Subsequent to his victory in the courts, Mr. Kowalski lost interest in tending to his daughter's needs. As a result, the courts opted to appoint as guardian a "friend" of the family, Karen

Tomberline, who had scarcely ever visited Sharon in the hospital, and had not even actually petitioned for guardianship. Although nine years after the accident the couple eventually succeeded in being reunited (*In re Guardianship of Kowalski*, 1992), what is so striking about their story is that the courts were prepared to appoint as guardians Donald Kowalski and Karen Tomberline, despite the fact that they both dealt with Sharon Kowalski as if she were nothing but a vehicle through which their homophobia might find expression, as if, that is, she were nothing but their chattel, their property.

What of the idea that the sanctity of the private sphere insulates batterers and entraps abused women? To put it bluntly, the notion that a lesbian's home is her castle, so to speak, and consequently, that state respect for lesbian privacy instills or reinforces battering lesbians' sense of entitlement to abuse their partners, is fanciful at best. As *Bowers v. Hardwick* (1986) so poignantly demonstrates, the state has no obligation to observe the boundaries separating public from private when it comes to "homosexuality." As is well known, Hardwick was charged with the crime of sodomy in violation of Georgia state law for engaging in sex with another man in the privacy of his own bedroom. Rejecting Hardwick's plea that the criminalization of homosexual sex violated the right to privacy established in other cases, the Supreme Court upheld the constitutionality of the statute. More than the legal holding of the case, the specific facts surrounding the prosecution of Michael Hardwick forcefully make the point that privacy is an inadequate conceptual device for analyzing same-sex abuse. Notably, the police's discovering Hardwick "in the act" involved more than investigative fortuity or, from the accused's point of view, inopportune hard luck. Mr. Hardwick's first encounter with the police took place outside a gay bar where Hardwick worked. Officer Torick of the Atlanta police witnessed Hardwick throw a beer bottle into a trashcan. He took Hardwick into custody in the back of his cruiser, questioned him, and charged him with drinking in a public place. Following this incident, Hardwick was subjected to a sustained pattern of harassment at the hands of the police. Due to a discrepancy on the charging ticket, Hardwick failed to present himself in court to answer to the public drinking charge. Very shortly thereafter, Officer Torick appeared at Hardwick's home with a warrant for his arrest. After having learned of the "visit," Hardwick immediately went to pay the fine. Some time later, Hardwick was severely beaten outside his home by three men who appeared to him to be police officers. It was only a few days after the beating that Officer Torick entered Hardwick's bedroom with a warrant for his arrest and charged Hardwick with sodomy.[19] Thus, when the Supreme Court upheld the constitutionality of the impugned law, it did more than deviate from established constitutional precedent:

by extension, it lent credence to the conduct of the police *vis-à-vis* Hardwick, and rendered ridiculous any suggestion that the "private" is available—as sword or shield—to lesbians and gays in their relations with the state.

Gender, Intimate Violence, and Lesbian Difference

Returning now to the framework for exploring questions of difference which I proposed at the beginning of this paper, where do these criticisms of existing accounts of domestic violence leave us? Self-evidently, since lesbian difference remains a problem for both individualist and systemic theories of abuse, neither can be preferred as more inclusive. It is not as if difference exists as a possible difficulty for one line of theory but not for the other. Somewhat less obviously, it does not appear to be the case that difference is less of a problem, quantitatively, for one genre of theorizing more than another. Thus, even if feminists were to make choices amongst competing accounts on the basis of an efficiency paradigm—and by no means am I suggesting that we should—considerations of economy would not resolve the difference dilemma.

An analysis of the kind of differences between the shortcomings made manifest by a critical review of prevailing accounts of domestic violence does not take one much further. Leaving aside any claim as to the relative superiority of systemic analyses of intimate abuse over individualist ones, it is impossible to choose between the competing accounts outlined here on the basis of the qualitative differences between the ways in which they deal with lesbian difference.[20]

For example, sex-role theorists' and gender detractors' neglect to attend to the possibility that intralesbian violence might not be sexualized in the same way as heterosexual violence is not an omission inconsequential to their theories. This sort of difference is not one which lies primarily within the realm of strategic choices but has substantive bearing on the validity of the paradigm as such. Much the same can be said of the systemic model's inability to account for lesbian specificity. Its insight that the ideologies of property and privacy play a key role in permitting domestic violence to continue are arguably of little explanatory force in the lesbian context. Given the centrality of notions of privacy and property to the systemic account of wife abuse, the notion that lesbian difference poses no fundamental challenge to the theory as such seems rather wishful. Nor do the differences which emerge from careful consideration of the adequacy with which feminist theories deal with differences of sexuality indicate that lesbians who are battered labor under a double burden—once as women and again as lesbians—and as such inhabit the bottom in some hierarchy of women who have been abused by their intimates. If, for example, it is true that intralesbian abuse is not sexualized as is heterosexual violence, would it not be possible to say that female-on-female violence is equally abusive but at the same time simply different from male-on-female violence? Or similarly, the systemic pressures which work to keep lesbians battering or being battered are clearly different from those which operate in heterosexual relations, but it is questionable whether they are necessarily worse. It seems to follow, then, that insofar as intralesbian violence is concerned, the shortcomings of extant feminist theories are not of mere formal omission that can be corrected by making the word "lesbian" part of an already established discourse. Likewise, it is doubtful that theorizing from the position of battered lesbians will produce an analysis which will be inclusive, in the sense that it will perforce speak to the experience of heterosexual women who have been victimized by their male lovers, as bottom-up theorizing tends to suggest.

It may well be that the inadequacies of existing feminist theories of domestic violence can be corrected, and a new, more inclusive paradigm created, but I leave that to others to attempt. Instead, I want to suggest that if one were to attend closely to the specificity of intralesbian violence and to conceptualize it as such, an account of lesbian battering as part and parcel of a larger pattern of antilesbian policies and practices suggests itself. My purpose in proceeding this way is neither to preempt efforts to produce umbrella theories nor to imply that the model I am about to outline is flawless. Indeed, I acknowledge that my model ought to undergo inquiry of the sort I detailed at the beginning of my paper: it, too, needs to be tested for its assumptions concerning different differences, different feminisms, and different contexts. Still, the advantage in articulating an account which seeks no more than to provide an understanding of the experiences of a circumscribed group of women is that it makes explicit the question of whether there is a basis upon which the construction of coalitional theories can proceed, a question that might otherwise be eclipsed in too determined a search for common ground.

There is an obvious connection between systemic homophobia/heterosexism and the vast silence which surrounds intralesbian abuse. Many lesbians are not "out," and coming out being diachronic in character in any event, no lesbian is "out" completely. To come out at any time is to make oneself vulnerable and to open oneself to disapprobation, discrimination, and violence. At risk is nothing less than the loss of emotional support of family and friends, the potential loss of one's children, the restriction of one's means to provide for oneself economically, and the sanctity of one' physical self. The difficulty is compounded in those situations where one publicly identifies as a lesbian in a time of crisis, as, for example, when one is abusing or being abused by one's lover. In order to get the particular kind of assistance they need, lesbians must come out as lesbians, because it is regularly assumed that all batterers are male and all victims, their female intimates (Chrystos 1986). Were it the case that lesbian abusers and victims received support and assistance for bringing to light the violent circumstances in which they find themselves, then perhaps coming out as a battered or battering lesbian would not be so fraught with risk. But the reality seems to be that those involved in violent lesbian relationships mostly do not make their troubles known, in large measure, because the responses to their attempts to seek assistance have been so sorely lacking. Indeed, the specific ways in which intralesbian violence has been greeted both by the lesbian community and by the "social problem apparatus"—legislatures, courts, shelters, and counselors—have encouraged continued silence around intralesbian violence.

For example, lesbians themselves have been less than enthusiastic about confronting the problem of intralesbian abuse. Lesbian unwillingness to accept that lesbians might deploy violence against one another stems in part from their ideals about what lesbian community is, can, and should be, and from concerns regarding the use to which such information might be put in a heterosexist/homophobic society. Victims have complained of the studied reluctance of their lesbian sisters to accept that they have been subjected to violence by their lovers, even in the face of such obvious and compelling physical evidence as prominent bruises and broken bones. Many lesbians, especially those who became lesbians through their involvement in feminist politics, have aspired to create a women's community superior to that of dominant heterosexual society, in the bosom of which each individual woman may pursue her own development free of inappropriate coercion and constraint by others. Confronted with the ugly reality that the creation of all-woman space did not necessarily promise an environment in which self-actualization would flourish, the problem of battering within lesbian communities was downplayed, even denied, by lesbians themselves. But aside from the failure of the utopian dream of a happy, healthy, women's community, the very real fear that knowledge of intralesbian violence would be ignored or misused by those hostile to lesbians also contributes to lesbians' desire to dismiss the existence and/or significance of lesbian battering.

In anecdotal accounts, lesbian victims of intimate abuse charge that victim services offered by feminists have been inappropriately denied them. The philosophical conundrum faced by shelter workers forced to choose between a pair of lesbian lovers, both claiming to be abused, and both seeking a safe place to stay, is not unknown. Even when lesbians claiming to be battered have approach shelters singly, they still have been denied entitlement to basic support services. Reports indicate that lesbians have been denied access to safe houses because it would be awkward to integrate them into the communal atmosphere shelters attempt to create. Shelter residents and workers would, it has been claimed, be forced into uncomfortable association with lesbians against their will. This discomfort has apparently been regarded as more terrible than the harm of denying a lesbian in danger safe refuge. As well, because many shelters have increasingly come to rely on state support to fund the services they provide, their activities have consequently come under more searching state review and regulation. Anxious about being forced to close their doors, and having been (perhaps inaccurately) accused of being man-hating lesbians themselves, some shelter staff have been known to deny lesbian access in order not to risk offending funders.

In the face of resistance from their own communities and from those who ostensibly were allies, some lesbians have found it necessary to invoke the power of law and other dominant institutions in the hope of securing the protection they need. Quite unsurprisingly, however, the response of these institutions to intralesbian violence has not been markedly different. "Law" has seemed basically unwilling to extend even rudimentary legal protections to lesbians who have been victimized by their intimates. Although there are exceptions,[21] most statutes regulating domestic violence services and providing for temporary restraining orders are limited in application to spouses.[22] A victim must, in other words, be involved in a legally recognized relationship with an abuser in order to gain access to these protections. But most marriage solemnization statutes are expressed in heterosexual terms. And even when open to more inclusive interpretation, courts have declined to read such legislation so as to allow state recognition of same-sex unions.[23] Constitutional challenges to heterosexual definitions of marriage[24] and common-law relationships[25] have almost uniformly failed.[26] The result, in many jurisdictions, then, is that a lesbian cannot even get a temporary restraining order to protect herself from her abuser.

To the extent that any relief to lesbian abusers and their victims has been forthcoming, it has been a mixed blessing. Assistance has often been conditioned on a construction of lesbian relationships as inherently pathological, thus contributing to lesbian reluctance to make lesbian violence public. Although sexual orientation was formerly removed as a psychiatric illness in and of itself in 1973, counselors, therapists, psychologists, and psychiatrists may nonetheless entertain discriminatory ideas about lesbians which can influence their judgment in dealing with lesbian clients. As Hammon (1988) notes, mainstream counselors may use the fact of violence to illustrate to the client the perverted or sick nature of lesbian relationships. She suggests that clients may be urged to change their sexual orientation or to put up with the abuse if they refuse, rather than to deal with the violence. Similarly, even in those instances where courts have the authority to issue a temporary restraining order against a lesbian who has abused her lover, they, seemingly, are unable to differentiate between the perpetrator and the victim in such cases, and tend to issue mutual orders (Corimer 1986). The cause of the courts' confusion is a matter of some mystery. It has been suggested that abused lesbians are inclined to fight back more than their heterosexual counterparts (Porat 1986), a fact which may account for judges' propensity to regard lesbian battery as a shared endeavor. That they do not experience the same difficulties in heterosexual cases suggests, however, that the problem resides more in their attitude towards lesbians and lesbianism than in the rhythm of intralesbian violence.

It is an insight of no profound dimension to suggest that systemic oppression of lesbians is bound up with the problem of lesbian battering and its reception in various public spheres. And perhaps because of its sheer obviousness, nothing much has been made of it by gender theorists of domestic violence. Here, however, I want to take what seems a rather quotidian insight and push it somewhat further.

The argument that erasure from the cultural imagination distinguishes lesbian oppression from other forms of systemic inequality is by no means novel: the observation that, unlike heterosexual women and gay men,[27] lesbians labor under the unique burden of being invisible has long been made by lesbian critics.[28] To the extent, then, that battering is connected with this notion of erasure, neither gender nor gay theories of intimate abuse, which do not factor enforced invisibility into their analyses, can speak fully to the experience of lesbians with domestic violence. And plainly, there is a relationship between invisibility and battering. If erasure is understood to exist on a continuum, from closetry at one pole to physical annihilation at the other, the phenomenon of intralesbian violence can be seen to span its entire spectrum. Battering complicates the difficult process of coming out, and contributes to the already widespread reticence to do so. Battered or battering lesbians have ample reason, as I have shown, not to come out as lesbians. The shame of individuals involved in such relationships, and the silence or ignorance with which their appeals for assistance are met, all foster closetry. Although the reluctance to announce one's lesbianism in problematic circumstances is understandable, if coming out is practised only by trouble-free lesbians on safe occasions, surely it is going to happen less often.

At the other extreme, battering fosters and sometimes accomplishes erasure in its most graphic and literal sense: dead lesbians are neither seen nor heard. Although one could say that it is internalized self-hatred, a belief that a lesbian really ought not to inhabit the earth, that feeds a battering lesbian's motivation to abuse and a battered lesbian decision to withstand her own violation, my point does not stop with such psycho-analytic insights. Whether or not it is self-loathing that drives the battering dynamic, the further question remains as to how to conceive of the response of the social problem apparatus, a response most often characterized by a seeming indifference. Societal willingness to allow lesbians to wreak destruction on one another unchecked and unabated begins to appear very much like a kind of genocidal practice. Sisters, as the song goes, are doin' it for themselves.

Conclusion

Taking account of lesbian specificity in the domestic violence context poses some rather profound difficulties for future feminist theorizing of intimate abuse. To the extent research on domestic violence suggests a common experience across sexualities, and hence a basis for coalition and shared struggle, it lies in the realm of individual experience, and more particularly, in the psychological impact on victims of sustained abuse. Beyond the unhappy irony of resolving dilemmas of difference by resort to such narrow conceptions of common ground, there is also the non-unimportant point that to do so obliterates much of what must be integral to lesbians' experiences of domestic violence. More fundamentally, though, there is a serious question as to why feminists should necessarily require commonality of experience among women as a basis for viable political unity.

My own tentative view is that heterosexual and lesbian feminists can join cause against domestic tyranny in a way that both attends to the specificity of male-on-female and female-on-female violence and respects what is common to both. Lesbians need our own conceptual paradigms for making sense of the particularities of intralesbian violence, and the notion of invisibility may serve us particularly well in that regard. So too, heterosexual women should not be required to forfeit too readily theoretical models which speak meaningfully to the violence of their intimate relations with men. What all of this means for feminist praxis in the future and, in particular, for the possibilities of dealing with lesbian batterers, is the challenge that remains to be confronted.

Notes

For their assistance, I would like to thank Roxanne Mykitiuk and Martha Fineman. Particular thanks are due, as always, to Sheila McIntyre. Support for this research was provided by the Social Sciences and Humanities Research Council of Canada and Columbia University in the City of New York.

1. My observation concerning common elisions within feminist writing on the difference question ought not to be taken as an indictment of individual authors. My intention,

rather, is to only to outline what I regard as general trends in the literature, to which there may of course be occasional exceptions.

2. The phrase is, of course, MacKinnon's (1987).

3. I do realize there are implications involved in the choice of language used to describe abuse of women at the hands of their intimates in the home, that there have been debates specifically around the issue of appropriate terminology, and that the linguistic choices I have made in this paper may consequently to a source of consternation to some. However, since may purpose is to explore the gender/heterosexuality of domestic violence, the use of gender or heterosexual specific labels like "wife abuse" seemed inappropriate.

4. For example, even of those who subscribe to the view that other systems of oppression combine together with sex inequality to create more burdensome experiences of gender domination, they are still allowing for the possibility that race etc. operate as connected but nonetheless separate systems.

5. That lesbian oppression can be accounted for under the theoretical paradigm of "gender" is not a claim unique to the domestic violence context. Much the same argument has been advanced within the specific phenomenological contexts of lesbian S/M, lesbian pornography, and indeed, as a general theoretical proposition. Given the methodological approach I am advocating, it follows that I make no claim here about the "gender" of lesbian pornography or lesbian S/M. Those phenomena, too, must be examined within and having regard to their own specifics.

6. The same problem is brought into sharper relief in the sexual harassment context; Remedies for sexual harassment were secured on the footing that sexual harassment was a gendered activity, and as such, amounted to sex discrimination in violation of civil rights law. The possible extension of remedies against sexual harassment beyond the male violator, female victim situation raises the question of whether sexual harassment was rightly conceived as a form of sex discrimination. For reasons which space does not permit me to detail here, there has been a greater reluctance to regard the battered woman defence as anything other than a plea of self-defence, cognizable within orthodox criminal doctrine,. and not a separate defence available only to women defendants. Nevertheless, to the extent that the theoretical foundations supporting the battered woman defence are similar to those which grounded a cause of action for sexual harassment, the risks engendered by opening up such pleas to all manner of people are the same.

7. The critical reader will notice that I rely on a notion of a "lesbian" class and its "experience" in my examination of intralesbian violence, without making any effort to interrogate or problematize either concept. I acknowledge that my use of the category "lesbian" betrays its own brand of essentialism (see Sullivan 1994), my invocation of their "experience" a kind of empiricism (see Scott 1992), and my developing a methodology which depends on such concepts, a sort of scientism. I use these notions only for their teleological value. I believe that without them, certain kinds of questions are not possible. And indeed, I do not understand the critique of feminism's own universalisms to be a command (see Butler 1992). I make no claim, therefore, to the transcendental soundness of my analysis, and specifically invite critique in the hopes that the questioning of foundations will continue.

8. Of the some 277 legal articles dealing with battered women that I reviewed, four papers dealt with lesbian or gay intimate abuse in a sustained way, and eight made passing reference to the phenomenon.

9. Interestingly, Suzanne Pharr's (1988) oft-cited generic analysis of heterosexism/homo-phobia as "a weapon" of sexism grew out of her struggle to bring lesbian issues to the attention of women working within the battered women's movement.

10. For a taxonomy of heterosexual intimate violence, see Straus and Gelles (1986).

11. Figures reflect percentages of respondents who answered yes to the query whether each type of violence happened "frequently/sometimes."

12. To be more precise, Renzetti's estimate was for those who had been in an abusive relationship for one to five years. The figures were considerably smaller for those who had been in an abusive relationship for less than one year (twenty-one percent) or for more than five years (fourteen percent).

13. In *Naming the Violence*, and to a lesser extent in Renzetti's work, contributors/respond-ents seemed also to be solidly feminist-identified. Many of the contributors to the anthology were active in the battered women's movement or other feminist endeavors prior to their involvement (political or experiential) with battered lesbians' issues: one was working in a battered women's shelter while simultaneously involved in a violent relationship, another was abused by a woman who earned her living as a therapist for battered women. A substantial number of Renzetti's contacts were gar-nered through lesbian feminist networks: questionnaires were sent to women's organi-zations and agencies, women's bookstores and bars, and a paid advertisement was taken out in *Off Our Backs*. I want to be cautious in raising this point. It is not my claim that the fact that such studies as there are suffer from feminist bias, and as such are not useful informational barometers. At the same time, I do think that the consequences of having a sample so weighted toward those schooled in feminist precepts need to be explored.

14. Similarly unexplored is the question whether there is a lesbian analog to "femicide." Although there are scattered reports of abusive lesbians taking their violence to the ultimate extreme, it is as yet unknown whether lesbian victims are murdered to the same horrifying extent as are women in relationships with abusive men (Côté 1992).

15. In a sense, the problem with labeling lesbian abusers "male" parallels the conceptual difficulty of how to account for the variety of female experience which has been generated by feminist attempts to theorize the impact of male violence against women. Some feminists suggested that women who were systematically abused lost the capacity to envision for themselves a way to escape the violence, but their model could not successfully account for the fact that at some point and for some reasons such women "victims" became their own agents and chose to act—indeed to act in definitive ways, either by finding the strength within themselves to leave, or by striking back fatally against their abusers. Relatedly, associating gender with the commission of socially "male" acts does not allow for he possibility that a lesbian who batters is also gendered female in other respects.

16. Since my purpose here is to test various feminist theories for their applicability to lesbian battery, I only sketch out those theories in a general and perfunctory way. In so doing, I hope I do not do a complete disservice to those who have detailed these accounts in much more sophisticated terms. For an excellent elaboration, refer-ence should be had to Olsen (1983).

17. The theoretical framework I have just sketched was plainly premised on the experi-ence of white, middle- and upper-class women. I have neglected to devote any textual space to race- and class-based critiques of this model, not because I find them uncon-vincing or in some sense ancillary, but because my purpose here is, in the tradition of those critiques, to test this analysis for its utility to lesbians.

18. A recent comparative study conducted in Canada found that "single" women fared better economically than divorced or separated women as well as divorced or separated men, although they of course lagged behind "single" men.

19. For a fuller telling of "the untold story" of *Bowers v. Hardwick*, 478 U.S. 186 (1986) see Thomas 1992.

20. Though these observations may seem somewhat self-evident, they may provide the foundation for a much broader point concerning the philosophy of theorizing difference. While they do indeed yield different differences, neither individualist nor systemic accounts fare better in terms of dealing with the differences their shortcomings reveal. This may suggest that classic divisions between "liberal" and more radical modes of theorizing "women," divisions which were so central, for instance, to the sexuality debates of the 1980s, apparently do not assist in coming to terms with the challenges of difference. Whether or not this will hold true in other contexts awaits further research.

21. For example, Ohio law provides that "no person shall knowing cause or attempt to cause physical harm to a family or household member" Ohio Rev. Code Ann. § 2919.25(A) (Page's 1991). Family or household member is defined in the legislation as a "spouse" or "person living as a spouse" (§ 2919.25(D)(1)(a)), and the latter, in turn, is defined as "a person who is living or has lived with the offender in a common law marital relationship, who otherwise is cohabiting with the offender, or who otherwise has cohabited with the offender within one year prior to the date of the alleged commission of the act in question" (§ 2919.25(D)(2)). In *State v. Hadinger* (1991), 373 N.E. 2d 1191 (Ohio Ct. App) the Ohio Court of Appeals interpreted the statutory definition of "person living as a spouse" to apply to a woman who had bitten the hand of the woman with whom she was living. Strausbaugh J. reasoned that two women who were "living together" could be considered persons living as spouses within the meaning of the legislation, since the term "cohabit" did not require the existence of sexual intercourse. Such, I suppose, are the spoils of legal victory.

22. See, for example, Cal. Penal Code § 273.5 (West 1985 & Supp. . 1992).

23. See, for instance, *Baker v. Nelson*, 191 N.W. 2d 185 (Minn. 1971), *Jones v. Hallahan*, 501 S.W. 2d 588 (KY 1973), and *Singer v. Hara*, 522 P. 2d 1187 (Wash. Ct. App. 1974).

24. *Ibid.*

25. *DeSanto v. Barnsley*, 476 A. 2d 952 (Pa. Super. Ct. 1984).

26. But, see, *Baehr v. Lewin*, 852 P. 2d 44 (Haw. 1993).

27. In saying this, I do not mean to suggest that lesbians alone experience deemed nonexistence by the dominant order. Invisibility also figures in the social subordination of people with disabilities, amongst others, but my sense is that it operates differently in those contexts.

28. See, for example, Frye 1983; and Eaton 1990. It may be that lesbian invisibility is an "intersectional" form of oppression (Crenshaw 1989), a product of the unique combination of sex inequality and heterosexism/homophobia, or that it constitutes a separate system of domination in its own right, but the investigation of such questions is beyond the scope of the present article.

The Death Penalty
and the Domestic Discount

by Elizabeth Rapaport

Introduction

The great majority of those sentenced to die in the United States, at least seventy-five percent, killed in the course of committing another serious felony.[1] Most often the victim is a stranger to his or her killer, less often an acquaintance. Domestic homicides, the killing of close kin and sexual intimates, rarely result in a death sentence. While such crimes can be predatory, for the most part they involve patterns of fact and motivation which Anglo-American law treats as mitigating moral blame and criminal liability. Hot-blooded killing, striking out in anger at one who has injured or inflamed his or her killer, is regarded as less reprehensible than premeditated or predatory killing. In this article I will argue that the traditional hot-blood/cold-blood dichotomy is an imperfect guide to the moral grading of homicide offenses. In particular, reliance on it has led to the underevaluation of the seriousness of some domestic homicides.

My thesis, then, is that the moral coherence of the law of homicide requires parity of offense seriousness as between the worst predatory and the worst domestic murders. To avoid misunderstanding I will enter some caveats at the outset: first, I do not advocate capital punishment. I focus on capital sentences because this allows the study of what we, as a society regard as the most reprehensible killing. My interest in isolating those domestic killings which rank among the most egregious offenses in contemporary American society should not be confused with endorsement of capital punishment. *Furman v. Georgia* condemned the former capital punishment regime for sending a few arbitrarily and capriciously selected wretches to die while the no less guilty received lesser sentences; the successor system retains the flaws condemned in *Furman* (Baldus 1990, Gross and Mauro 1991). Second, I make no brief that criminal

224

law is either the best or the only means of combating domestic violence—
or other forms of violence—much less that capital punishment enhances
the efficacy of our law of homicide. Nonetheless, the criminal law has
didactic as well as other powers that can be deployed to control domestic
violence; but the law itself must recognize the severity of domestic violence before it can best serve to combat it.

Although the capital sentencing of domestic killers is relatively unusual,
a small minority of convicted killers are sent to America's death rows.[2] My
study of domestic death row revealed that men and women (who comprise
a tiny fraction of the total death row population) are sent to death row for
strikingly different kinds of domestic murder.[3] This study was not designed to probe gender discrimination in capital sentencing (Rapaport
1991), but rather to determine what elevates a domestic homicide—normally the virtual antithesis of capital murder—to a capital offense.

In six states studied, male domestic killers comprised slightly less than
twelve percent of death-sentenced males, while female domestic killers
comprised almost half of all women sentenced to death in the United
States from 1978 to 1989. Female domestic killers comprise a much
larger fraction of the total death row population of their sex than do
male domestic killers. Almost half the women on death row killed family
or intimates; a far smaller proportion of the men are domestic killers.
Men and women are sent to death row for different sorts of domestic
crimes: almost half the men killed in retaliation for a woman's leaving a
sexual relationship,[4] while this pattern was quite rare among the women;
more than two-thirds of the women killed family and sexual intimates
for pecuniary gain, while this motive was rare among the men. The
following table displays the relationships between the type of domestic
murder and the gender of the offenders on death row.

Women who have killed for economic advantage, then, dominate female domestic death row. Here is the most abhorred female domestic
crime: dependence turned to gall and greed, trust betrayed, love and
duty mocked. The case of a North Carolina woman illustrates the female
domestic capital murderer of this type. Barbara Stager was sentenced
to die for shooting her sleeping husband to prevent him from discovering
her bad debts and to regain her financial poise (*Stager v. State*). Evidence
was heard at her trial from which it could be readily inferred that she
had killed her first husband in substantially the same way. While sixty-
nine percent of female domestic death row killed for profit, only thirteen
percent of male domestic death row killed for economic gain.

Almost half the men killed in retaliation for a wife or lover leaving
them, although the victims of these killers were sometimes the children
and relatives of the women as well as, or in place of, the women themselves.[5] These separation cases differ from stereotypical domestic killings

Table 1. Domestic Death Row by Gender and Type of Murder. Death-sentenced Men in AZ, GA, IL, NC, and PA, 1976 to 1991 and Women, nationwide, 1978 to 1989.

	MEN		WOMEN	
Total Number Death Row Offenders	699		54	
	#	%	#	%
Offenders Whose Victims Were Domestic	83	12%	26	48%
Type of Domestic Victim Murder:	#	%	#	%
Pecuniary Motive	11	13%	18	69%
Retaliatory Motive	40	48%	2	8%
Other	32	39%	6	23%
Total Domestic Victim Cases	83	100%	26	100%

that flow out of arguments in that they are planned, and follow the dissolution of a household or relationship by weeks or months.[6] The killer, having failed by threats or entreaties to dissuade a spouse or lover from leaving, executes her. Unlike the predatory killer sentenced to death row, these men killed out of consuming emotion. Many such killers show little interest in concealing their crimes or avoiding arrest; often the killer is so focused on his mission that he is indifferent to witnesses, unprepared for or interested in flight. There is a coda frequently heard in these cases, a statement to the arresting officer along the lines of: "I'm glad I killed her," or: "I'd do it again."

If the object in view is to understand domestic violence, and the law's role in defining, censuring, preventing (and perpetuating), and punishing domestic violence, the men's cases, the separation cases, are of considerably more theoretical interest than the women's cases, the cases of murder for money. The men are failed and defied patriarchs who have been publicly condemned, literally, for exacting retribution. The bulk of women's domestic death row cases are not politically resonant crimes of domestic violence, if they are properly classed as crimes of domestic violence at all within the relevant meaning of the term; they are economic crimes with intimate victims. It is of course possible, harking back to the ancient crime of petty treason, that is, the murder of a man by his wife, child, or servant to read these women's crimes as political acts, as acts of rebellion and usurpation of both the power and substance of men. In my view, however, the cases with political significance are the men's cases, while the women's cases are "common" crimes made spectacular by the sex of their perpetrators—women are supposed to nurture and support, not destroy and despoil—and by the intimate bond between the unfemale female killer and her prey—here are women who are predatory towards those who have most deeply engaged them as women, whether as wives and lovers, mothers, or in other familial roles.[7]

Our law of homicide generally exhibits a bias against treating domestic homicide as seriously as some other categories of arguably no more reprehensible homicide, notably predatory crime. I will support this claim by pursuing two lines of feminist critique. I will argue that skepticism is in order about the extent to which we allow heated anger to defend (the worst) hot-blooded domestic killers from more stringent accountability.[8] However, I will first argue that there is a tendency to discount the seriousness of cold-blooded domestic separation cases as well, to find mitigation in the pain and anger that are certainly experienced by the separation murderer. There is resistance to treating any sort of nonpredatory domestic homicide as of the first rank of seriousness. I call this phenomenon, whether enshrined in traditional doctrine or the impetus to new doctrine, "the domestic discount." This resistance can be found in the opinions of some appellate courts reviewing the death sentences meted out to men who have killed because women have left them. These courts have created doctrines and standards which discourage the future capital prosecution of domestic separation cases as capital murder.

The Domestic Discount in Appellate Review

The most well-known domestic separation death penalty case in the United States is *Godfrey v. Georgia. Godfrey* is a classic separation murder case. Godfrey's wife had left the marital home several weeks prior to her death at her husband's hands. She had filed for divorce and resisted repeated efforts on Godfrey's part to promote reconciliation. Godfrey went armed with his shotgun to his mother-in-law's trailer, where his wife was living. He shot his wife through the window, entered the trailer, swatted his fleeing eleven-year-old daughter with the barrel of his gun, and then shot his mother-in-law. Both women were shot in the head, and both died instantly. The police found Godfrey waiting for them. Godfrey told an officer that he had "done a hideous crime" and that he would "do it again."[9]

At issue in *Godfrey* was whether the supreme court of Georgia, in affirming Godfrey's death sentence, had relied on an overly broad and vague construction of an aggravating circumstance found in the Georgia capital statute, that the offense was "outrageously or wantonly vile, horrible or inhuman in that it involved torture, depravity of mind, or aggravated battery to the victim." (GA Code Ann., 1978, Section 27–

2534.1(b)(7). *Godfrey* is renowned not for its domestic subject matter, but because it establishes that the much-criticized "exceptional vileness" factor, which in substantially equivalent formulations—the language may invoke "cruelty," "heinousness," or "brutality"—is found in the statutes of the majority of death penalty states, has withstood concerted challenges from its critics; its critics had castigated the factor as vague and standardless. However, Justice Stewart's opinion in *Godfrey* also put prosecutors on notice that the tactic of relying on the especially vile or brutal factor as a handy catchall vehicle for bringing a domestic case forward capitally in the absence of evidence of other aggravating circumstances is problematic. Noting that Godfrey's victims "were members of his family who were causing him extreme emotional trauma,"[10] Justice Stewart concluded that the case could not be considered more brutal than the average run of murders where no death penalty was imposed.

A survey of the capital jurisdictions revealed three states, North Carolina, Illinois, and Florida, with judicially created exemption from capital punishment for domestic murderers. The absence of such doctrine in the remaining capital punishment states is by no means a clear indication that the domestic discount is recognized only in North Carolina, Illinois, and Florida. The domestic discount may well operate tacitly. And the evolution of contemporary capital punishment law, a regime not yet twenty years old, may see additional states develop formal domestic discount doctrines.

Godfrey in North Carolina: The Stanley Case

North Carolina v. Stanley is a capital domestic separation case whose facts are similar to those in *Godfrey*, and in which the sole aggravating circumstance, as in *Godfrey*, was extreme brutality, or in its North Carolina variant, that the murder was "especially heinous, atrocious or cruel." (N.C.G.S. 15A–2000(e)(9)). In an opinion which, more than *Godfrey* itself, emphasizes that the underlying murder is of the domestic separation type, the North Carolina Supreme court held the case was controlled by *Godfrey*. Stanley is situated as a killer who, like Godfrey, was responding to "extreme emotional trauma" caused by his wife/victim. The North Carolina Supreme Court forbade submitting the especially heinous factor to the jury in cases with fact patterns like *Godfrey* or *Stanley*. It held that such evidence could not support the conclusion that the extent of brutality exceeded that considerable quantum present in any first-degree murder.

Stanley is notable because it goes further than *Godfrey* in excluding domestic separation cases in which there are no traditional public enemy indicia of extreme reprehensibility, such as a record of prior felony convictions—which sometimes do encumber domestic killers as well as armed robbers—from capital adjudication, and therefore from the ranks of the most reprehensible murders known to our society. *Stanley* is more explicit than *Godfrey* in making domestic separation murder the paradigm case of the constitutionally improper punishment of ordinarily brutal murder as a death penalty offense.

In *Stanley*, as in *Godfrey*, the defendant's wife had left him and was seeking a divorce. Some six months after the couple separated Joyce Stanley was shot by her husband under the following circumstances: she had gone to her mother's home for Sunday dinner with members of her family. Stanley drove back and forth in front of the house five or six times. When the victim and some members of her family went outside to note Stanley's license plate number, Stanley drove up and shot her nine times from his car at close range. He was disarmed by two of his wife's relatives, remarked, "that's all right, I killed the bitch," then drove to the police station and surrendered.

The elastic extreme brutality aggravating circumstances, which encompasses psychological as well as physical suffering, is certainly copious enough to permit the development of an interpretation of the facts in cases like *Stanley* or *Godfrey* which find the basis of extreme brutality precisely in their being separation murders. The victims in each of these cases had been harassed and threatened by her husband in incidents involving weapons. In *Godfrey* the incident precipitating the wife's departure had been her husband's cutting some of the clothes she wore off her body with a knife; while in *Stanley* some six weeks before the murder Joyce Stanley observed her estranged husband first parked in front of her home, then standing in her yard with a rifle. Each woman had found it necessary to obtain warrants against her husband. The record also reveals that Godfrey had been a violent husband. These women may have lived and died with intense, well-founded fear of their husbands after separation. But as it happens, the imaginations of the authors of *Godfrey* and *Stanley* were attending not to the experience of the victims but to the rejection suffered by their killers.

It is possible to argue—I have just done it—that the experience of the victim in a separation murder can be one of painful suspense and intense suffering. And there certainly are separation murders that qualify as exceptionally brutal crimes by any measure of brutality. However, it obscures rather than captures the moral basis of ranking separation murders among the most reprehensible types of murders—where they may well deserve to be ranked—to focus exclusively on their degree of brutality.

If the capital murder statutes—or alternatively a noncapital homicide law regime—reflected a feminist sensibility, the murder of defecting spouses, lovers, and their surrogates might be ranked among the most reprehensible crimes, as reprehensible as predatory murder. From a feminist perspective, separation murder can be seen as the extreme of domestic tyranny, the refusal to acknowledge the independence of a woman from the will of her husband or lover at any price. If consuming a human life in appropriating the property of another is ranked among the most reprehensible murders, then deliberate destruction of another's life that cannot any longer otherwise be controlled is no less reprehensible.

Of course the law of homicide does not codify the just-stated feminist insight, if insight it is. Indeed, current law, when it focuses on separation murder as a distinct category of crime, tends to interpret it not from a feminist perspective but from a perspective of empathy with the pain caused the defendant by the defection of his spouse or lover. This is illustrated by *Carlson v. Illinois;* the Illinois Supreme Court saw Carlson's crime as one mitigated by the tragedy of his loss rather than aggravated by the enormity of murdering a woman who chose to be his wife no longer.

Tragedy in Illinois

Robert Carlson hoped to remarry the wife who had divorced him after nineteen years of marriage. The record reveals a man who was assiduously courting his ex-wife, running her errands, giving her money and gifts—there is no hint of abuse or intimidation—until the point at which he learned that another man was replacing him and that there would be no remarriage. The apparently callous and obtuse Rosemary Carlson rubbed salt in Carlson's wounds by complacently showing him her new diamond engagement ring and other gifts from his rival. Two days after Carlson was told there would be no remarriage he bought a gun, and the following day he bought two cans which he filled with gasoline and stowed in the trunk of his car. The next day, the day on which Rosemary displayed her diamond engagement ring and other symbols of her transfer of loyalties, Carlson shot her ten times, soaked three rooms with gasoline, and set fire to the house. When police officers came into the bar to arrest him, he shot and killed one of the officers. The two murder charges were consolidated. Carlson was actually sentenced to die for the murder of the officer and to fifty to one hundred years for the murder of his former wife.[11] Carlson fared better on direct appeal to the supreme court of Illinois.

The trial judge had concluded that the mitigating value of Carlson's lack of criminal history was "diminished greatly, if not totally extinguished, by the fact that a few hours before the murder of [the police officer] the defendant had with malice aforethought brutally murdered his wife and committed arson of the house in which her body lay." The Illinois Supreme Court held this was error. The Illinois Supreme Court described the arson and two murders as "a part of one unfortunate and tragic event precipitated by the events leading up to the killing of Rosemary." Carlson was entitled to mitigating credit for the conduct of his life prior to the tragedy. The testimony of Carlson's personal physician told more heavily with the appellate court:

> The doctor testified that for a year or two prior to [the murder] the defendant had deteriorated physically and emotionally . . . the doctor had counseled both Rosemary and the defendant concerning their marital difficulties . . . the defendant's two heart attacks had left him "partly disabled and really incapable of leading a complete and fulfilling life for a man in his early forties." He stated that the defendant, during this time, was undergoing a slow grieving process related to the loss of the affection of his wife.

Justice Ryan concludes his sympathetic recasting of Carlson's story with these words:

> These mitigating circumstances do not bespeak a man with a malignant heart who must be permanently eliminated from society . . . we see an individual with no past criminal record who would in all probability be leading a life acceptable to our society had not his unfortunate marital affair triggered this tragic sequence of events.

In 1986 the Illinois Supreme Court vacated the death sentence in another domestic murder case, *Illinois v. Buggs,* holding that the mitigating circumstances in that case "twin" those in *Carlson,* and entitled Buggs to similar sentencing relief. With the *Buggs* decision, the Illinois Supreme Court creates an exemption from capital punishment for nonpredatory spouse killers.

Buggs is not a separation murder case. Rather, it fits the pattern of what most people think of when they conjure up domestic homicide. The murder followed another 3 A.M. argument between Buggs and his wife about her infidelity—the fight was precipitated by a phone call from one of Loretta's boyfriends. The crime does, however, have some separationlike motifs. It was preceded not only by confirmation of his wife's extramarital interests but also by Loretta flinging at Buggs that two sons he thought were his were not in fact fathered by him. Buggs responded by pouring gasoline over Loretta and elsewhere in his home. As a result Loretta and a son were killed and a daughter severely burned.

Several children who had been asleep when the fire started escaped the burning house.

Although the majority opinion painted Buggs's crime as a lethal outburst, the spontaneous escalation of an argument between a faithless wife and an alcoholic husband, Justice Miller's dissent adduces parts of the record which cast the crime in a different light. Buggs had prepared for the confrontation by bringing gasoline into the house and hiding it in a closet. Despite his drinking problem, Buggs was not drunk on the night he set fire to his home. Apparently, Buggs did not strike out in reactive anger but executed a plan of action.

The Illinois Supreme Court set aside Buggs's death sentence because the tragic circumstances which led to it, as well as a life blameless, even admirable, in the world of men, precluded classifying Buggs as among the worst murderers. The majority emphasizes that, Buggs like Carlson, was a middle-aged man with a history of military service and no criminal history. Like Carlson, Buggs was in decline, drinking heavily enough to cause blackouts. Like Carlson, but for "marital disharmony" and "a dispute which triggered this tragic sequence of events" Buggs would presumably still be living "a life acceptable to society."

Justice Miller, in dissent, distinguishes *Buggs* and *Carlson*. Unlike Carlson, rather than show regard for his children, Buggs killed one, severely injured another, and put the lives of several others at risk. Unlike in *Carlson,* there was evidence in *Buggs* of a prior history of violence: Buggs had fired a gun between his son's legs some six months before the offense, and he had at one time stabbed a woman (his relationship to the woman is not clarified). To treat Buggs as a "twin" of Carlson renders the protection from capital punishment for domestic murderers more ample than that provided by *Carlson* standing alone.

Passion and Premeditation in Florida

The Florida capital statute includes as an aggravating circumstance that "the murder was committed in a cold, calculated, and premeditated manner without any moral or legal justification."[12] In 1991 the Florida Supreme Court held that this aggravator cannot be applied to murders performed in the grip of "heated passion" and arising from a "domestic dispute," regardless of the extent or strength of indicia of preplanning and calculation (*Santos v. State,* 1991; *Douglas v. State,* 1991). Prior to 1991, it was well established in Florida that domestic strife was a nonstatutory mitigating factor that could outweigh factors in aggravation, thus shielding a defendant from a death sentence (*Fead v. State,* 1987). But in *Santos v. State* and *Douglas v. State* the Florida Supreme Court enlarged its protection of domestic murderers from the death penalty: It held that domestic heat and cold deliberation were antithetical and thus that this aggravator was unavailable as a basis of capital prosecution in domestic murder cases.

The cold, calculated, and premeditated aggravator had been a convenient vehicle for the capital prosecution of domestic murder cases. The factor was typically applied to executions and contract murders (*Douglas v. State*, 1991). Domestic separation murder is aptly described as a species of execution, in retaliation for the pain of abandonment or the ultimate transgression against customary authority. However, the Florida Supreme Court reasoned that domestic murders are not cold, but passionate, or hot.

Carlos Santos's case was well suited for the development of Florida domestic discount doctrine. His mental condition and personal history rendered him a sympathetic defendant, at least to the extent of making the "cold, calculated, and premediated" aggravator seem incongruous and inapposite. Evidence was heard during the penalty phase of Santos's trial that Santos was vulnerable to succumbing to psychosis under stress, was probably psychotic when he killed Irma and their daughter, and plainly psychotic from the trauma of the loss and the crime after he killed them.

Irma, with whom Santos had lived for many years, left him. She avoided him after the breakup. He found Irma and threatened to kill her. Two days later Santos accosted her on the street and shot Irma and their daughter in the head at point-blank range with a gun bought for that purpose.

The Florida Supreme Court castigated the trial court for failing to credit Santos with the statutory mitigating factors, that he was suffering from extreme mental and emotional disturbance, and that his capacity to conform his conduct to the requirements of the law was substantially impaired. There was also evidence in the record that Santos had as a child suffered extreme physical and emotional abuse at the hands of his father, further mitigation unacknowledged by the trial court. This evidence lent further credibility to the defendant's claim that he was vulnerable to passages of derangement and had killed Irma and their child in the grip of such an episode.

The court concludes that killing arising from a domestic dispute, which in turn give rise to "violent' and "wild" emotions, and then to "mad acts," is neither cold nor genuinely premeditated. The court analogizes the facts in Santos to those in *Douglas v. State*, another 1991 case, and closely follows its analysis in that case, which also involved the rejection of the application of the cold, calculated, and premeditated aggravator. In 1992, the Florida Supreme Court applied the doctrine developed in *Santos* and *Douglas* in a more prosaic separation murder case (*Richardson v. State*, 1992). Tommy Richardson shot the woman with whom he had lived for some years several days after she had broken off their relationship and insisted he leave her trailer home. He killed her with a shotgun he concealed ready to hand for that purpose, having threatened to kill her the day before. Again the Florida Supreme Court held that this was a case of wild emotion in the context of a domestic dispute. The court concludes that: "the element of coldness, i.e., calm cool reflection, is not present here. The fact of cold, calculated premeditation thus is not permissible."

These three "domestic dispute" cases have in common that a woman's decision to leave is unacceptable to the defendants. The Florida Supreme Court held that "heated passion" immunized the defendants against the highest grade of criminal liability and punishment. The question I would like to address next is whether pain and anger kindled by the hazards of sexual love ought to be legally sufficient to reduce the grade of offense seriousness in domestic murder cases. Should loss and separation immunize defendants who are in a normal range of vulnerability (unlike in *Santos*), even when their pain, heat, and anger are accompanied by strong evidence of premeditation and deliberation?

The domestic discount that operates to reduce death sentences in appellate review by some state supreme courts has its roots in traditional homicide theory and doctrine, and in particular in the distinction between hot- and cold-blooded murder. This distinction invites feminist critique, the task to which I now turn.

Hot Blood, Cold Blood

I ask my readers to consider two murders, one a killing arising out of friction between a couple who lived together, for which the killer received a life sentence, and the other a robbery murder that resulted in a death sentence.

First consider the case of Michael Quesinberry (*Quesinberry v. State*, 1987). One day he took a break from work and drove up to a rural grocery store. Quesinberry sat there for a while, thinking about his money troubles. He then put a hammer in his pocket, walked into the store and asked the owner, a hale seventy-one-year-old man, for a Pepsi. Quesinberry then asked for some cigarettes, in order to induce the store-keeper to turn around and make himself vulnerable to attack. When the storekeeper turned, he struck him once on the head with a hammer. The owner fell, whereupon Quesinberry struck him on the head once more, and then took money from the till, and left.

Now consider the case of Bige Hamby (*Georgia v. Hamby*, 1978). Hamby killed his girlfriend. She had lived with him, although on an erratic basis, reflecting the ups and downs of their relationship. Bige and Margaret fought often, had called the law on each other; he had beaten her many times but she had always come back. The killing occurred in his trailer home under the following circumstances: Margaret was drinking in the next-door trailer. His neighbor asked Bige to make Margaret leave her trailer because Margaret was falling down drunk and making a nuisance of herself. He dragged the resisting woman out of the trailer by the leg. She hit her head on the concrete step. Bige kicked the side of the fallen Margaret with his booted foot. She was then unable to walk unsupported. He took her to his trailer and threw her inside at approximately 4:30 P.M. Bige called the police in the morning when Margaret failed to revive after a prolonged beating. Her entire body was covered with bruises and abrasions; she had been beaten with fists, a Pepsi bottle, the marks of whose crimped cap were clearly visible on her chest, and the buckle end of a belt, and she had been kicked or stomped on. Death was probably caused by particularly severe beating with fists administered to her head and face. Her face was one large undifferentiated bruise. There were cigarette burns on her inner thighs and the backs of her legs, and her vagina had been lacerated.

I do not rehearse these cases to point out that the crime for which Hamby drew a life sentence is morally as bad or worse than Quesinberry's robbery murder, although I believe this comparative statement to be true. Anyone familiar with the operation of the criminal law can easily produce pairs of cases which reflect haphazard and morally incoherent justice. My thesis rather is that the juxtaposition of these two cases illustrates a general proposition about the moral gradations embedded in our law of homicide, and the sentencing policies that follow from those moral judgments. Both Hamby and Quesinberry drew relatively stiff sentences for crimes of the type they committed. Both men could realistically have hoped to have been more fortunate; but neither should have been surprised by the severity of his sentence. Yet, arguably, crimes of Hamby's type are as reprehensible as Quesinberry's. Why then do the Hambys escape being treated as severely as the Quesinberrys? Why, also, are the Hambys, who kill women with whom they are living, at less risk of the most severe sentence than men who kill because women have left them? I will address the latter question first.

The Significance of the Threshold in Domestic Homicide

A man who kills a woman who lives with him is likely to be less severely sanctioned than one who kills a woman who has left him. The explanation for the significance of the (household) threshold in domestic homicide cases is less straightforward than it may appear to be at first blush. The expected explanation, which I would like to challenge, goes something like this: The worst homicides are premeditated crimes; common or garden-variety domestic homicides in which the killer lashes out at his partner-antagonist in explosive anger are the antithesis of premeditated murders. But the premeditated domestic murderer who also labors under the disadvantage of a prior violent felony conviction, or has some other aggravating factor in his case, may be selected for capital prosecution and eventually be sentenced to death.

The above explanation of the moral and legal basis for regarding murderous rage as less reprehensible than cold-blooded execution is unsatisfactory. Not all murder eligible for capital sentencing is premeditated. Michael Quesinberry, on the facts of his case, could have been prosecuted for capital murder in North Carolina on either a premeditation and deliberation theory or a felony murder theory. In most capital jurisdictions, robbery murders are eligible for capital prosecution as felony murders, murders committed in the course of another violent felony, regardless of whether the killing was premeditated. Unlike robbery, wife beating is not treated as a violent felony capable of elevating a homicide to capital murder. Admittedly, the ranking which treats robbery as more reprehensible than serious spouse battery is so familiar as to escape notice. Whether or not this ranking of domestic violence is defensible, it reflects a disposition to take predatory crime more seriously than domestic violence.

It is fair to conclude—regardless of whether one regards punishing lethal or other domestic violence more heavily as either morally justified or sound policy—that there is no wall between premeditated and unpremeditated murder that shelters domestic killers from capital responsibility; rather, our ranking of domestic violence as less serious than predatory crime reflects the moral assumptions embedded in our law of homicide. Were wife beating as disapproved as robbery, fatal wife beating could be capitally prosecuted on a felony murder theory. More needs to be said about the problematic concept of premeditation; however, my argument at this stage hinges on nothing more than the proposition that in our law of homicide, premeditation is not a necessary predicate of capital murder. We must seek explanations of the relatively low grade of offense seriousness assigned unpremeditated domestic murders elsewhere.

A second possible explanation of the reluctance to assign the highest degree of offense seriousness and punishment to (the worst) domestic homicides is that these crimes are thought to be difficult or impossible to deter (Fagan 1989, p. 377–425); hence the deterrence rationale for the *in terrorem* penalty—death—is unavailable. Recent research challenges three myths associated with the traditional view that domestic violence generally, and domestic homicide in particular, are not significantly deterrable:

(1) *The "out-of-control" domestic killer.* The image of the enraged domestic killer as "out of control," and hence beyond the reach of deterrent messages of the criminal law, has been rejected by researchers who argue that domestic violence generally is instrumental or purposive conduct. Batterers use violence because it works, because through it they achieve their objectives. These objectives include household dominance in general and the specific demands to which their victims accede under violent attack or threat.[13] One who launches a strategic assault, however, may yet find that he is not thoroughly in control of himself, or the situation, or the extent of damage done. Many lethal attacks should be understood as ill-calibrated, extremely reckless domestic violence in which death is risked by employing lethal weapons or severe beatings without firm determination to kill (Katz 1988, pp. 32–33).

(2) *Domestic killers tend to be otherwise peaceable men, who, having killed their provokers, pose little threat of future dangerousness.* Evidence is mounting that domestic killers have a very high incidence of prior assaults on their victims, histories of assault on other women with whom they are sexually intimate (Coker 1992),[14] and may beat their children as well as their wives and lovers (Hotaling and Strauss 1989). Far from posing no threat other than to their deceased victims, such men are dangerous in the domestic sphere, however peaceable they may be outside the home.[15] The emerging revisionist profile of male domestic killers as men who are habitually violent in the home suggest that deterrent criminal law strategies might aptly be applied in the domestic arena.

(3) *Domestic violence is deviant behavior.* Recent research has reported that domestic violence is more prevalent in all social classes than previously supposed.[16] These findings, if accurate, call for the reassessment of the image of batterers as members of deviant subcultures. Plausibly, a cultural transition is underway in which rejection of domestic violence is replacing acceptance of it. If this is so, then unambiguous stigmatization of such conduct by the criminal law may well prove an effective avenue of reform. Unambiguous and strong criminal law signals may prove a significant deterrent to significant numbers of individuals who are or should be absorbing new rules of family conduct.

In sum, if typical hot-blooded domestic homicides grow out of habitual, instrumental, and socially tolerated violence, the deterrence rationale for upgrading offense seriousness and severity of penalty is available.

From a feminist perspective, another explanation for the greater vulnerability to extreme sanction of separation killers, relative to killers as hot and hotter than Hamby, is discernible. A possible explanation of the lesser severity of the law's response to spousal as distinct from ex-spousal homicides is the continued influence of traditional patriarchal doctrines. Patriarchal law regards women as property of their husbands, and defers to male rule in the household.[17] These doctrines offer less protection to men who have lost the status of husband of their victims. Bige Hamby killed a woman who was socially recognized as his wife or wife equivalent; men like Godfrey killed women who had asserted their independent status—at least until death reversed their apparent success.

At common law, under the feudal doctrine of coverture, "the very being or legal existence of the woman is suspended during marriage."[18] In addition to the suspension of her independent civil identity, a married woman could not appeal to the law for protection from acts on the part of her husband that would otherwise be criminal. A husband had a right to force sexual intercourse upon his wife, to beat her, and to confine her (Blackstone's Commentaries 1803, pp. 444–445; Williams 1982). In the nineteenth century the Married Women's Property Acts improved the civil status of women (Williams 1982); but the criminal law continued to defer to the authority of men in the domestic sphere. It has continued to do so, although with abating force, into the contemporary era of sexual equality. Although the common-law marital exemption from rape prosecution has been significantly curtailed by contemporary statutes, the exemption is far from a dead letter (Buckborough 1989). Until the mid-1980s, domestic violence was treated by the police as a private matter; nonarrest of batterers and ignoring or delaying response to domestic violence calls were standard practices (Zorza, 1990). It is hardly surprising that domestic violence, not long recognized as crime, much less serious crime, is not found on statutory lists of felonies so reprehensible that death dealt during their commission can sustain a charge of capital murder.

Blood Heat

The question of why cold-blooded killings are more reprehensible than hot-blooded crimes is also less easily disposed of than may at first appear. If taken superficially as a question about traditional homicide doctrine, it is easily answered. The answer is that killing out of anger or other strong emotion tends to decrease the degree of moral blameworthiness attributed to the defendant, and hence to lower the rank of offense seriousness assigned to his crime along the entire scale of homicide offenses from capital murder to manslaughter. The law of homicide conceives that blood heat undermines or destroys an actor's rational capacity to deliberate and plan his actions; anger dethrones judgment.

The actor is imagined to lose control of his actions to his anger. Especially if the defendant is not wholly responsible for the situation that gave rise to his anger, his moral culpability is mitigated because his powers of agency, specifically self-restraint, are reduced by his passion and the circumstances inciting his passion.

Blood heat is a relative matter, ranging from the utter indifference that Quesinberry evinced toward his prey to the passionate wrath of the cuckold; it varies inversely with the degree of that elusive quality, premeditation. The cuckold who kills his wife or her paramour may be entitled to the maximum mitigation. The man who, for instance, kills his wife in the heat of an argument, but lacks sufficient provocation to reduce murder to manslaughter, may yet be provoked and passionate enough, in a sufficiently warm state of blood, to qualify for reduction from first- to second-degree murder. A Bige Hamby may have been too methodical, and too far outside the pale of a reasonable level of response to intimate discord, to qualify for reduction from first-degree murder to second, but may be given sufficient credit for the heat of his blood to avoid being tried for his life or to avoid a death sentence.[19] There may be sufficient evidence of premeditation in a domestic murder case to prove the element of premeditation; yet the anger or the pain out of which the defendant acted, the heat of his blood, may result in the killer being accorded less severe treatment than someone who was a cold-blooded predator.[20]

I will argue that, serviceable as the hot-blooded/cold-blooded distinction may be for some purposes of moral grading in homicide law, it has supplied a specious basis for the underevaluation of the seriousness of some classes of domestic homicides.

The history of the grading of homicide offenses in Anglo-American law has been that of successive attempts to align punishments meted out with notions of moral culpability, and in particular to avoid imposing capital punishment on insufficiently culpable killers. The first and most consequential innovation was the distinction between murder and manslaughter.[21] The common-law courts of the seventeenth century developed the distinction between capital murder, committed with malice aforethought, and noncapital criminal homicide (Ashworth 1976; Ashworth 1975, Kaye 1967).

Homicide committed upon a sudden quarrel or in the heat of passion upon adequate provocation was recognized as a defense or partial defense to murder, and as a less grave homicide offense.[22] These voluntary manslaughter doctrines are grounded in the hot-blood/cold-blood distinction; the same conceptual framework was the basis for the subsequent grading of murder offenses.

Heat of Passion

Manslaughter doctrine matured in the nineteenth century into the form in which it is preserved in most American jurisdictions. To qualify as heat-of-passion manslaughter, a killer must act out of anger induced by provocation which would move a reasonable man to lose his self-control, and in the space of time before a reasonable man's passion would have cooled. From the inception of the defense, the most important types of provocation held to be adequate to support heat of passion have included violent blows and assaults inflicted upon self or relative, mutual combat, and the sight of a wife taken in adultery.[23] In addition to fulfilling the objective test of provocation sufficient to induce a reasonable man to lose his self-control, the killer must actually be aroused to a pitch of anger or other violent emotion capable of overmastering the self-control of a reasonable man. This sudden emotion, rather than some antecedent plan, such as to take revenge, must actually supply the impetus for the crime (LaFave 1976, section 7.10(a)).

Commentators agree that the heat-of-passion defense functions to both partially excuse and partially justify the conduct of the provoked killer.[24] Both aspects are critical to the operation of the defense. The passionate killer is partially excused because he is less blameworthy than the cool killer for one or more of several reasons: either passion renders him incapable of premeditation, his passion renders his action less than fully voluntary, or because, while restraint is required by law, the law also recognizes that the ordinary law-abiding actor would find it difficult or impossible to conform his actions to the law were he subject to the provocation (Dressler 1982, p. 442). Blood heat clouds and overmasters judgment under circumstances which render the actor a suitable candidate for sympathy as well as blame.

Essential to the heat-of-passion defense is that the killer acts from moralized rage in circumstances in which his peers endorse his moral views, sympathize with his anger, and recognize that they might well prove no more equal to the law's demand for self-control if similarly situated. The defendant's lethal rage is rendered sympathetic, rather than, say, a symptom of a bullying temperament, by the serious injustice done him by his provoker. Under common-law rules no lawful action can be adequate provocation to sustain the defense of heat of passion (Ashworth 1976, p. 295; Dressler 1982, p. 439). Further, if the defendant provoked his provoker, if he brought his tormenter's affront upon himself, he could not establish the heat-of-passion defense (Ashworth 1976, p. 295). The victim of a heat-of-passion killing shares the blame for the lethal outcome, and may be more at fault than the provoked killer who dispatched him.[25] The heat-of-passion defense requires that the defendant acted under a claim of moral justification to reduce murder to manslaughter.

The scope of the provocation defense has expanded with the introduction of further gradations of homicide offenses in modern law. "Imperfect provocation,"[26] provocation insufficient to merit reduction to manslaughter, may yet suffice to avoid capital responsibility for death-eligible murder or reduce first-degree to second-degree murder. Provocation mitigates blame to the extent that the victim shares responsibility for his or her demise with the killer. At one end of the scale is cold-blooded murder: no morally cognizable provocation on the part of the victim is responsible for the lethal attack. The victim is wholly innocent. At the other end of scale is manslaughter; the victim is at least as responsible for his or her demise as the provoked killer.

As the moral justification for killing weakens, so does the excuse value to be derived from the provocation; mitigation varies inversely with the extent of moral wrong attributable to the victim. The degree of provocation necessary for manslaughter is that quantum of moral injury which would push the average, law-abiding person to the brink of homicidal rage. If the moral equation, as it were, is solved for any lesser value of injury, then reduction to second-degree murder is the best result the defendant should have. Thus insulting words are not considered injurious or threatening enough to reduce murder to manslaughter because we reject the culture of honor which ranks insult morally with injury or threat of injury (LaFave 1986, section 7.10(6)). The individual who explodes when insulted has a moral shortfall, cannot sufficiently justify his reaction, to avoid a murder conviction. But if the trier of fact concludes that, but for the victim's wilful insulting of the defendant, there would have been no attack, first-degree murder may be avoided.

The killer whose culpability is mitigated by imperfect provocation must, however, be in the same moral universe as ordinary, law-abiding citizens. What injures and provokes him, whether or not it rises to the level required for manslaughter, must be of a nature and quality to injure and provoke the ordinary run of people. The provocation must be capable of engaging common sympathy. Thus the Illinois Supreme Court sympathized with the tragic "twins," Carlson and Buggs, who killed in response to the taunting and exploitative behavior of their wives. The Illinois Supreme Court saw these crimes as "ignited by a flare-up of long lasting marital discord" (*Illinois v. Buggs*, 1986). Because they were suffering humiliation and rejection, their rage and their inability to master it were less blameworthy in the eyes of the state supreme court than would have been the case if they had not been emotionally assaulted by their wives. These men killed under the influence of extreme mental and emotional disturbance brought on at least in part by the morally repugnant conduct of Rosemary Carlson and Loretta Buggs.

Diminished Responsibility

Diminished responsibility is a novel basis for grading offenses, recently introduced into the law of homicide (Arenella 1977; Dix 1971; Lewin 1975). Like provocation, diminished responsibility provides a basis for diminution of moral culpability and, hence, of the grade of offense seriousness along the entire range of homicide offenses. Persons suffering from mental disease or defect, but not entitled to exoneration by reason of insanity, may be entitled to have charges reduced from first to second degree, or from murder to manslaughter. A death penalty may likewise be avoided by the mitigation of mental disease or defect. The reason of the mentally impaired killer is overwhelmed. But unlike in the case of the (normal) provoked killer, it is overwhelmed because the structures of self-control are abnormally weak or internal upheavals are abnormally powerful. Thus far only a minority of jurisdictions have adopted diminished responsibility as a basis of mitigation except for purposes of avoiding the death penalty.

The combination of imperfect provocation and diminished responsibility is a potent and protean basis for mitigation of domestic murder. There are certainly cases, like *Santos,* where both types of mitigation appear amply supported. Santos, driven into psychosis, could not subsequently understand that he had killed Irma, nor could he accept her death.

In *Buggs* and *Carlson,* the Illinois Supreme Court fuses imperfect provocation ("extreme mental and emotional disturbance" in the language of the widely adopted Model Penal Code formula) and diminished capacity to create a plausible rationale for sentence reduction in domestic capital cases: Carlson and Buggs were both men in decline, Carlson had suffered two heart attacks and, in his physician's words, was "partly disabled and really incapable of leading a complete and fulfilling life for a man in his early forties." Buggs was a severe enough alcoholic to have suffered blackouts. Ill-health and ill-fortune had deprived these men of the fortitude to endure blatant infidelity or callous abandonment for a more virile partner. They could not muster the self-control upon which normal, more fortunate men would be able to call.

The impairments attributed to Carlson and Buggs are tenuously linked to excusable absence of moral judgment and restraint; they hardly rise to the level of Santos's psychosis. It is certainly plausible, however, that declining men find rejection harder to bear than men secure in their social status and confident of their future prospects with women. In the eyes of the Illinois Supreme Court, decline, in combination with the provocation to which these men were subjected, add up to sufficient domestic mitigation to ward off capital liability.

In Florida, the "cold, calculated, and premeditated" aggravator cannot be applied to retaliatory domestic murder. A mitigating degree of impairment/provocation is ascribed to retaliatory domestic homicides. Murder of a wife or lover is itself taken as evidence that rational restraints were overwhelmed by mitigating rage. Rejection is taken as sufficient to impair the self-control of the average, law-abiding man.

The domestic discount of capital culpability is a post-*Furman* variant of the familiar syllogism: Hot-blooded killing is a less serious grade of offense than killing in cold blood, domestic killing is heated; therefore, domestic killing is mitigated.

I will argue against automatic mitigation—the imputation of diminished capacity or the moralized rage of provocation—simply because the relationship between victim and defendant is domestic or sexually intimate. In the worst cases of domestic murder, cases of retaliatory postseparation executions and of the last beating, the domestic relationship should, if anything, serve to aggravate murder. Such murders are among the worst expressions of domestic violence. They exploit the trust and vulnerability on which familial institutions are premised. They symbolize resistance to egalitarian marriage and to the recognition of the autonomy of wives within marriage. The *pro forma* discounting of the seriousness of such crimes reveals the ambivalence of society toward these egalitarian reforms and the incompleteness of their success.

If the law were purged of patriarchal values, the remaining principles that underlie our grading of homicide offenses would be consistent with the rejection of a domestic discount; the worst domestic murders, like the worst predatory murders, would rank among the most reprehensible crimes.

Cold Blood

The division of murder into degrees, as well as the most recent reform of capital punishment law, can be understood as an effort to reserve the highest grades of offense seriousness and highest degrees of culpability for cold-blooded murder.

All criminal homicide not manslaughter was murder at common law, defined as unlawful killing with malice aforethought (LaFave 1986, section 7.1(a), p. 605). Early common law probably understood "malice aforethought" to mean a preconceived intention or plan to kill (LaFave 1986, section 7.1(a), p. 605; Model Penal Code, 1980, section 210.6, p.

121). "Malice aforethought" lost the exclusive connotation of executing a preconceived plan as common law developed; none of the four types of common-law murder, express or implied, required that the defendant have a preconceived plan of killing his victim.[27] Any criminal homicide which failed to qualify as manslaughter under the rigid requirements of provocation doctrine was capital murder. Intentional homicides were exhaustively divided into two complementary classes, those committed in cold blood and those committed in the heat of adequately provoked passion. The inability of common law to reflect gradations of moral culpability among criminal homicides other than that between murder and manslaughter was a powerful impetus to reform.

Following the lead of Pennsylvania's 1794 statute, all but a handful of American jurisdictions introduced degrees of murder in order to reserve the death penalty for crimes deemed sufficiently reprehensible to merit the death penalty (Wechsler and Michael p. 703). The majority of states sought to define all first-degree murder save felony murder with the "deliberate and premeditated" formula. Although the defects of the formula have been well aired, its widespread continued use as the "chief criterion" (Model Penal Code, 1980, section 210.3, p. 67) of first-degree murder attests to the importance and durability of the connection between the first rank of offense seriousness and killing which proceeds from a cool mind rather than hot blood.

Two kinds of difficulties have frustrated efforts to use the premeditation and deliberation formula to explicate the basis for assigning murders to the highest grade of offense seriousness.

The first sort revolve around the lack of a clear and serviceable definition of the legal term of art. The legal definition of "premeditation and deliberation" has diverged from the ordinary definitions of these words, paralleling the similar denaturing of its common-law antecedent, "malice aforethought" (Wechsler and Michael pp. 707–8). "Premeditation" has been confusingly defined by courts as requiring little or no duration of thought; mere seconds suffice. This is of course contrary to the common significance of the term, "planned." Durationless "premeditation" is difficult to distinguish from the mental state necessary for the lesser offense of second-degree murder, which requires only the intent to kill. Consequently, juries are confounded between the common meaning of "premeditated," that is, "planned," and the legal significance of the term; the distinction between second-degree murder—merely intentional murder—and premeditated murder evaporates in definitional confusion.[28] "Deliberation" appears be little more than a synonym for "done by a cool mind" or "in a cool state of blood."

More importantly for the present inquiry, some of the worst murders apparently lack the quality of premediation.

Two types of murder not requiring premeditation are ranked among first-degree murders, felony murder and depraved-heart murder. These types of murder are cold-blooded crimes in the sense that the victims are wholly innocent. The victims share no part of the moral responsibility for their deaths. "Cold-blooded" has another meaning, synonymous with the common meaning of "deliberate and premeditated," something like, "planned and carried forward with a firm and fixed purpose." The worst murders known to our law, with the exception of the category of revenge murders, are cold-blooded in the first sense but not necessarily the second. The absence of reflection and firm purpose does not improve the moral quality of crimes which take the lives of innocent victims.

The common-law felony murder rule has been severely criticized because it imposes strict liability for an unintended death occurring during the commission of a felony (Model Penal Code, 1980, section 210.2, p. 29–42). Yet felony murder survives in most American jurisdictions as first-degree murder, although with scope curtailed to lesser or greater extent (LaFave 1986, section 7.5). The survival of the felony murder rule can be explained by the failure of the concept of premeditation to capture all the qualities associated with murders of the worst kind in our culture. The taking of life, innocent of any affront to the killer or complicity in its own destruction, is assigned the highest grade of offense seriousness. The application of the felony murder rule is morally defensible, insofar as the defendant may be fairly charged with knowledge that a very substantial risk of lethal harm attached to his or her felonious activities; reform of the felony murder rule has been in the direction of applying it only to cases where the defendant evinced reckless indifference to great risk to human life.[29] In this sense, felony murder is cold-blooded; the depth of our revulsion from such crime is revealed by our placing strict liability upon those whose predatory ventures result in the foreseeable loss of innocent life.

A similar analysis accounts for the appearance of depraved-heart murder, unintentional killing which manifests an extreme indifference to the value of human life, as first-degree murder in the statutes of a minority of states (LaFave 1986, section 7.4). Examples of such extremely reckless murder include shooting into a room in which several persons are known to be (*People v. Jernatowski*, 1924), and shooting into a moving automobile (*Wiley v. State*, 1918). As with felony murder, life innocent of any morally cognizable offense against the killer is taken.

There are also unplanned, impulsive murders which rank on a par morally with planned murders. The legal definition of premeditation in some jurisdictions may allow impulsive murders to be graded as first-degree murder due to premeditation; this would be true wherever the definition of "premeditation" collapses planned and merely intentional murder. But the moral basis of the inclusion of some impulsive murders in the highest grade of offense seriousness is obscured by the semantics of the legal definition of "premeditation."

Sir James Fitzjames Stephen argued that impulsive murders can be as morally reprehensible and bespeak characters as dangerous to society as premeditated murders. Consider two of Stephen's examples:

> A man passing along the road, sees a boy sitting on a bridge over a deep river and, out of mere wanton barbarity, pushes him in and so drowns him. A man makes advances to a girl who repels him. He deliberately but instantly cuts her throat.[30]

Such easy cruelty in response to the sheer vulnerability of a child or the legitimate assertiveness of a woman displays a frightening lack of moral inhibition. In addition to the taking of innocent life, these impulsive murders display cold-bloodedness in the lack of the moral emotions that normally create visceral barriers to acting on antisocial impulses.

Revenge murders deviate from the otherwise typical worse murders in that their victims may indeed have wronged their killers, and hence lack the innocence that outrages our moral sensibility in other kinds of cases. Assuming that the victim has committed some atrocious wrong—killed or terribly injured a relative of his murderer, for example—there may be no moral content underwriting the ranking of the crime among the worst murders, other than the violation of the critical norms of our civilization that retribution belongs to the state and requires due process of law. If the magnitude and quality of the wrong done by the killer is morally sufficient—a war crime, a murder unreachable by the law—or is popularly regarded as having been insufficiently punished by official justice, the lack of moral innocence on the part of the victim may hamper prosecution to the fullest extent permitted by the law.

A Feminist Critique of the Domestic Discount

I now reach the question, should a domestic discount operate to exclude domestic murder from the highest grade of offense seriousness—from capital liability under the present dispensation? Should blood heated by the negative and painful emotions of intimate and familial life shield a defendant from the highest degree of criminal liability? I will argue that the worst cases of domestic murder, postseparation executions and murder arising out of habitual wife beating, should be counted among the worst murders, absent legitimate mitigating circumstances. There should be no blanket or automatic extension of imperfect provocation or diminished capacity, or the two in combination, to domestic killers merely in virtue of the domestic relationship.

Heat-of-passion doctrine is the conceptual fount of all provocation doctrine. Heat-of-passion doctrine grants mitigation to a killer reacting to assault on his person or that of a close relative. Adultery is sufficient provocation by virtue of being assimilated to assault: the blow administered to the husband is moral, not physical (Coker 1992). Adultery derogates from his manhood, which both entitles him and requires him to control his wife, sexually and otherwise. Within the patriarchal conception of marriage, any challenge to masculine control—adulterous behavior or inclinations, contesting household authority, leaving—is an assault on both legitimate prerogatives and the very masculinity of the husband. Traditionally, violence to reassert possession or punish defiance has been considered legitimate masculine behavior. It is the rootedness of adultery provocation in patriarchal norms which explains why the extension of this mitigation to women who kill adulterous husbands did not occur until law began to undergo the transition toward gender egalitarianism. It was not pain and anger at betrayal, which either husband or wife may feel, which mitigated culpability at classical common law; rather it was the defense of masculinity and its prerogatives, and the legitimacy of violence as a vehicle of male control of the family (*Homstead v. Director of Public Prosecution,* 1946).

In contemporary society, patriarchal values have no more legitimate place in criminal law than they do in family law. Particularized inquiry, not patriarchical values, should determine whether there are grounds for mitigation of blame for a killing rage. A wife/victim may have asserted her own autonomous judgment. Or she may have provoked her husband to a degree which mitigates his culpability. The blood of a Godfrey may be hot, but his wife may yet be as morally innocent of complicity in her own death as are the victims of cold-blooded killers. Society has, in effect, asked men to relinquish patriarchal conceptions of masculinity, at least in domestic life: consistency and efficacy in the reform effort requires that our law not legitimate retaliation against spouses whose provocation can be seen only through a patriarchal lens.

Nor should diminished capacity mitigation be so liberally interpreted as to permit virtually any nonpredatory domestic murderer to avoid the full measure of culpability on the grounds that rejection triggered powerful emotions he could not control. The Florida Supreme Court, for example, refuses to assign premeditated nonpredatory domestic murder the highest grade of offense seriousness because such crimes are "mad acts prompted by wild emotions." (*Santos v. State,* 1991). The Illinois Supreme Court held that Carlson, who was suffering the constriction of his life due to two disabling heart attacks, was on that account impaired in his ability to endure peaceably the defection of his wife. These courts should not be emulated. Patriarchal conceptions of masculine identity are constituent of a moral outlook which makes wifely defection hard or impossible to bear peaceably. The too-ready ascription of "impairment" to domestic killers may result in a disguised reintroduction of the ancient permission to take revenge upon a wife who defies patriarchal norms.

The law should impose new standards of peaceful deportment, rather than accept adherence to the old norms as mitigating. In analogous fashion, reformed rape law imposes new standards of sexual conduct on men who may find them alien to their traditional moral outlook. The law of rape no longer allows, for example, a woman's consent to be inferred from her reputation for unchastity.[31] Being mired in sexual oldthink is not a defense to a charge of rape. Similarly, the wild and violent—and murderous—responses to rejection which are mitigating in the eyes of the Florida Supreme Court are readable as such only within a patriarchal moral framework which it is the work of the criminal law in this period of social transition to delegitimate and transcend.

The moral culture that supported the justification of the domestic discount, of marital mitigation, is fading. Contemporary society officially recognizes sexual equality in marriage and in divorce, and is liberal in allowing divorce. Property rights in wives as the ground of mitigation have lapsed; indeed, what was traditionally universally accepted morality has become a profound affront to the newly recognized rights of women. Further, the remaining justification leg on which the extent of mitigation granted to domestic homicide now stands, the pain and anger suffered by the defied or abandoned spouse, cannot provide sufficient justification standing alone. What gave male anger justificatory force was its rootedness in rights; without these patriarchal rights it becomes harder to make out a case for sufficient provocation for mitigation of domestic homicide of any rank of offense severity. It is especially hard if a court or jury does not slip into a narrowly male perspective, if attention is paid to the quality of the victim's actions and experiences. The doctrine of mitigation has traditionally required that the killer's reactions reflect those of the morality of the typical member of his society. In a world which repudiates traditional patriarchal rights in marriage, the homicidal rage of the defied or abandoned spouse loses its moral force.

What remains for both sexes when confronted with the loss of a spouse is, of course, primal suffering. But excessive psychologizing and individualized consideration of the suffering of denied domestic killers tends to allow men to retain by force and threat of force that which the equality of the sexes and the reform of marriage was designed to remove: their right to control the women in their lives. It also continues to give a degree of sanction to male styles, deployment of force and threat of force, which the reforms undertaken presumably commit our society to combatting. Finally, too great a rein for subjective analysis again creates a lack of parity between predatory and spousal homicides. Predators also have emotional lives; but the criminal law has been more resistant to folding the emotional life of predators into calculations of culpability and offense severity than it has with domestic crime.

I conclude that an automatic domestic discount has no place in contemporary homicide law. But the translation of moral argument into policy is too complex and difficult a matter to be done woodenly, especially since moral analysis does not automatically answer a large range of questions about efficacy in achieving the goals of criminal law. Getting the jurisprudence right is a necessary first step.

Notes

This article is an abbreviated adaptation of "Passion and Premeditation: Capital Domestic Murder in the Post-*Furman* Era." I would like to thank Elizabeth Hudgins and Anna Tefft for research assistance in preparing this article.

1. Gross & Mauro report that in 1976 to 1980 over eighty percent of the death penalties in Florida and Georgia were in cases involving another serious felony, as were seventy-five percent in Illinois. See S. Gross and R. Mauro, *Death and Discrimination* 45 (1989). Ekland-Olson (1988) reports that in Texas from 1974 to 1983, seventy-two percent of death sentences involved the felonies of robbery, burglary, and sexual assault. S. Ekland-Olsen, "Structured Discretion, Racial Bias and the Death Penalty," 69 *Social Science Quarterly* 853 (1988). According to the NAACP Legal Defense and Education Fund, which monitors death row, in 1986 more than seventy-five percent of death row cases nationwide involved a separate felony. See Baldus, Pulaski, and Woodworth, "Arbitrariness and Discrimination in the Administration of the Death Penalty: A Challenge to State Supreme Courts," 15 *Stetson Law Review* 133 (1986).

2. Capital sentences are unusual for all types of homicide (Baldus 1990, pp. 394–425).

3. A full report and analysis of the results of the study of domestic death row from which this account is drawn can be found in, "Passion and Premeditation: Capital Domestic Murder in the Post-*Furman* Era" (Rapaport forthcoming).

4. Under the rubric "sexual relationship" I group spouses and ex-spouses, couples who lived together without marriage, and couples who did not share a household but had a durable relationship. Both hetero- and homosexual relationships are included.

5. Perhaps the old adage that "hell hath no fury like a woman scorned" is in need of revision.

6. Separation has been identified as a dangerous passage in domestic relations (Mahoney 1991).

7. The women's cases raise other issues about gender and the law of homicide (Rapaport 1991 and 1990).

8. I am not of course advocating that every domestic homicide be treated as aggravated first-degree murder. In a regime in which there was parity of offense seriousness between predatory and domestic homicide, a small minority of domestic crimes would

lend themselves to processing as aggravated first-degree murders, just as a small minority of predatory crimes are in fact so processed in the current regime.

9. In other states, no doubt the fact that two people were killed and a third assaulted would have made it possible to sentence Godfrey to death on the strength of a multiple murder or risk-to-lives-in-addition-to-that-of-the-victim(s) factor; but in Georgia the multiple murder/risk-to-others factor was then qualified (it has since been amended) so that it applied only to murders occurring "in a public place," rendering it inapplicable to the trailer home setting of the murders in *Godfrey* (see Georgia Code Annotate, section 27–2534.1(b)(3).

10. 466 U.S. at 433.

11. With the Carlson case I have made an exception to my otherwise strict policy of counting a murder as a capital domestic case only if the death sentence is pronounced for the murder of an intimate. I do so because the issues on which the appellate review of Carlson's sentence turn, and the reasons why the Illinois Supreme Court reduced the death sentence, concern the domestic murder. The Illinois Supreme Court itself treats *Carlson* as a domestic capital case precedent in *Buggs v. Illinois,* 493 N.E.2d 332 (1986).

12. Section 921.141(5)(h), Florida Statutes (1985). The "cold, calculated, and premeditated" factor requires a heightened level of premeditation, exceeding that needed to convict for first-degree murder. *Preston v. State,* 1984.

13. This conclusion has been reached by researchers using a range of disparate methodologies, including traditional clinical psychology, sociobiology, and phenomenological sociology. See Donna Coker's review and assessment of recent literature on the psychology of batterers and her exploration of the psychology of heat-of-passion wife killers (Coker 1992). Margo Daly's and Donald Wilson's sociobiological account of male violence, concludes that domestic violence persists because it works; it tends to achieve the purposes of its perpetrators. Jack Katz's analysis of domestic homicide also finds it to be purposive, although not instrumental in the manner of the rational utility maximizer (Katz 1988).

14. A study of Kansas City found that police had intervened in domestic disturbances at the address of suspect or victim in ninety percent of domestic homicide cases and had done so more than five times for approximately half the cases (Breedlove, Kennish, Sandker, and Sawtell 1977). Also see J. Katz 1988.

15. Researchers observe that there are two types of batterers: those who confine their violence to the home, and those who are violent outside the home as well (Hotaling and Straus 1989. p. 357, a compilation of statistics reported in research on the proportion of domestic batterers who are also violent outside the home).

16. According to Bureau of Justice Statistics (1991) a woman is beaten in the United States approximately every fifty-two seconds. Hotaling and Strauss (1989 pp. 336–337) report, based on a 1985 national survey of family violence, that child or spousal abuse occurs in over thirty percent of American homes in any year. Gelles and Straus (1988 p. 43) report that, while abuse is more likely to occur among the poor, it is not confined to their ranks.

17. Isabel Marcus sharpened my appreciation of the importance of the continuing influence of patriarchal legal doctrine in contemporary homicide law.

18. 2 Blackstone's Commentaries [443] (St. George Tucker ed. 1803). Blackstone elaborates the legal relationship of wife to husband, ". . . under whose wing, protection and *cover*, she performs everything; and is therefore called in our law-french a *feme-*

covert, foemina viro co-operta; is said to be *covert baron,* or under the protection of her husband, her *baron,* or lord; and her condition during her marriage is called *coverture.*"

19. This is not an issue in the Hamby case, because Georgia does not recognize degrees of murder; the Georgia statute preserves the common-law definition of murder.

20. In *State v. Huffstetler,* Chief Justice Exum argued, in dissent, that a death penalty in a domestic murder case ought not to survive proportionality review. *Preston v. State* distinguished between the heightened level of premeditation necessary to elevate murder to the death penalty range of crimes, and ordinary first-degree-murder-caliber premeditation.

21. A series of statutes, the first in 1496, denying benefit of clergy for "murder upon malice prepensed" introduced the distinction between murder and less grave homicide offenses (Model Penal Code, 1980, section 210.6, p. 121).

22. Ashworth 1976, Dressler 1982 and Kaye 1967. A second type of manslaughter was recognized which need not concern us here: involuntary manslaughter; see LaFave and Scott 1986, sections 7.12 & 7.13. Provocation is a defense in that, if made out, the defendant is exonerated as to the offense of murder, but only a partial defense in that he may still be guilty of the lesser criminal homicide offense of manslaughter.

23. The common-law categories of adequate provocation are summarized by Lord Hale in *Regina v. Mawbridge,* (1707) Kel. J. 119, 130–37. See LaFave 1986, section 7.10(b)(1)-(7).

24. Ashworth, 1976, argues that the mixture of justification and excuse is a virtue of the law of provocation. Dressler, 1982, argues that heat of passion should be reformed to make it a pure excuse doctrine.

25. Ashworth 1976, p. 292, invokes Aristotle, who says that "it is apparent injustice that occasions rage," *Nichomachean Ethics* Bk V, 8.

26. This felicitous phrase is used and perhaps coined by the Model Penal Code Commentators at 138.

27. Wechsler and Michael, p. 707. The four types of common-law murder are the following: 1) intent-to-kill murder; 2) intent-to-do-serious-bodily-injury murder; 3) depraved-heart murder; and 4) felony murder; See LaFave 1986, section 7.1, p. 605.

28. Cardozo, indeed, remarked that he himself was not confident he grasped the distinction between first- and second-degree murder, hinging as it did on the definition of premeditation: "I am not at all sure that I understand it myself after trying to apply it for many years and after diligent study of what has been written in books" (1931, pp. 100–101).

29. The Model Penal Code Commentary argues that it would be preferable to eliminate felony murder as a separate category of murder offense altogether, and subsume it under reckless murder committed with extreme indifference to human life. (1980, section 2.10.2, pp. 29–30).

30. Stephen's (1883) argument is quoted and endorsed by the Model Penal Code, section 210.6, p. 128.

31. So-called rape shield laws forbid reputation evidence about alleged victims' past sexual behavior (other than with the defendant), thereby blocking the ancient unchastity defense predicated on the syllogism, "the victim slept with Tom, she slept with Harry, therefore she slept with the defendant" (Federal Rules of Evidence, 412).

Section III

International and Comparative Perspectives on Domestic Violence

Introduction

by Michele E. Beasley

This section provides an opportunity for our examination of how different cultural and national perspectives influence analyses of domestic or "private" violence against women. The chapters also reveal the common difficulties facing women's global efforts to analyze domestic violence, and to combat its structural causes and devastating effects. These, then, are the common threads: the difficulty of naming domestic violence, and the mismatch between the severity of the experience of abuse and the weakness of the legal and social tools that exist to address that abuse.

These common threads are tied together by the "context" in which each thread—the experience, its naming, the solution—appears. By context is meant the particular position—in society, in small community, in profession, in advocacy stance, in theoretical viewpoint—from which each writer sees and writes about domestic violence. What we discover from this section is that each writer is influenced (as are we) by the context in which she finds herself even at the moment that she critiques some aspect of that context in her analysis. Context, whether or not consciously acknowledged, dictates both the way each writer conceptualizes her issues as well as the way in which she proposes to solve them. Context affects each writer's (and our) vision of domestic violence, by either expanding or limiting our ability to define the problem and how we relate to it. Thus context formulates our actions, which actions in turn affect the context out of which those actions arose, creating a circle where cause and effect are difficult to distinguish and sometimes serve to disguise the truth of what is happening, that women are subjected to violent attacks without recourse. This circularity can make it difficult to step aside and see the whole. However, we can see, in each essay in this section, the context the writer inhabits and how it affects her and her definition of and approach to domestic violence.

This ability to see clearly and describe the effects of context is, as Celina Romany points out, the crucial step for the feminist endeavor in this area: "feminism cannot afford to surrender definitional control" (p. 298). Only by holding firm our ability and right to name and define domestic violence can we hope to begin to overcome the contextual limitations that have (so far) impeded the struggle to end it, of which these writers are a part.

The comparative endeavor of this section reveals not only the consonances of contexts, but also the dissimilarities of the particulars. It is perhaps in the dissimilarity of the facts (and, therefore, the dissimilarity of the theories and perspectives to which those facts give rise) that the greatest benefits lie for creative thinking and new solutions to the problem of violence against women.

The contributors describe a broad range of analytical and advocacy problems in addressing domestic violence, problems that have their root in structures that privilege men and disempower women. These structures exist in law—in the entrenched dichotomy between a public sphere of legal rights and power and a private sphere deemed untouchable by civil society, where the experiences of those disempowered within it are ignored in the legal constructions presumed useful to defend it. The structures exist in the "helping professions"—in a view of violence as pathology, not crime, and, in the words of Romany, defiance as deviance (p. 292). The structures exist in social systems—in the acceptance of the idea that women are not capable of making decisions, and therefore must be "disciplined," and that there is self-evident justification for the (male) use of violence to control (female) others.

This section raises the issue of to what extent the context each writer inhabits recognizes or fails to recognize that domestic violence is a "harm"; what the nature of the harm is (legal, moral, physical, psychological); who it is that is harmed (the state, society, the "victim," privacy itself); and how or whether such harm should be remedied, and by whom. The particular analyses contained in each chapter demonstrate the powerful vise of patriarchy over every facet of the struggle to end domestic violence, from identification of the issues to strategies to combat it.

However, they also raise the problem of being outside the context of the violence and attempting to name it or address it. Speaking of women's oppression in many contexts carries with it the risk of imperialism and the potential destruction of the traditions that go into making up the fabric of a particular society. Thus, context is seen in these pieces to shape the debate, the solutions, and even our own participation and understanding as readers and observers.

Ofei-Aboagye offers an overview inquiry into the status and oppression of women in Ghana, wherein "the largest problem in (not) talking about domestic violence is its (not) problem status" (p. 261). Naming domestic violence, as violence, as a social and moral wrong, and thereby overtly questioning it as a "natural" phenomenon of social and marital relations, is the heart of her inquiry. She finds that there are extraordinary barriers that inhibit women themselves from talking about the abuse they experience, or from questioning its occurrence. Only two of her fifty Ghanaian interlocutors emphatically believed that "any beating at all transcends the norm" (p. 264). She describes a situation in which the general social oppression of Ghanaian women directly stalls any attempt even to discuss the problem, or to name it.

Ofei-Aboagye also offers thoughts of how to approach the necessary (re)analysis of "wife beating" in Ghana. She posits both changes to and retention of the very culture that permits wife beating and calls it natural. Through reference to the traditional "Ananse" spider children's stories, she shows how tradition reinforces the acceptance of the premise that "wives ha[ve] to bow in submission to husbands, however clumsy those men [are]." In contrast, she offers us Wole Soyinka's metaphor of change without "uprooting the plaintain sucker" (p. 269 & n. 12) and a vision of Ghanaian society as a piece of *Kente* cloth that can have a portion removed and another piece woven into its place without destroying the beauty of the whole. She points out that the greatest difficulty in speaking about the oppression of African women is that the act of labeling "the way things are" as problematic has imperialist implications for many (both men and women) who hear the charge. Questioning of tradition can be viewed as an attempt to destroy the traditions that otherwise strengthen Ghanaian society and give it its communal character. Her vision of changing Ghanaian society without destroying its fabric offers an alternative model to the frontal approach of "top-down" legal reform that seeks to change laws and then enforce them in order to change society.

Romany offers a vision of such "top-down" reform, and the difficulties that inhere in such an approach when the "discourse of extended patriarchy" (p. 285) continues to pervade the law, its application, and the thinking of its supposed adherents and experts. She documents the analytical clash between feminist groups that confront the political nature of violence and its roots in an overarching patriarchy, and law enforcement officials who see domestic violence as merely a "social problem" that should be dealt with by the "helping professions."

Although Romany chronicles the successful implementation of legal reform in Puerto Rico in 1989, she also reports the lack of fundamental progress rooted in the compromise made by Puerto Rican feminists to allow the divorce of legal reforms from an understanding of the gendered and political nature of domestic violence:

> In obscuring the political dimension of violence against women, the normalizing impulse of the helping professions, interacting with the ruling social institutions, buttress the patriarchal assignment of roles within the family. The political act of defiance is coined deviant. . . . Looking back . . . I see how the deradicalization of violence from a gender perspective strikes back and haunts us, despite its usefulness as a tactic towards legislative approval. (p. 292)

Additional difficulties arise even in a legal system that recognizes domestic violence as a crime. Des Rosiers writes of the disparity between the legal remedies that exist for children (girls) who have suffered incest and sexual abuse, and a legal framework that does not reflect the needs of those who seek justice within it. In her analysis of existing remedies, for assault and battery, intentional infliction of emotional distress and negligent failure to exercise reasonable care, and their inadequacies, Des Rosiers reveals the failure of the Canadian legal system to acknowledge the existence of gender-aligned power imbalances in familial relations. She quotes a judge who, in dismissing the action of a girl against her father, reasoned that the girl "was asked, and given time and opportunity, to think about the sexual involvement . . . [and that] the acts complained of were not against the will of the plaintiff but rather with her consent" (p. 308). This example of the "myth of the seductress daughter" is but one that demonstrates a misunderstanding of the dynamic of power in families and in gender relations generally. The Canadian legal system's failure to accurately reflect the realities of patriarchal hierarchies leads Des Rosiers to posit new legal remedies—such as the tort of incest—as necessary to provide effective legal remedies for victims of childhood sexual abuse.

Des Rosiers decries the Canadian courts' rigid and narrow interpretation of rules which serves to shut out a vulnerable group in Canadian society. However, by its nature, her criticism reveals her place in a particular context—the Canadian legal system—that can only view domestic violence through the lens of rules, procedures, and an existing power structure that is firmly based in patriarchy. Des Rosiers's chapter offers us the view of a system that can only recognize concepts it already understands. Often, like the jurist, that system cannot see its own gender bias or that of those whom it judges. In the analyses of Des Rosiers, and Thomas and myself, we can see that changing the inner workings of an existing system can result in an analysis complicated by the attempt to fit a true understanding of gender violence into preexisting pigeonholes.

Thomas and I also write from the perspective of a particular community: the international human rights community. From that perspective, we take the existing language and tools of a given system of advocacy and law to analyze domestic violence, although we explicitly note the limitations inherent in an "inside job." We demonstrate that domestic violence is an issue of state responsibility, and that the state's failure to prosecute cases of domestic violence and failure to provide equal protection of the law to women victims of violent crime violate international law. The human rights context incorporates certain limitations in the analysis of domestic violence, in particular because international human rights law is law that binds *states,* not law that binds individuals, and this focus at present necessitates a complicated analysis to demonstrate state accountability. On the other hand, while unwieldy in certain ways, a human rights approach to combating domestic violence "provides an opportunity for local institutions and activists to supplement their efforts with support from the international community" (p. 342).

We focus on the problem of discriminatory prosecution of gender-violence in Brazil, where the honor defense is used to exculpate men accused of killing their wives, and where the criminal justice system generally fails to investigate and prosecute wife murder, battery, and rape. The crafting of a human rights analysis of domestic violence in Brazil afforded an opportunity to expand human rights practice, as well as to support local struggles. The report itself, coinciding with increased activism by local women's and human rights groups, resulted in new training programs in domestic violence for local police, and the consideration of a state convention prohibiting discrimination against women.

By focusing on the struggle to name and characterize gender-violence in many of its forms, the authors of the following chapters retain their mastery of the cultural, national, and systemic contexts in which they exist. Their assessments, of both the practical problems they face as well as the theoretical limitations under which they labor, reveal common problems and various solutions. Together, the chapters show us that we can change our worlds, whatever they may be.

Domestic Violence in Ghana: Some Initial Questions

by Rosemary Ofeibea Ofei-Aboagye

Focusing

In this chapter I attempt to pull together diverse threads which depict instances of the repression of women in the Ghanaian home, and thereby to examine a problem which remains unidentified, unexplored, un-named, and therefore unsolved. The chapter focuses on some of the initial questions that can be asked about domestic violence in Ghana. Because the pressing and very real concerns of Ghanaian women are treated in a lukewarm manner (at best), this work attempts to expose the anxiety of abused women in Ghana. The challenging concepts that are identified and discussed come as a result of the very novel nature of research on domestic violence in Ghana. The woefully inadequate research findings and, indeed, the lack of substantial evidence about the concerns of Ghanaian women indicate that research on women and the status of law must become an urgent priority in Ghana.

For there to be the requisite priority exposure, it is important to focus on ways in which the concept of domestic violence has been addressed and examined in other jurisdictions. A case in point is Justice Bertha Wilson's judgment in *R. v. Lavallee* (1990), 1 S.C.R. 852. The Supreme Court of Canada's keynote decision in *Lavallee,* in May 1990, emphasizes the importance of examining wife assault in divorce cultural contexts to see if the victory "scored" on behalf of battered women could be applied as a standard test. Justice Bertha Wilson in this decision, wrote:

> The average member of the public (or of the jury) can be forgiven for asking: Why would the woman put up with this kind of treatment; why would she continue to live with such a man? How could she love a partner who beat her to the point of requiring hospitalization? Where is her self-respect? [Why doesn't she] cut loose and make a new life for

herself? Such is the reaction of the average person. ((1990), 1 S.C.R. 852)

R. v. Lavallee is an attempt to incorporate new meaning to the previously codified definition of self-defence by the Supreme Court of Canada. Its relevance in the present paper lies in its detailed discussion of the plight of the battered woman.

The *Lavallee* case concerned the application of the self-defence provision of Canada's Criminal Code[1] to an abused woman who killed her batterer by shooting him in the back as he was leaving their bedroom after threatening her life. Angelique Lavallee was charged with murder. She sought at her trial to adduce expert testimony to show that, as a battered woman, she believed that there was imminent danger to her life, and that her actions were taken in self-defence. The trial judge admitted evidence of what was described as the "battered woman syndrome," and the jury acquitted Lavallee. The Manitoba Court of Appeal, however, held that such evidence should not have been admitted, and ordered a new trial ((1989) 44 C.C.C. (3d)). The refusal to allow expert testimony was the major issue in the appeal to the Supreme Court of Canada. The Supreme Court affirmed the decision of the trial judge. Justice Wilson wrote a year later:

> Angelique Lavallee was acquitted when the social reality of wife battering and its documented effects on women victims was not only taken into account but was incorporated into the legal concept of self-defence.[2]

The dimensions of the *Lavallee* case are numerous and thought-provoking. However, the many inferences that could be drawn from the decision snowballed into one important deduction for me. If Lyn Angelique Lavallee could successfully assert self-defence based on her suffering from battered woman syndrome, this was a clear and basic indication that there was such a phenomenon as a "battered woman." Abused women were finally recognized as such. Recognition that there is such a person as a "battered woman" (indeed, that there is even the phenomenon of domestic violence) rarely occurs to most people in Ghana. My own realization that I knew women who would fall within the category of "battered women," but whom I had never thought of as such, and certainly whom the law had *never* recognized as such, seems a good focal point for my inquiry into women's status and oppression in Ghana.

Yet, was this examination of battered women a possible (and plausible) area of research, especially in Ghana? The largest problem in (not) talking about domestic violence is its (not) problem status. It is *wished* out of existence. There are reasons to deny its existence and to deliberately downplay its visibility. There is pain in recounting the violence for women (and some men). There is the embarrassment that the victim has been a "bad" wife: slothful, lazy, and argumentative, according to her husband's "standards." These may well be acceptable causes for punishing a recalcitrant wife. Again, there is the vulnerability that comes from exposure, as well as the fact that there is no place to turn—there has been the brainwashing and the conditioning that that is the way things are, and the way that things will always be. There is another problem. In defining domestic violence in Ghana, there is the difficulty in defining the actors, for domestic violence may include numerous activities and victims.[3]

Extant knowledge has made me aware that there are Ghanaian women being beaten by their husbands every day.[4] Neither the men nor their wives seem to question the phenomenon of beating as discipline, and they would not thank me for my interference. Despite this, the questions still reverberated: And what about the hurting women? Where was the "justice" that I imagined should be done—not only for North American women but for their Ghanaian (and African) counterparts as well? For *all* women?

Invisibility

The invisibility of domestic violence in Ghana has to be questioned. The difficulty lies in how to approach the study. If there had been studies previously that argued that there was no domestic violence, then arguments to refute those claims could be the focus of legal questioning. But there were (and still are) none. Logically this leads to the need to identify and, possibly, to explore the viability of naming the phenomenon, so that it would be easier to examine. For, after much searching, it appears that there are women who will talk about domestic violence, if sufficiently persuaded that their accounts will remain anonymous.

Descriptions of domestic violence can be elaborated by excerpts from interviews held with battered women in Ghana.

> He links giving me maintenance money with whether or not I have sex with him. He's violent with the children. I'd advise young women to marry God-fearing men, who go to their church. . . . He even attempts to sleep with our daughters . . . we should know people for a long time before we marry them.
>
> He refuses to accept his faults so that mediation and counselling were out of the question. Anytime my sisters suggested that I complain about his behavior, he grew wild and the treatment I would receive at home was so bad that I can't even talk about it now. Anytime I tried to talk

to him I would get a beating worse than the one I was complaining about. I finally fled the matrimonial home after I had been driven nearly insane.

But one woman who accepts that beating is a part of married life had this comment to make:

> It happens to a lot of people. If your husband gets annoyed don't respond to him. Just leave him and go out. If you reply he might beat you. So do not give him the opportunity to beat you.

This is the situation in Ghana. Most women will not talk about their experiences at the hands of abusive partners, nor will they question the existence of domestic violence in their lives or in their communities. This could be the result of traditional precedents of remaining at home, the inability of living an independent life, and, to some measure, may be attributable to religion. Whatever the reasons are as to why domestic violence is a taboo area in Ghana, an analysis of existing evidence of domestic violence remains vital. The following is a transcription of the responses of fifty women clients of the legal aid unit of FIDA, Ghana (The International Federation of Women Lawyers) to an informal survey on domestic violence (Appendix A).

In response to the survey question: "What do you understand by domestic violence?" all of the women interviewed understood domestic violence to mean the beating of a wife by her husband. However, thirty-two of them saw domestic violence as the beating of a wife by her husband only;[5] the rest added the variations of the beating of a husband by his wife, and the beating of the children by either parent.

To the question, "In your culture/tribe, is it "usual/accepted" for a woman to be beaten by her husband?" only five women out of the fifty answered "yes." All of the others stated that it was not the norm of their tribe. Yet this response was not supported by the answers to the question: "When does it transcend the norm and become a violent action—that is, assuming that it is the usual thing for women to accept some disciplining at the hands of her husband?"[6] The answers reflected that there was a norm: a point to which beating was acceptable, even expected, to keep the woman in line. But when:

> he injures her. . . . She is hurt or experiences any pain. . . . He beats her to leave a scar or deformity. . . . He leaves her with a fracture. . . . He beats her publicly. . . . The beating is more than three slaps or he beats her three or four times. . . .

then it "transcends the norm." One woman said that "a slap or two to discipline a wife is acceptable." Only two women emphatically stated that "any beating" at all transcends the norm. "Beating" was seen as any hitting. Slapping with the hands or with a weapon such as a belt, a cane, or shoes were all given as examples of beatings. In some cases some of the women admitted to being whipped or "booted."[7] All the women saw the *excessive* beating of a woman by her husband as an action to be deplored. The reasons were varied:

> A man should not use his strength to "cheat" a woman. . . . It is wrong. . . . He may injure her. . . . She is not a slave. . . . In the event of misunderstandings they should have discussions. . . . She is his partner and not his child. . . . The beating can result in death. . . . It does not show respect for the woman. . . . God made women the weaker vessels. . . . It has an adverse effect on the children. . . . It is not fair. . . .

All of the respondents had been struck by their partners during the course of the marriage. Three of them had not gone through the traditional marriage, even though they were living with their assaulters. For all purposes they were treated as "married" women, and therefore, had been beaten or "disciplined" several times. Only four women called the beating "one isolated incident," but five of them had endured more than ten years of beating. In most cases they had lost count of the number of times they had been beaten. The incidents that caused the beatings varied:

> He would beat me whenever he was drunk. . . . When I confronted him with evidence of his sleeping with another woman. . . . When I asked him for chop money [housekeeping money] . . . When I refused to have sex. . . . There was no particular reason. . . . Because I was pregnant. . . . He accused me of sleeping with another man. . . . Because my cooking was not to his taste. . . . He said I was rude in public. . . . I had insulted his mother. . . . I spent too much money. . . .

None of the women had left her abusive marriage, for a variety of reasons:

> I felt shy at my "failure" to keep my husband happy. . . . I would not be able to keep the children in the comfort to which they were accustomed. . . . So long as the danger to my health was not so bad I felt that I could manage. . . . My family would not support me if I left. . . . I did not want my children to have different fathers. . . . I had no money to sue him in court. . . . We have to be obedient to our husbands. . . .

I know of no organization that could advise and support me if I left.
. . .

The general consensus to questions such as:

Do you consider the beating(s) serious enough to warrant any action against him? How long would you experience the violence before you would think of reporting him? What would eventually cause you to come out of your silence to report him? and What are the sort of actions that would be taken?

was that all the women who had been beaten saw that the beatings were serious enough to warrant some outsider action, but said they had never really thought about "serious action" because that was just not the way things were done, and that "it could be worse."[8]

The form of action to be taken by the women posed the biggest problem. They had little or no information about what to do or whether, indeed, they had the "right" to do anything. Each woman had reported the incidents to some relatives, usually her own, at one time or another. In nine cases the women had reported their husbands to the chief of the village where he came from, though it had not helped much. One of fifty women, only four of them saw their first option as reporting the violence to the police. Two women had reported the incidents to their husbands' superiors at work. Two had sought the assistance of the Department of Social Welfare, but had had no meaningful response. Ten women had chosen to report the abuse to their priests as a first effort, but none could report to their doctors because "they felt shy." All of the women felt that once they had been to FIDA they could seek out FIDA lawyers for advice: specifically on the sort of legal action to take, and the kind of redress they could secure.

The women were asked the question:

Stepping out to report domestic violence entails great determination and courage. It can lead to a number of repercussions against you and possibly your children. What would be the final step against you that would encourage you to take this move?

All the women interviewed felt that they had endured enough pain and humiliation to come out of their silence to report the abuse, and possibly leave the relationship with their assaulter. Asked why they now felt they could break their silence, all of them ascribed their fears to the danger being done to their health. One woman felt "she was going insane." More than half felt that the repeated abuse to them was detrimental to the atmosphere in which their children were growing up.

Finally, when asked if they would opt for mediation and counseling to repair the marriage, most of them found that such a step would be "useless," since they had, for the most part, always been blamed for the breakdown of the relationship by their partners and both families. Though most of them wanted the violence to stop, they were not clear what alternatives there were, and apart from three who were definitely leaving their marriages, the others had not ever considered any other options but to remain with their partners.

Fifty cases are not enough upon which to make any definitive statement about domestic violence in Ghana, except that it is experienced by some women. However, these interviews do document the fact of domestic violence among the respondents. The problem now is how to deal with it.

The Trends

There are two possible trends in describing "domestic violence" in Ghana. If the words "domestic violence" and/or "wife beating" are used to describe the violence that women feel at the hands of their partners, there would be no affirmative responses by Ghanaian battered women to assertions that they are being abused. There seems to be no consensus that a Ghanaian wife is beaten merely for the sake of *beating*. According to this way of naming the problem, most Ghanaian women would deny that they are abused. If on the other hand, the violence was referred to as "discipline" which wives received at the hands of their husbands, the women would possibly tell their stories, but always with the anxiety that they were washing their dirty linen in public.

The difficulty lay—and still lies—in the fact that, for the most part, speaking about any form of oppression of the African woman implies an importation of Western academic values into traditional African beliefs. It follows that generally, feminist analysis is anathema to the culture, because it questions the *status quo* and ripples the smooth surface of tradition. Following this logic, any inquiry into domestic violence is an importation of "foreign" values into the traditional culture.

It is a common expectation of the current social order in Ghana, that a woman must wait for her husband to lead the way in all that she does. There is a dominant view that, without him, she is incapable of even small decisions. This is a social order that must go, and along with it the customs and folklore that condition people into thinking that wife beating is acceptable.

Since there is a dearth of reported cases and studies on domestic violence in Ghana, an illustration from traditional Ghanaian folklore seems effective here. There are stories which most children in a Ghanaian community are told, in the evening, just before they go to bed, and often by their grandmothers (or Nana). They cover a wide range of issues about our ways of life. Children assimilate the lessons of these stories subconsciously. But those children can, if need be, recall them as illustrations of how the people in the culture should act. There are no stories labelled "domestic violence," but there are stories about how a man beats his wife to maintain "law and order." Here is such a story.

Ananse

Ghanaian children's stories usually revolve around the figure Ananse[9] and the traditional songs about him. It is incredible how, as children, we accept certain things as a matter of course. Children laugh at the amusing incidents that occur in Ananse's colorful existence, and never question the role of Yaa, his wife, in it. She is stoic and uncomplaining. There are stories in which their seemingly endless poverty and hunger would have ended if Yaa's ideas had been accepted by Ananse.[10] But no, Ananse's grand gestures always take precedence. When things go wrong, Yaa always takes a beating, for Ananse is quick with his fists, and never accepts his faults.

Seated at the feet of Nana, we learned at the end of the story, every time, that it was splendid to be as daring as Ananse, since he always escaped in the nick of time. But more germane to the present context, we learned that wives had to bow in submission to husbands, however clumsy those men were. Ananse was always right. We never questioned the basis of this premise—it conditioned the boys, it conditioned the girls. Yaa was a colorless, beaten woman; she was always in Ananse's shadow. This conditioned the boys, it conditioned the girls.

> Ananse went to transact business in town, about three days' journey from his village. At that time, he was a wealthy cocoa owner, and the crop had been gathered and the beans were being dried. It meant a huge sum of money if he saved all the beans. He left Yaa in charge of the beans to guard them with her life and to make sure that no water spilt on them, since water would destroy the fermentation process.
>
> His business went well in town, so he bought himself a pair of dark glasses which made the world look stormy and mysterious. He went back home, donning the glasses as he approached the homestead. As he got near the cocoa beans he realized that it was about to rain and he yelled for Yaa to take the beans in. She did so quickly yet he mercilessly beat her up. She picked herself off the ground as she had done many times before, and waited to know the nature of her offence.

How could you leave the beans out when it is going to rain? My Lord, it is not going to rain. It is, it is; are you arguing with me? I'll teach you. At that point, his dark glasses slipped off his nose and he saw the sun was suddenly as bright as always.

This is a traditional folktale teaching the subservience of wives, even in the height of a husband's blunders. But for children it is a hilarious story. I remember how we laughed at Ananse's blunder, while admiring his control over Yaa. Yaa's feelings were never at issue. There were always songs and refrains encouraging this mastery of wives.

It is noteworthy that a number of these songs are songs that educate on marriage in the Ghanaian society. However, they are also songs which, should they disturb the ideological facade of male superiority, endanger the power relationship between wives and husbands. Even women, therefore, prefer to keep the facade intact in order to safeguard their interests. Asante Darko and Van der Geest record a report by Kleinkowski which is atypical of this:

> For the annual meeting of a Ghanaian women's organization a song was composed which said "The belief of the past that men are superior to women gives way to a new era: men and women are equal." The women liked the song but did not want to sing it because, as they said, their husbands would stop giving them chop money [housekeeping money] if they heard the song. (Asante Darko and Van der Geest, 1984, p. 248)

The palpable oppression that is recorded here cannot be discounted. Yet, there persists in Ghana the belief that stifling the truths about the society, including those about the oppression of women, prevents strife and discord. Women have always borne the brunt of this denial, and, it seems, will continue to do so. Male superiority has always prevailed, and does not show any sign of abating in Ghana.

Ghanaian women might say:

> It is true, without him I cannot function and he knows that I need him for that. Yesterday, he said as much—and I fully endorsed what he said. Our culture knows that we need our men to take decisions for us.

And they must be told:

> Then you must be "radicalized" yourself . . . to know that you are capable of taking these decisions . . . all decisions.

This "radicalization" must proceed from awareness—awareness of things that need to be examined. A good place to start is with the recognition of domestic violence as a problem and not as a way of life.

The women would say:

> So are you saying that after we have recognized within ourselves the need to undergo a transformation to "improve our lot," and to see some self-worth in ourselves, we must seek a forum for defining the shortcomings (the flaws in the fabric) and attempt to put some semblance of order in the regulation of these shortcomings?
> Yes, that is what I am saying.
> And you say that it is not too different from the weaving of our traditional *Kente?*[11] and that we must add to and subtract from the original fabric in order to create a masterpiece? That I think we can do. The important thing is to achieve its beauty for the good of all. Well, we are doing our best, but you should understand that it is not easy. In a way you are trying to undo our cultural values. You are trying to uproot the plantain sucker[12] and you know what that means.

I would reply:

> I am only trying to remove one sucker and replace it with another. How can I attempt to uproot the mother? Did you not hear? I am only giving you a choice out of many. You know that my whole aim is to have the strongest plantain tree. . . .

A major difficulty lies in the often unreceptive attitude of Ghanaian *women* to the idea of an awareness which is not necessarily harmful to them. It is my view that domestic violence exists in all Ghanaian communities—whatever form it may take—and it must be exposed and brought to the awareness of Ghanaian women. Further, searching for and addressing issues of domestic violence must not be dismissed as the figments of the overheated imaginations of a few female malcontents. If such sentiments belonged solely to men, it would be easier, in a sense, to understand. The greater challenge comes from women who draw negative conclusions about the need for change. Yet, ironically, these women are also victims of the rules and abuses of the society.[13]

Domestic violence is a form of violence that robs women of their very soul and reason for being. It reduces them to a nothingness, and often renders them useless in their societies. Women so situated are like the "living dead," and as long as they remain in that position they cannot function as they should: full of confidence and working to their fullest capacities.

While I would say that most of the laws in force in Ghana are in need of a careful reworking to dispel the notion of the inferiority of Ghanaian women, in the present context, I dwell on initial inquiries into the problem of wife beating. First, I question the fact that wife beating has never been examined under Ghana's laws; second, I ask whether its eradication should be controlled by the activities of Ghanaian women's organizations, or by self-help and education projects to uplift and upgrade the status of Ghanaian women. Finally, I ask whether it will be necessary to promulgate new laws to eradicate wife beating.

It is my current aim to draw attention to wife beating as an area of distress that requires rethinking and social change in Ghana. While an instant solution to this problem cannot be formulated, thinking about it as an example of the need for social reform and substantive equality for Ghanaian women is important.

Wife Battering: An Area of Distress

In his introduction to a study on interval and transition houses for battered women in Canada, T. Don observed that:

> woman battering is a crime and a social problem, not a private affair. Therefore all levels of government and society must share the responsibility to eliminate it. (Don 1986, p. 8)

This may be seen as an urgent appeal to address the problem of domestic violence in Canada, a country where efforts have been made to expose the phenomenon in the last fifteen to twenty years (McGillivray 1987, pp. 14–45). It is precisely such an appeal that is needed in Ghana, where the issue has not been addressed at all.

Some of the questions that come to mind when beginning to think about the problem of wife beating in Ghana are: What can be done to identify and define the problems of wife beating to make them visible to Ghanaians generally? What legislation can be structured to support the bid to eradicate it? And, even if legislation is passed to eradicate it, how can we ensure that following such legislation will create peace for women? What can be used to bring awareness of domestic violence to the forefront? And what social policies can be taken to counter the problem?

As I have suggested, domestic violence has not been regarded as a problem in Ghana, and has certainly not been given the same exposure as it has in Canada.[14] Moreover, it is not likely that, were the same exposure to be given, the same measures would necessarily be taken to address domestic violence in Ghana. There is not yet a felt need for a redefinition of the crime in Ghana; indeed, it is not defined as a crime.

The Canadian Law Reform Commission has written about domestic violence that:

> in general, public education is essential to prevent such attacks from being somehow different from ordinary assaults and more acceptable than ordinary violence (Law Reform Commission of Canada 1984, p. 38).

This statement sums up what can be the only possible antidote to the problem of domestic violence. It is my view that an emphasis on "public education" through the activities of some women's organizations is vital. These activities can be used to bring attention to the problem of domestic violence in Ghana. I submit that only through some form of public education, awareness, and social change process can domestic violence be eradicated, and the status of Ghanaian women upgraded. I will consider how far community-based organizations in Ghana can be used to disseminate the message that women should be free from domestic violence. The education of the Ghanaian woman about her self-worth as an independent human being is a necessary starting point, in my view, for any efforts to address and eradicate domestic violence from Ghana.

The attitude of resigned hopelessness must go. The most vital step is the need to remove, from the minds of the women themselves, the conditioned helplessness which seems to pervade them regardless of their differing levels of education. As Justice Anne Jiagge pointed out in a talk given at the World Council of Churches' Fifth Plenary Presentation on "Women in a Changing World" in Nairobi, in 1975:

> [W]omen have accepted the inferior status imposed upon them as an inescapable part of life. Wives are proud to be treated as appendages of their husbands. A wife will bask in the glory of her husband's achievements without giving a thought to her own capabilities and native wisdom. Even where the creative urge is strong and she is aware of her own potential she is inhibited within herself and suppresses what is crying to be let out for fear of being regarded as out of the ordinary. (Arthur, 1976, p. 149)

And Lucy Arthur, speaking at an African Conference on the need for the African Woman to speak out more boldly than the tradition has previously allowed her, had this to say about the Ghanaian woman:

> [W]e realised too that woman herself should be awakened from her long sleep. We did not lose sight of the fact that centuries of discrimination and deep-rooted prejudice have conditioned the women themselves. (Arthur, 1976, p. 149)

I believe both of these observations to be true. If it is the general attitude of Ghanaian women to believe that they are mere appendages to their husbands, and if this is the conditioning of centuries of prejudice, both must be changed. For these attitudes lead to the oppression of women to such an extent that they feel that their oppression is part of "the way life is."

Marilyn Frye compares the oppression of women to the structure of a bird cage (Frye 1983). She notes that if you examine closely any one wire or each of the wires of the cage individually and in sequence, you will be unable to figure out why the bird cannot escape. If however, you stand back and view the cage as a whole it becomes perfectly obvious that the bird is surrounded by a network of systematically related barriers—not one of which by itself would be the least hinderance to the bird's flight, but which, by their interwoven relations, become as confining as the solid walls of the dungeon. This graphic description could be said to apply to the situation of Ghanaian women who seek to flee from circumstances of abuse. For them, the "cage wires" include being ostracized by family; economic hardships generated by the battered wife's quest for independence; a fear of further abuse if she attempts to leave; loss of custody of children; and, importantly, the "learned helplessness" (Walker 1979) which the society has conditioned a woman to feel and which renders her unable to do many things for herself. Perhaps, taken individually, these factors would be no bar to the woman's escape. However, taken as a whole, the cage is a permanent prison, and there is indeed no escape.

Despite the power of Frye's analogy, I wonder if the Ghanaian woman sees herself as a bird in a cage. First, she is not aware of confinement. What Frye describes as "a network of systematically related barriers" would be interpreted as a way of life . . . *the* way of life. Second, the individual strands of the cage (that is, the factors which discourage her from leaving an abusive marriage) may be seen as only minor irritations to be taken in stride as the hazards to expect in a marriage. Hence, there is the larger problem: How do you free someone from bondage, who does not experience herself in bondage?

Towards Addressing Domestic Violence in Ghana

In order to free Ghanaian women from the oppression of domestic violence we need to understand their needs and fears. Proposals to address and counter domestic violence could be made to the police, to the legislature, or to the judiciary in a bid to do away with it. However, if such proposals do not reflect what women think or feel, this goal may not be achieved. Projects which embrace the needs of Ghanaian women without tearing apart the fabric of Ghana's undoubtedly rich tradition are needed to enhance and encourage the development of Ghanaian women, and to bring domestic violence into the open. There can be no meaningful solution to the problem of wife beating unless an entire community pitches in to help.

This belief is based on my knowledge that generally Ghanaians have a sense of the communal well-being of their society. On the whole, society in Ghana is not individualistic, and members of a particular community are ready, for the most part, to assist each other. I find it interesting that the same community which takes a keen interest in a bereaved neighbor's plight may be reticent in intervening when a man is beating up his wife. Perhaps, with the right education, the community can harness its energies to alleviate the anguish of a battered wife.

Self-awareness and, therefore, self-help could be more readily achieved by strengthening female organizations in Ghana. Organizations established to meet the needs of women should be functional, technically competent, and, most importantly, should reach rural women.[15] The Ghana National Council on Women and Development (NCWD) is one such organization that can help bring an awareness about the plight of battered women in Ghana.[16] Since most of the women in Ghana belong to a local voluntary organization, either in the church or at their work-place—be it the market, a factory, or an office—the council tries to work through these organizations to reach women (Dolphyne 1987, p. 214).

The first major task of the NCWD was to create public awareness about the plight of Ghanaian women. It launched a program of education in 1975 to eradicate prejudices through public lectures and discussions on radio and television, in English and in the Ghanaian languages. One result of this educational program was a healthy debate that went on in schools and in the newspapers about women's capabilities and their role in the society (Dolphyne 1987, p. 214).

An illustration of some of its other concerns may help to show how the NCWD could be important as a means of reform in the arena of domestic violence in Ghana—especially where the productive and repro-ductive roles of Ghanaian women in the development of the country are so vital. If domestic violence is one of the reasons why women's full productive potential has not been realized, then a policy to eradicate it must be undertaken to facilitate their development.[17]

The specific question of wife beating or domestic violence has never, to my knowledge, been addressed as a matter of primary consideration by the NCWD. However, the NCWD is one forum that could begin to teach the Ghanaian people that domestic violence should not be accepted as part of marriage in both rural and urban settings. Even though domes-tic violence has hitherto been seen as a private matter, and, consequently, has not been regarded as falling within the scope of National and Developmental Organizations such as the NCWD, it should be treated as a public development issue. Women in Ghana could contribute more effectively to Ghana's development if they did not have the threat and experiences of domestic violence to contend with.

One of the long-term plans of the NCWD is to embark on functional literacy programs for illiterate women. In addition, the NCWD has, from time to time, made recommendations to the government about issues affecting the education and training of girls, especially regarding the creation of an educational program relevant to the educational needs of young girls. This has included suggestions to diversify vocational training programs for girls to include nontraditional courses. A series of seminars, consultations, and public discussions have been held throughout the country to identify the needs of Ghanaian women with respect to training, income generation, employment, health, and family welfare (Dolphyne 1987).

The cynicism with which people greeted the launching of the International Women's Year in Ghana soon gave way to sober reflection and an understanding of the issues that the NCWD programs for the year were designed to highlight. This reflection and greater understanding could happen, too, in the case of domestic violence if it were given wide exposure and coverage. It is true that there will be an initial cynicism and opposition to such a change in the existing culture, but with perseverance this can be altered (Dolphyne 1987).

Ghana has been a member of FIDA (Federation International de Abogadas), the International Federation of Women Lawyers, for over a decade. The federation was born some thirty years ago in Mexico. Its membership stretches over seventy countries, and it has among its aims the need to promote and enhance the welfare of women and children upon whose well-being the happiness of the home and the strength of society depends (Arthur 1976).

It is my view that FIDA could be an ideal organization for the exposure of domestic violence in Ghana. This is because it is a high-powered organization of which some of Ghana's best-educated women are members. These women are in a position to propose many measures which their colleagues in other countries have proposed to stop the oppression of women. Moreover, it is not an organization of lawyers exclusively. Female judges are also members. All these women could be very influential with respect to this issue if they were so inclined. At the moment FIDA is devoted, along with the Legal Aid Clinic in Ghana, to assisting Ghanaian women with their legal problems. Its engagement with the issue of domestic violence would convey the message that it is a problem which must be exposed and eradicated. As a legal matter, this in itself would further the sense of self-worth of women in their own environments. If organizations such as the NCWD and FIDA help to deal with the issue of domestic violence, the awareness that is needed to break through the "culture of silence" that surrounds this deeply private crime against women could be generated.

Community Education

While the NCWD and FIDA can help draw awareness to domestic violence in Ghana, and attempt to draw women out of their oppression, I acknowledge that all of this cannot be done if Ghanaian men, who control the resources of the society, are not educated about the outrage of domestic violence. Public education must be given priority in Ghana. The most obvious solution is to place posters in public places berating the evils of wife abuse. The radio and television stations could also be used as a way of reaching out. Dramas acted out on the television often have tremendous impact on the viewing public.[18] If these programs were to focus on the wrongfulness of domestic violence, they could be an effective part of a campaign to educate the public. This could be a campaign drawn up by FIDA and the Adult Education Unit of the Ghana Broadcasting Corporation. However, there will be great financial costs involved. Running television and radio programs as well as designing posters could further deplete the almost empty coffers of the state. Thus, though media exposure is a solution, what must be undertaken is a more inexpensive communitarian approach.

One way of educating the people of Ghana about the evils of domestic violence is to use the medium of the chieftaincy. It is my view that the power of the chief in Ghana can be used in a positive way to help address and alleviate the hardships and horrors of domestic violence.

Susan Hare, President of the Ontario Native Women's Association, once stated that:

> It [the Association] should draw heavily on the resources of elders and the most respected members of the community, who can assist aboriginal men in overcoming their anger, frustration and destructive behavior towards their families.[19]

Hare's recommendation, that the resources of First Nations elders be used to address the problem of domestic violence among Canada's native people, supports my view that chiefs of Ghana may be able to assist in addressing and eradicating the problem of domestic violence in Ghana. The chiefs of Ghana are deeply revered,[20] and the entire institution of the chieftaincy is felt to be a sublime one.[21] It is an institution that is felt to be ordained by God. For the most part, it is regarded as superior to the human-made choices of the three democratic governments that Ghana has had, and also to the military governments which have arisen from the coups that have besieged Ghana since its independence in 1957. For these reasons, even though I consider possible government legislation and the paragovernmental policies that can be taken, I believe that edicts from the chieftaincy to stop domestic violence will be taken seriously.[22]

Education of the Men (Without Uprooting the Plantain Sucker)

The task of introducing novel ways of thinking about male/female roles is not an easy one. A reason for this could be that questions about gender roles have not been a priority issue for the women with whose safety I am concerned. The primary concern of the majority of Ghanaian women in the rural areas and in the poor areas of the urban centers has been for employment, in particular self-employment (Dolphyne 1987, p. 215). Many of them are too preoccupied with obtaining money to feed themselves and their children to worry about why they are beaten. Furthermore, the boldness it requires to disagree with "enshrined" principles of established tradition is not easy to come by. There would need to be a massive educational campaign guaranteed to change beliefs and practices which have been held since time immemorial about the place of a woman and the right of her husband to assault her. This reeducation has to be done without unduly upsetting the tradition (without uprooting the plantain sucker). Or, to use another metaphor, it must be done in such a way that changing a strand in the *Kente* fabric and altering the pattern does not destroy the fabric. The educational campaigns must come from the NCWD and FIDA, together with the National House of Chiefs. It will be a slow process, but not an impossible one.

Other Recommendations

I have argued that organizations like the National Council for Women and Development (NCWD) and the International Federation of Women Lawyers (FIDA) can educate Ghanaian communities about the harms of domestic violence. This role is in keeping with similar efforts which have been made by women and women's movements elsewhere. Undoubtedly, it was such early efforts that led to the exposure of domestic violence in other countries. I believe the same exposure can be accomplished in Ghana.

There are other recommendations to combat domestic violence in Ghana that can be made. These are longer-term solutions to domestic violence, and must wait until there is a greater awareness about domestic violence in Ghana before they can be put into place. However, they can ultimately help to eradicate domestic violence in Ghana. These measures include the introduction of the specific crime of wife beating in the Criminal Code; a definition of cruelty in the Matrimonial Causes Act; and the education of the police and the judiciary about the need to eradicate domestic violence. Ultimately, the setting up of transition houses for battered women and rehabilitation homes for battering men are also necessary. I will discuss these "solutions" briefly.

The Police

Upon interviewing fifty Ghanaian women, in May 1991, it was found that only four of them would report domestic violence to the police. This finding could stem from an attitude that "other" people should not be involved in domestic matters, or from the fact that any punishment or stigma attaching to the husband as a result of such a report would be the fault of the woman and would operate to her detriment and that of her children. Yet, unless the police are utilized, there can be no meaningful eradication of the problem of domestic violence. The Police Service Act of Ghana could be a medium for channeling the services of the police in Ghana into restraining and controlling domestic violence. As a first step FIDA, in conjunction with the police service, could organize education programs to educate police officers about the need to treat domestic violence as a public matter, and to engage in discourse about the dangers and unfairness of the traditional idea of discipline of wives by beating. Undoubtedly these would be uphill tasks, but important ones. A second step would be to issue directives for the compulsory charging of spousal abuse offenses in Ghana. Ultimately, a project such as the London, Ontario Integrated Community Project, which has been tried in Canada, might be of immense help in Ghana. In May 1981, the London, Ontario City Police Force, in conjunction with the University of Western Ontario and several community services, came together to fight the problem of wife abuse in the area. This is a project which took the approach that the community, through the leadership and advocacy of criminal justice officers, could improve services to victims of family violence if people became more aware of the dynamics of the problem and realized the limitations of existing services.

Policies were put in place to encourage and empower officers to lay charges of assault in domestic situations. The program did not result from changes in legislation, but was undertaken by the police department in response to research which indicated that victims wanted officers to lay charges, and that the necessary grounds for laying charges often existed. The police perceived this policy to reflect a change in attitude about the seriousness of wife assault cases (Burris and Jaffe 1982, 1983, 1984). This project is worth studying in the hope that in future it can be made applicable to the Ghanaian situation.

Legislation

There is no specific legislation in the Criminal Code of Ghana to deter husbands from beating their wives. While assault is categorized under three main headings as Assault and Battery, Assault without Actual Battery, and Imprisonment, none of these is clearly designed to cover the crime of domestic violence. It is submitted that the legislative body in Ghana should consider the creation and definition of a crime of wife beating in the Ghanaian Criminal Code and introduce the mandatory prosecution of such assaults.

In addition, I believe that, if any meaningful headway is to be made in identifying, restricting, and restraining domestic violence, eventually there should be clear provisions within the Matrimonial Causes Act of Ghana which make battering a ground of divorce, regardless of the status of the victim.

The NCWD has done research which documents the absence of women on the country's decision-making bodies at all levels. Few women hold positions of seniority and authority in the medical, legal, and educational fields, or the civil service (Dolphyne 1987, p. 214). It is submitted that legislative organs must have the representation of both women and men if laws are to be designed effectively, to consider the position and well-being of women. The present government of Ghana is alleged to have pledged its commitment to women.[23] If this is so, then with the enhanced participation of women in the decision-making process, there is a chance that more may be done to alleviate the hardships of women.[24]

The Judiciary

In the Ghana Law Reports there are few reported cases on domestic violence. However, some reported divorce law cases indicate that some judges believe that a woman's social standing and education should determine whether assaults by her husband are cruel or not.[25] This finding can be illustrated with statements from the judgments of two selected cases.[26] In *Manu v. Manu,* a European wife petitioned for a divorce on the ground of cruelty. She complained that, among other grievances, she had been beaten by her Ghanaian husband. A deciding factor in the Chief Justice's ruling was his observation that:

... the petitioner is a university graduate and must be a person of considerable culture and intelligence. In our opinion, conduct of the kind complained of ... having regard to her class and standing, amounted to mental cruelty. ([1959] Ghana Law Reports, 21)

The petitioner was, in the opinion of the judge, subjected to the indignity of *mental cruelty* which was not befitting her status. His words seem to imply that such treatment might be more appropriate for or less cruel to women who do not fall within Manu's class and standing. In *Osei-Koom v. Osei-Koom*, Edusei J. said:

... here are a man and a woman trained in the best traditions of English life and urbanity. And their standard of culture, no doubt is on a higher plane than that of a couple quartered in a remote Ghanaiain village. ... ([1967] Ghana Law Reports, 274)

In both cases the battered wives got the divorces they sought. But it is the comments of the judges which set me thinking. Are there categories of women who should be beaten, and women who should not? If a meaningful policing of domestic violence is to be pursued, it must be on the premise that no woman should be excluded from legal protection against assault. Will there be a time in Ghana when all women will be seen as "equal"—all deserving of a basic freedom from domestic oppression, and not dichotomised by virtue of their position in Ghanaian society? Will a time come when there will no longer be a stoic acceptance that all women are inferior to men, and that among the inferior, there are still some more inferior than others? To my mind, when judges identify people by their class and standing, they cease to be impartial referees dispensing justice. This detracts from the purpose of the law. There must be a reeducation of the judiciary, so that all Ghanaian women can be seen by judges as equal to each other and entitled to equal protection of the laws. This could be one of the projects that I would recommend that FIDA, in conjunction with the judicial service of Ghana, take on, to educate the judiciary about the horrors of domestic violence.

Last Words

There is a need to deal with the problems that face Ghanaian women with regard to the oppression of domestic violence. The questions which arise are many: What is the nature and incidence of domestic violence in Ghana? Why do the cases not get to the courts? What are the sociological and the psychological constraints? What are the attitudes of the authorities on the issue—the judges, the police, the lawmakers, and the extended family? What lessons can be learned from other jurisdictions which have taken the bold plunge to examine questions of domestic violence?

It is my hope that the above discussion will generate serious and widespread interest in domestic violence. Perhaps this discussion will also help us to focus on the practical efforts to address this problem. Issues such as the education of the public about the right to be free from such abuse; the upgrading of the educational and employment level of women to help reduce their economic dependence on their husbands; the enactment of provisions within the Ghanaian Criminal Code and the Matrimonial Causes Act to deter and punish wife battering; the education of the police and the judiciary about the concept of domestic violence and its attendant remedies, all should be considered.

At present, the paucity of information on domestic violence in Ghana indicates how compelling it is that studies be carried out about this problem. Whatever I have written here about domestic violence in Ghana is the result of piecing together information from a few interviews with Ghanaian women, from divorce cases, and from folklore. It is evident that much more work needs to be undertaken on the subject. To merely make pronouncements about how heinous the crime of domestic violence is will not solve it. There is every need to address it by engaging in research, self-help, and communal and traditional education. Only once these measures have demonstrated clearly that the problem of domestic violence does exist in Ghana, and that it is wrong, will the legislative, prosecutorial, and judicial controls be drawn up and enforced.

Domestic violence can no longer be accepted as an "occupational hazard" of marriage in Ghana. The time has come to name it and address it, and for its eradication.

Appendix A

The idea of a questionnaire to be administered to Ghanaian women who had been assaulted by their husbands was born out of my need for some "evidence" to support the fact that there was indeed a lot of wife assault occurring in Ghana.

The Legal Aid Clinic of FIDA seemed an adequate forum for finding women who had been victims of domestic violence. FIDA is the abbreviated name for the International Federation of Female Lawyers, of which Ghana is a member. Among other duties they run a legal aid clinic for women with domestic or marital problems.

In May 1991, I discussed the possibility of administering such a questionnaire with Ms. Doe Tsikata, a colleague in Ghana. Both Ms. Tsikata and Ms. Sheila Gyimah were working at the legal aid clinic of FIDA between May 1991 and August 1991.

They assured me that there were a substantial number of women coming to the clinic with marital problems. Thus, it would not be difficult to do an informal survey of some of those women to identify whether they were victims of their husband's violence, and further, to ascertain their views on what domestic violence entailed and whether it could be considered a problem or not. I make no claim to sophistication in the design of the questionnaire which I sent to Ms. Tsikata in May. It is simply presented as a number of questions about women's experiences with views about their reactions to domestic violence.

The respondents were, at the time of their interviews, all old clients of the legal aid clinic of FIDA. The questionnaires were administered to the women as and when they came to the clinic for their first (but previously scheduled) appointment between the months of May and August. These women were selected on the basis of their willingness to answer questions on domestic violence. It was explained to them that the interview had nothing to do with their individual cases but was to support a study of domestic violence in Ghana being done in Canada.

The women were assured of anonymity in answer to their fears that the questionnaire would expose their private domestic affairs. The interviewers assured the respondents that they understood that domestic violence was not a topic about which women could express their viewpoints openly. In spite of the assurances, out of the approximately two hundred women who were clients with domestic problems at FIDA during the time of the interviews, only fifty of them agreed to do the interview. All the others refused on the basis that they did not wish to have any answers recorded "against them." Those who agreed to do the interviews felt they had "nothing to lose" if their views were recorded.

The respondents came from all sorts of backgrounds. They did not belong to a particular income bracket, did not have a common educational background, nor did they belong to one particular tribe. However, what these women had in common was the fact that they were all consulting FIDA about marital problems. This was in itself quite unusual, as women are not encouraged to discuss their domestic affairs with "strangers" as opposed to family members. Yet all these women had gone through a form of abuse by their partners which had taken them to the point that they felt that they had to seek recourse from the legal aid clinic of FIDA.

All the respondents were encouraged to air their views and to relive their experiences through the medium of the questions asked. There were a number of illiterate women among the sample group. For this reason, about a third of the respondents had oral interviews. Wherever

282 / *Rosemary Ofeibea Ofei-Aboagye*

possible, the Ghanaian dialect that the respondent was most familiar with was spoken. Transcription and where necessary, translation were done by the two lawyers who assisted me.

Notes

Paper presented at the Domestic Violence Conference: Columbia Law School, New York. (3 & 4 April 1992)

1. The Revised Statutes of Canada, 1985, c. C–46, S.34.

2. Madame Justice Bertha Wilson, "Women, the Family and the Constitutional Protection of Privacy," speech delivered in Hong Kong in June 1991, pp. 24–25.

3. Whenever I talk about domestic violence in this paper, I am referring to physical abuse of women by their partners.

4. In an interview held with fifty Ghanaian women in Ghana, at least thirty-six of them did not hesitate to describe domestic violence *solely* as the physical abuse of a female by her male partner.

5. Interestingly the word "beating" was used interchangeably with "disciplining."

6. I believe that the reason for this discrepancy may lie in the framing of the question. The women were asked if "*beating* was the norm". If they had been asked if "*disciplining* was the norm" more might have replied "yes." This is because most of them accept some beating as "discipline."

7. Usual slang in Ghana for kicking.

8. These are the condensed answers of the women. The individual responses are more graphic and revealing than are transcribed here.

9. *Ananse* means spider. Kweku Ananse is the Spider-man. He has an overworked hapless wife (Yaa) and a brood of malformed children. There are several stories which depict Ananse as an inept, bumbling, greedy man—full of cunning with which he attempts to cheat the rest of the world. His pranks are often traced back to him, but he always manages to escape by the skin of his teeth, leaving his wife to take the blame. Despite his clumsiness, there are also a number of stories which show him as a formidable disciplinarian to his wife Yaa and their children. They all stand in awe of him, and the underlying message is that the man of the house, regardless of his social position, has the untrammelled mandate to control the household as he will.

10. Ideas such as cultivating a farm of their own instead of plundering their neighbor's; or of engaging in some profitable business venture instead of living on the gifts made to them by sympathetic passersby, as Ananse pretended that all of his family were lepers and beggars.

11. *Kente* is the traditional cloth of Ghana, originating from the powerful Ashanti Empire. It entirely defies description in the beauty of its weave. It is as much a tradition as the very essence of the people themselves, and the mystery of its quality is handed down from generation to generation, not through words but through a picturesque weave which speaks for itself.

12. Plantain trees grow out of plantain suckers in tropical forests. There is usually a clump of suckers from which the strongest sucker grows over and above the others to become the dominant tree. The plantain sucker is a particularly difficult sucker to uproot; hence the expression "Uprooting the sucker" is a popular traditional saying

which refers to a person's stubborn desire to uproot and change the firmly entrenched *status quo*.

13. It is not unknown for some women to see other women who question the inequality between the sexes as frustrated malcontents. This is so especially in a country where there has not been an active rethinking of women's issues to date. It is interesting to note the different reasons that some women will ascribe to others who seek to address the oppression of women. Lahey (1985, p. 521) describes this situation aptly. Interestingly, it seems that in Ghana the few women who have been exposed to the rethinking of women's issues in other cultures cannot or do not think that they are the ones to introduce the "change." In my view, the choice of domestic violence as a way of introducing topical and essential questions about equality into the Ghanaian culture seems apt.

14. As demonstrated for example, in the groundbreaking work on domestic violence by Macleod 1984; Jaffe and Burris 1984; and Dutton 1988. Macleod, for example, takes the issues in context—examining and identifying the problems of wife assault and stressing the urgent need for women to become aware of the fact that it is a crime.

    Rather than wait for wholesale directives to be issued by provincial and federal governments, Burris and Jaffe use the community model of combined assistance by the police and the community of London, Ontario. This project, now over a decade old, has been described as an unqualified success. Dutton begins with the hypothesis that domestic assault is dependent, to a large extent, on psychological factors. He examines this hypothesis from the criminal justice viewpoint.

15. The aim of incorporating women on an equal basis with men into development planning as decision-makers, administrators, and beneficiaries has been a recurrent theme of national and international meetings held in the past decade, and was repeatedly emphasized by country delegations in July 1985. The world conference to "Appraise the Achievements of the UN Decade for Women: Equality, Development and Peace," held in Nairobi in July 1985, was one such example. The Organization of African Unity (OAU) passed a resolution which resolved that the "establishment or strengthening of the women's unit in collaboration with member states will be a major preoccupation of the OAU and the Economic Commission of Africa in the second half of the nineteen eighties." That they achieved this within that time is doubtful. At the present time, it is impossible to say, with any certainty, that it was a "major preoccupation."

16. Following the celebration of the International Women's Year in 1975, and the focus on the need to integrate women into national development at all levels, the Government of Ghana, by National Redemption Council Decree 322, established the National Council on Women and Development. It was set up as the national machinery to advise government on all issues affecting the full participation of women in National Development.

17. What I mean here is that if the women are so beaten by their husbands that it detracts from the level of self-confidence and assertion with which they pursue their productive skills, which boost the Ghanaian economy, then such violence must be addressed so as to permit more freedom and morale for the women.

18. In 1989 I remember watching a drama on Ghanaian television which had a tremendous impact on my way of thinking about domestic violence. Interestingly, the story line was about a man who got drunk and beat his wife to death with his young son looking on and screaming. Later, the priest of the church the family attended had to counsel the man. I listened with fascination, as the priest pedantically berated the vices of drinking—not the horrors of domestic violence.

19. Quoted from H. Borden, "8 in 10 native wives found abused by husband," *The Toronto Star,* January 19, 1990.

20. The office of the chief is hereditary but is believed, at the same time, to be God-given and therefore sacred (Warren 1973, pp. 38–39).

21. I must point out that the sacred power, tied in with the secular power of Stools—as the lineage is known—is most puissant in areas where the Stool is wealthy. It has been seen to happen in recent times, with the diaspora to the urban areas, that there are no attendants to labor on royal farms or other investments to replenish the Stool's coffers. In that case the Stool is not very powerful economically, and the citizens of the town do not accord it all the respect due. Such Stools are relatively few. For the most part the chiefs continue, all over Ghana, to have a very powerful influence.

22. I concede that the question: Who will educate the chiefs? is an involved one, to which I do not have a ready or simple answer. There is a National House of Chiefs to which all the chiefs of Ghana belong. There are also regional houses. While I could say that the Committee of the National House will organize the Committees of the Regional Houses to educate their members, who then educates the Committees of the National House? It may help to know that, for some reason, a number of the chiefs of Ghana are lawyers. Indeed, the President of the National House of Chiefs is a lawyer. These are people with whom FIDA could discuss the problem of domestic violence.

23. Indeed the Chairman of the PNDC is reported to have said in August of 1982 (nearly a year after assuming office) that the revolution could not succeed without the involvement of women. *Daily Graphic,* August 2, 1982.

24. Of course it is important not to rely on the equal representation of women and men on decision-making panels as constituting the ultimate solution for women's problems. The society is a male-oriented one, and will need a major revolution to ensure that the women on the board are not there merely as tokens.

25. It would seem from my personal experience that this viewpoint reflects the general opinion of Ghanaians as a whole—women included. The irony is that there is a passive acceptance that some are different (better?) than others—that some women may be human while some are not quite human beings. Questions about whether this might relate to internalized racism are beyond the scope of this paper.

26. *Manu v. Manu* (1959) Ghana Law Reports, 21; and *Osei-Koom v. Osei-Koom* (1967) Ghana Law Reports, 274.

Killing "the Angel in the House": Digging for the Political Vortex of Male Violence Against Women

by Celina Romany

A Personal Failure Story

Carmen sits next to me in one of those crowded basements which house courtrooms in the Hato Rey section of San Juan, and listens in total despair and disbelief to a judge (the black robe and gavel serve as the *erga-omnes-reminders* of the symbols of power) as he expounds his views about the lack of adequate rehabilitation for offenders and the preservation of the sacrosanct family. She hears the discourse of extended patriarchy distilled through the cross-fertilization of morality, scientific knowledge, and objectivity; while the judge regurgitates the words of the "professionals" of the world: the psychologists, the psychiatrists, the social workers, the counselors, the media experts, the priests, and the spiritualists.

Carmen is the expert. But her eyes seem to dwell in nothingness, the nothingness of dead ends. And I am the eternal optimist, the woman who learned to respect her by witnessing her struggles against all brands of pressure: relatives, children, income inequalities, as well as a husband's lawyer, with his bag full of the dirtiest tricks of the trade. After watching her struggle with every kind of weapon and manipulation, I experience abysmal failure, one that could cost her life. Yet again, I encounter the familiar "special treatment" afforded to gender crimes. An occasion for judges and prosecutors to assume a blanket license to pontificate about crime and punishment. An acquittal yet again dismisses gender crimes, relegates them to the basement of tropically hot and humid Hato Rey, trivializing the "private" infernos that only women know about.

The judge's face was familiar to Carmen. He could easily switch places with the physician who attended her in an emergency room of a public hospital in San Juan or with the Family Institute counselor. He could as easily be the physician who fails to see the bruises which fit the gender

285

crime, black and blue breasts, or a pregnant belly brutally kicked, the physician who fails to see how the commodity gets her due for defying her role.[1] The respective theories and practices of the physician, the psychologist, and the social worker view socialization as if coming from a cultural planet devoid of material foundations.

Once again Carmen has to submerge the political dimension of her abuse.

Depoliticization and the Helping Professions

The increasing consciousness in the 1990s of the gender dimension of the violence against women (breaking the silence, exposing women's dirty little secrets) takes place against a social backdrop of privatization, where the cultural discourse travels an autonomous roadway from social forces of domination, and entrenches images of private wrongs. With the (so-called) end of ideologies, the private sphere grows, while the public state is dismantled. The accomplishments of social movements and struggles which "publicized" wrongs historically labelled as private, and which pushed to the center of state responsibility and intervention areas of our lives that had been left to the vagaries of a feudalism dressed in liberal robes, or to the vagaries of a market wearing apolitical masks, grow increasingly threatened. Civil rights, race relations, workers rights, reproductive rights, to name a few, are increasingly privatized. Even privacy is privatized (Romany 1990a) as the historical struggles waged for the recognition of state responsibility become dimmer voices in our consciousness.

The current popularity enjoyed by privatization in the traditional political arena presents a strong force to be reckoned with. While we reap the accomplishments of a women's movement that has exposed the public nature of violence against women, we swim against a strong current of privatization.

The achievements of women's movements, while significant, are increasingly threatened by the discourses of the helping professions, despite increasing numbers of feminist professionals. The patriarchal constraints of the disciplines within which they operate have proven difficult to shed. Professional intervention is threatening to undermine the significant revelations brought about by that unique feminist methodology called consciousness-raising. It was consciousness-raising which gave voice to the experience of women, and served as a springboard for the critique of the artificial divisions between the public and the private spheres. The battered women's movement in particular, coming as it did from experience-based knowledge, challenged the patriarchal basis of violence against women. It was a conceptualization that served to name such violence as political, and thus paved the way for the state's responsibility.

The feminist *exposé* of the sexist foundations underlying the artificial division of social spheres in the violence scenario reveal the urgency of the need to rewrite the social script in a way that accounts for differences while underscoring the commonalities. Violence against women presents a fertile context for a dialogue on the nature of those common denominators. As a prime suspect stands a stubborn liberal state which guards the borders of a private world where women lose their lives, their dignity, their self-determination; where women's bodies and souls are consistently mutilated. It is this stubbornness that has kept a whole variety of feminists holding to a common ground which critiques the sanctity of artificial social spheres.[2]

My aim in this chapter is to bring to the surface the tensions, contradictions, and dilemmas brought about by the criminalization of violence.[3] To demonstrate how, in the act of coming together, the multiplicity of discourses deployed for the design of a state's strategy in addressing violence reveal their ideological foundations, their respective discipline's genealogy in a world of compartmentalized professional knowledges.

My point of entry will be a discussion of the Puerto Rican experience with domestic violence three years after the enactment of comprehensive legislation.[4] This experience revealed to me the need to expose and ultimately expunge the strong influence exerted by specialized conceptual formulations that exclude women's voices. The claims of objectivity and expertise by the helping professions tend to "normalize" the very phenomenon we are pledged to eradicate.

Criminalization is a significant step in the politicization of violence against women, yet it must be exorcised of the imperial intervention of the helping professions. First, the criminal justice system, by relying on the allegedly ungendered discourse of the helping professions, undercuts the criminalization agenda and obscures its social control functions. Second, the helping profession's discourse impacts on the legal system to privilege the dysfunctional and pathological over the gender dimensions of violence. This blurs the boundaries between the legal, the therapeutic, and the political which must be maintained to address the problem of domestic violence. Third, the mediation of women's experience through the discourse of the helping professions dispossesses women of the definitional control essential to the politicization of violence. We increasingly witness the devastating consequences of professional discourse's trespasses: the relegation of the legal guarantees of women's dignity, bodily integrity, and self-determination to the alleys while the rehabilitation of the family unit or of the victims of "psychological dysfunction" travel the main roads.

The systemic influence which the helping professions have had on the characterization of women's battering throughout the social institutions currently dealing with the problem, and specifically within the legal system, is significant. These characterizations, which are embedded in practices that ignore the knowledge derived from the experience of battered women and waves of impersonal professional categorizations, make us invisible and silent.

The helping professions' characterizations portray a contradictory picture of the abused women where, on the one hand, she is responsible for the abuse and thus exerts some kind of agency over the violent cycle, while on the other hand her "praxis" is considered pathological, a "weakness" that needs to be treated. As Evan Stark points out:

> her persistence leads to her recognition as a person, not simply as a complex of incongruous symptoms, but her personhood is acknowledged as itself symptomatic of a more profound disorder. (Stark 1973, p. 473)

Through the infiltration of the helping professions, the public character of violence against women is diluted and sabotaged. The politicization that brings to the fore issues of legal responsibility, and which underscore the political nature of violence, is obscured and ultimately shot down. Legal responsibility in no way denies the social ramifications of violence. Rather it deals with the exercise of the coercive power of the state to control conduct that infringes society's shared values. The infringement of social norms by those under the influence of alcohol or other substances continues to be subject to coercive social control without contradicting their diagnosis as social ills; why should violence against women be different?

Notwithstanding the inroads of feminist critiques of the public and private divide, the professional discourse generated by these helping professions strongly reverberates in the halls of Puerto Rican police precincts, prosecutors offices, courthouses, the ministry of justice, and the department of corrections. It is this reverberation which contributes to the harmony of the current chorus of privatization that spills into all spheres of our lives.

Without oversimplifying the complexities that the enforcement of new legislation entails, the Puerto Rican experience gave me a contextual understanding of the particularly detrimental impact that conceptual arrangements which neglect the experience of women have upon the legal characterization of violence against women. It made me concentrate on this dimension of the problem since, in spite of the multiple obstacles that the enforcement of this legislation confronts (most of them stemming from the trivialization women's issues typically confront), the most visible attack launched against the legislation involved the refusal to accept the real consequences of the criminalization of violence. Criminal conviction for domestic violence is criticized as the wrong solution for what is regarded primarily as a social problem. Law enforcement officials have strongly argued for amendments to the new statute that allow for diversion without a criminal conviction. The discourse that invariably permeates the discussion in support of this amendment is that of the helping professions.

I am not arguing that criminalization is a panacea. The critique of criminalization cannot stem, however, from the privatization of this kind of violence through the discourse of the helping professions. Discussions about the wisdom of crime and punishment, of crime and rehabilitation, of the legal and nonlegal institutional frameworks that are to be entrusted with the regulation of violence, must take place against the backdrop of women's experience and not against that of professional discourses which organize knowledge based on the erasure of women's experience. The criminalization of violence needs problematization (particularly if we care to factor in the interplay of sexism, racism, and economic inequality in the criminal justice system) but one that is grounded in a dialogue where the key factor of gender is not silenced. A discussion around these issues should not, as Dorothy Smith points out, be "condemned forever to a borrowed language" (Smith 1990, p. 4).[5]

An open critique of professional assumptions, backed by the political clout that strong movements can bring about, is essential for exposing the political nature of violence. This can, in turn, impact on codes of cultural discourse and enable actors to deal with psychosocial ramifications without jeopardizing women's lives and psyches.

The Puerto Rican Experience

The Puerto Rican experience shows how deeply ingrained dysfunctional characterizations of woman battering are, and the significant role the helping professions have played in maintaining them. The so-called objective findings of professionals in charge of the process become the oracle of scientific authority and expertise to which policymakers and legal enforcers defer.[6] Expert authority ultimately places the violent family at the top of the ladder of social institutions to be *preserved.*

The scientific "objectivity" of professionals, recognized by ruling elites and buttressed by public discourse, does its share to silence and exclude women's experience.[7] The treatment of male violence against women in the media and in the multiple scenarios of popular culture speaks for itself. Take, for instance, the "trauma bonding" characterization which, although helpful in the reconceptualization of legal norms such as self-defense (through the battered woman syndrome), nevertheless constitutes a slippery road and must be traveled with caution. While it can provide the courts with a broader picture that uncovers the subjugation of women within the sacrosanct family, it invites them to pursue the tempting paths of psychological accounts that overly victimize women, and deny them any form of agency. It can also serve to overemphasize the dysfunctionality inherent in the interpersonal relationship that portrays men as victims of such an aberrant dynamic. Trauma bonding is based on studies of hostages with the "Stockholm" syndrome, where male rage is reduced to stress and the "interpersonal aspect of the battering relationship" affects the legal discourse of responsibility. Once "past the rage threshold," men "have no control over and no memory of their actions and thus presumably no responsibility for them," while "women are helplessly unable to escape because of their own trauma" (Walker 1990, p. 106).

Law 54: Legislation Gets Approved

In 1989, after several years of bringing violence against women to the fore of public discussion under the leadership of the Women's Affairs Commission, a governmental institution that operates under the direct supervision of the Governor, Act No. 54 for the Prevention of and Intervention in Domestic Violence was approved. Several women's organizations, under the umbrella group called *Coordinadora de Paz para la Mujer* (Coalition on Peace for Women), along with government agencies that dealt with violence from their respective mandates, endorsed the idea of legislation.

The statute was the product of negotiations among diverse governmental and nongovernmental sectors dealing with violence. At the forefront of the criminalization route were feminist groups and the Governor's Women's Affairs Commission, which clearly saw the political nature of violence and its patriarchal foundations. For them, dealing exclusively with the therapeutic, social service perspective had run its course and had proven to be ineffective in the eradication and prevention of this violence. Oppositional attack came primarily from law enforcement officials, who saw no need to criminalize what was "a social problem." The department of corrections and the Police Commissioner joined forces in exposing the lack of resources available to deal with the enforcement of the proposed legislation.

After intense lobbying and evaluation of reports on the seriousness of this kind of violence, the Puerto Rican legislature approved comprehensive legislation which incorporated civil and criminal remedies for domestic violence as well as preventive mechanisms. Law 54 criminalizes any kind of physical or psychological violence among intimates (in past or in present relationships) by incorporating five different felonies for its occurrence, including marital rape. It provides for mandatory arrest, and allows for diversion after conviction or upon entering a guilty plea. The state is the entity that brings charges initiated by the signing of a complaint by the prosecutor. In addition, it provides for the expedition of orders of protection.[8]

The Sacrosanct Family is Alive and Well

The interaction between the predominant family narratives and the helping professions' discourse lies at the vortex of the depoliticization of male violence against women. The helping professions operate within a social context that takes as natural—a given—the heterosexual nuclear family (Cott 1977; Okin 1989), and thus professional accounts of violence within that unit rarely challenge its contingent character. Master narratives on the family of the liberal state get translated into the accepted discourse of the discipline.

Nowhere is this extrapolation of natural foundations more lethal than in the scenario of male violence against women. The family, "the most violent group or setting that a typical citizen is likely to encounter" (Walker 1990, p. 64, citing Murray Straus's *Report of the Task Force on Family Violence in Canada*) is revered and glorified.

Home, the sacred site of the family, the "shelter for those moral and spiritual values which the commercial spirit and the critical spirit are threatening to destroy" (Olsen 1983, p. 1499), becomes the contested terrain of state intervention. As long as it fits the natural model which suppresses oppositional and/or different configurations, the family will remain the "sanctuary of privacy into which one can retreat to avoid state regulation" (Olsen 1990, p. 1504). As long as the family remains the consolidating unit of male hierarchy, the state can remain neutral (Olsen 1990, p. 1504).

The politicization of the family, the indictment of its foundational ideology as the *status quo*, threatens core narratives of liberalism. Individual freedom, the clear demarcation lines between the political, the economic, and the metaphysical are central themes in the conceptualization of liberalism's social institutions. As with market transactions, the master liberal narrative highlights the battered woman's formal freedom in establishing relations. Fran Olsen's analogy captures this dimension when she notes that:

> The wife who does not leave her battering husband is in a position
> analogous to that of the weaker party entering a contract characterized

by unequal bargaining power. Just as the fact that the weaker party chose to enter into the contract suggests that he thought he would profit from it, so the fact that the wife remains in her marriage suggests that, in her own estimation, she gains more from the relationship than she loses. (Olsen 1990, p. 1507)

With the transformations of liberalism, the contingency of such liberal foundations have been gradually exposed. With the advent of higher levels of state intervention—via the welfare state—we are better able to see, through the apparent inconsistencies of the state regulation of women, how the regulation of family life remains embedded in a static division of gender roles.

In obscuring the political dimension of violence against women, the normalizing impulse of the helping professions, interacting with the ruling social institutions, buttress the patriarchal assignment of roles within the family. The political act of defiance is coined deviant. *Defiance* becomes *deviance* in the public discourse, which cackles the scientific discourse of the helping professions.

As Gillian Walker states:

> The issue of men's violence against women in the family setting is being transformed into a professional psychiatric or counselling problem. The "battered wife" concept is substituted for the political analysis of violence by men against women. There are conferences, a literature, the elaboration of a professional practice (often focusing more on men than on women). . . . Wife-beating or battering might perhaps have some claim to the status of mere description, but the "battered wife" is clearly a social construction. Its ideological properties as a category removed from the social relation of women's lives allows "the battered wife" to be treated as an instance of family violence, or any other larger theoretical framework implicated in the ideological process of separating out features of people's lives into manageable administrative portions. (Walker 1990, p. 102)

Looking back at the Puerto Rican process with the benefit of three years experience of implementation, I see how the deradicalization of violence from a gender perspective strikes back and haunts us, despite its usefulness as tactic towards legislative approval.

A Representative Sample

Despite the victory in the outcome, the statute's Statement of Purpose is the prologue for the dilemmas and contradictions which arise in the social regulation of this type of violence. Take for example, a preamble that addresses "the seriousness of violence as it affects women and children," which lumps together women and children as victims of violence within the family unit. Traditionally, when the rights of women and the rights of children are treated together, the rights of children tend to draw more attention, and women take a backseat. Violence against female children, and particularly sexual violence, on the other hand—pervasive in our societies—rarely get explicit attention in domestic violence legislation. The dilution of the gender-specific nature of violence in the Puerto Rico legislation's preamble contributes to its depoliticization, and turns the primary attention to the family unit.

Women's experiences of gender-based violence remain invisible or hidden beneath the violence that plagues the family unit,[9] or beneath the state's primary concern with criminality as it affects the family unit (Preamble, Law 54). Consider this chorus of criticism. The Department of Corrections is still complaining of lack of resources. Despite persistent voices of criticism, the Department of Corrections Administrator has not yet asked the legislature to allocate resources for the specific needs of batterer's rehabilitation, which in turn is grounds for challenging the criminalization of violence. The Police Commissioner has openly criticized the legislation, and thus has sent a clear message to the rank and file regarding the forcefulness of its implementation.[10]

The experience with protective orders is a showcase of the resistance displayed by enforcement agents. Women engage in forum shopping for sympathetic judges, since they are frequently confronted with judges' reluctance to deal with the serious implications of violence with its lethal nature. At times judges make derogatory comments about Law 54, revoke orders granted by other courts, while granting the batterer temporary custody of the children. They attempt to reconcile the couple, advising women to give their husbands or partners another opportunity; grant the order for a relatively short period of time; grant "mutual orders of protection" ordering both parties "to refrain from harming each other." In short, battered women are not given adequate protection.[11]

Legal arguments are also advanced to prevent women from obtaining protective orders. Due process objections to *ex parte* hearings, as well as the access right of the male partner to his property, are given precedence over the rights of women to be free from attack under the statute.

Police officers often complain of the lack of resources for dealing with the problem in a coordinated fashion. This is a serious critique that addresses the importance of dealing with violence from a multipronged perspective. The critique, however, crosses the boundaries, attacking the criminalization route and deflecting attention from the need to allocate sufficient resources to implement the law adequately. The inadequacy of resources becomes the smokescreen for maintaining the preeminence of the social over the criminal nature of violence. Several officers have gone as far as to criticize the lack of discretion and flexibility they have in attempting to "save the family," given the ramifications brought about by the removal of the father.[12]

The inscription in our psyches of the dysfunctional-pathology narrative that clouds the labeling process comes to the fore in discussions around the wisdom of crime and punishment. As responses to woman battering get shuffled along the social spectrum, particularly within the legal system, the debate between punitive versus rehabilitative measures emerges. This hides, once again, the multiple layers of complexity which surround woman battering, and which, more significantly, disguise its sex-specific character.

The legislative mandate is also sabotaged by the legal activism of judges who revel in discovering anew the role of rehabilitation within the criminal justice system. In a passionate defense of rehabilitation (absent in other criminal offense contexts) men who beat women are singled out, are spared the inadequacies of the system, and are saved from the oppressive conditions of prisons. Legal realism makes a comeback and with a vengeance. But this is a dose of legal realism denied in other criminal justice contexts, and selectively invoked for the protection of men who batter women. Adequate rehabilitation, a right guaranteed in Puerto Rico's Constitution, and which, for the most part, remains in the gulag of oblivion, gains stature and captures the attention of the judicial system here. The virtual nonexistence of a rehabilitation system becomes the center of heated public debates on the wisdom of the criminalization of domestic violence. It is the basis for the public outcry demanding the statute's amendment.

The Police Commissioner, the Secretary of Justice, and the Head of the Department of Corrections join ranks in criticizing the diversion mechanism after convictions, setting the "tone" for the statute's enforcement. Their recommendation of mandatory diversion without conviction is couched in the discourse of the helping professions. Indeed, they are on the record, reiterating as essential, that "professional help" be given to both the perpetrator *and* the victim.[13]

The Police Commissioner's recommendations include that the charge, though criminal, be evaluated by a nonlegal body before reaching the judicial level, so that nonlegal solutions are first exhausted; that a procedure be established whereby the prosecutor, after evaluating the case legally but before filing charges, could refer it to helping professionals, such as couples counselors; that couple counseling be court-mandated in those instances where the couple refuses voluntary submission; and that the Social Services Department be the government institution in charge of coordinating the administration of such counseling (Puerto Rico Women's Affairs Commission 1991, pp. 61–66).

In addition, the Department of Justice has essentially ignored the myriad factors that make many women drop charges against their partners, and instead focuses on these statistics in order to undercut Law 54.[14] Prosecutors publicly vent their frustrations with women's withdrawal of charges (when women's lives just don't fit into those manageable administrative portions) (Walker 1990, p. 102) and with the judicial response in those cases which they manage to take to trial. The common experience is for a judge to dismiss "at the slightest provocation," especially when women say in court what all battered women know, that their primary concern is their protection and not retaliation—when women affirm that recourse to the courts is their last resort. Like some of the Police Commissioners' recommendations, prosecutors have recommended screening the complaints with the input of the helping professions, counseling, and the transfer of the Womens' Affairs Commission's advocacy functions to the Family Institute.[15]

In spite of the dramatic examples of lack of awareness and sensitivity in dealing with this statute, judges exhibit the strongest resistance against education on the subject, which they characterize as an undue intrusion on their judicial freedom and discretion—a breach of the government separation of powers. The experience of the Women's Commission in attempting to reach out to judges has received a cool and often openly hostile reception.[16]

Digging for the Political Vortex of Violence Against Women

Several narratives about the relationship between the self and the state, and between civil society and the state, account for the allocation of boundaries between the public and private spheres in the democratic liberal state. A common thread of those narratives is the objective, neutral, and universal portrayal of the individual as an abstract and autonomous self that freely hires the state to provide her with those minimum guarantees of peaceful and civilized social interaction. State responsibility with respect to social spheres has been the target of critiques aimed at exposing the value-laden nature of the equation, and its complicity with a market economic system. These critiques have also exposed the exclusionary foundations for social citizenship, the exclusionary basis for the issuance of the equal participation *carnet*.

Feminist theory has been at the forefront of such critiques. Women throughout history have experienced a marginal position. Women have been consistently relegated to the private sphere that lies outside the boundaries of state intervention. Women exist within that civil society which, by virtue of its increasing depoliticization, does not constitute a social force which can forcefully claim authority and challenge the legitimation of state activities. The self-impairing depoliticization of civil society has dispossessed it of its power to make the state accountable.

The male-centered foundations of the social contract have been critiqued, in an effort to contribute to a deeper understanding of how the personal is the political (Romany 1990b, 1991a; Pateman 1988; Okin 1989). I have also challenged those foundations in the context of the articulation of a constitutional privacy right that, although responsive to the state's masculine control of women's reproductive choices, has failed to account for the equally significant task of providing the affirmative conditions for women's full incorporation in society (Romany 1990a).

Although the institutionalization of gender subordination constitutes a central piece of this analysis, it joins forces with the institutionalization of other forms of oppression, and compounds the effect of violence among diverse women. The intersection of racism and sexism constitutes a powerful example (hooks 1984, 1989, 1990, 1992; Crenshaw 1988; Matsuda 1989; Williams 1991; Harris 1990; Kline 1989; Romany 1990, 1991a). Without losing sight of those differences, commonalities at the baseline need to be underscored since they lie at the core of liberal conceptualizations of the private, with professional discourses leading the discussion.

Women's lives-in-violence, their stories of survival and resistance, are filtered through the lens of expert categorizations—a logical consequence in a society compartmentalized by expert knowledge, giving preeminence to the scientific, objective, and primarily male ways of knowing (Harding 1986; Smith 1990; Fox-Keller 1985). Our society dichotomizes and assigns priority to reason over emotion, and personal experiences are confined to the realm of contradiction and indeterminancy (Unger 1975, 1982). Along with many other feminist scholars, activists, and women survivors of violence, I opt to privilege the experience of women (Walker 1990, p. 66). As Dorothy Smith points out:

> The standpoint of women discloses the distinctive power relations of professionalism—hierarchy preserving the authority of theory where theory is ideology, in preference to the working knowledge of an actual everyday world; in rationality having as its secret form opposition to those who take up the side of the oppressed; neutrality having as its secret form taking sides against those who take the side of the oppressed. (Walker, 1990 p. 66)

The increasing literature on violence against women reveals the paths walked in refining the understanding of violence as applied to women.

In underscoring the *leitmotif* of the dysfunctional/aberrant nature of violence, one loses sight of the logical normalizing role it plays in the gender scenario, by preserving categories of social stratification. By highlighting the dysfunctional/pathological aspect of violence, professional disciplines, armed with their respective cognitive arsenal, deflect attention from the implication of society in its use of multiple manifestations of force and abuse that maintain the *status quo* of female subordination (Pleck 1987, pp. 145–163).

Without denying the specific pathological/dysfunctional proportions that the infliction of violence against women may acquire, the overemphasis on the psychological or psychosocial dynamics unleashed in women battering contributes to a mere peripheral attack on gender social stratification, and obstructs the task of exposing its public character, its politicization, and its connection with the requirements for full social citizenship. This overemphasis on the psychosocial dynamics within the family, including child abuse, also serves to deflect attention away from the many diverse scenarios in which violence against women occurs for reasons well beyond those of family structure.

The Lockean conception of civil society remains intact when violence against women is overly psychologized. This script retains the family and its traditional role in the market—violence becomes aberrant or exceptional, when we know this not to be the case. In advocating for a political construction of violence against women, I want to underscore the importance of naming the issue without neglecting the myriad strategies to be explored for its eradication. My critique of the overly psychologized nature of the professional discourses' response to domestic violence is intended to expose the damaging ramifications of this approach on the design, formulation, and implementation of public policy. My ultimate aim is to redefine legal principles from a feminist perspective.

Lessons to be Learned

The lack of a strong movement within a civil society, where voices of consciousness emerge and consolidate, essential sentinels of the materialization of social change through law, sentinels which create structures that facilitate the "catching-up" adjustments, can hurt the successful implementation of progressive domestic violence legislation. This is a basic lesson on law and social change. The Puerto Rican experience is no exception. A problematic situation becomes compounded by Puerto Rico's lack of a significant public interest infrastructure. Puerto Rico lacks a network of public interest law centers functioning as independent watchdogs and advocates in the advancement of a women's rights agenda. Notwithstanding the militancy and best intentions of feminist government officials, their governmental-structural constraints prevent them from pushing far enough. The Women's Commission operates within the Governor's office and, as such, is subject to its discretionary oversight. The commission has less independence than other executive and independent governmental agencies. Thus, the feminist side of the Women's Commission officer is always trailing behind by the sheer reality of her position.

However, a feminist governmental Women's Commission[17] can claim much of the credit for the statute's resounding success in breaking women's silence.[18] The commission has done extraordinary work in raising public consciousness and in attempting to educate law enforcement officials and judges. It has designed a comprehensive set of minimum guidelines for the rehabilitation treatment of batterers who qualify for postsentencing diversion. At the prevention stage, the commission is designing and coordinating the implementation of a special school curriculum that approaches the political nature of gender-based violence.

One of the tangible successes of the statute is that, in the relatively short period of time since its implementation, the number of cases reported to the police has increased by forty-four percent (Puerto Rico Women's Affairs Commission Report 1991, p. 34). Two legislators have been criminally charged (one of them the Speaker of the House of Representatives), a development that a few years ago would have belonged to the domain of a feminist's wildest fantasies. This is a resounding success, given the contextual scenario of a society that still operates under the residues of *caudillismo*. It has also been a resounding success in terms of the free press coverage, and the street discussions it has generated about domestic violence throughout the island.

The feminist movement (regardless of the wave it is currently riding on) cannot afford to endorse indulgent self-explorations that dim the political spark which ignited significant reforms and recognized the political nature of women's social subordination. Feminism cannot afford to surrender definitional control.[19] To talk of paths of self-exploration, and the psychological adventures that await by recovering our wounded self-esteem through the invocation of our inner child, is to personalize the political, a dangerous detour in the development of civil society's conscience, and weakens the alliance we require to compel the state to assume its responsibility in addressing the residues of the naked power of patriarchy in this century.[20]

I have stressed in this essay the need to politicize violence against women, and have used my experience in Puerto Rico to argue for the need to raise the level of legal protection for women. I have concentrated on the common denominators women share when dealing with male violence. In doing so, however, I am not overlooking the intersection of colonialism and economic inequality in the conceptualization of gender violence and in the design of strategies for its eradication and prevention.

I have dealt with this subject elsewhere (Romany 1991b, 1992). My objective in this essay was to isolate what I see as a stumbling block which affects all women. This in no way should mean that I am endorsing an essentialist conceptualization of violence against women (Romany 1991a). The need to problematize that common denominator through the filter of the broader social picture and women's positionality within it remains urgent. In the case of Puerto Rico, like in many Third World countries, we need to grapple with structural violence, with poverty, with political, economic, and cultural imperialism. When evaluating recourse to the criminal justice system, we need to grapple with the role law enforcement plays in the repression of challenges to the social *status quo*. We also need to grapple with the "ideological blame-shifting" that plagues the discourse and praxis surrounding people of color, such as when the black family is represented as "the heart of dangerous dysfunctions that affect the moral well-being of U.S. society" (Davis 1989, pp. 75–76).

Conclusion

To expose the strong influence exerted by specialized conceptual formulations of violence that exclude women's voices barely scratches the surface of the damaging and often lethal effects of its depoliticization. An *exposé* merely scratches the surface of how these specialized disciplines often serve as legitimating grounds in sabotage campaigns against legal reform in this area.

In Puerto Rico, the criminalization route has definitely brought to the fore of public discourse the political connotations of male violence against women. As pointed out earlier, it is not the magic solution, nor does it deal with the individualistic tone which permeates legal discourse and which hides structural subordination. In our attempts to address the lethal nature of male violence against women, we have positioned ourselves within unholy alliances of the state (Walker 1990, p. 109). However, until consciousness of the marriage of patriarchy with other forces of domination is anchored in social discourses and practices, the criminalization of violence is imperative.[21] It is an important first step in acknowledging that male violence against women is a gender crime.

Notes

1. Carmen knows very well about the "angel in the house" that Virginia Woolf so eloquently describes as threatening to annihilate a woman's soul:

She was immensely charming. She was utterly unselfish. She excelled in the difficult art of family life. She sacrificed herself daily. If there was chicken, she took the leg: if there was a draught she sat in it—in short she was so constituted that she never had a mind or a wish of her own, but preferred to sympathize always with the minds and wishes of others. Above all—I need to say it—she was pure. . . . I turned upon her and caught her by the throat. I did my best to kill her. My excuse, if I were to be held up in a court of law, would be that I acted in self-defense, had I not killed her she would have killed me. (Woolf 1984, p. 278–9)

2. This in no way means that there is a totalizing account of the critique of the public and the private which universally triggers a formula for evaluating state's responsibility. A clear example that comes to mind is the multiple set of criteria that guide an understanding of the constitutional right of privacy. I am not arguing, either, for the eradication of public private distinctions, but rather for "a recasting of their boundaries and a disentangling from institutional designations," for the acknowledgment of the "public and private aspects of what has been labelled as private life" (Ostrander 1989).

3. I deal with the patriarchal dimensions of male violence against women, and do not address violence in nonheterosexual relationships.

4. I spent the summer of 1991 as a consultant to Puerto Rico's Women's Affairs Commission, interviewing judges, prosecutors, psychologists, social workers, and women's groups, and gave training seminars to law enforcement officials on domestic violence. I was also present at several criminal hearings against women batterers.

5. Smith refers to language as it is situated within the relations of ruling, what Julia Kristeva's work has unearthed as the "father tongue" (p. 5).

6. Martha Fineman correctly criticizes this deference in child custody cases. The tension that lies between the professional and the legal discourse should facilitate a dialogue whereby the legal values embodied in procedural due process, the right to hearsay, the right to cross-examine witnesses, currently trashed as "the vestiges of an arcane system," are recognized as important values in our society (Fineman 1988, p. 770). For an analysis of how professional scenarios often have little to do with rational decision-making, how these belief structures are difficult to revise since the constitutive role of groups ensures that shared beliefs intensify when challenged, see Margulies 1992; Mahoney, 1991.

7. By ruling elites I refer to what Gillian Walker describes as "a complex of relations, including the state, the managerial, and administrative processes, education, the professions, the media, and so on, that organize and control contemporary capitalist society." (Walker 1990, p. 8). With regard to the medical profession's response to abused women, Evan Stark, Anne Flitcraft, and William Frazier also recognize the importance of structural societal forms of domination. Medicine, in order to reaffirm its peculiar brand of mystification, must align its structure, procedures, and ideology with the overall structure of domination in bourgeois society (Stark 1979, p. 473).

Objectivity, on the other hand, is about that view from nowhere which feminists have systematically attacked. Issues are selected for their administrative relevance, while their importance in terms of real-life consequences is considered as secondary. Dorothy Smith notes how professionals are "paid to pursue a knowledge to which they are otherwise indifferent. What they feel and think about society can be kept out of what they are professionally or academically interested in. Correlatively, if they are interested in exploring a topic sociologically, they must find ways of converting their private interest into an objectified, unbiased form" (Smith 1990, p. 15).

8. From November 1989 to December 1990, approximately fourteen months from its enactment, 39.6 percent of the 15,594 cases in which the police intervened requested protective orders. The increase in requests for orders of protection was significative, from 20.3 percent in November 1989 to 52.9 percent in December 1990 (Puerto Rico Women's Affairs Commission, 1991, p. 34).

9. Preamble Law 54 for the Prevention of and Intervention in Domestic Violence (August 15, 1989), hereinafter Preamble, Law 54. In quoting an excerpt from James Q. Wilson's essay "Violence," appearing in *Toward The Year 2000* (ed. Daniel Bell, 1969), Dorothy Smith highlights the burial of women's experience in sociological presentations, in which wife beatings are still not considered "domestic violence":

   There are two kinds of domestic violence for which we would like to estimate future rates and thus two kinds of problems that make such estimates very difficult, if not impossible. The first kind is individual violence—murders, suicides, assaults, child-beatings—and the second is collective violence—riots, civil insurrections, internal wars, and the like. (Smith 1990, p. 55)

10. In a letter to the Women's Affairs Commission Executive Director, the Police Commissioner indicated his frustration with the use of scarce resources for these type of cases, given the number of women who eventually drop charges, and given that criminalization "does not address the root of the problem" (Puerto Rico Women's Affairs Commission Report 1991, p. 53).

11. This is from both my own observation of the hearings and the findings Gillian Walker reports from the Canadian study.

12. "Entendemos que el proposito de la Ley 54 no ha logrado su objetivo. Continua el maltrato conyugal. Esta ley en vez de unir al nucleo familiar ha sido lo contrario. Una vez se aplica la Ley, estas personas quedan afectadas en forma negativa - hijos, suegros y esposos. Economicamente se afecta el nucleo familiar. La relacion paternal se afecta. Al implantar la ley no hay flexiblidad en la policia para tomar medidas de reconciliacion familiar." Letter of Ismael Rivera Betancourt to the Executive Director of the Women's Affairs Commission (Puerto Rico Women's Affairs Commission Report 1991, p. 56).

13. The Police Commissioner expresses his concern for the children, "the real victims of domestic violence . . . for the thousands of innocent victims who have suffered the law's impact and for whom no professional help has been provided" (Puerto Rico Women's Affairs Commission Report 1991, p. 61). He recommends the decision to file remain in the hands of the police supervisor; that the statute be amended to require a previous police record of violence for conviction, so "that the law is not used as a subterfuge by women for the eviction of their partner from their shared residence" (Puerto Rico Women's Affairs Commission Report 1991, p. 56, my translation).

14. Statistics are also distorted in public debates, and convictions become the exclusive measuring rod for the statute's effectiveness. During the first fourteen months of implementation, of the 2,136 charges filed by prosecutors, 1,529 were finally disposed of. Within those, 1,108 (72.5 percent) ended in convictions, 96 (6.1 percent) ended in acquittals, 320 (20.9 percent) were filed and seven (0.5 percent) were transferred; 588 cases remained pending for trial (Puerto Rico Women's Affairs Commission Report 1991, p. 69).

15. Puerto Rico Women's Affairs Commission Report 1991, pp. 82–84; Celina Romany, Training Session Conducted for Island-wide Prosecutors, cosponsored by the Department of Justice and the Women Affairs Commission, August 1991.

16. Interview with the Executive Director of the Puerto Rico Women's Affairs Commission, Yolanda Zayas.

17. The commission, according to the review of some feminists, in recruiting the most experienced feminists in town, has depopulated the movement of its leaders, and has coopted the articulation of a nongovernmental voice.

18. Although men are covered by the legislation, ninety-seven percent of the cases reported to the police are women. (Puerto Rico Women's Affairs Commission Report 1991, p. 7).

19. Feminism cannot dress in professional robes that bury the gendered nature of male violence against women. Labels have been extremely important ("gender crimes, crimes against women, torture, terrorism") in the indictment of the helping professions (Walker 1990, p. 105).

20. Although not representing a movement, the popular reception that Gloria Steinman's latest book has had is a good example of the privatization that is part of the global political mood. Consider excerpts of her personal journey:

    I used to feel impatient with her: Why was she wasting time? Why was she with this man? At that appointment? Forgetting to say the most important thing? Why wasn't she wiser, more reproductive, happier? But lately, I've begun to feel a tenderness, a welling of tears in the back of my throat, when I see her. I think: She's doing the best she can. She's survived and she's trying so hard. Sometimes, I wish I could go back and put my arms around her. . . . (Steinem 1992). For a provocative review of Ms. Steinem's book, see Judith Levine, The Personal is the Personal," *Village Voice*, (March 17, 1992), p. 65.

    Schecter also insists on the need for a movement that challenges the ideological framework which justifies violence. As she points out: "without a reference point to a movement organizing to change conditions for all women, even self-help, a liberating model for assisting women can move in a dangerously apolitical direction." (Schecter 1982, p. 241).

21. A criminalization that will not erect roadblocks against its problematization. For a critical-criminological analysis within colonialism, see Romany, 1989.

Civil Remedies for Childhood Sexual Abuse in Canada: Trying to Break the Silence

by Nathalie Des Rosiers

The emergence of a civil right of action for survivors of childhood sexual abuse has been slow in Canada. It is not only economic and cultural difficulties in accessing the courts which explain the lack of court actions by women,[1] but also the legal system's lack of receptiveness to this type of action. Through the operation of limitations periods, in particular, the legal system has perpetuated the silence surrounding child sexual abuse. This chapter describes the legal barriers to a right of civil action. It also suggests ways to circumvent them.

In the first part of this study, the psychological reality which explains a survivor's enforced silence and her delay and reluctance in bringing a civil action will be described. Second, arguments will be developed to suggest ways in which a civil action should be framed so as to recognize this psychological reality of victims, both in common-law jurisdictions and in Québec, which has a civil law tradition. The different types of causes of action which may be brought will be examined. The issues of limitation periods and damage awards, the most difficult legal hurdles to overcome in successfully instituting a civil action, will also be addressed.

The Reality of Sexual Abuse

The adverse effects of child sexual abuse are extensive, both in childhood and adulthood. As a child, the victim may experience anxiety, remorse, shame, feelings of inferiority, and lack of self-esteem. Adult survivors typically have difficulties with romantic relationships (whether heterosexual or lesbian), have a tendency to become involved in abusive relationships (James and Meyerding 1977, p. 1383), or have an exaggerated mistrust of other people (Allen 1983, p. 616). Women who have problems with drugs, alcoholism, or prostitution have often been victims of sexual abuse as children. Other noted consequences include depression, self-mutilation, suicidal tendencies, bulimia, anorexia, and insomnia (Finkelhor 1986, p. 152).

Finkelhor and Browne regroup the different symptoms affecting children into four dynamics (Finkelhor and Browne 1985): the dynamic of traumatic sexualization, the dynamic of betrayal, the dynamic of powerlessness, and the dynamic of stigmatization. Adult women who were abused as children also experience similar symptoms. Traumatic sexualization corresponds to the abnormal sexual development of a child exposed to sexual behavior much too early. When, for example, a child receives gifts, affection, or compensation in exchange for sexual favors, the child develops the idea of offering her sexuality in order to satisfy other emotional needs. Traumatic sexualization is also associated with the victim's confusion about sexual and moral norms and the role of sexual relations in social interactions. The child believes that offering her body is the only way to obtain love and affection, and continues to maintain this image of relationships between people. This confusion about moral norms clouds her ability to realize that she has suffered a "wrong." Until she comprehends that having sexual relations with a child is not a normal loving gesture, she is unlikely to see herself as a "victim," and is unlikely to institute legal proceedings, criminal or civil (Harshaw 1989, p. 756).

The betrayal dynamic comes from the child's unarticulated understanding that someone she is completely dependant upon has betrayed and hurt her. The child can understand that the adult has lied about the normal character of their relationship. The betrayal is not only by the aggressor but also by other members of the family or society who have participated in the assault through their silence. The intensity of the feeling of betrayal will also depend on the family's response when the sexual assault comes to light. A child who is not believed or who is blamed feels all the more betrayed. It is likely that she will take longer to trust authorities and reveal the abuse (Harshaw 1989).

The symptoms associated with the dynamic of betrayal include excessive dependence on or lack of judgment concerning the value of other individuals. Childhood sexual abuse victims will have a tendency to continue to maintain abusive or dead-end relationships. The betrayal dynamic can also explain contradictory feelings of complete lack of confidence in others and purposeful isolation. This, in part, explains the victim's inability to contact the appropriate authorities in a timely fashion.

The dynamic of powerlessness is easily understood. It has its roots in the relationship between the all-powerful aggressor who abuses his power and the child who must suffer the abuse without being able to do anything about it. In a patriarchal society like ours, the feeling and position of powerlessness may be reinforced by the daily experience of the subjugation of women, of the victim's mother or of any other female figure in the child's life.

The symptoms associated with this experience of powerlessness include a profound lack of self-esteem. The victim sees herself as an object to be used, as opposed to a person with rights. Consequently, she may not be able to assert her own will because of that perception. This feeling of powerlessness is accentuated when the child is confronted with a system which reinforces the psychological power and predominant place of the aggressor. The criminal justice system may contribute to the feeling of powerlessness, since it is based on the presumption of innocence which favors the position of the aggressor-accused.

Finally, the dynamic of stigmatization identifies the psychological effects on a young child of experiencing sexuality prematurely. The feeling of social isolation often contributes to the development of a double personality: the young girl who can exist in society and the one who must secretly live the fantasies of her aggressor. This feeling may be reinforced by social mechanisms which isolate the child, for example, the withdrawal of the child from the family home to "protect" her from the aggressor's attacks. The symptoms which one associates with this dynamic include feelings of guilt and shame, a lack of self-confidence, and a tendency to associate with groups stigmatized by society, in the world of drugs or prostitution. Again, this perception of the abused girl as the "bad person" hinders her from being able to bring an action until such perception has been altered. She will continue to keep silent about the abuse.

The intensity of the symptoms experienced may vary according to several indicators, which include economic dependency upon the aggressor, other physical assaults by the aggressor, age of the abused child, and length of the abuse. While research continues on these subjects, certain data are already well documented. It has been found that the girls most seriously traumatized are those subjected to vaginal penetration during heterosexual intercourse (Russell 1986, p. 144). However, Russell concludes that other factors are sometimes more important, for example, economic dependency. The abused girl might experience a very high degree of powerlessness when the aggressor is not a stranger or a distant relative but her father or stepfather, upon whom she is economically dependent.

Likewise, the length and frequency of the assault are not entirely conclusive factors, even though, generally, an abusive relationship which includes repetitive incidents of assault and which lasts several years has more impact than an isolated incident of assault (Russell 1986, p. 147). Victims of multiple sexual assaults (by several different aggressors) are more traumatized. Russell concludes that victims of sexual abuse are less capable of preventing new sexual assaults. This is compatible with the dynamics of premature sexualization and powerlessness.

Studies suggest that filiation is not in itself a determinant factor of the severity of the trauma, as sexual abuse committed by an uncle or a stepfather can be just as traumatic as that committed by the natural father (Russell 1986, p. 149). As Judith Herman explains, it is "the relation that exists by virtue of the power of the adult and the dependence of the child" which explains the trauma, and not just the violation of family rules of relationships between blood relatives (Herman 1981, p. 70). Finally, Russell (1986, pp. 147–150) documents that the economic dependence of the victim on the aggressor definitely constitutes an aggravating factor, as does the use of force.

In summary, the intensity of feelings experienced by a child victim may have a direct impact on the timing of disclosure of the abuse: the more intense the symptoms of betrayal and powerlessness, the lengthier the delay before the victim will be able to face the reality of the abuse. Victims often "repress" the memories of the abuse. They survive by burying in their subconscious the images of the abuse. They may block the negative experience completely or partially (Donaldson and Gardner 1985, p. 356). Victims may ignore the significance of the abuse as an explanation of continuously experienced symptoms until it is less dangerous to recognize the traumatic events. This latter type of accommodation, called post-traumatic stress disorder (PTSD), describes victims who continue to experience symptoms but are unable to relate them to the painful and traumatic events of abuse (Napier 1990, p. 1005).

The psychological effects of child sexual abuse briefly canvased above document why it is often impossible for victims of incest to sue their aggressor within statutorily defined limitation periods. Survivors keep silent because the law tells them that their stories of abuse are too old to be told, and that their years of suffering are no longer relevant to the public discourse of right and wrong and of justice.

The remainder of this essay attempts to reconcile the psychological realities of the child victim with the current legal framework to provide an effective legal remedy.

Civil Remedies for Survivors

The Common-law Response in Canada

The traditional actions brought by Canadian common-law victims of violence remain assault and battery. The use of these intentional torts as they are presently constituted is problematic for the child sexual abuse survivor, as is the limitations defence which is raised, generally, in the context of an assault or battery. The following is a description of the legal and symbolic difficulties that confront the survivor of childhood sexual abuse when instituting an assault or battery action. We also attempt to suggest solutions to remedy the difficulties.

ACTION FOR ASSAULT AND BATTERY

In Canadian common law, the tort of battery is committed when a person intentionally causes a traumatic contact to another. The assault, which consists of gestures and threats bringing on the apprehension of contact, occurs before the battery. There is no doubt that incest and sexual abuse are traumatic contacts and therefore batteries giving rise to a cause of action.

One of the defenses to a battery action is that of consent: that the victim consented to the touching or traumatic contact and therefore cannot later complain. One important question that arises in this context is whether a girl under the age of majority can give *consent* to sexual fondling. Traditionally, there is no consent if the person who gave the agreement is legally incapable of giving it. This legal incapacity to consent is ascribed to young children because of their immaturity. However, one becomes able to give a valid consent before the age of majority, and adolescents can give valid consent in certain circumstances.[2] Therefore the question of whether it is possible for an adolescent to consent to sexual contacts remains. Although the case of *Norberg v. Wynrib* (1992, 2 S.C.R. 224), of the Supreme Court of Canada in 1992, sheds some light on the question of consent in sexual batteries, it is still necessary to examine previous case law, since there are three different opinions rendered in the case, and it does not deal with a case of child sexual abuse.

In *M. (M.) v. K. (K.)* (1987, 11 B.C.L.R. (2d) 90), the child plaintiff was placed in the home of the defendant by the Children's Aid provincial authority when she was six years old. The plaintiff began having sexual relations with the defendant at the age of fifteen, shortly after the defendant's wife left him. The relations continued for two and a half years, until the plaintiff reported the sexual relationship to a counselor at school. She was removed from the defendant's home, and the defendant pleaded guilty to the charge of having sexual relations with his ward.

One month after attaining the age of majority, the plaintiff brought an action against the defendant, the provincial Children's Aid authority and the Ministry of Human Resources. Mr. Justice A. G. MacKinnon dismissed the action against the ministry and the respondent Children's Aid authority. The judge admitted that these authorities had not followed their own directives for the plaintiff's development: they had not visited the home annually, nor had they developed a placement plan. However, the judge concluded that these deficiencies did not necessarily constitute negligence. Moreover, he was not convinced that visits would have changed matters, since the defendant and the plaintiff had concealed their relationship not only from the neighbors but also from the plaintiff's sister, who still lived in the house.

The judge also dismissed the action brought against the defendant, because the young girl had "consented" to the sexual relations. In his judgment, he provided a detailed description of the "facts" which surrounded the beginning of the relationship. It is important to relay Mac-Kinnon's discussion of the facts and law, as they illustrate his complete misunderstanding of the inequality in power between the parties. Even though the judge notes the difference in age of the parties, the foster father being forty-one and the girl fifteen, he considers the plaintiff responsible for the first undisguised sexual overture:

> The plaintiff says she was coerced into acting as she did; there was an imbalance of power in her relationship making her susceptible to coercion. Such a relationship may exist in some circumstances. But, I do not, however, find that coercion by reason of the relationship between the plaintiff and the defendant. If she felt obliged against her will to comply with the requests of her foster father, it would be a form of coercion. . . .
>
> However, [the defendant] at the outset did state to the plaintiff there should be reflection on the actions upon which they were about to embark. He suggested she might regret what they might do. She assured him she would not. She was asked, and given time and opportunity, to think about the sexual involvement. She demonstrated before and after the relationship that she participated because she wanted the attention of the defendant and not because she was coerced into it.
>
> On the whole of the evidence I am satisfied that sexual abuse occurred at a time when the plaintiff was possessed of a sufficient degree of intelligence and maturity to understand the nature and consequences of the sexual activity in which she was involved. She was mentally and physically capable of assessing the situation and able to make a free choice as to whether or not she would become a part of the activity.
>
> I am driven to conclude that the acts complained of were not against the will of the plaintiff but rather with her consent. Accordingly, her action must be dismissed. The defendant K. is not entitled to costs. (1987, 11 B.C.L.R. (2d) 105)

One can see, in the judgment of the British Columbia Supreme Court, one real problem of childhood sexual abuse victims: the complete misunderstanding by the judiciary of the dynamics of power in the family.[3]

Girls raised to respect their father, and who understand at an early age that the only way to survive is to obey their parent's desires, must also know when the desires of their parents are harmful. It is sufficient for the parent to say to them: "Maybe you will regret it. . . ."

The case of *M. (M.) v. K. (K.)* is a good example of the myth of the seductress daughter (Herman 1981, p. 36). According to this myth, the father is not responsible for his behavior; it is his daughter who desires and collaborates in establishing the sexual relationship. The victim is judged to have consented if she does not protest. Her silence is proof of complicity. When, finally, the victim does complain, her complaints are attributed to jealousy or to something other than the incest or abuse. In the case of M., the judge considered that M. decided to unveil the relationship after a disagreement with her foster father regarding financial matters, and because of her jealousy. However, in its narration of the facts on appeal, the Court of Appeal mentions the adverse effects of the supposedly "consensual relationship": M. is seeing a psychologist, and is experiencing depression and problems of self-esteem. These adverse effects are not mentioned by the trial judge because their existence is incompatible with the finding of a "consensual" sexual relationship.

Fortunately and importantly, the British Columbia Court of Appeal reversed the decision of the trial court with respect to the defence of consent.[4] The Court of Appeal concluded that the trial judge erred in accepting the defence of consent after having concluded that the defendant had committed sexual assault, abused the plaintiff's confidence, and contravened his duty to act in the best interest of the plaintiff. According to the Court of Appeal, the defendant could not argue a defence of consent by relying on his abuse of trust and the contravention of his duty to act in the best interest of the child. The court referred to *Prosser on Torts* to conclude that it was contrary to the public interest to recognize consent to a criminal act as a defence to a civil action in battery. The court concluded that the plaintiff would have won an action for breach of the fiduciary duties of her foster father, and declared that it would be prepared to allow the amendment of the pleading to this end. It allowed the appeal, and sent the question of damages back to trial.

Although the decision of the Court of Appeal must be applauded in the hope that it will guide trial courts in the future, one can question the basis of reasoning advanced by the court. Tying the question of consent to the criminal aspect of the activities of the defendant does not resolve the issue of the power inequality between the parties, except in the narrow sense where the Criminal Code recognizes this inequality of power. The Criminal Code now recognizes the offence of having sexual contacts with a person between the ages of fourteen and eighteen who is in a position of dependency.[5] However, what will happen if these provisions are eliminated? Will the defence of consent reappear in tort law? What if they are restrictively amended? The defence of consent should not be rejected simply because of the operation of criminal provisions, but because the concept of consent must reflect the power realities of a sexual relationship. It must take into account not only the criminal conduct of the defendant but also the perception of the victim.

More recently, the Supreme Court of Canada has further addressed the issue of consent in sexual batteries. In *Norberg v. Wynrib*, three members of the Supreme Court of Canada recognized that the issue of consent must take into account the power relationship between the parties.[6] In the *Norberg* case, a chemically dependent woman patient agreed to have sex with her doctor in exchange for drugs. After her rehabilitation, she sued the doctor for sexual assault, negligence, and breach of fiduciary duty. Her action was unsuccessful at both the trial and appellate levels. There were three opinions from the Supreme Court, all in favor of the plaintiff. Three members of the court decided the issue on the basis of the battery claim, and concluded either that the plaintiff had not validly consented to the sexual contacts, or that for reasons of public policy it was unwise to uphold the consent when the positions of the parties were so unequal.

The three justices advanced a test suggesting that, if 1) the parties were in an unequal position of power, and 2) there was exploitation, that is, "if the type of sexual relationship at issue is one that is sufficiently divergent from community standards of conduct" (1992, 2 S.C.R.), the apparent consent should be set aside.

This recent decision could eliminate the possibility of a consent defence being raised in response to allegations of childhood sexual abuse, since the difference in age will often justify a finding that the parties are in an unequal position of power. However, the second criterion merely reproduces a standard of general good behavior in society. It misses altogether the real problem of exploitation. It is unclear whether conduct which is *not* prohibited by the Criminal Code or by a professional disciplinary code of conduct could ever be deemed to be "sufficiently divergent from community standards of conduct." For example, will dating practices which have a coercive effect be considered to be behavior which "is sufficiently divergent from community standards of conduct"? In that sense the second criterion is subject to the same critique as the British Columbia Court of Appeal decision in *M. (M.) v. K. (K)*; that is, that it is unsatisfactory to tie the unavailability of consent to the existence of community prohibitions against the defendant's conduct without also looking at the impressions of the victim. The linkage with criminal law should not replace a proper analysis of the issue of consent in torts: criminal prohibitions constitute a minimal threshold of behavior in our society and not the sole extent to which citizens are entitled to compensation for wrongs they have suffered. Therefore, it is unfair for victims of sexual batteries to see the analysis of their tort action limited to the extent of the defendant's criminal conduct. Furthermore, the criterion leaves the judiciary in a powerful position *vis-à-vis* the plaintiff survivor: it is the judge who will determine whether the behavior is divergent from community standards of conduct, not the plaintiff. The criterion leaves no place for the survivor's perception; it is completely focused on the defendant's conduct.

One might consider reformulating the criteria in the following way:

(1) were the parties in an unequal position of power *psychologically, physically, or economically?* and

(2) was there exploitation? That is, whether the type of sexual relationship at issue is one that is sufficiently divergent from community standards of conduct *or whether the relationship was harmful to this victim.*

The new test would attempt to add to the community standards the issue of harm to the victim. It would be closer to the concept of exploitation, which is not concerned solely with breaches of community standards but also with preventing harm to victims. It is important to stay away from abstract tests, which leave the victim powerless and lead to conclusions that her perception of exploitation is wrong or that her difficulties are self-inflicted. One might even argue that not only must the test move toward a victim/survivor-centered test, but also that it must include a more subjective approach to the issue of consent. Exploitation should not be assessed in the abstract, for instance, was the relationship likely to cause harm? It is important that the story of the survivor be told, her story, not the story of the objective reasonable victim, probably a white, middle-class, heterosexual woman. Unless the test is focused as well on the victim's perception, we will never learn about the pervasiveness of exploitation which occurred. The story of exploitation will remain silenced. It is the perception of the survivor which needs to be heard, not the community's perception, nor the intellectually constructed response of a "reasonable victim."

THE LIMITATION OF ACTION PROBLEM

Assaults and batteries are subject to a limitation period under various limitation statutes. For example, in Ontario, an action for assault and battery must be commenced within four years of the event, and a negligence action will be subject to a six-year limitation period.[7] In cases of intentional torts, the limitation period will start to run from the time of the wrongful act, since it creates an immediate right to nominal damages. A negligence action will arise when damages are discovered. In Ontario, the limitation period does not run during childhood. The child victim of sexual abuse will, therefore, have the right to commence her action in assault and battery against the aggressor up to four years after the age of majority, and in negligence up to six years after the age of majority.[8]

However, as discussed in the first part of this chapter, it is by no means evident that adult survivors of childhood sexual abuse will even be aware of the past abuse by the time they reach the age of twenty-two or twenty-four. Examples may be found in case law of adult survivors not remembering the traumatic event, or not being able to connect their injuries to the trauma, until they are in their late twenties and early thirties.[9] One question facing the courts is whether it is rational and just to refuse access to the courts to a victim because the intensity and nature of her trauma (and presumably of her damages) are so great that they precluded her from being aware of the injury and therefore from being able to bring an action within the requisite limitation period.

In Canada, victims have had difficulty extending the limitation period. This question was finally resolved by the Supreme Court of Canada in the *M. (K.) v. M. (H.)* case (1992, 3 S.C.R. 6) (hereinafter the *M. (K.)* case). K. M. sued her father and her mother twelve years after the end of an incestuous relationship. After the jury concluded that incest had occurred, and awarded the plaintiff more than fifty thousand dollars in damages, the trial judge decided that the action ought to be rejected pursuant to the Limitations Act of Ontario. He concluded that the plaintiff should have brought her claim on or before the age of twenty-two, and rejected the argument that her psychological condition amounted to "unsoundness of mind," which would have justified delaying the application of the limitation period until the "unsoundness of the mind" had disappeared. In the judge's view, since K. M. had been able to work, to get married, and to have children, she could not claim to have been of unsound mind.

The Ontario Court of Appeal confirmed the decision of the trial court, and the Supreme Court of Canada granted K. M. permission to appeal in November 1990, with leave to intervene also granted to the Women's Legal Education and Action Fund (LEAF). The court reversed the decision of the Ontario Court of Appeal in November 1992. The court considered that the theory of late discovery of harm should be applicable to incest cases, and applied a presumption that the plaintiff could not have known that her damages were related to the incest or that the incest was a wrongful conduct until she entered into therapy. As Mr. Justice La Forest explains:

... I am satisfied that the issue properly turns on the question of when the victim becomes fully cognizant of who bears the responsibility for her childhood abuse, for it is then that she realizes the nature of the wrong done to her. (1992, 3 S.C.R. 45)

Mr. Justice La Forest went on to conclude that there should be a presumption that, when a survivor suffers from "post-incest syndrome," as defined in the medical literature, she will be found to have been unable to discover her cause of action until she entered therapy. "Of course, it will be open to the defendant to refute the presumption by leading evidence showing that the plaintiff appreciated the causal link between the harm and its origin without the benefit of therapy" (1992, 3 S.C.R. 48).

The establishment of this presumption was a point of disagreement for two members of the seven-judge panel. Mr. Justice Sopinka considered the establishment of such a presumption unnecessary and unwise, since the survivor was in possession of the evidence necessary to make her claim of late discovery, that is, her absence of knowledge of the connection between the harm and the trauma suffered during a certain period of time. Madam Justice McLachlin also agreed that the presumption might be unnecessary. She would also have preferred that a broader number of criteria be used to determine whether a survivor is able to discover a cause of action other than simply entering into therapy. Her concern was that survivors who commence an action after several different therapies might be disadvantaged by this presumption.

These interpretations and criticisms of the presumption cannot be substantiated by a proper reading of Mr. Justice La Forest's decision and the facts of the *M. (K.)* case. For example, evidence advanced at trial established that K. M. had commenced several therapy efforts before engaging in a trusting therapeutic relationship that allowed her to confront the incest. Further, there already existed in the case law, which was relied upon by Mr. Justice La Forest, a recognition that not all therapeutic relationships have the potential to empower the survivor to assign blame properly upon the perpetrator.[10] It must be remembered that the basis for the presumption is the "close connection between therapy and the shifting of responsibility [which] is typical in incest cases" (*M. (K.)* 1992, 3 S.C.R. 48); it is therefore only those therapeutic efforts that have the potential of empowering the survivor which must be considered.

The *M. (K.)* decision will be helpful to survivors. It removes unequivocally, at least in incest cases, the hurdle of limitation periods. The majority's discussion of late discoverability and the post-incest syndrome presumption are definitely valuable tools for the incest survivor. An obiter

discussion of the doctrine of fraudulent concealment,[11] presented in the
M. (K.) decision, may also be useful. In the decision, Mr. Justice La Forest
explains in detail why, in his opinion, incest cases will often be amenable
to the application of the doctrine of fraudulent concealment as a response
to a limitations defence. As he states:

> Incest takes place in a climate of secrecy, and the victim's silence is
> attained through various insidious measures. As we have seen, these
> actions by the perpetrator of the incest condition the victim to conceal
> the wrong from herself. The fact that the abuser is a trusted family
> authority figure in and of itself masks the wrongfulness of the conduct
> in the child's eyes, thus fraudulently concealing her cause of action.
> (1992, 3 S.C.R. 56)

In his view, it is the nature of the concealment in abuse cases, that is,
the denial of the harm done, which is significant in an assessment of the
doctrine of fraudulent concealment. In addition to its practical significance, fraudulent concealment as a response to the limitation defense
produces substantial gains to the symbolic reinforcement of the survivor's
position. Fraudulent concealment refers to the defendant's conduct, and
not to the weakness, delay, or inability to remember of the survivor. In
that sense, it is a much more potent argument and probably one which
is closer to reality, since it blames the defendant and not the survivor
for the incestuous conduct and resulting trauma (Rosenfeld 1989, p.
206).

Although it is not technically necessary for legislatures to intervene in
this limitation debate, it might be politically important that they do so.
The most efficacious method of responding to the problem would be to
exempt from the operation of the Limitations Act childhood sexual abuse
and abuse by persons in positions of authority. This solution would not
leave any discretion to the judiciary, and, to that extent, would be both
symbolically affirming as well as safe in its application. This is the solution
adopted recently in British Columbia[12] and in the Consultation Draft
of the Ontario Government, published in 1990 and now tabled as an
amendment to the Limitations Act.[13]

Apart from such legislative developments, improvements to torts doctrine will need to be made to enable survivors to have a meaningful right
of action against the perpetrator. The emergence of a new tort might
be considered, as well as the development and sophistication of an action
for breach of fiduciary duty.

A NEW TORT OF SEXUAL ABUSE

In the M. (K.) decision, Mr. Justice La Forest expressly rejected the
proposition that incest could constitute a distinct tort. As he states: "I

am of the view that incest does not constitute a distinct tort, separate and apart from the intentional tort of assault and battery, and the continuous nature of the tort need not be decided in this case" (1992, 3 S.C.R. 24). Such a statement was unnecessary, since he allowed the appeal on other grounds. It might be possible to argue for the development of, not a tort of incest, but a more general tort of sexual abuse. This new tort of sexual abuse should be proposed to remedy the problems associated with the use of the tort of battery, and in particular the defense of consent associated with it. A new tort could focus on the distinct problems of sexual abuse: its sometimes continuous nature as opposed to the "isolated occurrence" model of battery, and the issue of exploitation which, thus far, eludes a determination of consent. However, the question remains whether Mr. Justice La Forest's rejection of a tort of incest in the *M. (K.)* case definitively closes the door to any development in this area. Attention should be given, therefore, to the alternative cause of action which *was* provided by the Supreme Court—the breach of fiduciary duty.

BREACH OF FIDUCIARY DUTY

The concept of fiduciary duty results from one principle: a fiduciary relationship will exist when a person has an obligation to act in the best interests of another (Fridman 1992, p. 371), because the latter is at the mercy of the discretion of the former (Weinrib 1975, p. 7). The Supreme Court of Canada has detailed the elements to consider in determining whether a fiduciary relationship exists:

(1) The fiduciary has scope for the exercise of some discretion or power.

(2) The fiduciary can unilaterally exercise that power or discretion so as to affect the beneficiary's legal or practical interests.

(3) The beneficiary is peculiarly vulnerable to or at the mercy of the fiduciary holding the discretion or power.[14]

It is possible for a fiduciary relationship to exist even if one or two of the above elements is absent; however, the fundamental characteristic of vulnerability or dependency of the beneficiary must be present. It is clear that the parent-child relationship engenders the qualities of a fiduciary relationship. Indeed, it is arguable that relationships between teachers, caregivers, and close relatives and children could constitute a fiduciary relationship where the requisite elements are present.

Once the existence of a fiduciary relationship has been established, the extent of the duty of the fiduciary must be determined to establish whether the duty has been violated, and what compensation is warranted.

Only the violation of an obligation arising from a fiduciary relationship will constitute a "breach of fiduciary duty."[15]

The fiduciary obligation of a parent or any person in a position of authority *vis-à-vis* a child is to tend to the needs of the child and to not act in a matter contrary to his or her interests. Clearly, a sexual relationship with the child or any sexual assault constitutes a breach of the duty to act in the best interests of the child. A sexual relation is hardly compatible with the duty to act with the utmost loyalty (duty to act *uberrimae fides*) (Ellis 1988, pp. 1–4 and 1–5), or with the duty to avoid any potential conflict of interest. A breach of fiduciary duty was recognized in the *M. (K.)* decision of the Supreme Court.

The advantage of an action for breach of fiduciary duty lies in its equitable nature. In Ontario, equitable actions are not subject to the Limitations Act.[16] Equitable defences will be available to a defendant accused of breaching a fiduciary duty, and, of those which are possible, the laches doctrine will most likely be advanced. However, the defence can be resisted by arguing, as was recognized in the *M. (K.)* case, that "a reasonable . . . survivor is incapable of appreciating her rights in equity or in law, and as such is incapable of acquiescing to the conduct that has breached those rights" (1992, 3 S.C.R. 79). Therefore the defence of laches should be unavailable to most defendants.

An action for breach of fiduciary duty has symbolic advantages as well, in that it correctly identifies the real harm—the violation of a relationship of trust, as well as the powerlessness of the victim. Technically, in the area of limitations of actions, it might also have an advantage, despite the development of the presumption of unawareness in the *M. (K.)* decision. If a perpetrator was able to rebut the presumption, an action in breach of fiduciary duty might be more favorable to the survivor. Arguably, the only cases where an action in breach of a fiduciary duty might be more difficult would be where the perpetrator is not acting as a parent towards the child: friends of the family who are visiting the family, brothers and stepbrothers, for example. These cases justify an argument for the development of a new tort of sexual abuse.

DAMAGE AWARDS

Another impediment to a meaningful right of action for incest survivors consists in the paucity of the damage awards awarded to successful survivors. A complete study of the inadequacies of the law of damages in this regard is beyond the scope of this paper. However, two decisions merit treatment in this context. In the *M. (K.)* case, the jury had made an award of ten thousand dollars compensatory damages and forty thousand dollars for punitive damages. The Supreme Court of Canada considered that the award was probably insufficient, but since the plaintiff had not appealed the award, there was no jurisdiction to increase the amount of damages. The Supreme Court provided little guidance for future awards of damages, even though it cited the British Columbia Supreme Court decision in *Gray v. Reeves.*[17] In my opinion, the law of damages was grossly misapplied in *Gray,* where the trial judge refused to recognize the economic impact of childhood sexual abuse. Further, the judge justified the award of damages for pain and suffering on a comparative analysis of defendants' conduct in different sexual abuse cases rather than looking at the plaintiff's needs and particular situation.

Both of these errors plague decisions in cases of childhood sexual abuse. It is particularly upsetting to see courts ignore the psychological literature detailing the impact of childhood sexual abuse on self-esteem and the development of the abused child's potential. By limiting recovery to emotional damage and the future costs of therapy, and by refusing to award damages for economic loss or loss of competitiveness in the marketplace, the courts are sending troublesome messages to survivors. Their failure to access high-paying jobs or to complete their schooling is again deemed to be their sole responsibility. The message conveyed is that it is solely the fault of incest survivors if their life is a mess, and not the fault of their perpetrator. The establishment of a more appropriate conception of damages is the next battle that survivors will have to fight, in both the common-law and civil-law systems.

The Québec Civil-law Response

RIGHT OF ACTION PURSUANT TO THE CIVIL CODE

Under the Québec civil-law system, one option for survivors of childhood sexual abuse is to institute an action *in delict* under section 1457 of the Civil Code of Québec.[18] Such action requires the establishment of a fault, damages, and a causal connection between the fault and the damages. The concept of fault incorporates both intentional and nonintentional actions: the question to be determined is whether the conduct of the defendant was conduct to be expected from a reasonable person in the circumstances.

It is quite clear that the sexual assault of children would constitute a fault giving rise to an action *in delict.* As in the common-law jurisdictions, the difficulty will be in recovering sufficient damages to make the exercise of the right of action worthwhile. Traditionally, *dommages moraux* (moral damages), which include those for pain and suffering, are low. A crucial issue will be to demonstrate a causal connection between the assault and the loss of self-esteem of the survivor which would establish a compensable economic loss. To date, there is no civil-law case awarding a child sexual abuse survivor substantial damages as a result of an action *in delict*.

The obstacle posed by limitation periods (prescription of action) is also very substantial in civil law. The Civil Code of Québec provides for a three-year limitation period for causes of action involving personal rights of action, such as *delict* for personal injuries (section 2925). The child who has not reached the age of majority benefits from a "suspension" of the prescriptive period when suing a person entrusted with her custody (section 2905). As set out in the Code, the limitation period is fixed from the day on which the right of action arises (section 2880), except when damages are progressively discovered. In that case, the period runs from the day the damage appears for the first time (section 2926). The spirit of the Code is to oblige the plaintiff to pursue her claim in a diligent fashion once she has discovered the damages. Therefore, a childhood sexual abuse survivor who, in her late twenties, finally recognizes the connection between her lack of self-esteem, for example, and past incidents of childhood sexual abuse must pursue her claim within three years after the connection is first discovered. However, she might have difficulty claiming damages for losses which have occurred prior to the last three years (for instance, failure to complete high school) since such claims would contradict her assertion that her damages "appeared for the first time" within the last three years. However, failure to argue past harm such as the failure to complete high school will limit her damage recovery for economic losses. The remedy provided by the Code could lead to very unsatisfactory damage awards.

Another avenue for avoiding the limitation problem would be to argue the "incapacity" of the survivor to act. In Québec, the Civil Code of Lower Canada referred to the absolute impossibility of a plaintiff, in law and in fact, to act (section 2232). The new Civil Code refers simply to the factual impossibility of the plaintiff to act. It is possible to argue that, until a survivor is able to assign blame to her perpetrator, it is impossible for her to pursue her claim. One obstacle a survivor will have to overcome in advancing this argument is that psychological incapacity to sue was seen as not sufficient to meet the standard set out in the old Civil Code of Lower Canada. It is unclear at this point the extent to which case law under the old Code will bind courts interpreting the provisions of the new *Civil Code of Québec*.

Right of Action Pursuant to the Québec Charter of Rights

Probably the most creative and best recourse for a survivor would be to use the Québec Charter of Rights and Freedoms of Persons,[19] which provides in section 39 that "[e]very child has a right to the protection, security and attention that his parents or the persons acting in their place are capable of providing." Section 49 provides for a right of action for any unlawful interference with a right recognized by the Charter. It entitles a victim to obtain a cessation of any interference with her section 39 right, and compensation for the moral and material prejudice resulting from the interference with her rights.

Such a right of action entitles the plaintiff to punitive damages if warranted, and might not be subject to a limitation period. Therefore, section 49 appears to be a good tool for child sexual abuse survivors wishing to sue their perpetrator in the civil courts. Up to now, no childhood sexual abuse survivor has brought an action under these provisions. However, with the increasing strength of the feminist movement in Québec, and increased awareness of the incidents and trauma of childhood sexual abuse, it is hoped that such actions will be instituted and well received.

Finally, under the Criminal Injuries Compensation Act, the Québec *Commission des affaires sociales* has recognized the possibility of ignoring limitation deadlines in cases of sexual assault.[20] Hopefully, this development by the administrative tribunal responsible for providing compensation to victims of criminal injuries could be relied upon by a survivor attempting to exercise her right of action against the perpetrator in civil courts.

Conclusion

Several objections are generally raised when one attempts to suggest the development of a meaningful tort remedy for childhood sexual abuse survivors. Practitioners first argue that it is unsavory and socially unproductive to allow children to sue their parents. However, they do not attempt to justify the social usefulness of tort actions which already keep courts busy: occupiers' liability, tavern brawls, and the like. The desire to insulate the family from lawsuits is very much the result of the traditional private-public distinction which has operated to make invisible some of the horrors of family life. What is unsavory is that the sexual abuse happened, not that it is talked about in public or in court.

A second, more substantial objection to the development of civil actions for survivors of childhood sexual abuse is the "middle-class" nature of this type of lawsuit. Even if problems of damage awards were to be resolved, and even if legal assistance were available to plaintiffs, the only adult children who would benefit from the evolution of such case law would be the children of parents with material assets or who have substantial savings. A large class of plaintiffs who have been hurt or abused, or whose development was thwarted by penniless parents would not benefit from such legal developments.

Such criticism is valid, and suggests that other legal mechanisms for addressing childhood sexual abuse must be reinforced and developed (the criminal law being one of them). However, I would suggest that advances in the area of civil liability would have advantages for survivors. One such advantage of a civil action might be the independence that it would give to the survivor: unlike criminal procedures, which are controlled by the police and Crown attorneys, civil proceedings would give the plaintiff, probably with the aid of a lawyer, some control over the process (Cole 1989, p. 96). Publicized lawsuits crowned with appropriate damage awards could affirm publicly the survivor's reality, break the silence which had surrounded her life, and could have an added deterrent effect.

The best possible remedy for the childhood sexual abuse victim remains the early intervention of child protection authorities to stop the abuse and assist the victim in developing a coping strategy. However, child protection laws are insufficient to solve all child abuse cases, and, in fact, it is likely that some sexually abused children will not be reached by them. Moreover, the impact of the criminal justice system will not always be sufficient to empower the victim. Therefore a meaningful civil remedy is necessary for survivors, although one should not overemphasize the benefits of such recourse when the perpetrator is improvident or in jail.

Great efforts will need to be directed in order for the survivors to obtain the monetary compensation which they deserve and need. Although the limitation problem in common-law jurisdictions has diminished, the paucity of damage awards continues to discourage resort to the courts. In Québec, the civil remedy has not been tried yet, and it might take some time for survivors to begin using civil courts. The failure of both the common-law and civil-law systems to provide for meaningful compensation to survivors is not only unfair to them, but also continues to perpetuate the silence surrounding childhood sexual abuse.

Notes

I want to acknowledge the help of my research assistant, Monica Song, and the financial support of the Law Foundation of Ontario and the Faculty of Law of the University of Western Ontario.

1. The victims described in this paper are persons who have been sexually abused as children. They include survivors of incest and other sexual exploitation of children by persons in authority (school teachers, foster parents, caregivers, old friends of the family). The victims are predominantly women, although there are instances of sexual

abuse of young boys for whom the present work might be helpful. Because of the gender-specificity of the problem, I will be using the feminine to describe the survivor.

2. In *Johnston v. Wellesley Hospital*, 1971, 2 O.R. 103; 17 D.L.R. (3d) 139 (H.C.), the court decided that a twenty-year-old girl could validly consent to a dermatologist's treatment of acne, even though the age of majority was twenty one years. The girl had the capacity to fully appreciate the nature and consequences of the treatment. The result of this case was followed in numerous other cases and statutes, and most common-law jurisdictions have recognized the same principle.

3. A similar problem pervades the American judiciary as well, since, despite some break-throughs, the major problems facing survivors continue to be the lack of knowledge about their trauma and the mistrust that courts entertain toward victims of sexual assault. Traditional arguments about the untrustworthy character of victims are still found. In *Tyson v. Tyson*, 727 P.2d 226 (Wash. 1986), for example, the court found that "the lack of objective, verifiable evidence, the necessary reliance of fallible memo-ries and dubious expert testimony" unacceptably increased the risk of spurious claims proceeding to trial. See also the decision in *Meiers-Post v. Schafer*, 427 N.W.2d 606 (Mich. App. 1988), where the court considered that the victim had been incapable to pursue her claims earlier, and rejected the defendant's motion for summary judgment, only after being convinced that there was *corroborative evidence* of the assault.

4. 1989, 38 B.C.L.R. (2d) 273; 61 D.L.R. (4th) 382 (C.A.). Nevertheless, the Court of Appeal rejected the appeal of the dismissal of the action against the provincial authori-ties and the ministry. The Appeal Court held that the factual conclusion of the trial judge, that the social workers were not negligent and had acted in good faith, could not be displaced, absent proof that the evaluation of facts was completely unreasonable.

5. *Criminal Code*, R.S.C. 1985, c. C–46, s. 153 as am. by R.S.C. 1985, c. 19 (3rd Supp.), s.1.

6. One other member of the court, Mr. Justice Sopinka, disagreed with this view of consent, but allowed the appeal based on the failure of the physician to provide adequate care for his patient, that is, his failure to direct her to a detoxication centre. Mr. Justice Sopinka considered that the sexual contact was a consequence of a breach of care, and the plaintiff was therefore entitled to damages. The two women on the court, Justices L'Heureux-Dubé and McLachlin, filed a concurrent opinion which would have awarded punitive damages as well as compensatory damages. For Madam Justice McLachlin, the only way to look at this case was as one involving a breach of fiduciary duty. Viewed through the lenses of breach of fiduciary duty, the issue of consent was irrelevant.

7. See Ontario Limitations Act, R.S.O. 1990, c. L.15, s. 45(1)(j) and 45(1)(g), for example. Section 45(1)(g) of the Limitations Act provides for a six-year limitation period for actions on the case. Negligence actions have grown out of the old action on the case and are subject to the same limitation period. See Ontario Law Reform Commission, *Report on Limitation of Actions*, 1969, p. 35.

8. See R.S.O. 1990, c. L.15, s. 47, for example.

9. In *Gray v. Reeves*, 1992, 64 B.C.L.R. (2d) 275, the victim was in her late twenties, and K. M. was twenty-eight when she instituted her action. For U.S. examples, see *Marsha v. Gardner*, 281 Cal. Rptr. 473 (Cal. App. 2 Dist. 1991) and *Baily v. Lewis*, 763 F. Supp. 802 (E.D.Pa. 1991) where the survivors were thirty-two.

10. For example, in *Gray v. Reeves*, relied upon by Mr. Justice La Forest, the British Columbia trial court found that a plaintiff could benefit from an extension of the

limitation period pursuant to the theory of late discovery of damages, even if she had entered into several therapeutic relationships prior to commencing her action. The court considered that the first therapeutic relationship with a male doctor had proved unsatisfactory, and had not helped the plaintiff understand the connection between her injury and the childhood sexual abuse. Only the last therapeutic relationship, with a female psychologist, had allowed the plaintiff to understand the impact of the abuse.

11. At common law, if a plaintiff had been unable to discover that she had a cause of action because of the actions of the defendant, the courts could conclude that the defendant had fraudulently concealed to the plaintiff her cause of action, and he could not claim the benefit of the expiration of the limitation period. See *King v. Victor Parsons & Co.*, 1973, 1 All.E.R. 206 (C.A.).

12. See Limitation Amendment Act, 1992, S.B.C. 1992, c. 44, s. 1.

13. Bill 99, An Act to Revise the Limitations Act, 2nd Sess., 35th Leg., Ontario, 1992 (1st reading 25 November 1992).

14. *Frame v. Smith*, 1987, 2 S.C.R. 99 at 136; 78 N.R. 40, Madam Justice Wilson, where the question was whether the custodial parent stood in a fiduciary relationship toward the noncustodial parent. In the *M. (K.)* decision, Mr. Justice La Forest again applied these criteria to find the existence of a breach of fiduciary relationship in the context of incest.

15. See *Lac Minerals v. International Corona Resources*, 1989, 2 S.C.R. 574, at 647, Mr. Justice La Forest.

16. Ontario appears to be in a unique position, in that its Limitations Act does not generally apply to equitable causes of action. The reform to the Limitations Act, currently in front of the legislature, would make the Act applicable to both equitable and common-law claims.

17. In the *Gray* case, the trial judge awarded damages to the plaintiff for her inability to form relationships with men. This bias in terms of defining "improvement" in terms of ability to form heterosexual relationships is dangerous. It obviously contributes to a discourse which defines normality in terms of heterosexuality. However, it appears that the plaintiff in the *Gray* case considered that this was an important loss to her and raised the issue.

18. An action *in delict* arises when a person has breached a duty imposed upon her, and has thereby caused injury to another person. It replaces the common-law categories of both intentional torts and negligence. I will refer to the sections of the new Civil Code of Québec, S.Q. 1980, c. 39, coming into force January 1st, 1994.

19. R.S.Q. 1977, C–12.

20. *Sauveteurs et victimes d'actes criminels—9*, 1990, C.A.S. 46; *Sauveteurs et victimes d'actes criminels—24*, 1991, C.A.S. 116.

Domestic Violence as a Human Rights Issue

by Michele E. Beasley and Dorothy Q. Thomas

Maria was brutally assaulted in her own kitchen in England by a man wielding two knives. He held one of the weapons at her throat, while raping her with the other. After he finished, the man doused her with alcohol and set her alight with a blow torch. Maria lived through the assault to prosecute the man, although seventy percent of her body is now covered with scars. But because they were married, he could not be charged with rape. He received a ten-year sentence for bodily injury, of which he will only serve five years (Reynolds 1990).[1]

In 1990 in the Brazilian state of Maranhão, women registered over four thousand complaints of battery and sexual abuse in the home at the main police station. Of those complaints, only three hundred—less than eight percent—were forwarded to the court for processing and only two men were ever convicted and sent to prison (Brazil Report 1991, pp. 48–49).

In Pakistan, Muhammad Younis killed his wife, claiming that he found her in the act of adultery. The court found his defense untrue, in part because the woman was fully dressed when she was killed, and sentenced him to life imprisonment. However, on appeal the Lahore High Court reduced his sentence to ten years at hard labor, stating that "the appellant had two children from his deceased wife and when he took the extreme step of taking her life by giving her repeated knife blows on different parts of her body, she must have done something to enrage him to that extent."[2]

It has been observed that "the concept of human rights is one of the few moral visions ascribed to internationally" (Bunch/WILDAF 1992, p. 4). Domestic violence violates the principles that lie at the heart of this moral vision: the inherent dignity and worth of all members of the human family, the inalienable right to freedom from fear and want, and the equal rights of men and women (Universal Declaration 1948). Yet until recently, it has been difficult to conceive of domestic violence as a human rights issue under international law. In exploring some of the reasons why such a conceptualization has been so problematic, we stress that the methods of combatting domestic violence under international law are still emerging and that the strategies set forth in this chapter mark only one step in this process.

Problems with Understanding Domestic Violence as a Proper Human Rights Issue

The Scope of International Human Rights Law

Domestic violence has not traditionally been analyzed as a human rights issue because it has been understood, both at the domestic and international levels, to be a "private" issue and, as such, outside the scope of international human rights law. The concept of human rights developed largely from ideas in Western political theory about rights of the individual to autonomy and freedom (Peterson 1990, pp. 308–310). International human rights law evolved in order to protect those individual rights from limitations that might be imposed on them by states. States are bound by international law to respect the individual rights of each and every person, and are thus accountable for abuses of those rights. The aim of the human rights movement is to enforce states' obligations in this regard by denouncing violations of their duties under international law (Eisler 1987, p. 287). The exclusive focus on the behavior of states confines the operation of international human rights law entirely within the public sphere. The purpose of this chapter, and the domestic violence report described herein, is to reveal the gender-based character of the public/private sphere division, to expose the "public" aspects of "private" violence, and, ultimately, to demonstrate the state's responsibility for domestic violence under its international human rights obligations.

Gender-neutral Law, Gender-biased Application

International human rights law is ostensibly gender-neutral. The rights embodied in the Universal Declaration of Human Rights are defined as belonging to "all human beings," not just to men.[3] All the major human rights instruments include sex as one of the grounds on which states are prohibited from discrimination in enforcing the rights set forth. Although international law is gender-neutral in theory, in practice it interacts with gender-biased domestic laws and social structures that relegate women and men to separate spheres of existence: private and public. Men exist as public, legal entities in all countries, and, barring an overt abuse by the state, participate in public life and enjoy the full extent of whatever civil and political rights exist. Women, however, even when not explicitly excluded from protection by law, are in every country

socially and economically disadvantaged in practice and in fact. Therefore, women's capacity to participate in public life is routinely circumscribed (Charlesworth et al., 1991, pp. 25–30).

This gender bias, if unchallenged, becomes so embedded in the social
structure that it often assumes the form of a social or cultural norm
seemingly beyond the purview of the state's responsibility, rather than
a violation of women's human rights for which the state is accountable.
In some cases, even civil and political rights violations committed directly
by state actors have been shrugged off as acceptable. For example, in
1986 a Peruvian prosecutor told an Amnesty International delegation
visiting the state of Ayacucho that rape of civilian women by soldiers
"was to be expected" when troops were conducting counterinsurgency
operations (Amnesty, December 1991, p. 1).

When gender-neutral international human rights law is applied in
these gender-biased social contexts, those making the application—both
governments and nongovernmental organizations—do not necessarily
challenge the gender bias embedded in the social structure or in the
state's determination of its responsibilities. In past human rights practice,
human rights organizations often have not challenged the relegation of
women and what happens to them to the private sphere, and have allowed
social or cultural justifications to deter them from denouncing restrictions
on women's capacity to participate in public life. Even where abuses
against women have occurred in realms they traditionally monitor, such
as police custody, organizations have not consistently reported them. For
example, only very recently have human rights organizations begun to
report on rape of women prisoners as a form of torture (Amnesty, March
1991, p. 18; Blatt 1992).

In the absence of a challenge to states' consistent relegation of women
to the private sphere, international law's application can have the effect
of reinforcing, even replicating, the exclusion of women's rights abuses
from the public sphere and, therefore, from the state's international
obligations.[4] In a very real sense, gender-specific abuses—even those
directly attributable to states—have until recently been "privatized" internationally, and either go unchallenged or are left out of human rights
practice altogether.

Nowhere is the effect on international human rights practice of the
public/private split more evident than in the case of domestic violence—
which literally happens "in private." For example, blatant and frequent
crimes, including murder, rape, and physical abuse of women in the
home, are dismissed by states as private, family matters, and routinely
escape government action. Moreover, the state's failure to prosecute
violence against women equally with other similar crimes or to guarantee
women the fundamental civil and political right to equal protection of

the law without regard to sex have largely escaped international condemnation.

At least four interrelated factors have caused the exclusion of domestic violence, in particular, from international human rights practice: traditional concepts of state responsibility under international law and practice; misconceptions about the nature and extent of domestic violence and states' responses to it; the neglect of equality before and equal protection of the law without regard to sex as a governing human rights principle; and the failure of states to recognize their affirmative obligation to provide remedies for domestic violence crimes. These factors, independently and in relation to one another, are beginning to change and, with them, so is the treatment of domestic violence under international law. The following sections attempt to trace the course and direction of this emerging change.

The Concept of State Responsibility

The concept of state responsibility defines the limits of a government's accountability under international law for human rights abuses.[5] Of course, all acts are done by real people, individually or with others, and not by the fictive "person" of the state. Therefore, responsibility is generally understood to arise only when an act by a real person or persons can be imputed to the state (Brownlie 1990, p. 435). Traditionally, the idea of vicarious responsibility for acts is a perfectly acceptable one: such responsibility flows from the authorized acts of agents of the state, or persons acting with the apparent authority or condonation of the state (Brownlie 1990, pp. 435–436). In traditional human rights practice, states are held accountable for what they do directly or through an agent, rendering acts of purely private individuals—such as domestic violence crimes—outside the scope of state responsibility (ILC Yearbook 1972, pp. 95–125).

More recently, however, the concept of state responsibility has expanded to include not only actions directly committed by states, but also states' systematic failure to prosecute acts committed either by low-level or parastatal agents, or by private actors. In these situations, although the state may not actually be committing the primary abuse, its failure to prosecute the abuse amounts to complicity in it. For instance, in three significant cases, *Velásquez*, *Godínez*, and *Fairén and Solís*,[6] decided by the Inter-American Court on Human Rights in 1988 to 89, the tribunal found that the government of Honduras was responsible for a series of forced disappearances carried out between 1981 and 1984 by members of the Honduran military who were acting as private individuals (Shelton 1990; Drucker 1989; Mendez and Vivanco 1990). The test of the state's responsibility for an act differs depending upon whether the actor is the state or a private individual.

To hold a state accountable for the actions of state actors, one of two things must be shown: 1) the state explicitly authorized the act (that is, a senior official committed or authorized it), *or* 2) the state systematically failed to prosecute abuses committed by its agents, whether or not these acts were ordered by senior officials. In the latter case, it is usually necessary to show a pattern of nonprosecution of acts that violate human rights that the state has agreed to enforce.[7] For example, the state is responsible if it fails systematically to prohibit or prosecute torture, because the right to be free of torture is guaranteed under international law. Governments have agreed not to torture people themselves, and have undertaken to ensure that no one else in the state tortures (Convention Against Torture, Article 2). If the state failed to prosecute torturers, it would be in violation of its international obligations.

The test is different when the actors are private. For example, systematic nonenforcement of laws against armed robbery by private actors alone would not constitute a human rights problem; it would merely indicate a serious common-crime problem. Nonprosecution of the crimes of private individuals becomes a human rights issue (assuming no state action or direct complicity) *only* if the reason for the state's failure to prosecute can be shown to be rooted in discrimination along prohibited lines, such as those set forth in Article 26 of the Covenant on Civil and Political Rights.

It is true that there are rights to bodily integrity in international human rights law which armed robbery would appear to violate. However, these are rights *against the state,* not rights that states must enforce against all other persons. States cannot be directly accountable for violent acts of all private individuals, because *all* violent crime would then constitute a human rights abuse for which states could be held directly accountable under international law. The state's international obligation with regard to the acts of private individuals is to ensure that, where it *does* protect people's lives, liberty, and security against private depredations, it must do so equally, without discrimination on prohibited grounds (CCPR, Article 26). Therefore, there would have to be systematic, discriminatory nonenforcement of the domestic criminal law against murder or assault for domestic violence to constitute a human rights issue, not merely a showing that the victims' lives ended or their bodies were harmed.[8]

The expansion of state responsibility to include accountability for some acts of private individuals as described here was one of the factors necessary to permit analysis of domestic violence as a human rights violation. However, in many cases it was still necessary to show a pattern of discriminatory nonprosecution which amounted to a failure to guarantee equal protection of the law to women victims. The following section is an overview of new information about the vast extent of violence experienced by women and the frequency of its discriminatory or nonprosecution, which was revealed as a general characteristic, not merely a rare anomaly of domestic criminal law.

Widespread Violence and a Pattern of Nonprosecution

As noted, domestic violence generally has been understood as a "private" matter, in which governments should not interfere, and for which they are not accountable (Finesmith 1983). The home is traditionally idealized as a place of safety and security, a sanctuary from duty, responsibility, and work. Moreover, the relationships between members of the family were also idealized as respectful and supportive. Needless to say, the reality is quite different, and "modern studies suggest . . . that far from being a place of safety, the family can be a 'cradle of violence' and that much of this violence is directed at female members of the family." (UN Report 1989, p. 14.)

New information on domestic violence surfaced as a result of a long, international campaign by women's rights groups to raise consciousness about women's issues and problems. After successfully pushing for the inclusion of a commitment to equal rights for women in the UN Charter and Universal Declaration of Human Rights, women's organizations worked for the establishment of the UN Commission on the Status of Women and other formal mechanisms for the advancement of women's status (Fraser 1983, p. i). The commission and affiliated nongovernmental organizations (NGOs) drafted a variety of conventions to combat discrimination against women internationally, and pressed for the General Assembly to declare a Decade for Women program. It was the international resurgence of women's activism in the 1960s and 1970s, and the pressure generated by women's organizations internationally, that made the UN Decade for Women (1975 to 1985) a reality (Fraser 1983, p. v). As the decade unfolded, women's rights activists coordinated international efforts to study the position of women in all societies and the reasons for their subordinate status. By 1985, at the Final Conference of the Decade for Women in Nairobi, Kenya, a consensus was reached that violence against women:

> exists in various forms in everyday life in all societies. Women are beaten, mutilated, burned, sexually abused and raped. Such violence is a major obstacle to the achievement of peace and other objectives of the Decade and should be given special attention. . . . National machinery should be established in order to deal with the question of violence against

women within the family. . . . (UN Nairobi Report 1986, paragraph 258.)

In 1989, the UN Commission on the Status of Women in Vienna compiled a mass of statistics and analyses of domestic violence by women's rights activists and academics, and published its report, *Violence Against Women in the Family.* The report's author reviewed over 250 articles, books, and studies of various aspects of domestic violence, of which only ten had been published earlier than 1971 (UN Report 1989, pp. 95– 107). This was only a small sample of the huge amount of new material being published about this old problem (Schuler 1992, p. 1). The report concluded that

> Women . . . have been revealed as seriously deprived of basic human rights. Not only are women denied equality with the balance of the world's population, men, but also they are often denied liberty and dignity, and in many situations suffer direct violations of their physical and mental autonomy (UN Report 1989, p. 3).

The nature of domestic violence was revealed as widespread and gender-specific. For example, in the United States, a 1984 National Crime Survey found that women were victims of family violence at a rate three times that of men, and that of all spousal violence crimes, ninety-one percent were victimizations of women by their husbands or ex-husbands (Klaus 1984, p. 4). In Colombia, during 1982 and 1983, the Forensic Institute of Bogota found that out of 1,170 cases of bodily injury, twenty percent were due to marital violence against women. The Forensic Institute also determined that *ninety-four percent* of persons hospitalized in bodily injury cases were battered women (World's Women 1991, p. 19). In Thailand, a study in Bangkok discovered that more than fifty percent of married women were beaten regularly by their husbands (World's Women 1991, p. 19). And the number of women being killed in disputes over their dowries in India almost doubled between 1985 and 1987, rising from 999 reports to 1,786 reports per year (World's Women 1991, p. 19).

This is only a small sampling of the emerging information on domestic violence. Certain characteristics of the problem became clear from the overall research: domestic violence is not unusual or an exception to normal private family life; the vast majority of crimes against women occur in the home and are usually committed by a spouse or relative in the form of murder, battery, or rape; domestic violence is endemic to all societies (Schuler 1992). The immensity of the problem led researchers to conclude that:

> If you are one of only five hundred women in a population of fifty million then you have certainly been more than unlucky and there may perhaps be something very peculiar about your husband, or unusual about your circumstances, or about you; on the other hand, if you are one of 500,000 women then that suggests something very different— that there is something wrong not with a few individual men, or women, or marriages, but with the situation. . . . (Wilson 1976, pp. 5–6.)

If violence against women in the home is inherent to the position of women in all societies, then domestic violence can no longer be dismissed as something private beyond the scope of state responsibility. Although information about government responses to this problem is still minimal, the research suggests that investigation, prosecution, and sentencing of domestic violence crimes occurs with much less frequency than other similar crimes. As the examples at the beginning of this paper indicate, wife-murderers receive greatly reduced sentences, domestic battery is rarely investigated, and rape frequently goes unpunished. Marital rape is often not seen as a crime.[9] These examples stand in contrast to the treatment of violent crimes against male victims (a comparison now made possible by the new data on violence against women). The widespread absence of state intervention in crimes against women is not merely the result of governments' failure to criminalize a class of behavior (since the violent acts themselves *are* crimes), but rather is the result of governments' failure to enforce laws equitably across gender lines. The next section explains how gender-discrimination in enforcement of criminal law constitutes a human rights issue, and applies that analysis to domestic violence.

Right to Equal Protection of the Law as the Underlying Right

As we indicated above, the inclusion of failure to prosecute human rights abusers, whether state agents or private individuals, within the limits of state responsibility is not at present—in and of itself—enough to position domestic violence within the human rights framework. Evidence of a state's failure to prosecute is not sufficient *unless a pattern can be shown that reveals the failure to be gender-discriminatory, and thereby a violation of the internationally guaranteed right to equal protection of the law.* However, even though increased research into and understanding of domestic violence indicated that states were discriminating against women in the enforcement of criminal laws, gender-discrimination under international law was not a central human rights concern. Thus, domestic violence continued to fall outside human rights practice.

Until recently, sex discrimination has been visibly absent from the agendas of most governmental and nongovernmental bodies concerned with human rights, with the exception of the Committee on the Elimination of All Forms of Discrimination Against Women, the UN body which oversees the Convention on the Elimination of All Forms of Discrimination Against Women (CEDAW, Part V, Article 17). The committee and the other women's rights bodies located in Vienna have undertaken landmark work in holding governments accountable for discrimination on the basis of sex, whether by commission or omission. These organizations have made notable progress, despite insufficient resources (Byrnes 1989, pp. 56–59) and limited enforcement mechanisms in the instruments they oversee (Byrnes 1989, pp. 42–45).

However, and more importantly for the purposes of this paper, the mainstream, Geneva-based, human rights bodies, which oversee instruments that have stronger protective mechanisms, have used the existence of this separate women's human rights regime as an excuse to marginalize sex discrimination and most other women's human rights violations that fall clearly within their own mandates.[10] Within the cumulative human rights practices of governments and governmental bodies, sex discrimination has been deemphasized and placed outside the rubric of central human rights concerns. This trend has been reflected and perpetuated, until recently, by the international nongovernmental human rights organizations, including the two largest international groups, Amnesty International and Human Rights Watch.[11]

By failing to focus on the sex-discriminatory practices of governments, human rights organizations have neither challenged the broadest form of sex discrimination that relegates women and what happens to them to the "private" sphere, nor denounced one of its immediate effects: the devaluation of women by governments, and their resulting failure to prosecute violence against women equally with other similar crimes. Instead, human rights organizations have allowed a pattern of discriminatory nonprosecution of such violence to flourish unchecked. This is uncharacteristic, because in other areas where governments discriminate on a prohibited basis, such as race or ethnicity, NGO interventions have been effective in exposing and reversing these violations.[12] However, in the case of domestic violence, the widespread failure by states to prosecute such violence and fulfill their international obligations to guarantee women equal protection of the law has gone largely undenounced.

Ultimately, women's rights activists internationally condemned many of the international governmental and nongovernmental human rights bodies for gender bias and, among other things, their failure adequately to promote and protect women's rights to nondiscrimination and equal protection of the law (Charlesworth, et al. 1986). Largely as a result of this increasing pressure from women's rights activists internationally, and heightened awareness of the extent of violence against women and government tolerance of it, the nongovernmental human rights organizations began to highlight these issues within their overall human rights practice.

These separate but interrelated developments allowed domestic violence to be placed within the context of international human rights law and practice. Developments in the concept of state responsibility, new information about the gender-specific nature of domestic violence, its pervasiveness and frequent discriminatory or nonprosecution by governments, and a new emphasis on equal protection of the law as a central human rights concern made it possible to conceptualize domestic violence as a human rights issue, and to hold governments accountable for the pervasive abuse of women worldwide. In addition, there is a nascent movement to interpret international human rights law to assign accountability to governments directly for their failure to protect women from what has been revealed to be the leading form of violence experienced by women everywhere.

Although not all states have acknowledged that they have an underlying obligation to provide substantive protection to women from domestic violence, there is support in international human rights jurisprudence for the idea that states have an affirmative obligation to criminalize domestic violence crimes.[13] For example, in the case of *X and Y v. The Netherlands*,[14] Y, a mentally handicapped girl, was allegedly sexually assaulted by someone at the private facility where she lived. Her father, Mr. X, attempted to file a claim on her behalf with local police, but it was rejected because the girl did not file it herself. Mr. X brought suit under the European Convention on Human Rights. The European Court on Human Rights found that "although article 8 [of the European convention] is primarily concerned with protecting individuals from arbitrary interference by public authorities, *it also may impose positive obligations on contracting states to insure effective respect for private and family life.*" (Cook 1990, p. 800.) Article 8 of the European Convention is equivalent to Article 17 of the Covenant on Civil and Political Rights in Article 12 of the Universal Declaration of Human Rights, in that both contain the further guarantee of the protection of law against such interference or attacks. These provisions, if interpreted as was their sister provision by the European Court would seem to provide direct shelter from domestic violence crimes, in addition to the indirect shelter provided by the equal protection provisions contained in every human rights instrument.

This language would seem to indicate that there is some obligation under international human rights law to at least provide a real remedy for private violence that extends beyond the duty to provide equal protection. The European Court described the general parameters of that duty in the *X and Y* case, finding that, while recourse to criminal law might not always be required to "ensure effective respect for private and family life,"[15] sexual assault "involved [such] fundamental values and essential aspects of private life" (Cook 1990, p. 800) that effective deterrence was particularly crucial. Domestic violence might similarly be said to violate fundamental values of personal safety in one's private life, and thus similarly require that states provide recourse to victims through provisions of criminal law.

While states themselves may not always bear responsibility for the violent acts of private individuals, this case implies that the rights contained in the major human rights source documents do establish state responsibility for more than just equal protection with regard to abuse committed by private actors. This interpretation is borne out by Article 2 of the Covenant on Civil and Political Rights which requires each state party "to ensure to all individuals within its territory and subject to its jurisdiction the rights recognized in the present covenant . . . " and provides that the state "adopt such legislative or other measures as may be necessary to give effect to the rights recognized in the present covenant."

However, although approaches to combatting domestic violence through the application of human rights law are still evolving, this point of view is far from universally held. So far, initial applications of human rights law to domestic violence have used an equal-protection framework. One practical application of this equal-protection human rights methodology, as explained above, is examined in the following section. It describes the first time human rights law was used by an international human rights organization to reveal a state's systematic nonprosecution of domestic violence crimes, and gives an analysis of that failure as a violation of the fundamental right to equal protection without regard to sex.

Applying the Human Rights Methodology to Domestic Violence: A Case Study

In April 1991, a delegation from Americas Watch and the Women's Rights Project of Human Rights Watch[16] traveled to Brazil to assess the government's response to domestic violence. Brazil was chosen because it has a serious and mounting problem of domestic violence, made visible largely through the efforts of a vigorous national women's movement, and because of the degree to which such violence received the explicit and implicit sanction of the state. The delegation investigated the problem of discriminatory prosecution of violence against women in Brazil, reflected primarily in the use of the honor defense, which has been used to exculpate men accused of killing their wives. It also looked at the failure of the Brazilian criminal justice system to investigate and prosecute domestic violence generally, with particular regard to wife-murder, battery, and rape.

Domestic Violence and State Responsibility: Nonprosecution and Equal Protection

Existing information indicates that wife-murder is a common crime in Brazil, and reveals a pattern of impunity or undue mitigation of sentence in homicides where the victim is a woman.[17] In cases of spousal murder, men are able to obtain an acquittal based on the theory that the killing was justified to defend the man's "honor" after the wife's alleged adultery. The reverse is rarely true (Brazil Report 1991, p. 35). The honor defense is rooted in proprietary attitudes towards women, such that many Brazilians believe that any action by the woman has the potential to so mortally offend her husband that he is within his rights to execute her, in what is then interpreted by the courts as an act of self-defense.[18] And, in general, a defendant will not be held accountable for a homicide if, among other things, it was committed in legitimate self-defense (Brazil Report 1991, p. 18).

In a 1990 spousal-murder case, in the Brazilian city of Apucarana, a man murdered his wife and her lover after stalking them for two days. The defendant was unanimously acquitted on the grounds of honor, and the acquittal was upheld on appeal. Brazil's highest court overturned the lower courts' decisions, on the grounds that murder is not a legitimate response to adultery, and that what is being defended in this type of crime is not honor, but "self-esteem, vanity and the pride of the Lord who sees his wife as property."[19] Despite the court's clear denunciation of the honor defense, when the case was retried, the defendant was again acquitted on the grounds of the "legitimate defense of honor." (Brazil Report 1991, p. 19.) This demonstrates, in its most extreme form, the grip on Brazil's criminal justice system of discriminatory attitudes towards women.

Even when the honor defense is not invoked, there is ample evidence that the Brazilian courts treat defendants in wife-murder cases more leniently than others arrested for murder, largely through misuse of a "violent emotion" defense to allow sentence mitigation (Brazil Report 1991, p. 29).[20] In wife-murder cases, Brazilian courts ignored evidence of premeditation and intent to kill, and focused instead on the behavior of the victim.[21] The same was not found to be true in cases where a wife murdered her husband (Brazil Report 1991, p. 35). There was also evidence that men who murdered their wives were often arraigned on reduced charges, although the information about this problem was scarce

(Brazil Report 1991, pp. 36–39). Even when the murderer is not exculpated, the notion that the victim "provoked" the murder frequently results in unduly short prison terms for wife-murderers, irrespective of the degree of premeditation involved. In cases where wife-murderers are prosecuted, their crime is often reclassified as a less serious charge, and defendants, who are usually first-time offenders, receive preferential treatment from the courts, despite the extreme gravity of their crimes (Brazil Report 1991, pp. 36–39).

Like spousal-murder, punishment of domestic abuse of women that falls short of death is also the exception rather than the rule in Brazil. Brazil's 1988 census, the first to collect data by gender on incidents of physical abuse, found that between October 1987 and September 1988, over 1.1 million people declared that they had been victims of physical abuse (Brazil Report 1991, p. 14). Of that number, forty percent were women (Brazil Report 1991, p. 14), and the violence they experienced was markedly different from that suffered by men. Available statistics show that over seventy percent of all reported incidents of violence against women in Brazil take place in the home (Brazil Report 1991, p. 4), versus ten percent for men (Brazil Report 1991, p. 14).

Despite the prevalence of violence in the home, police rarely investigated such crimes prior to 1985 (Brazil Report 1991, p. 43). Studies from 1981 and 1983 show that "when [women] tried to report aggressions" to the police, they often turned female victims away on the grounds that domestic violence was "a private problem." (Brazil Report 1991, p. 43.) When the police did register domestic abuse crimes, they frequently failed to follow standard procedures, leaving out pertinent information about the circumstances of the abuse or subjecting the victim to abusive treatment aimed at implicating her in the crime (Brazil Report 1991, pp. 43–44). These biased police attitudes were a major deterrent to women seeking the government's protection.

Some positive steps were taken to address the issue in 1985 (Brazil Report 1991, p. 43). After a nationwide campaign by the women's rights movement,[22] the government instituted women's police stations—*delegacias*—to deal exclusively with crimes of violence against women (Brazil Report 1991, p. 43). Reports of violence against women immediately increased, and the treatment of female victims by police markedly improved. However, although the *delegacias* have been successful in raising social consciousness of domestic abuse as a crime, they have been less successful in changing institutional attitudes necessary for criminalization of the abuse, even in police stations run by women (Brazil Report 1991, p. 45).

The work of the *delegacias* is further inhibited by the fact that abuse of women, even if investigated, is rarely prosecuted. The chief of the women's police station in Rio de Janeiro stated that, of the over two thousand battery cases she investigated in 1990, none resulted in punishment of the accused (Brazil Report 1991, p. 48). In the main *delegacia* in São Luis, Maranhão, of over four thousand battery complaints registered by women from 1988 to 1990, only three hundred were forwarded for processing by the court, and only two men were convicted and sent to prison (US DOS Country Reports 1991, p. 531). These figures indicate the persistent failure by the judiciary to see violence against women in the home as a crime, rather than a mere "domestic dispute" in which the government should not interfere (Brazil Report 1991, p. 48).

The government of Brazil also treats victims of rape in a discriminatory manner, by making it difficult to prove rape, and by encouraging intrusive inquiries into the victim's life of a sort that are not made in cases in which men have experienced a form of physical violence. For example, the definition of rape in Brazil is confined to sexual intercourse with a woman involving violence or serious threat of violence (Brazil Report 1991, p. 53). Proof of rape requires a demonstration of penetration and serious bodily injury or a serious threat (Brazil Report 1991, pp. 53, 61). While rape has always been viewed as a grave crime in Brazil, the penalties have in the past varied according to the "honesty" of the victim (Brazil Report 1991, p. 54), because most sexual assault crimes are deemed crimes only if the victim is an "honest" woman (Brazil Report 1991, p. 5). Although explicit requirements that the victim be an "honest" woman (that is, a virgin) have been removed from the penal law regarding rape, if the rape survivor does not fit this stereotype, she is likely to be accused of having consented to the crime, and the rape is unlikely to be investigated and prosecuted. There is strong evidence that the distinction between honest and dishonest women continues to influence the way rape is treated by the Brazilian criminal justice system (Brazil Report 1991, pp. 54–55).

It is also important to note that the legal definition of rape treats it as a crime against custom, rather than as a crime against an individual; this signifies that the victim is society, not the woman. Under the law, the woman's individual rights are regarded as less important than the social order that her abuse is understood to violate. This conception of rape lends legitimacy to the "honest" woman distinction, and makes it more difficult for a woman who does not fit the stereotype to prove that she was raped (Brazil Report 1991, p. 55). It also dramatically highlights the discriminatory attitude towards women that permeates this system.

Conclusions and Recommendations of the Brazil Report

Because of the Brazilian government's discrimination against women victims of domestic violence, as displayed in these substantial barriers to investigation and prosecution[23] of battery and rape, impunity or undue mitigation of sentence for these crimes—and for wife-murder—is commonplace in Brazil.[24] The study of domestic violence in Brazil demonstrates that the nonprosecution of these crimes is directly related to the gender of the victims. The state's refusal to prosecute, or its more lenient treatment of gender-specific violence, denies women the equal protection of criminal law in violation of Brazil's international obligations.[25] This denial is evident both in Brazil's failure to prosecute—or even investigate—most reported complaints of domestic violence crimes against women, and in its legitimization of discriminatory legal concepts, such as the honor defense, that deny female victims of crime the same protection afforded to male victims, and further institutionalize gender bias in Brazilian law.

By denouncing the Brazilian government's failure to meet its obligations in this regard, the report lends the persuasive force of public embarrassment—the major tool of nongovernmental human rights organizations—to the dual tasks of ensuring the application of international human rights guarantees and addressing the problem of domestic violence as a worldwide human rights issue. Additionally, this application of international human rights law to the problem of domestic violence in Brazil highlighted some of the practical problems and limitations of the human rights approach as a tool for social change regarding domestic violence, as well as the enormous power of utilizing this framework. This next section discusses these more general questions raised by the Brazil report about the limits and overall usefulness of the human rights approach.

Conclusions: The Limits and Value of the Equal Protection-Human Rights Approach to Combatting Domestic Violence

Practical Problems

Human rights practice is a method of reporting facts to promote change. The influence of nongovernmental human rights organizations is intimately linked to the rigor of their research methodology (Orentlicher 1990, p. 84). One typical method of reporting human rights violations in specific countries is to investigate individual cases of human rights violations through interviews with victims and witnesses, supported by research of other credible sources of information about the abuse.

The analysis of domestic violence as a human rights abuse depends not only on proving a pattern of violence, but also on demonstrating a systematic failure by the state to afford women equal protection of the law against those abuses. Without detailed statistical information concerning both the incidence of wife-murder, battery, and rape, and the criminal justice system's response to those crimes, it can be difficult to make a solid case against a government for its failure to guarantee equal protection of the law. The problem of inadequate documentation of abuses of women's human rights is common to countries throughout the world.

As noted earlier, information about the nature and extent of domestic violence has been available for only a relatively short period of time. For example, in Brazil, although anecdotal evidence of an overwhelming incidence of domestic violence exists, hard facts or large-scale surveys of specific aspects of spousal-murder, battery, or rape were often hard to obtain or altogether unavailable. At present, national homicide data by gender has not been collected, and statistics regarding battery and rape, where available, are usually compiled by hand, and rarely in a systematic way (Brazil Report 1991, pp. 67–68). In addition, individual cases have not always been well documented or pursued beyond the original report that the abuse occurred—there is often no information about how the government responded, particularly as regards prosecution and sentencing.

Inadequate documentation is a function of another practical problem which is equally common internationally: the lack of cooperation between women's rights and human rights groups on both a national and international level. In Brazil, for example, the human rights and women's rights groups had no history at all of working together, and, in fact, often saw their aims as antagonistic. For example, efforts to emphasize the equal rights of women in the context of the struggle against military dictatorship were often perceived by the human rights community as divisive and marginal to the central issue of creating a nonoppressive (and in this case, democratic) form of government. The result of this split is that, not only do human rights organizations lack information pertaining to violations of women rights, but women's rights organizations often have neither the training nor the resources to document abuses as required to make a case under international law (Consultation Report 1991, pp. 8–11).

One of the important practical advances resulting from fieldwork on women's human rights was the realization that, to address abuses against women adequately in the context of international human rights practice, women's rights and human rights organizations at the national and international level need to work together to locate and develop the data and methods necessary for the rigorous fact-finding and analysis on which human rights reporting is based (Consultation Report 1991, pp. 8–11).

Given some attention and concerted effort, these and other emerging practical problems can be overcome. However, some profound methodological limits to the human rights approach also need to be examined and addressed.

Methodological Limitations

In addition to the quality of its facts, the efficacy of the human rights method depends on the solidity of the legal principles on which arguments are made that governments are in violation of their international obligations and should change their practices. Consequently, any changes in the human rights method must be developed from those legal principles, or they will be ineffective to condemn states.

The most general methodological problem with applying human rights to domestic violence is not specific to domestic violence *per se*, but is a function of the general focus of human rights law: international human rights law is law that binds *states*, not law that binds individuals. As we discussed at length earlier, the focus of human rights law on states and the fact that domestic violence and other abuses of women's human rights are often committed by private individuals necessitate a complicated analysis to demonstrate state accountability. The requirements of building a case for state responsibility can often appear daunting, particularly when coupled with the documentary problems detailed above.

Another limitation is that human rights practice tends to focus on individual acts (whether by state or nonstate actors), and not on the causes of those acts. Documentation of a government's failure to prosecute domestic violence does not directly address the causes of that violence, which are rooted in social, economic, and legal structures that discriminate against women, and in widely held attitudes about women's inferior status. The inability, in current human rights practice, to hold governments accountable for the broad economic and social inequities that underlie those abuses has at least two consequences. First, it may lead governments to the false conclusion that all they need to do to eliminate domestic violence is prosecute aggressors equally with other violent criminals. Second, it largely limits human rights organizations to denouncing abuses after they have already occurred and the victim is hurt or dead.[26]

To put it another way, it is very difficult to use the human rights approach to prevent domestic violence. Positive state responsibilities, such as education or economic support programs, that might help eliminate the causes of domestic violence are less clearly prescribed by international law than prohibitions of certain abuses, even where the state may be domestically obligated to undertake certain functions. It is one thing for a human rights organization to address the state's discriminatory application of law; it is quite another to direct a state to adopt a particular social program to change discriminatory attitudes. The first is, in a sense, a "negative" injunction: stop violating international human rights law; while the second is more of a "positive" exhortation: adopt this policy. The latter statement has a more amorphous basis in international legal principles, and requires a less straightforward remedy. It is more difficult for an international human rights organization to be persuasive positively than negatively.[27]

Increasingly, the positive responsibilities of states are being incorporated into international human rights law and practice. The Convention on the Elimination of All Forms of Discrimination Against Women (CEDAW), for example, requires governments to take positive measures to end legal, social, and economic gender inequality (CEDAW, Article 3). There is no current consensus in the international human rights community about the ability of human rights organizations to advocate positive measures, or about states' responsibility under international law to take such actions. However, as the concept of state responsibility in international law evolves further, it may be more possible to hold governments accountable for failing actively to counter the social, economic, and attitudinal biases which underpin and perpetuate domestic violence.

Finally, and perhaps most importantly, the current human rights approach to domestic violence and state responsibility only addresses the problem of equal protection; it usually cannot hold governments accountable for the domestic violence itself, just as it could not hold governments accountable internationally for other violent crimes committed by private individuals. Given the current state of international human rights jurisprudence, the nondiscrimination approach most closely resembles current thinking as regards state responsibility for private actions. This is not to say that it is impossible to derive concepts of direct state accountability for private acts from human rights law, as we discussed above, nor that it might not be preferable to undertake such an analytic endeavor.

Addressing the state's responsibility for domestic violence *per se* would entail investigating in more detail the particular characteristics of domestic violence, as distinguished from, for example, other violent crime. To some extent domestic violence is not random, that is, it is directed at women because they are women, and is committed to impede women from exercising their rights. As such, it is an essential factor in maintaining women's subordinate status, as well as in the resulting domestic and international privatization of gender-specific abuse,[28]—the problem with which this paper began and which the integration of women's rights into human rights practice seeks to counter. In this sense, domestic violence is different from other violent crimes. Treating domestic violence as merely an issue of equal protection, and by inference, therefore, setting up the treatment of men as the standard by which we ought to measure the treatment of women in our societies, may in fact disserve women and mask the ways in which domestic violence is not just another common crime. The norm of gender-neutrality itself, embodied in the human rights treaties and international customary law, may unintentionally reinforce gender bias in the law's application, and obscure the fact that human rights laws ought to deal directly with gender-specific abuse, and not just gender-specific failures to provide equal protection. The gender-neutral norm may appear to require only identical treatment of men and women, when in fact, equal treatment in many cases is not adequate.

These limitations to the approach used in the Brazil case study outlined herein are grave. However, they should not obscure the viability of the equal-protection approach and the important step that was taken in using human rights law in any capacity to address domestic violence. Nor should they detract from the real value to using human rights law in general as a tool to combatting violence against women in the home.

Value of the Human Rights Approach

The practical and methodological problems outlined above are no inherent deterrent to integrating domestic violence into human rights practice. To identify practical obstacles and understand the methodological limits of the current human rights approach is to expand human rights practice, which is far from static, that much further. Moreover, to understand the limits of the human rights approach is also to clarify the particular contributions it can make as part of broader local and international efforts to combat domestic violence.

"Human rights is a prominent subject of international diplomacy" (Orentlicher 1990, p. 83), and the prestige and influence of nongovernmental international human rights organizations is great. Heads of state pay significant attention to the findings and recommendations of such NGOs, even if only to deny their validity,[29] and states regularly monitor whether other states have successfully met their international obligations to uphold the human rights of their citizens.[30] Human rights activists have shown the effectiveness of prompting governments to curb human rights violations by aiming the spotlight of public scrutiny on the depredations (Orentlicher 1990, p. 84). Therefore, the potential power of the human rights machinery to combat domestic violence is a strong incentive to use this approach.

The human rights approach employs a preexisting international system to bring pressure to bear on governments that routinely fail to prosecute domestic violence equally with other similar crimes. This provides an opportunity for local institutions and activists to supplement their efforts with support from the international community. The effect is twofold: local struggles are enhanced, and domestic protections available to women may improve. For example, following the publication of the Brazil report discussed above, and the surrounding activism by local women's and human rights groups, the state of Rio initiated training programs in domestic violence with women's rights activists and local police.[31] In addition, the report's release helped encourage efforts in São Paulo to draft a state convention to eliminate discrimination against women. It also served as a catalyst to further research in Brazil on the "legitimate defense of honor" and on the criminal justice system's failure to punish domestic violence crimes. Finally, it provided an opportunity for local women's rights and human rights organizations to cooperate in these efforts.

The human rights approach to domestic violence may also have the effect of improving international protections for women. Although, until recently, "women's issues" have been seen as marginal to the "real" issues of human rights, placing domestic violence within the mainstream of the theory and practice of international human rights draws attention to the extent and seriousness of the problem. This not only points out the past failure of the human rights community adequately to counter the problem, but brings to light the urgent need for the international human rights system to function more effectively on behalf of women.

The most compelling advantage to utilizing a human rights approach to oppose domestic violence may be that it simultaneously raises women's issues in the mainstream of human rights practice, while it broadens the mainstream's perceived scope. Applying this approach to domestic violence produces the insight that the incorporation of women's rights issues into human rights practice is a (r)evolutionary process, and that the process itself will provide new ideas and identify unsuspected obstacles at each step along the way. Ultimately, together with developments in other areas of law and activism, this dynamic may help transform the international human rights system, so that it honors the Universal Declaration of Human Rights, and protects more than the rights of man.

Notes

1. It should be noted that, since this case, England's House of Lords has abolished the marital rape exception. See *The Independent* 1991.

2. *Muhammad Younis alias Joona v. The State,* 1989 Pakistan Criminal Law Journal 1747 (Lahore).

3. Universal Declaration of Human Rights, Article 1. It should be noted that the declaration was originally drafted in terms of the eighteenth-century concept of "the rights of man." The language was only expanded at the insistence of Eleanor Roosevelt and a group of Latin American women who fought for the use of the term "human" rights and the inclusion of sex in the declaration (see Bunch 1990, p. 487).

4. Some notable exceptions to this general practice are detailed in the section below that discusses equal protection.

5. See Spanish Zone of Morocco Claims, Judge Huber, translation of French text, *UN Reports of International Arbitral Awards* ii. 615, p. 641.

6. *Inter-Am. Ct. H.R.* (ser. C) No. 4 (1988).

7. This requirement was established in the context of widespread activism on the problem of disappearances, which was the occasion for some of the expansion of the concept of state responsibility (see Méndez & Vivanco 1990, pp. 542–3).

8. Such as race, color, sex, language, religion, political, or other opinion, national or social origin, property, birth or other status. CCPR, Article 26. Note that under this discrimination approach, it is irrelevant whether the harm to the victim implicates some other right guaranteed by international human rights law, because CCPR, Article 26, prohibits discrimination in the enforcement of *any* law, not just in the enforcement of the other rights guaranteed by the covenant itself.

9. The authors wish to thank Jane Connors for her generosity in sharing with us a recent unpublished paper, in which she notes that "In most jurisdictions, non-consensual sexual activity which takes place in marriage is not subject to legal sanction."

10. For example, the United Nations Human Rights Commission established an Ad Hoc Working Group of Experts in 1967 to investigate various aspects of human rights and racial discrimination in South African and other parts of Southern Africa (see Human Rights Commission Report 1983). No such similar group has ever been established by the Human Rights Commission to study discrimination on the basis of sex, internationally or even regionally.

11. Amnesty International (AI) is an international human rights organization with a research staff based in London, many national sections, and a large grass-roots membership. AI works to free political prisoners, and focuses on specific issues affecting prisoners, such as torture, executions, and disappearances. It also reports on violations of the laws of war by both sides, monitors violence against lesbians and gays and HIV-positive persons, and works to abolish the death penalty.

    Human Rights Watch (HRW) is a U.S.-based international human rights organization. It is composed of five regional divisions—African Watch, Americas Watch, Asia Watch, Helsinki Watch, and Middle East Watch—and three thematic projects: the Fund for Free Expression, the Prison Project, and the Women's Rights Project. HRW monitors the human rights practices of governments, focusing mainly on politically motivated abuses of human rights, but also monitoring such abuses as summary executions, torture, and cruel conditions of imprisonment, regardless of the victim. In situations of sustained armed conflict, HRW monitors violations of the laws of war not only by governments but also by rebel groups.

12. For example, Americas Watch's denunciations in the mid-1980s of government-sponsored discrimination against Miskito and Sumu indigenous peoples in Nicaragua and Honduras and attendant international pressure resulted in substantial concessions of territory to those peoples (see Americas Watch 1984; Americas Watch 1987). Similarly, monitoring by human rights organizations of the effects of apartheid and

344 / Michele E. Beasley and Dorothy Q. Thomas

of state-sponsored racial violence in South Africa pressured governments into sustaining a widespread international boycott against South African products, and led ultimately to the formal dismantling of apartheid in that country.

13. Some states' constitutions even contain provisions providing substantive protection to women from domestic violence. See, e.g., Constitution of the Federative Republic of Brazil, Article 226, Section 8 (1988) ("the state should assist the family, in the person of each of its members, and should create mechanisms so as to impede violence in the sphere of its relationships."); Colombian Constitution of 1989, Article 42 ("Family relations are based on the equality of rights and duties of the couple and on the reciprocal rights of all its members. Any form of violence in the family is considered destructive of its harmony and unity and will be sanctioned according to law.").

14. 91 Eur. Ct. H.R. (ser. A) (1985).

15. *X and Y v. The Netherlands*, 91 Eur. Ct. H. R. (ser. A) (1985), paras. 23–4.

16. Americas Watch is one of the regional committees of Human Rights Watch. It monitors human rights in Latin America and the Caribbean. The Women's Rights Project is a division of Human Rights Watch. This mission was the first undertaken by the Women's Rights Project, which was formed in 1990 to monitor violence against women and discrimination on the basis of sex throughout the world. For other reports by the Women's Rights Project and various regional Watch Committees, see WRP/Asia Watch 1992; WRP/Helsinki Watch 1992; WRP/Middle East Watch 1992.

17. This is particularly true in Brazil's interior, where one state prosecutor told Americas Watch that the honor defense is successful in eighty percent of the cases in which it is invoked (Brazil Report 1991, p. 44).

18. In wife-murder cases, defense attorneys usually characterize the killing as an unintentional or "privileged homicide." In these honor defense cases, the idea is that the man acted in legitimate self-defense of his honor in killing his wife. This concept effectively collapses the honor defense into the realm of legitimate self-defense by equating the wife's adulterous (or allegedly adulterous) act with a physical act of aggression towards the accused, against which he is permitted to respond with violence.

Although the theory of legitimate defense of honor existed in Portuguese colonial law, it was abolished in 1830 with the enactment of Brazil's first postindependence Penal Code (Brazil Report 1991, p. 20). A subsequent similar theory, that a man could be acquitted of killing his adulterous wife if he murdered her in the "heat of passion," was similarly done away with by Brazil's Third Penal Code in 1940. Today, strong emotion or passion no longer excuses criminal responsibility for murder, although it can be used to mitigate sentence (Brazil Report 1991, p. 21). The delegation found that despite a history of Brazilian jurisprudence that has unequivocally declared that the honor defense has no basis in law, men such as João Lopes are still regularly acquitted under this defense (Brazil Report 1991, pp. 26–28).

19. These attitudes are deeply rooted in Brazilian society and law. Brazil's first Civil Code (1914) treated women like minors. Women did not achieve the vote until 1932 and could not work outside the home without their husbands' permission until 1962. Although the country's 1988 Constitution granted full equality to men, the Civil Code still deems the husband to be the head of the family, and therefore the only one authorized to represent the family legally and administer family finances (Brazil Report 1991, pp. 16–17).

20. There is evidence that similar patterns of using violent emotion defenses to privilege male defendants over female defendants in spousal-murder cases exist in other countries, such as Pakistan and Canada (see WRP/Asia Watch 1992, p. 46; Cote 1991).

21. Courts have considered the victim's clothing, her level of independence, or her initiative in separating from her husband, treating these factors as if they justified her death (Brazil Report 1991, pp. 23, 30).

22. The women's movement in Brazil emerged in the context of the gradual liberalization of Brazil's polity and the country's shift towards democracy in the late 1970s and early 1980s. Reports on sexual abuse, torture, and murder of political prisoners during the previous military dictatorship led to national debate about violence, and to the proliferation of women's organizations during that same period (see Stepan 1989). During the first sets of direct elections in 1982, gender-specific issues were incorporated into the platforms of various political parties, and in 1983, the first state council on the condition of women (*Conselho Estadual da Condição Feminina*) was formed in São Paulo. Its primary goal was to increase women's access to the policy-making process, and to promote women's interests within state administration. By 1985, a national women's council (CDNM) was formed that made domestic violence its number-one priority. Women's increased power during this period enabled the women's movement to press for the establishment of women's police stations in a few states, staffed entirely by women and dedicated solely to crimes of violence against women, excluding homicide (which was not then viewed as a gender-specific crime) (see Stepan 1989; Medeiros de Fonseca 1977, p. 14).

23. There is a larger problem of nonreported cases of domestic abuse, which in part reflects the state's failure to make reporting possible. This is especially a problem as regards battery and rape. Rape and battery victims in general often lack any confidence that they will receive justice, either because they view the violence they experience as "normal" (or fear the authorities so view it) or because they fear ill-treatment at the hands of the police (Brazil Report 1991, pp. 50–51). In addition, women are reluctant to report being battered or raped in the home because they are economically dependent upon the abuser (Brazil Report 1991, at p. 51).

24. This paper does not mean to suggest that Brazil is unique in this regard. Discrimination in the state's treatment of violence against women in the home is also prevalent in the United States, among other states.

25. Brazil has ratified the International Covenant on Civil and Political Rights and the Convention to End All Forms of Discrimination Against Women, both of which guarantee the right to equal protection of the law without regard to sex.

26. It is also important to note that, just as the human rights approach does not focus on the social causes of domestic violence, it does little to directly address the needs of women victims of such crimes. The approach cannot help with the provision of medical care, psychological counseling, or economic support that would enable women to leave the homes in which they are battered or pursue other options, because these aspects of the state's provision of services are beyond the reach of international human rights practice as currently constituted. Yet, to a large extent, it is these social services that are most immediately needed by domestic violence survivors.

27. That is in large part because positive exhortations usually imply that a state ought to spend its money in a particular way. Human rights practice loses its moral force when it attempts to direct spending policies; the practice is then attempting to insert itself into what is purely an internal state matter of distributive justice.

28. The Committee on Elimination of All Forms of Discrimination Against Women adopted a general recommendation on violence against women that stated: "gender-based violence is a form of discrimination which seriously inhibits women's ability to enjoy rights and freedoms on a basis of equality with men." See *General Recommendation No. 19*, 11th Session, 1992. Further discussion of violence against women as a means "of maintaining [women] in sex-stereotyped roles, or of denying her human dignity . . . " can be found in the Expert Group Report 1991, pp. 14–15.

29. For example, Peruvian President Alberto Fujimori strongly criticized Amnesty International and Americas Watch for damaging Peru's international reputation by issuing reports describing his government's abuses of Peruvians' human rights (Lokken 1991). The severity of his criticism indicates how seriously such denunciations are taken by world leaders.

30. For instance, the United States in many cases ties its provision of foreign aid to the recipient country's human rights record, and publishes a yearly country-by-country report detailing and analyzing the status of internationally recognized human rights in countries that receive such assistance. See The Foreign Assistance Act, Sections 116(d)(1) and 502(B)(b).

31. A more recent Women's Rights Project of Human Rights Watch report on discrimination against women in post-Communist Poland has similarly received local and international attention, and affords local women's activists another tool for compelling the government to guarantee women equal protection of the law and make elimination of sex discrimination and violence against women a clear national priority (WRP/ Helsinki Watch 1992).

Section IV

Policy Postscript

Private Violence and Public Obligation: The Fulcrum of Reason

by Jane Maslow Cohen

Introduction

In this concluding essay, I intend to recast our titular theme, the public nature of private violence, into an exploration of the reasons that private violence is a matter of public obligation, and I shall seek to impress a host of public policy recommendations with a sense of powerful public obligation. For these purposes, the devices I shall forge into method include, on the one hand, a feminist perspective—a necessarily telescoped perspective—on history, law, politics, and economics; and on the other, a fundamental reliance on reason—the grounds and the processes of reason.

My hope is that the reasons I will propose for public obligation in the matter of private violence will animate the changes in public attitudes and actions that I will go on to describe. But if some of these changes seem harsh, impractical, or otherwise unwelcome, I remain hopeful that the compelling nature of the reasons themselves will inspire both a more coherent program and, within it, new directives to redress the private violence crisis we are in.

To inaugurate the inquiry in appropriate terms, I shall first offer my reasons for grounding this effort in reason.

What Drove Me to This Place

(A)

The engine that drives this essay contains four cylinders. The first consists of my growing sense that, after a decade marked by new and diverse public policy initiatives, institutional responses to private violence have begun to lack momentum and have developed an obvious lack of coherence. The second is that the extraordinarily rapid development of both real-world initiatives and a social science research program in private violence have led to problems in the consistency and reliability of facts, interpretations, and evaluations in design and in the field made worse by informational deficits unremedied by government. The third is that, despite the powerful contributions of multitudes of concerned persons, feminists and nonfeminists alike, we enter the mid-1990s with private violence retaining the upper hand. The fourth and last is that American feminism, the chief motive force behind the changes we have experienced in public responses to private violence, could, in addition to its other ongoing efforts, help to remotivate the further shaping of public policy with an approach that is based in public reason.

The need for an approach from reason—a kind of back-to-basics emphasis on public obligation—is, in part, backward-looking. To that extent, it depends on the view that, throughout the 1980s, the weak defense of violence as a male prerogative, in the teeth of the newly aggressive feminist attack on the problem, correspondingly weakened public deliberation over its causes, its effects, and the efforts needed to effectuate any significant alteration in its modes of existence. But on grounds independent of the past, the need for an approach from reason is forward-looking. It responds to the amalgam of social, economic, political, and legal experiences that we have had with private violence and seeks to organize and make use of these experiences in ways that are responsive to their logic. Taken together, these four matters constitute my departure-point for what follows; I shall further address them below, but in amalgamated terms.

(B)

If private violence toward women has become a matter of recognition and response, it is because American feminism became our tutor. Through its involvement in both scholarship and activism and its prime tutelary emotion—anger[1]—feminism broke open the convenient, conventional understandings that, blanketed in denial, had masked any meaningful opportunity for knowledge and understanding of the central condition of many women's lives: that they are ruled by male violence. Building on the consciousness-raising of the sixties' women's movement by insisting on the truth of women's accounts, feminism nurtured the social conditions that enabled these women to speak. Armed with a new vocabulary that, with the aid of social science, soon came to specify the descriptive and evaluative terms needed to frame these accounts, feminist activists helped women, whose numbers grew exponentially throughout the breakaway 1980s, to petition legislatures and courts for redress from the effects, collective and personal, of violence.

There can be no doubt that the aggregate effects of group conscious-ness-raising and individual and collective pleas for action would eventu-ally have given rise to some response. But feminism called also for the public conscience to rise above the singularity of each newly told version of a woman's fear and horror to take account of history. The definition of the plight of abused women is to be found in the history of all women, feminism reminded all those who had not had to learn this lesson by living it. The inquiries done to abused women within the privacy of home and intimate relationship must, therefore, be understood not as atomistic events of no acknowledged meaning to the social order but, rather, as class-based wrongs that help, the way that gender-based workplace harassment and gender-stratified career options and wage scales help, to define the place of women in that order.

What feminism had to teach was that the norm of privacy and its opposite face—public denial—were shielding from the reach of law and from the legal norms of fairness and equality a clear paradigm of social and psychological subordination, subordination that achieves its ritual and nonritual ends in relationships where one or more persons are cast by a domineering individual as the objects of chronically frightening and often physically injurious attention. Over the course of history, religious dogma, scientific precept, the pontifications of early research medicine, legal rules, and the reinforcing tendencies of social practice—sex-differ-entiated role expectations, gender-differentated etiquette, early preg-nancy and unremitted childbearing, and height and weight averages inferior to men—had yielded an ideology of female inferiority that seemed to translate with no lack of fluency into the subordination para-digm.[2] Still, the further translation of subordination into actual physical violence within intimate relationships required address before it could begin to achieve redress. Statistics and the effort to obtain them became an obvious form of address. Thus, it was found in the early 1980s in a state in the Northeast—regionally less gender-violent than the West and the South—that there was a female victim in eighty-three percent of *reported* cases of private violence, even as the FBI estimated wife abuse to be the most *unreported* crime in the United States (Schneider 1986, p. 212, n. 109).

But legal feminist tutoring also took a multitude of more specific forms. Joined by activist lawyers and policy planners unaffiliated with feminism more generally, feminists began to craft an articulated body of responses to private abuse and violence. Only then did the institutional behemoths of law and politics begin to move. Seen from the vantage point of the denial, distraction, and defensiveness that had blanketed these institu-tions only a decade earlier, the initiatives that were put into operation during the 1980s and early nineties seem quite remarkable. These included the retraction in some states of the criminal law's exclusion of rape in marriage (Note 1986, p. 1255); efforts to recontour the plea of self-defense, primarily through the use of expert testimony about the "learned helplessness" syndrome (Walker 1979, 1984); the development of domestic abuse as a tort (Developments 1993, pp. 1498, 1530–33); the imposition of police and other public liability through the use of 42 U.S.C. § 1983; the use of judicial restraining orders (see Chaudhuri and Daly, in Buzawa and Buzawa 1992, pp. 227–252 and Finn, in Steinman 1991, pp. 155–189); efforts to integrate concerns about private violence with judgments about child custody and access to children (Developments 1993, pp. 1603–1611); the implementation of training programs for the police and the judiciary (Bouza, in Steinman 1991, p. 198; Developments 1993, pp. 1555);[3] the funding and provision of public shelters for battered women and their children (see Dutton-Douglas and Dionne, in Steinman 1991, pp. 113–130); mandated treatment for batterers (see Dutton and McGregor, in Steinman 1991, pp. 131–154, but see Ford, in Knudsen and Miller 1991, pp. 191–210); mandated detention for batterers;[4] and the initiation, however tentative, of efforts to reach out to ethnic women and women of color in context-sensitive ways (Edleston, in Steinman 1991, p. 211).

But the work of articulating and experimenting with policy initiatives has not the ringing clarification of a paradigm shift. With the use of each new strategy, each effort at change, has come an awareness of the need for further articulation, further experiment, further change. These revised forms of awareness have come to include pragmatic and conceptual concerns raised by the "learned helplessness" syndrome (Schneider 1986, 1992; Littleton 1989; Maguigan 1991; Mahoney 1991, *infra*); concerns over the appropriate boundaries of privacy doctrine in its application to the family (McClain 1992; Schneider 1991, *infra;* Zimring 1987); the need to abandon or curtail mediation as a vehicle for public response (Lerman 1984); the need for concerted and much revised public activity within ethnic and minority communities (Crenshaw, *infra*); and concerns over the fragmented, sometimes competitive, often unorganized nature of police and judicial efforts involving both the prosecution of batterers and the prevention of further harm (Steinman 1991, pp. 7–12).

To these concerns must be added a layer of increasing awareness about the kinds of difficulty in making forward progress that are the products of inertia, resistance, retrenchment, and the occasional genuinely retrograde, if well-intentioned, innovation. In some instances, inertia and resistance by police and judicial departments have occasioned litigations. The most powerful of these systemic indictments included *Bruno v. Codd* (1979), a vanguard class-action suit against the heads of the New York Police Department and Family Court for a pattern of conduct intended to deter the redress of private violence through the justice system, and *Thurman v. Torrington* (1984), a suit which alleged federal civil rights violations by police and city government when an estranged wife's complaints of death threats and murderous physical attacks were rejected and ignored. The fact that these cases were favorably settled pointed toward change; a 1968 precursor of *Codd, Riss v. City of New York* (1968), had been turned away by the courts on the ground that gender-biased police priorities were judicially unreviewable (this during the heyday of court-supervised school desegregation). But studies of these matters, conducted during the mid-eighties, confirmed the pandemic extent of victim-blaming, identification with the aggressor, and brute unresponsiveness by police and the judiciary,[5] thereby disproving on the ground the Supreme Court's optimistic assessment that "any notion of a husband's prerogative to physically discipline his wife is an 'increasingly outdated misconception'." (*Thurman v. Torrington*, 1984, p. 1528, citing *Craig v. Boren*, 1976, pp. 198–99).

But perhaps the most haunting as well as problematic example of retrenchment was the Seventh Circuit's sharp recasting of the "special duty" rule so as to reduce or even nullify the basis for federal judicial redress of failures of public protection. The case was *DeShaney v. Winnebago County Department of Social Services* (1989), which a Supreme Court majority, without evident discomfort, upheld. Given the Court's explicit concern with the "razor's edge" problem of parental custody and state intervention,[6] the extent of the retrenchment that the ruling will occasion in non-child-related cases of private violence remains to be determined. But its potential for removing a check on a justice system still mired in patriarchal norms is a powerful cause for concern (see Borgmann 1990).

However, *DeShaney* presents evidence of yet another source of concern, one that received surprisingly little attention in the considerable commentary the case generated. This involves the functions of punishment as they relate to private violence. For battering his small, defenseless son into insentience—the child was deprived of most cognitive function and will be institutionalized for as long as he lives—the father received a prison term of two to four years (DeShaney 1989, p. 300). Since judicial discretion in sentencing is almost entirely immune from review, even an overruling of *DeShaney* will do nothing to address this aspect of institutional resistance, one that is replicated whenever a recidivist batterer violates a court's restraining order and is left undetained.

The tail that wags the dog of retrogression is the poorly conceived innovation. While others have undoubted candidates for the honor, perhaps an award belongs to those states which reconsidered the marital rape exclusion only to widen it, on equal protection grounds, to include nonmarital cohabitants.[7]

The social science research efforts that have accompanied and helped to foster the feminist efforts at change have encountered difficulties of their own over the same brief interval of time. These include problems of description and, therefore, of management. There is no doubt that for the design of public policy we need to know, to a reliable degree of accuracy, about the overall prevalence as well as incidence of private violence,[8] the rate of underreporting, the extent of serious as well as nonserious injury, and the extent to which serious and nonserious injuries are inflicted by women as well as by men. But the definitions of each such category and the methodologies of data collection have fallen into considerable contest, while the problem of underreporting has left major attempts at fact-finding in substantial disrepute.[9]

Just by way of example, estimates of degree of injury and the monetized cost of private violence that are based on the National Crime Survey are criticized as "based on limited and questionable data" and "undemonstrated assumptions" (Straus and Gelles 1987). When it turns out that the National Crime Survey makes no attempt to take underreporting into account, these changes achieve an immediate degree of salience. When it further turns out that the most accurate NCS statistic is thought to be its measure of intrafamilial homicide despite the fact that nonmarital family units are not included in the measure, a strong basis for distrust is established.

Then again, one of the coauthors of this NCS critique (Straus) has generated a statistical measure of private violence, the Conflict Tactics Scale (Straus 1979), the use of which revealed that women engage in more separate incidents of husband abuse than men engage in incidences of wife abuse. But the Conflict Tactics Scale has been sharply criticized for failing to make distinctions between offensive and defensive violence (Russell, in Yllö and Bograd 1988) and for failing even to attempt to measure the consequences of abuse, which tends to injure women far more severely than men (Yllö, in Yllö and Bograd 1988, pp. 40–41). Yet its creator has not seen fit to modify his scale (Straus and Gelles 1990), leading one commentator to observe, "It becomes clear that just as the problem of battered wives cannot be eradicated as long as men have the power in the family and in society, so the problem of patriarchal research on 'family violence' will not easily be transformed by feminist critiques" (Russell, in Yllö and Bograd 1988, p. 8).

But perhaps the most embarrassing and fettering problem pertains to the dearth of federal governmental activity. The problem of private violence is national; data-gathering, however, is local or, on a highly extrapolated basis, regional. As of the date of this writing, there is still no commitment to federal data collection concerning the extent, the causes, or the effects—even the readily monetized effects—of private violence. In 1991, a member of the United States Senate introduced sweeping legislation concerning violence against women.[10] Its sweep did not, however, include the provision of a significant federal effort at data-gathering so that the first comprehensive understanding of the phenomenon of private violence could be had. Thus does federal inactivity join intradisciplinary controversy and institutional resistance, retrenchment, and retrograde innovation in creating drag within the already fragmented and considerably unorganized forces for serious change.

There is also a certain sense of early and perhaps too-graceful resignation. This does not shout its way out of the literature. It is more to be heard in muffled cries and lowest whispers, the sighs of one practiced observer about another's characterization of current policy interventions as " 'mired in self-indulgence' " and about his own characterization of the difficulties in achieving interagency coordination "in a fragmented response system . . . when events and their consequences are perceived and assessed differently" (Steinman 1991, p. 10). Or it might appear as a matter of accidental syncopation, as in the sentence, "Family violence, like the poor, may be always with us, but in different proportions and with different outcomes" (Zimring 1987, p. 539). Surely, it is the second half of this compound that is meant for emphasis, but the first keeps ringing in our ears.

But perhaps the reason that the first phrase will not stop ringing is not its threat of resignation. Perhaps it is because we are assaulted daily—indeed, we are collectively victimized—by accounts of new and extreme violence, the forms and amounts of which suggest, in ways the fragmented statistical evidence does not contest, that private violence is on the rise. Women are not the only victims of this violence, nor are men their only batterers. Violence between same-sex partners is just now being acknowledged as a more than rare phenomenon (see Eaton *infra*). Intergenerational violence—child abuse and elder abuse, as well—are matters of ever-rising and newly risen notice, respectively. In the face of all of this, it is indeed difficult to decide where and how to go about a renewed set of efforts to combat and redress private violence, difficult, as one researcher writes, to make "rational assessments of how to make progress in a less than rational world" (Steinman 1991, p. 10).

I think that we should begin by pulling apart the very idea of "rational assessment." I propose to explore this notion by revisiting some very basic reasons that we must engage in the fullest possible forms of public response to private violence. Once we have renewed our commitment to these reasons for public obligation, we can begin to assess the possibilities for policy innovations that public reasons of this highly germinal kind give onto. Because violence toward women and toward female children remains a matter of staggering disproportion, by most measures and as a matter of common awareness, and because one of its sources of issuance, the paradigm of female subordination, remains an uneradicated norm, I, like the other contributors to this volume, will treat private violence toward women as my chief, though not my exclusive concern.

The object of my effort, then, is first to offer public reasons of a very basic kind for a highly energized recommitment to public engagement with the problem of private violence. Second, I shall seek to derive particular policy initiatives from the public reasons that give them force.

But why this insistence on "basic" reasons and "public" reasons, as I keep promising? The next section speaks to these insistences in two different ways.

The What and the Why of Public Reason

Here, I need to offer some explanation for what I mean by "basic, public" reasons, why I see a need to rely on them for the derivation of public policies toward private violence, and what my deployment of "reason" has to do with my title reference to "the fulcrum of reason." I should probably add that, by "public reason," I do not mean what John Rawls means by public reason (see Rawls 1993, pp. 212–254), though it was tempting to bathe in his glow. My difference in conception will be plain enough in moments.

Because I intend to put pressure on the law and, broadly conceived, the politics of public institutional response, the few reasons that I have chosen to elaborate are those that seem to qualify without question as public reasons. By public reasons I mean reasons that seek to justify the need for public action. Implicitly or explicitly, they operate so as to hold up for comparison to public norms—justice, social welfare, public order, to name but three—circumstances as they are and circumstances as they might be. If present circumstances be found unattractive, in light of our desired adherence to these norms, then the public reasons that give rise to the comparison will *commend* public action, though they may suggest, rather than *command,* some particular action. The degree of suggestiveness, giving onto the possibility of a specific command, may depend on which norm constitutes the lens of inquiry and how badly the present circumstance fails by the light of careful examination under it. But it is also the case that there will be a very considerable gap between the broad, categorical terms of public reasons and the detailed terms of most public-policy initiatives in the agency-laden and faction-dense public-policy arenas within which initiatives evolve into actions. It is fact and argument, in an infinitude of combinations, that serve to bridge that gap. In light of the constraints of space and the awkward scope of this project, this layer of pursuit is one I shall present only in suggestive terms here, an introduction, at best, to the deliberations I mean to invite.

Yet, I do intend my terse arguments from reason to be robust enough to perform the largest task at hand. This task is to achieve the hypothetical equivalent of actionable political consensus from a majority of both men and women concerning the legitimacy of employing the coercive powers of the state, as well as some private institutional mechanisms, to combat private violence. This consensus on legitimacy is the essence, the basic goal, of political morality; but it is a goal we must understand as problematized by the existence of private violence. The reason, as we have previously noted through some of its manifestations—widespread denial, the protection of traditional norms, physical escalation—is easy to describe. Private violence is a way of life, a way of social life. Moreover, it has functioned as a kind of benefit—an outlet for aggression, a means of self-aggrandizement, an opportunity for social and psychological bonding—for approximately half the population, to whatever extent they have chosen to lay claim to it. Female subordination is rooted in history, in culture, in our culture, in our subcultures. The job of separating our present attitudes and institutions from their roots and from the fruit that domination continues to bear for those who enjoy it is, as I see things, the meanest task at hand. It is on that account that the reasons I offer for public action are big, brawny reasons, sounding in well-accepted principle and the necessary and obvious aims of public policy.

But there is another powerful reason to adopt a back-to-basics approach, as I have called it. The general process of public-policy determination resembles its smaller cousin, legal process. At the core of legal process—I mean here to reference American legal process only—stands the practice of adversariness. Across the fulcrum of reason, as the title of this essay adverts and as the scales of justice more graphically depict, parties with substantial interests in the matter in contest offer to those who occupy the conjoint roles of norm-givers and dispute-resolvers arguments for the doing of justice that are grounded in reason. The more strongly the reasons called forth in contest are able to evoke the compelling purposes or goals of our common political morality, the more likely they are to persuade the justice-giver of the desirability of a particular outcome, while providing the justificatory basis—the legitimating rationale—for the end that she commands. By extension, the process of reason that should animate all decisions to do justice in the coercion-wielding state should seek to balance, not power against power or level of influence against level of influence—the models of aggression and a certain version of politics, respectively—but reason against reason, because the process of reason is invaluable to public action that is based upon the identification, sorting of, and eventual commitment to the principles that underlie our collective moral life.

It is this process of coming to terms with ourselves through a commitment to reason balanced against reason, under conditions of fair process I have not the space here to stipulate, that should lead not only to public commitments to social projects, but to complex judgments through which to order social priorities among a range of projects and outcomes. This is the background condition that should operate in conjunction with any decision, however large or small, over the public response to private violence; the public funding of any such response; the overall design of social change.

It must not be forgotten, moreover, that the public reasons that support public action in responses to private violence must contend not only with the forces of satisfaction and inertia that are destined to exist in respect to any culturally rooted epiphenomenon, but also to the more volatile and attractive forces of reason that compel the expenditure of public resources on other worthy candidates for social change—the crying needs of public education, for example; higher levels of breast cancer research funding, to name a second; public support for the elderly poor, by way of a third. It is well and good to here object that government aid is not a frozen pie, that the general welfare is not a zero-sum game, but such stipulations fail to turn aside the fact that it is a competitive, aggressively argumentative social universe into which the issue of public obligation in the matter of private violence was born and must be nurtured.

What I will next argue is that the birth process of that debate was, in an important sense, too easy: that feminism—for present purposes, the mother of public reason—defined its early role in relation to the fat and lazy targets of institutional self-satisfaction and inertia, leaving the harder case of competition-worthy reasons for public obligation to be developed at a later stage. It is now that later stage, a time to sample and deliberate anew, on the basis of public reasons, the nature and consequences of public obligation in the matter of private violence.

Public Reason, Then and Now

(A)

The most basic and interesting fact about the process of reasoning that undertook to create the new political and legal responses to domestic violence out of the raw artifacts of feminist theory and horrific personal experience was not so much the crude moral power of the arguments in favor of change but, rather, the ludicrous weakness of the reasons that were mustered to support the *status quo*. Absolutely no one in any legal or political text that achieved publication in any form attempted to mount an argument in favor of the need for men to subordinate women through violent means. Nor did anyone try to make out an argument that such means, though not necessary, were desirable. Nor did anyone attempt the more refined argument from domestic rather than from gender hierarchy: that the social foundation of contemporary democracy could or should be a marriage of institutionalized despotism, since shared power between partner-equals—its idealized counterconception—is obviously problematic to achieve.

It was as if all who maintained any degree of belief in gender hierarchy or male superiority had listened with a common ear to the fulminations of the eminent Victorian moralist James Fitzjames Stephen (uncle, as the worm turns, of Virginia Woolf) who, in 1873, had sought to defend the institution of male-hegemonic marriage from the withering, equality-based attack of John Stuart Mill, in the latter's recently published *The Subjection of Women*. Mill had written:

> The equality of married persons before the law . . . is the only means of rendering the daily life of mankind in any high sense a school of moral cultivation. . . . Already in modern life, and more and more as it progressively improves, command and obedience become exceptional facts in life, equal association its general rule. . . . We have had the morality of submission and the morality of chivalry and generosity; the time is now come for the morality of justice. (Okin, ed. 1988, pp. 45–46)

Stephen's response to Mill's then-utopian-seeming eloquence was that gender equality represented "a grotesquely distorted view of facts," these being the ineluctable weakness and inferiority of women and the equally ineluctable strength and superiority of men, giving on to the obvious necessity for the latter to rule the former. Of course, he continued, far better for women to acknowledge their deficiencies and submit willingly to their appropriate fate than to exhibit, through resistance, "a base, unworthy, mutinous disposition." But here, Stephen's argument hit a wall of his own earlier and undoubtedly self-enlightened devising, for, just before his mention of this possibility of resistance and rebellion, he had cautiously intoned, "No one contends that a man ought to have power to order his wife about like a slave and beat her if she disobeys him." Then, without proffering a way out of the impasse that would arise under conditions of disobedience, Stephen silently backed away from the difficulty (1873, pp. 188–198).

By the time the judges, lawyers, and legislators of the 1980s returned, just over a century later, to the argument over the relationship among marriage, gender inequality, and female "disobedience," the public endorsement, as a means of control, of male violence justified in the terms of "private" male supremacy had become literally unthinkable. But with the looming presence of just such violence a matter of increasing public awareness, what reasoned arguments for its institutional toleration remained to be offered? There were but two. One amounted to a celebration of the importance of a private realm free from state intervention. But to offer such an argument was either ludicrous or, since it amounted to a state license for any level of aggression, monstrous. Still, out of the mouths of some untold number of judges, this reason for inaction—obeisance to privacy—was offered.[11]

The remaining argument rested still more strongly on the ostensible benefit of public inaction. Here, the idea was that restraining orders and other forms of statist intervention could upset the delicate mechanisms of marital and intrafamilial negotiation, thereby lessening the likelihood of reconciliation. But the "any marriage is better than no marriage" mind-frame that anchored this argument to social purpose had already seen defeat in the debate over no-fault divorce (Cohen 1989, pp. 1257–1263). Even the most conservative advocates of a return to high-barrier divorce—the most conservative secular advocates, that is—were not tempted, it seems, to see the argument from reconciliation in the setting of domestic violence as useful. (Religious counseling, on the other hand, continued to emphasize reconciliation even within violent marriages. Survey evidence has come to find pastoral counseling the least effective form of response to private violence against women (Bowker and Maurer 1986; cf. Dutton-Douglas and Dionne, in Steinman 1991, p. 124)).

Then, too, marriage did not maintain a monopoly on this particular form of misery. Domestic abuse was as likely to occur in nonconjugal relationships as in those endorsed by the state. Thus, the marriage-biased argument for reconciliation was, in many instances, irrelevant.

More important, perhaps, than either of these factors, sociological and psychological studies were beginning to provide troubling evidence of the "cycle" that typifies domestic violence, a cycle in which the insults and threats of the first phase are followed, in the second, by verbal and physical violence—violence which may lead to injury—only to be followed by a third phase typified by apparent remorse and contrition. After this, the cycle begins again (Walker 1979, 1984). In the face of this evidence of repetitive, cyclical violence, it would not have been other than sadistic for law or for politics to invoke reconciliation in the name of public reason.

As we have seen, the two arguments from privacy and from marital conservatism delegitimated themselves on account of their lack of moral substance, and, therefore, collapsed of their own weightlessness. Into the public-policy void created by this departure of alleged principle in a time of mounting concern came the plethora of initiatives mentioned in the second section of this chapter. But the lack of coherent organizing strategies for these initiatives and the host of other problems also mentioned there provides strong reason to begin the articulation of public-policy rationales in a new way now. My effort to begin this process commences below.

(B)

Here, I shall offer four public reasons for the deployment of the coercive powers of the state and the deployment of other social mechanisms against private violence. In structural terms, two of these reasons—state sovereignty and institutional fit—are meant to illustrate a class of reasons (paternalism would be another) for the just state to require actions against private violence as a matter of justice. A third of the reasons—evolutionary malfunction—is intended to deepen the case for state obligation and contend for coercive engagement by the state as a type of reparation for past and present injury. The fourth reason—economic disutility—forsakes argument from high principle to enlist one grounded in statist self-interest. For reasons of overall coherence, these reasons appear below in a revised order (evolutionary malfunction, state sovereignty, institutional fit, and economic disutility). Afterwards, in the next section, I will explore the public policy choices these reasons seem to me to commend.

(1) The Evolutionary Malfunction of the Family as Public Reason:

Like the persons of whom they are composed, families are capable of doing both good and bad. The latter tendency has inspired much great literature and some interesting philosophy. Some critical observers—Plato and Karl Marx, for two—have considered the family to *be* a form of the bad, a blight on the prospects for human community. Even present-day political theorists are put to some hard strategic choices in regard to the family. Either they have to curry favor for theories that explain why individuals should be entitled to bestow privilege and wealth on those they call their own in the face of the painfully distorted wealth distributions that characterize our society (Fishkin 1983; Nagel 1981), or they have to try to displace our strong and resilient human habit of wealth aggregation—hence, selfishness—by attempting to subvert its role, along with our social identity (Rawls 1971).

What the feminist view of history adds to the already problematic picture is the second of the following two observations: the family is an institution the actual behavior of which can go bad in two dichotomous ways: either by privileging its own members to excess and, therefore, squelching such distributions of wealth as might serve to help equalize human flourishing across families and communities (or, to broaden our outlook, across cultures); or by violating and even destroying the possibilities for safety and security of some of its members, thereby squelching the possibility of fair wealth enjoyment within the family unit, whatever its level of wealth. It hardly need be added that the unmediated presence of materialism and patriarchy can generate *both* forms of badness, excess financial privilege and excess personal vulnerability, even within the same family group.

Moreover, from a bottom-up rather than a top-down perspective, the separation of material possibility from patriarchal possibility gives ground to another version of harm, this time by instilling the notion that power within the family *is* wealth—indeed, that patriarchal power may be the only form of widely proliferated wealth that the dominant culture is happy to share. In this way, the men of subcultures in which material affluence remains a rarity may become understandably reluctant to relinquish the only form of "wealth" that, on account of nonscarcity, has been unreluctantly ceded to them—power over "their" women.

It may be that patriarchy could have been more lucky or more talented than to have given onto the malignancy of the abusive male presence in the family. Perhaps a more well-defined and well-maintained theoretical tie to benevolence, coupled with some strong policing mechanism for contravening lapses from benevolence, would have helped. But patriarchy, in its American incarnation, never set out to design or to enforce a model of benevolent despotism (see the discussion of institutional fit at (3) below). And even if it had, the corruption of benevolent despotism is only a fist-length away.

In fact, to give patriarchy its due, its intended model, from the late-feudal period to and including the last gasp of its serious public defense, as earlier illustrated by means of the Mill-Stephen debate, was not despotism at all. Rather, incorporating by reference the teachings of the early Christian church, it was monarchy. Just as God was denominated King within the doctrines of the Church, with the vertical chain of all Being under Him, so did earthly monarchs, not least the kings of England, claim to derive their rule from God, with all lesser links on the chain of Being under them.[12]

But now let us conduct a highly abbreviated thought experiment. Suppose that, when this theory of necessary hierarchy—necessary, because ordained by God, according to the foundation myth—was first proposed, it did not sit well with some of the plotting, scheming, competitive, and highly aggressive squirearchy on whom the early post-feudal kings, bereft of sufficient wealth to raise up an independent army, had need to rely. What bone of wealth and succor could be thrown to them by a king-in-need that would provide some satisfaction? Why, what about an analog of the foundation myth itself, one that would nicely supplement kingly acquiescence in the squires' private armies by offering them the possibility of unlimited family wealth aggregation, subject only to the king's direct and indirect levies, and a faithful replication of monarchical privilege over all within their estate? Translated into middle-class terms to accommodate the needs, soon to follow, of the rising burghers, the reduced, though still-grandiose ideal became: "A man's home is his castle."

The translation of the ideal to the real did not require much institutional effort, at least on behalf of the primary patrons of formal institutions, the upper classes, so long as the custom of rape-kidnap stood in for parental consent, when the male marriage proponent was unacceptable to the proposed bride's family, and arranged marriage performed the more regular tasks. Still, one stands in awe of the energy that the common law began to apply, as early as the thirteenth century, to the outfitting of patriarchy in full legal regalia. This soon came to include the classification of marriage as a form of wardship and the creative fiction of the merger of the wife's legal identity into the husband's. By these strokes of ingenuity, the domestic sphere became the only widely acceptable place, outside nunneries, for women to be. Deprived of contract, property, and, until much later, the vote or any other form of legal or political autonomy, women became far less than the subjects of the male head of household, though never the intended equivalents of slaves. Not utter disempowerment but social weakness—a mirror of the physical and psychological models of weakness the guild of physicians contributed to the picture—became the self-fulfilling prophecy of women's lot.

Even under the relatively benign conditions of benevolent monarchy, the stasis that was the official design of gender arrangements gave onto the possibility of utter madness for women who could think their way outside this prison. That possibility was lofted over the *fin-de-siècle* transom in Charlotte Perkins Gilman's *The Yellow Wallpaper* (1899), as riveting as a nightmare in its presentation of the plight of women under even the most benevolent of patriarchal marriages.

But patriarchy fell into ruin for practices that were corrupt, not merely for the failure of the ideal that Gilman pilloried. Under the good-natured umbrella of privacy, males abused the privileges of patriarchy as they came—increasingly, it seems—to physically and emotionally abuse "their" women within the private havens that many versions of American political theory endorsed for autonomous persons to enjoy.

Here, from a very recent newspaper account about private male abu-

364 / Jane Maslow Cohen

siveness, is the sound of a gauntlet hitting the ground before the state, whose positive law and acquiescent norms became the master design that led us to this pass:

> "I don't think women belong to anybody, but she should have been paying more attention to me," explained Jim, who gave his now ex-girlfriend a black eye when he caught her talking to another guy. "It wasn't like I felt I owned her, but, I felt like she was mine, that she should be for me more, you know." (Gorov 1993)

The "you know" that ends Jim's statement is the knowing echo of history, the history of legal patriarchy and what it has given onto through the neglect and denial of its own corruption into violence. Perhaps no more could be expected of a system that functioned without the counsel of women from the start, that functioned on the basis of forced marriage, that functioned on the basis of a proliferation of institutional excuses—those conveniently served up by religion, law, and medicine—for treating all members of the female sex as weak and inferior to the male.

The obligation that the state must assume to cure the practices that have devolved from this malformation of the reigning ideology should be clear, though the ideology may no longer officially reign. In case it is not, there is this further reminder from the article that begins with "Jim": "Even in 1993, boys learn that girls are there to serve them. . . . We have another generation of batterers coming up" (Gorov 1993).

(2) State Sovereignty as Public Reason:

The sovereignty of the modern state, which includes its monopoly on the legitimate use of coercion has been long justified in relation to a single purpose: the personal safety of its citizens. It was on this basis that Thomas Hobbes sought, in his peculiarly eclectic way, to justify the sovereignty of monarchy.[13] After a century and a half of experience with governance by remote and otherwise unsatisfactory monarchs, the Framers attempted the creation of a different sort of sovereign, yet stayed glued to citizen safety as the central justification of governments. Thus, while liberty and equality were saluted as the hallmarks of democratic government and the basis for monarchical overthrow in the American Colonies, the Federalists based the need for a strong, central government on the same concern that Hobbes's various arguments for obeisance to authority had rallied round. Here, couched in a capacious understanding of "property," is Madison on the subject:

> Government is instituted to protect property of every sort. . . . [T]he praise of affording a just security to property, should be sparingly

bestowed on a government which, however scrupulously guarding the possessions of individuals, does not protect them in the enjoyment and communication of their opinions, in which they have an equal, and in the estimation of some, a more valuable property. . . . That is not a just government . . . where the property which a man has in his personal safety and personal liberty, is violated by arbitrary seizures of one class of citizens for the service of the rest. (Rossiter 1961, p. 79)

Hamilton captured the matter more succinctly: "[the] [o]ne great ob[ject] of Gov[ernment] is personal protection and the security of Property" (Farrand 1911, p. 302).

The attempt of these great men was to weave into whole cloth a concept of democratic personhood fashioned from the ideals of equality and autonomy but rendered wearable only by the protections of government. That is still the nature of our ongoing projects in governance. It is why even libertarians accept the need for a state which performs the role—albeit, for libertarians, the sole and minimal role—of watchman: the maintenance of safety is the very nub of government.[14]

From the standpoint of women, the state can hardly be said to have satisfied even this minimal condition of and justification for its existence. The history of women's experience marks out for serious concern the mere referential commonality that would otherwise treat "watchman," like "mankind," or Madison's "man . . . in his personal safety," as the standard terminological blanket for women. The early normative view seems more closely to have approximated this: the state should undertake to protect the personal welfare of men and their property from the manifold predations of other men. But the state need not concern itself with the welfare of women because men will, and should, undertake to protect their women and the property of their women from the predations of other men.

On this account, the positive state is properly held responsible for creating a state-authorized status out of the private social norm by which men have historically treated themselves as entitled both to more political power than women and to physical power over women. In positively endowing all men with power over the lives of all women, the state deputizes men as its agents, and legitimates the use of force by one class of citizens over another. The fact that foundational arguments over the structure of government and over the perceived need for acquiescence in the existence of slavery helped to render the gender issue invisible to the Framers does nothing to hide, from our eyes, anyway, its existence. What is more, in an era of belief in merged gender identity through marriage, the appeal of such a gestural reflection of paternalism would have required no notice. But the obsession with ideological neatness that permitted all known forms of marital misery to be swept under the rug of coherence could only have belonged to a theory unchallenged by popular, or at least audible dissent. Since the economic, social, and psychological oppression of women as a class rendered political dissent functionally impossible until the middle of the nineteenth century, it is not surprising that, in the case of women, the less-than-minimal state watchman could have held his job for so long.

Today's feminism has undertaken to redefine that job. As should have been obvious to anyone not blinkered by ideology, every class of persons throughout the history of culture that has attempted to wield unchecked, unreviewed power over another class has fallen prey to the corruption that excessive power entails. From the ancient Roman skepticism embodied in *"quis custodiet custodes?"* to the contemporary significance of the ideal of autonomy, we are reminded of the need to redistribute power that has been badly distributed along gendered lines. That gendered power is a corruption of government is, in light of our history, foundational to any claim that feminism might make regarding either the ideal or the actual distribution of power between men and women.

It should be equally clear that both the ideal and the actual distribution of power must travel through the concept of equality—a concept that must continue to mature as the practice of our ideals causes this society to mature. Thus, it must be taken as a social truth, a contemporary truth itself intended for governance, that the state-sanctioned relations between men and women must intend an equal distribution of the power the state can authorize. This truth requires that government assume the obligation to place its coercion-wielding resources in the service of gender-equilibrating power.

But it should be no less obvious that, as contemporary feminists have often noted, we find ourselves mired in problems of transition. One such problem—the problem of private violence—represents a severe impediment to the equal distribution of power.

(3) INSTITUTIONAL FIT AS PUBLIC REASON:

In the first subsection, I offered the hypothesis that patriarchal marriage was intended to resemble a small mirror of monarchy. In the next, I referred to our obviously antimonarchical political history and yet our blind inattendance to male sovereignty. Even under the most benign hypothesis of intended benevolence, however, there is a radical issue of fit between the family—the veritable cradle of political ideals under patriarchy—and the ideals the family is supposed, in theory, to cradle.

One glance at *Meyer v. State of Nebraska* (1923), the progenitor of our sustaining constitutional devotion to such emanations of liberty as can fend off the wrongfully intrusive state, confirms this view. There, we find a state's distrust of its citizens, on the one hand, motivated by a misguided regulatory impulse toward patriotism and, on the other hand, poised across the fulcrum of reason, Justice McReynold's faith in the family to guide our future citizens in their primary experiences with democracy.

Yet nothing about the model of patriarchy even begins to suggest how the mothers into whose care the males of our society entrust our future citizens can likely inculcate in them a love of the liberty and equality that these same women have been denied. On this broad sweep through the field, it is remarkable that the young of this society ever grow up to be democrats, although it is possible, to be sure, to surmount one's past. Explanations are afoot, of course. The roles of religion, ethics, morality, and even patriotism in women's lives may offset the experiential difficulty. Alternatively, some active form of cultural schizophrenia may be at work. From a yet-more-cynical perspective, perhaps we teach our children—our boys, anyway—to look beyond women and their democratic circumscription to find their sources of ideals.

But nothing in the practical world suggests any basis for reliance on these matters of hypothesis. From a practical standpoint, therefore, it can be nothing other than a mistake for democracy to be married to patriarchy, since patriarchy is barren of democratic values and cannot, therefore, reproduce them. From a normative standpoint, it is a wrong— one that, having been fostered by the state, requires the state to oblige itself to right.

(4) Economic Disutility as Public Reason:

Even if the state were to flout the obligations based on right that I have described, a reason for robust state activity to counter the existence of private violence would persist. This reason sounds in utility. Moreover, it sounds in statist self-interest of a particularly acute sort. Here we are, the largest debtor nation in the world, threatened by a flagging economy, a creeping economic growth rate, naked extremes of wealth inequality, serious adult literacy problems, and a rising poverty rate for women and children. The form of illiteracy that we, the happenstantial guardians of this society, exhibit in regard to all manners of violence, however, is pervasive. Aside from stranger violence and the costs that that incurs, the directly and indirectly monetizable costs[15] of private violence are staggering.

Consider these representative submissions from a 1993 report published by the U.S. Department of Health and Human Services:

(1) Approximately one American household in three is the seat of private violence.

(2) Twenty-five to fifty percent of homeless families headed by women left home to escape private violence.

(3) According to one state study, thirty-four percent of the private violence calls to police were repeat calls. According to another state's study, the figure was eighty-five percent.

(4) Half of the murdered women in the United States—many of them economic providers—are killed by a current or former domestic partner.

(5) Women commit just eight percent of all homicides; fifty-one percent of these are against partners with a history of abusing them.

(6) As many as half of all women alcoholics are battered women.

(7) Between thirty-five and forty percent of battered women attempt suicide.

(8) Nearly one million children experienced demonstrated harm as a result of abuse or neglect in one recent year. That same year, 1,100 of those children died from these causes.

(9) Forty thousand children a year, it is estimated, are raped by a caregiver.

(10) Males who had abusive childhoods have a high rate of alcoholism, mental illness, and early death.

(11) Approximately three quarters of a million to a million of the elderly are abused or physically neglected by a caregiver.

(12) Violence is a learned response to the human condition. Men who have experienced violence in their childhoods are ten times as likely as other men to abuse their women partners. Forty percent of the women who abuse their children were abused as children. More than half of the men who abuse their women partners also abuse their children (Mason 1993, pp. 1–3).

A smaller-scale study conducted at a Minneapolis hospital, as published in the prestigious *Journal of the American Medical Association*, reported these findings:

(1) Sixty percent of the hospital's emergency department staff said they perceived abuse occurring at home monthly or more often.

(2) Sixty-seven percent of that staff reported that abuse occurred at work monthly or more often.

(3) Ninety-one percent said that abuse at home leads to abuse at work and the reverse.

(4) One hundred percent of those reporting abuse at home also re-

ported that the abuse had led to medical problems. Ninety-four percent of those reporting abuse at work also report consequent medical problems.

(5) More than eighty percent of those in the study reported abuse as the cause of one or more of the following: reduced productivity, increased absenteeism, inability to complete tasks, reduced communication, a negative effect on staff morale, and increased staff turnover. A smaller percentage reported visits to the doctor, use of chemical dependencies, and involvement in lawsuits.

(6) Sixty-nine percent of those in the study said they do not seek help for home-life abuse because of embarrassment; fifty-three percent because of shame; forty-three percent because of guilt; and thirty-two percent because of denial.

(7) Forty-four percent of those studied said the workplace should be very involved or extremely involved with the issues of home-life abuse (Randall 1992, pp. 1439–40).

A 1990 report from the Bureau of National Affairs states the direct cost of private violence to U.S. companies at between three and five billion dollars annually (Randall 1992). A 1989 report from the Center for Disease Control, based primarily on directly associated medical costs, assessed the direct annual cost of private violence at forty-five billion dollars (Randall 1992). A 1993 report from the American Medical Association found 5.3 billion dollars of U.S. annual health costs to be directly attributable to street and private violence. It stated that these are America's fastest growing public health problems. It alleged that the financial protection offered by insurance screens many of these costs from individuals and therefore discourages cost-conscious decisions.[16]

But that form of discouragement has been able to operate within the arena of individual and private-sector policy-making because of the inadequacy of public policy. Public policy, in turn, has been aided in its inadequacy by the nonexistence of a national surveillance system to help to define and monitor private violence and by the nonexistence of a federal policy-making presence to articulate, inspire, cajole, threaten, and help to deliver responses that are as bold and as coherent as the depth and breadth of public obligation should demand.

I now turn to some suggestions for the revision of public policy, based on the public reasons given here. With this herald must come the acknowledgment, as offered in a different form in my introduction, that the recommendations that follow are not strictly entailed by the reasons that have helped to generate them, nor do they follow as inevitably as the night the day.

What Yield From Public Reason?

(A)

The argument from state sovereignty yields this much: on all foundational accounts, the primary justification of government is to provide for the safety of its citizens. If that is government's justification, then that is its obligation. It is in service of that obligation that we grant to government a monopoly over the use of coercive force, except on the individualizing excuse of necessity.

Government did not license the use of violence as a male prerogative on the basis of necessity. It deputized males as coercion-wielding agents of the state in deference to the legal and social norms of male superiority, female subordination, the ideal of family privacy, and the ideal peculiarly derived from Christian monarchy of male hegemony over a stringently hierarchical family. In the absence of state superintendence, the license for male hegemony over the family, in combination with the norm of female subordination, gave onto a practice norm that came to accept private violence as a means of family governance beyond the state's control.

Only when the arguments from evolutionary malformation, state sovereignty, and institutional fit are arrayed in combination do we see the state's utter complicity in this outcome. Whether understood as a matter of state instigation, or state dereliction, or both is a matter of interpretive refinement that does not compromise the analysis: the state's obligation to abolish the prerogative of private violence is clear. Seen in the light of economic disutility, moreover, the state's fulfillment of this obligation becomes urgent, and the problem before the state, one of more than individual justice. Private violence cripples economic productivity. Because it is contagious and is passed from generation to generation, it bids fair to cripple our future.

Earlier, I outlined some of the ways that the state has already become involved in responding to private violence. But initiative, coherence, and, at the federal level, basic attentiveness are missing from the present picture of state response. The paradigm shift from a model of private female subordination within an abusive family hierarchy to a model of government superintendence of citizen safety throughout all realms of social life demands much more effort from government. It demands qualitative and quantitative changes that truly represent a paradigm shift.

What might these changes look like? Elbowing aside nice questions of constitutional constraint (this is an essay on the derivation of policy!) as well as the methodological disagreements rife in the basic and applied studies of private violence to date (the endurance of these must undergo scrutiny elsewhere), I offer some proposals for change. To put my intentions more directly, I see the problem of private violence as urgent and underattended. I see the paradigm of private safety as still inchoate, as a matter of state obligation. For these reasons, I have treated brashness as the order of the day.

(B)

The misuse of state sovereignty requires three large-scale recastings. One involves a federal executive presence. The second involves the gender of the local sovereign. The third requires the attainment of responsive consistency within the justice system. I shall address each in turn.

(1)

The design of any policy-based response to private violence depends in the most obvious and fundamental way on a comprehensive understanding of the nature of the problem and its impacts. It is impossible to achieve that kind of understanding without the energy and consistency of unified scope and design. Without continual national surveillance, it is impossible to gauge the efficacy of basic ongoing policy responses, let alone new, experimental ones. The lack of federal data-gathering about a problem as socially and economically devastating as this one is both inexcusable and shocking. The urgency of any appeal, the necessity of any design, the commitment of public zeal—all are rendered insecure by the epistemic issue beneath.

My first and most comprehensive call is for the federal surveillance of private violence through the imposition of a uniform reporting scheme made mandatory on all the states and ongoing federal evaluation of the findings.

A federal clearinghouse for information on all federal and state-sponsored public activities involving responses to private violence is the next obvious need, together with the commitment of high-level executive concern and involvement. The natural homes for this involvement are the Justice Department and the Department of Health and Human Services, but it does not seem out of place to suppose that the President of the United States—the commander, *inter alia*, of the armed services, should issue and maintain the call to arms in service of the domestic safety of our citizens—safety that would render us safe from each other and, therefore, able to face the world.

(2)

As a matter of the most elemental justice, for the state to continue to claim its monopoly over the use of force in the pursuit of an antisubordination agenda on behalf of women, it seems reasonable to suppose that state sovereignty must alter its human form. The sovereign's coercion-wielding agents must be no more male than female, but rather, in rough proportion to the population, half of each. While a politics of wealth and power place this goal at an obviously distant remove in the case of the executive (here is one place that monarchy surpasses us), there are no such impediments to an equality-based regendering of the justice system. Indeed, while the significance of seniority within police and, to some extent, judicial hierarchies will take greater time to gender-balance, it is the policeperson on the beat and the lowest-status judge—the family court or criminal court judge—to whom abuse victims first turn. These ranks should not be difficult to half-fill with women. Similarly, the ranks of prosecutors cannot be hard to half-fill with women. Special strike forces half-composed of women—the sort of strike forces quickly composed and deployed to meet the savings-and-loan crisis, for example—would not be difficult to create, to provide strong and innovative leadership for the private violence crisis.

The position I take here does not rest on naive or essentialist assumptions to the effect that all women or only women can best respond to the victimization of women, or that truly gender-specific forms of pain and experience are necessarily translatable into other, nongender-specific forms of pain and experience. In fact, to the extent that private violence is based on deeply rooted beliefs in female subordination, it may well *be* a gender-specific experience; but not all private violence against women has those roots; and not all private violence directs itself at women.

Short of naiveté and essentialism, the need for gender balance within the justice system rests on these assumptions:

(1) It is just that there be gender balance, as one manifestation of a comprehensive agenda of gender equality.

(2) There is real symbolic importance in gender balance within the justice system, on account of the gender inequalities that have been directly tied to the misuse of state sovereignty.

(3) There is a wealth of perspectives to be gained from gender balance, provided it is accompanied by ethnic and racial balance.

(4) It is likely that gender balance, particularly as it trickles up the seniority system, can strongly affect the resistance and even the

engagement in private violence that continue to plague justice officialdom, particularly, it seems, in the lower ranks.

(5) Given the timidity that is a female norm within some subcultures, the habit of isolation that is common to abused women, and the overarching norm of privacy that is pervasive within our culture, a female officer at the door and on the bench may well encourage steps to change on the part of female victims of violence.

(6) Gender balance within the justice system, in the presence of consistent negative incentives for violent behavior, should change the risk-reward assessments of many abusers.

(3)

The justice system must counter private violence with clear and consistent negative incentives for abusive and violent behavior. It is not the case that all abusers are rational in their determination of whether, when, and how to abuse their victims. But neither should justice system policymakers assume that they are irrational, or that a rational assessment of risks and rewards plays no role whatever in this aspect of their lives.

At the most fundamental level, the licensing of male superiority over females as an instantiation of state sovereignty has helped to sustain social norms that gave an appearance of order and rationality to earlier social norms of female subordination that are at odds with the principle of equality, including gender equality, that is foundational to liberal justice. This level of sovereign support must, in tangible form, be ripped out of the justice system, root and branch.

Moreover, there is empirical support for the proposition that many abusers engage in rational assessments of risk. Experimental programs in two cities have strongly demonstrated that mandatory detention lowers recidivism within the population of private violence perpetrators.[17] Other evidence points in the same direction, suggesting that in communities where women have internalized strong traditional biases against going to court, where punishments cannot, therefore, be dealt with, recidivism may be highest (see Crenshaw *infra*). Also, men with jobs have been found less recidivistic in the face of criminal punishment than men without jobs (Developments 1993, p. 1539). Perhaps this is because they have more to lose when their conduct is brought to light—a matter I will return to in subsection (E).

I do not mean by these casual references to suggest that mandatory detention is the only means or is necessarily the best means of criminal justice response. Sophisticated research has already added important reasons to qualify this blunt approach (Ford, in Knudsen & Miller 1991, pp. 191–210). But nothing in the social science literature that I have read does anything to blunt my enthusiasm for far greater consistency than we now have on offer in the design and delivery of negative incentives for violent behavior. That matter stands apart from the details of design.

(C)

This essay is about reason. The previous subsection took on board the likelihood that some amount of private violence is the product of rational risk assessment and can be curtailed by higher risk. But the evolutionary malfunction of the family is a dark subject. It embraces the darkness of human conduct when one person makes another his prisoner, when terror produces silence, when the need to hurt someone creates pain, injury, and even death. It would be irrational to portray this subject as altogether rational. Yet the justice system must seek to respond with the only tools it has—rational ones. It must, therefore, find ways to respond to the evolved circumstances that women are the victims of private violence, and of seriously injurious violence, far more often than men. And it must respond to the fact that, with or without succumbing to the learned helplessness syndrome, some women have learned to become violent. I shall take up these aspects in turn.

(1)

Far more than men, women have been and continue to be the victims of violent acts. Public policy cannot but respond to that fact. And then there is the fact of physical disparities in size and weight, the ease with which many women can be overcome. Add to these the inevitable facts of timing errors—some women will misjudge the chances of putting an end to the violence inside their relationships, wrongly evaluating the likelihood that they can find ways to stop or decrease the extent of the violence or keep it from escalating. Add to all of this the very real possibility of human error on other sides: a restraining order will be too narrow in its terms, will be interpreted too narrowly, or will be unaccompanied by appropriate judicial demeanor, and, in any event, will fail to stop the violence. In some instances, then, women will take matters into their own hands and defend themselves. Their ultimate defense is to kill their aggressors. Much recent scholarly and activist effort has been devoted to the appropriate normative boundaries of the doctrine of self-defense. The need to give doctrinal content to the unsafety of women is clear. How this should be accomplished is less clear. My suggestions, here, are two.

The first is that evidence of justice system failures should be treated as an element of self-defense. That is, whenever a woman can prove by competent evidence that the police failed to respond, or responded in ways dismissive of threats or acts against her safety, or responded significantly later than their average emergency response time in the community, or whenever, through other means, the justice system can be shown to have contributed to a reasonable sense on the part of the victim that the most rational defense is self-defense, the proof should be admissible as an element of the excuse.

My second suggestion I will call "the superrestraining order." In the event that some number of restraining orders have been violated—one or more is a matter I leave for discussion elsewhere—and the basis for these orders involves threats or acts of serious bodily injury, or death threats without more, then I propose that judges issue, and that the orders give due notice of same, a "superrestraining order." This order would prohibit any contact by the perpetrator of violence with his victim for an appropriately long period in any and all settings, *and* it would serve, in the event of its violation, as presumptive evidence that the victim acted in self-defense for causing the physical repulsion of her perpetrator, including, if need be, his death. This presumption of self-defense is not intended as a license to kill. Rather, it should serve as a warning to would-be violators of state restraint—and a reminder to the state itself—of the need, under extraordinary circumstances—perhaps made ordinary by the prior misdeeds of the state—for victims to engage in self-defense.

(2)

I shall treat it as a straightforward proposition in need of little argument that to the extent the evolutionary malfunction of the family has caused some women to become violent abusers of other family members, they must be dealt with by the justice system in the same way as men. I hope not to stumble across cases at the margin. It is certainly true that, to the extent women are primary child-care providers, our norms concerning children continue to tolerate their physical discipline, and that "discipline" may also be a matter of community norms. So there is cause to be sensitive in drawing the abuse/nonabuse boundary. Similarly, there is empirical evidence that men who engage in physical violence toward women have a pronounced tendency to treat criticism, hectoring, and sexual refusal as types of abuse (Ptacek, in Yllö and Bograd 1988, pp. 144–145). That practice of interpretation also has consequences for public policy, but it is not my focus here.

In nonmarginal cases of violence committed by women, my position is that there can be no period of transition, no offer of special excuse.

To the extent the violence is directed at men and is not within the boundaries of self-defense, as I have extended them above, the justice system must respond to women on equal terms to men. Any separate, gender-based response is unjust. It is also unworkable, in that it gives onto an obvious problem of regression: I, a woman, claim my abuse of my husband should be excused because I was abused by my father, from whom I learned this behavior. But there is evidence to show that my father was abused by his mother and, meanwhile, husbands other than mine are claiming that their violence toward women is the result of abuse by their mothers. . . . The problem will not quit unless, as a matter of corrective justice, gender equality ends it.

As to violence toward children, I have only the obvious to say. We know that private abuse is largely a form of learned behavior. There can be no excuse for teaching it. There can be no excuse for engaging in abuse or violence toward children, one's own or anyone else's, except on defense of necessity. That defense is nonoperative in most cases of severe physical abuse, which occurs disproportionately toward very young children, and is equally unavailing in the other greatest category of child abuse, child sexual abuse (Straus, in Knudsen and Miller 1992, pp. 28–29). The evolutionary malfunction of the family must be stopped from evolving further.

(D)

The argument from institutional fit—institutional ill-fit, that is—should cause us to reflect on the need to reeducate adults and to find ways to educate children about the meaning of democratic family. The democratic family is not ruled by a sovereign. Although its children occupy a dependent status, it is otherwise nonhierarchical. This means that neither of the adults in an intimate relationship are entitled, as a matter of status, to hegemony, to coercion as a prerogative, or to gender-based authority as such. Such distribution of power and authority as may eventuate between them must be a matter of private consent that, however culturally conditioned, has to be deprived of any ability to reference gender bias as a social norm.

To accomplish this deprivation, the state's opposition to gender bias as a matter of power and status within the family must be made clear. I will go so far as to suggest that the misuse of state sovereignty in these terms gives onto a state obligation to mandate instruction for children in the endowments of democracy, among which is the democratic family. But the lesser-included case that is the subject of this essay is also the easier case to make out in a society of religious and ethnic diversity. That case is that the democratic state cannot tolerate the existence of private violence as a norm or as a practice. To do so would violate our commitment to personal safety, the basis for liberty and equality, and, therefore, the primary justification for the state. Thus, the state must insist that personal safety is an endowment of democracy and that no personal, social, or cultural commitment of a democratic citizen may contravene it.

To accomplish this educative goal, the state should engage in three forms of activity. One is a curricular mandate for children concerning the democratic family. The second is an attempt to garner the support and aid of religious and other cultural institutions. The third is for the state to mount an antiviolence educational campaign of its own. The courts, especially the appellate courts, can certainly serve a didactic function in this regard. We might suppose they are didactically engaged generally when they articulate their reasons for a (as well as the) rule of law. That these reasons include matters of policy as well as principle is no longer a matter of controversy. The need to articulate concerns for private safety that sound in democratic value is clearly an issue of both policy and principle. In high-visibility cases, such as *DeShaney*, the need could be said to be strongest, but I see the didactic function of the courts of *first* resort, the family and criminal courts, to be at least as compelling a site for this effort.

At relatively little cost, the state can do more. It can create an antiviolence literature and incorporate it within the licensure requirements for marriage. Given the misuse of state sovereignty, the state should assume the obligation to educate its citizens that it is not licensing the private use of coercive force any longer; that, to the extent the state ever stood behind the norm of power in marriage as a male prerogative, and to the extent it failed to enforce any norms of private safety and gender equality in marriage, it has reformed. This literature should make express reference to the kinds of state aid and state sanction that are available for private abuse, and the recommended ways to invoke them.

And the state—some states, anyway—have now created another way station and temporal space for the dissemination of such literature. In those that have legislated a mandatory waiting period for abortion, the distribution of literature specially devised to help pregnant women who are the victims of private violence—an astonishing thirty-seven percent of all pregnant women (Mason 1993, p. 1)—should be mandated in all relevant places: hospitals and abortion clinics, especially. Given the rate of adolescent pregnancy in this country, literature designed especially for young pregnant women, making clear the nature of the state's aid in the case of violence, should also be widely disseminated, perhaps through the schools.

Beyond the education of its citizens, including its youngest citizens, the state needs to do more to educate itself. Why does private violence tend to escalate? Why are pregnant women so greatly at risk? What feasible measures can most effectively screen children from this violence? What kind of antiviolence literacy campaign can provide the most help? The need for research in these areas is obvious. Support for innovative policy research must be a matter of greater obligation than it is now.

(E)

Current efforts to improve the economy, its performance, and its future are focused on job security and health security. But economic policy has no hope of stability and, therefore, success unless it rests on a third leg. Workers cannot perform productively if they are the victims of private violence. Whether they are out sick on this account or are merely dragging themselves through the day, in hospital beds or merely hospital emergency rooms, in our congested courts or merely in lawyers' or prosecutors' offices, whether they have made a break for a shelter or are cringing inside their rooms, workers cannot work productively under conditions of fear and violence. Their children cannot perform productively in schools under these conditions; neither can their teachers.

Private safety is as much a matter of our economic status as are job security and health security. For this reason, the state must seek to engage all sectors of the private and public economy in responding to the crisis. The largest or, in any case, the most obvious pieces of needed response are job training, job security, and equality-based job status for women.[18] It is a commonplace that women are reluctant to leave abusers if they cannot afford to take care of themselves—there is no reason, after all, to trust the public safety net, and certainly not for long. It is equally clear that women who are primary child-care providers cannot be economically self-sufficient without outside sources of child care. These issues can no longer afford to be understood as women's issues or feminist issues. It is, in effect, a form of low treason to treat them as other than national issues of crucial importance to our general welfare.

At the level of policy initiative, I can only add small suggestions for now. One is for the state to involve employers in the antiviolence educational campaign I have suggested. A second is for the state to encourage employers to take stringent measures—suspensions, fines, firings—against employees who are convicted of private violence. The deterrent effect is likely to be greatest if the policies apply to everyone in the organization, including those at its top. Since private violence is not a class issue, one way to demonstrate an equality of concern for its victims is to meaningfully democratize the enforcement of its penalties in the labor market. If, as I have noted, those abusers with jobs are more responsive to negative incentives than those without, the noncriminal imposition of costs on them can help to create the mutuality of reinforcement that policymakers already seek (Steinman 1991, p. 10).

Lastly, premium rate adjustments within the medical insurance system for those who perpetrate violence may be a useful means of obtaining the internalization of at least some of its costs. Such a scheme would also help to enlist insurance providers in both the study of the overall costs of private violence and the design and implementation of effective strategies of response.

Afterword

In this essay, I first sought to examine, from a critical perspective, issues and problems in the public response to private violence. Then, from an avowedly feminist perspective, I offered four large-scale public reasons to reenergize our public response. Next and last, from an untimidly creative perspective, I placed four sets of public policy proposals on the examining table, each set generated by one or more of the public reasons presented earlier. My aim throughout was to treat the horrific occurrence of private violence and the norms that have nurtured its existence as matters of public obligation, obligation in urgent need of examination, understanding, and policy-based reformulation on the basis of public reason.

Casting a look back at the materials that must be absorbed, the stories that need be heard, the terrors that must be faced to develop a commitment to this issue, I end from a humanist perspective. There seems no end to human folly, to the waste and carnage that are the living—and no longer living—remnants of our folly. I wonder whether a corrective justice system that reconciles its concerns for deterrence, rehabilitation, and, in its candid moments, retribution through a primary reliance on detention might not be better served by causing the perpetrators of private violence to hear and see, and, therefore, relive the pain and fear and shrunken sense of self that the victims of this violence hardly cease to experience. I wonder whether there is not some way for the perpetrators of this violence to be caused to weep, along with their victims, for the children they are destroying, for the future of this country that they are burning.

When Aeneas looked back at flaming Troy, a civilization, as much as a city, in ruin, he hoisted his old father over his shoulders and he turned to seek out the future. Aeneas left Troy weeping—a man, a hero, weeping on account of human folly. *Lacrimae rerum.*[19] The tears in mortal things.[20]

Notes

My thanks go to Clay Gillette, Bill Nelson, Derek Parfit, Amelie Rorty, Larry Sager, and Kate Silbaugh for helpful conversations about and readings of this chapter, to Jon Fernald, Glen Sarka, and Lindsay Smith for research assistance, and to William Kaleva for preparation of the manuscript.

1. All of feminist scholarship has by no means been framed by a rhetoric of anger. But the feminist whose speeches and writings have most widely captured popular and academic attention and have, in that sense, been tutelary is Catherine MacKinnon, whose tone of engagement has unmistakably and definingly been angry. See, e.g., C. MacKinnon 1984, 1987 and Buffalo Symposium, 1985. See, also, A. Dworkin 1987.

2. I provide the facts and circumstances that give substance to this position in Cohen 1993, pp. 175, 193–217.

3. R. I. Gen Laws § 12–29–6 (C)–(D) (Supp. 1992) and W. Va. Code § 48–2A–13 (Supp. 1992).

4. See Quincy Court Model Domestic Abuse Program, Trial Court of the Commonwealth of Massachusetts, Innovations in State and Local Government: Semifinalist Application, 1992 (application for award, on file at the Harvard Law School Library).

5. See, e.g., Governor's Battered Women's Working Group, Massachusetts, 1985, which documented, within a half-year period, some 250 complaints involving gender- or race-bias on the part of police, judges, and court clerks.

6. Writing for the majority, Chief Justice Rehnquist worried that, while moving against an abusive parent too late might subject the state to the charge of failure to provide protection, moving against a parent too soon might generate the charge of improper interference with parental rights. *DeShaney* 1989, p. 1007. The term "razor's edge" was actually used by the Seventh Circuit in its opinion in *DeShaney* (7th Cir. 1987).

7. See state statutes cited in Note 1986, p. 1260 n. 37. I have not updated these citations to see whether any of the states noted have since seen the error of their ways.

8. "Incidence" rates attempt to record each occurrence of abuse or violence, however defined, during a given year. "Prevalence" rates are used to indicate the proportion of couples, which, during the course of their relationship, experience the researcher's defined version of abuse or violence. See Straus, in D. Knudsen and J. Miller 1991, p. 21.

9. These methodological issues and problems are dealt with in a burgeoning social science literature. See, e.g., Halsted, in Buzawa and Buzawa 1992; Miller, Straus, and Webster, in D. Knudsen and J. Miller 1991; Steinman, in Steinman 1991; and Yllö, in K. Yllö and M. Bograd 1988.

10. The bill, which includes five titles, is known as the Violence Against Women Act of 1991, S.15, 102nd Congress, 1st Sess. (1991). It did not pass in that session and has, with one modification, been reintroduced as the Violence Against Women Act of 1993, S.11, 103rd Congress, 1st Sess. (1993).

11. The example that will live always in my memory involved a judge's rebuke of a young woman who sought protection orders four times from a judge who, though he finally granted one, rebuked her in her husband's presence for wasting his time and the taxpayers' money on her petty domestic problems. The pregnant woman was murdered by her husband shortly thereafter. He left her body at the town dump. The

judge, who had behaved similarly in other woman-abuse cases, received a private reprimand from the state's high court. See E. McNamara 1988, p. 17.

12. For a succinct discussion of the relationship between Christian dogma and the absolutist claims of the English monarchy, see Stone 1977, pp. 152–4, 667–68.

13. Admittedly, Hobbes's concerns about safety were more consistent than were his arguments in favor of monarchy. The latter, it has seemed reasonable to suppose, floated on the political tide of his tumultuous times. Thus, in his earliest significant writings, Hobbes urged that the will of the majority could give onto the creation of a democracy, an oligarchy, or a monarchy, and that any of these could be supplanted by one of the others on a change of majority sentiment (Hobbes, *The Elements of Law: Natural and Politic*, part 2, ch. 1, section 2–5, pp. 108–110, (ed. F. Tönnies 1969)). Later, in *Behemoth*, Hobbes extolled a natural law view of the divine nature of Christian monarchy (Hobbes, *Behemoth, or the Long Parliament*, (1682), ed. F. Tönnies (1969). Still later, in *Leviathan*, Hobbes opined that monarchy could only be replaced on the monarch's consent (Hobbes, *Leviathan*, p. 229, ed. MacPherson, (1984). Meanwhile, as monarchy took a more rooted hold, Hobbes upped the ante in terms of the *need* for a monarchically led Christian Commonwealth: whereas his earliest arguments had treated the threats to men's safety as coming from individual enemies within and common enemies outside the Commonwealth, the energized conclusion to *Leviathan* elaborates men's need to defend against a yet more plenipotential enemy, the "Kingdome of Darknesse" (*Id.*, pp. 627–729).

14. Of course, libertarians are content to have the watchman state safeguard unequal distributions of wealth and power. The contemporary locus classicus of libertarianism is Robert Nozick's *Anarchy, State and Utopia*, New York, 1974. The locus classicus by way of critique is, in my view, Thomas Nagel's "Libertarianism Without Foundations," 85 *Yale Law Journal* 136 (1975).

15. Indirectly monetizable costs include workdays lost due to injuries or other problems attributable to private violence. One estimate places total workdays lost annually at 175,500 days lost from paid work. This figure is a decade old and is, therefore, most likely far too low. See S. McLeer and R. Anwar, "A Study of Battered Women Presenting in an Emergency Department," 79 *Amer. J. of Public Health*, pp. 65–66, n.13 (1989).

16. "AMA study says lifestyle pushing up health care bill," U.P.I., February 22, 1993.

17. These programs have operated in Minneapolis, Minnesota and in Quincy, Massachusetts. The Minneapolis program is frequently cited in the research literature on private violence. See, e.g., L. Sherman, *Policing Domestic Violence Experiments and Dilemmas*, p. 2 (1992), where the author reports that a single night in jail reduced the risk of further violence from twenty to ten percent, according to the Minneapolis study.

18. On the present inequalities that plague women workers, see M. Becker, "Politics, Differences and Economic Rights," 1989 *Univ. of Chicago L. Forum*, pp. 169–90.

19. Vergils' *Aeneid*, in *Latin Poetry*, Carr and Wedeck (eds.) (1940). Since there is much folly, both human and divine, recounted in the Aeneid, the phrase *"lacrimae rerum"* appears quite often in the text.

20. The nonliteral translation is that of Matthew Arnold, whose full phrase reads: "That liquid, melancholy eye / From whose pathetic, soul-fed springs / Seemed surging the Virgilian cry / The sense of tears in mortal things—," "Geist's Grave," in Allott 1965, p. 547.

References

Abraham, W. E. 1962. *The Mind of Africa*. Chicago: University of Chicago Press.

Abrams, Kathryn. 1990. "Ideology and Women's Choice." *Georgia Law Review* 24:761.

———. 1991. "Hearing the Call of Stories." *California Law Review* 79:971.

Adams, David. 1988. "Treatment Models of Men Who Batter: A Profeminist Analysis." In *Feminist Perspectives on Wife Abuse*, eds. K. Ylló and M. Bograd. Newbury Park: Sage Publications.

Ali, Shahrazad. 1989. *The Blackman's Guide to Understanding the Blackwoman*. Philadelphia: Civilized Publications.

Allard, Sharon. 1991. "Rethinking Battered Women Syndrome: A Black Feminist Perspective." *University of California at Los Angeles Women's Law Journal* 1:191–207.

Allen, Anita. 1988. *Uneasy Access: Privacy for Women in a Free Society*. Ottawa: Rowman & Littlefield.

Allen, M. J. 1983. "Tort Remedies for Incestuous Abuse." Golden Gate University Law Review. 13:609.

Allott, Kenneth, ed. 1965. *The Poems of Matthew Arnold*. New York: Barnes & Noble.

Alschuler, Albert. 1991. "The Failure of Sentencing Guidelines: A Plea for Less Aggregation." *University of Chicago Law Review* 58:901.

Americas Watch. 1984. *The Miskitos in Nicaragua, 1981–1984*. New York: Human Rights Watch.

———. 1987. *The Sumus in Nicaragua and Honduras: An Endangered People*. New York: Human Rights Watch.

Amnesty. December 1991. "Rape and Sexual Abuse: Torture and Ill-Treatment of Women in Detention." *AI Index* ACT 77/11/91.

———. March 1991. "Women in the Front Line." *AI Index* 77/01/91.

Anderson, Erich D. and Anne Read Anderson. 1992. "Constitutional Dimensions of the Battered Woman Syndrome." *Ohio State Law Journal* 53:363.

Areen, J. 1975. "Intervention Between Parent and Child: A Reappraisal of the State's Role in Child Neglect and Abuse Cases." *Georgetown Law Journal* 63:887.

Arenella, P. 1977. "The Diminished Capacity and Diminished Responsibility Defenses: Two Children of a Doomed Marriage." *Columbia Law Review* 77:827.

Aristotle, *Nichomachean Ethics* Bk. V, 8.

Arthur, L. F. 1976. "African Regional Conference on the Federation of Women Lawyers (FIDA)." *Review of Ghana Law* 8:140–42.

Asante-Darko, N. and S. Van der Geest. 1983. "Male Chauvinism: Men and Women in Ghanaian Highlife Songs." In *Male and Female in West Africa,* ed. Christine Oppong. London: George Allen and Unwin.

Ashe, Marie. 1987. "Mind's Opportunity: Birthing a Post-Structuralist Feminist Jurisprudence." *Syracuse Law Review* 38:1129.

———. 1991. "Abortion of Narrative: A Reading of the Judgment of Solomon." *Yale Journal of Law and Feminism* 4:81.

———. 1992. "The 'Bad Mother' in Law and Literature: A Problem of Representation." *Hastings Law Journal* 43:1017.

Ashworth, A. J. 1975. "Sentencing in Provocation." *Criminal Law Review:* 553.

———. 1976. "The Doctrine of Provocation." *Cambridge Law Journal.* 35:292.

Attorney General of the U.S. Department of Justice. 1984. *Task Force on Family Violence: Final Report.* Washington, DC: Government Printing Office.

Avery, Billye. 1991. "Empowerment Through Wellness." *Yale Journal of Law and Feminism.* 4:147.

Baldus, D., C. Pulaski and G. Woodworth. 1986. "Arbitrariness and Discrimination in the Administration of the Death Penalty: A Challenge to State Supreme Courts." *Stetson Law Review* 15:133.

———. 1990. *Equal Justice and the Law.* Boston: Northeastern University Press.

Banales, Jorge. 1990. "Abuse Among Immigrants; As Their Numbers Grow So Does the Need for Services." *Washington Post.* October 16:E5.

Baron, Jane. 1991. "The Many Promises of Storytelling in the Law." *Rutgers Law Journal* 23:79.

Bartlett, Katharine. 1990. "Feminist Legal Methods." *Harvard Law Review* 103:829.

Bass, Ellen and Louise Thornton, eds. 1983. *I Never Told Anyone.* New York: Harper & Row.

Bates, Jeanne-Marie. 1991. "Expert Testimony on the Battered Woman Syndrome in Maryland." *Maryland Law Review* 50:920–944.

Becker, Mary. 1989. "Politics, Differences and Economic Rights." *University of Chicago Law Forum* 1989:169–190.

Benowitz, Mindy. 1990. "How Homophobia Affects Lesbians' Response to Violence in Lesbian Relationships." In *Confronting Lesbian Battering,* ed. Pamela Elliott. St. Paul, Minnesota Coalition for Battered Women, Lesbian Battering Intervention Project.

Bernard, George, W., et al. 1982. "Till Death Do Us Part: A Study of Spouse Murder." *Bulletin of American Academy of Psychiatry and Law* 10:271.

Bettelheim, Bruno. 1976. *The Uses of Enchantment: The Meaning and Importance of Fairy Tales.* New York: Knopf.

Bilionis, Louis, 1993. "Legitimizing Death." *Michigan Law Review* 91:1643.

Blackmun, Julie. 1989. *Intimate Violence.* New York: Columbia University Press.

Blackstone, W. 1765. *Commentaries on the Laws of England.* London.

Blatt, D. 1992. "Recognizing Rape as a Method of Torture." *N.Y.U. Review of Law and Social Change* 19.

Blumstein, A., J. Cohen, S. Martin and M. Tonry. 1983. "Determinants of Sentences." 1 *Research on Sentencing: The Search for Reform.* Washington, DC: National Academy Press.

Bochnak, Elizabeth, et al. 1981. "Case Preparation and Development." In *Women's Self-Defense Cases: Theory and Practice,* ed. E. Bochnak. Charlottesville: Michie Co.

Bograd, Michele. 1988. "Feminist Perspectives on Wife Abuse: An Introduction." In *Feminist Perspectives on Wife Abuse,* ed. K. Yllö and M. Bograd. Newbury Park: Sage Publications.

Borgmann, Caitlin. 1990. "Battered Women's Substantive Due Process Claims: Can Orders of Protection Deflect DeShaney?" *N.Y.U. Law Review* 65:1280–1323.

Boston Globe. 1989. August 23:1.

———. 1991. February 11:12.

Bowker, Lee H. 1983. *Beating Wife-Beating.* Lexington: D.C. Heath.

———, and L. Maurer. 1986. "The Effectiveness of Counseling Services Utilized by Battered Women." *Women & Therapy* 5(4):65–82.

Brazil Report. 1991. "Criminal Injustice: Violence Against Women in Brazil." New York: Americas Watch.

Breedlove, Kennish, Sandker and Sawtell. 1977. "Domestic Violence and the Police: Kansas City." In *Domestic Violence and the Police.*

Browne, Angela. 1987. *When Battered Women Kill.* New York: Free Press.

Brownlie, I. 1990. *Principles of Public International Law.* Oxford: Clarendon Press (4th ed.).

Brownmiller, Susan. 1989. "Hedda Nussbaum, Hardly a Heroine . . ." *New York Times.* February 2:A25.

Brownstein, Alan E. 1990. "Harmonizing the Heavenly and Earthly Spheres: The Fragmentation and Synthesis of Religion, Equality, and Speech in the Constitution." *Ohio State Law Journal* 51:89.

Buckborough, A. "Family Law: Recent Developments in the Law of Marital Rape." *Ann. Surv. Am. L.* 1989:343.

Buel, Sara. 1988. "Mandatory Arrest for Domestic Violence." *Harvard Women's Law Journal* 11:213–226.

Buffalo Symposium. 1985. "Feminist Discourse, Moral Values, and the Law—A Conversation." *Buffalo Law Review* 34:11–87.

Bunch, C. 1989. "Global Feminism, Human Rights and Sexual Violence." In *First Annual Women's Policy Research Conference Proceedings.* Washington, DC: Institute for Women's Policy Research.

———. 1990. "Women's Rights as Human Rights: Towards a Re-Vision of Human Rights." *Human Rights Quarterly* 12:486.

———. 1992. Quoted in "Violence Against Women is a Violation of Human Rights," 2 *Women in Law and Development in Africa News,* p. 4.

———, and R. Carrillo. 1991. "Gender Violence: A Development and Human Rights Issue." New Brunswick, NJ: Center for Women's Global Leadership.

Bureau of Justice Statistics, U.S. Department of Justice. 1983. *Report to the Nation on Crime and Justice: The Data.*

———. 1991A. *Capital Punishment.*

———. 1991B. *Female Victims of Violent Crime.*

Burgess, Ann and Holstram. 1974. "Rape Trauma Syndrome." *American Journal of Psychiatry* 131:981.

Burris, C. A. and P. Jaffe. 1982. *Family Consultant Service with the London Police Force: A Prescriptive Package.* Ottawa: Ministry of the Solicitor General.

———. 1983. "Wife Abuse as a Crime: The Impact of Police Laying Charges." In *Canadian Journal of Crime and Criminology* 25:309.

———. 1984a. "Crisis Intervention on the London Family Consultant Model." 46 *RCMP Gazette.*

———. 1984b. *An Integrated Response to Wife Assault: A Community Model.* Ottawa: Ministry of the Solicitor General.

Busia, K. A. 1951. *The Position of the Chief in the Modern Political System of Ashanti.* London: Frank Cass.

Butler, Judith. 1992. "Contingent Foundations: Feminism and the Question of Postmodernism." In *Feminists Theorize the Political,* eds. J. Butler and J. Scott. New York: Routledge.

Buzawa, Eve S. and C. Buzawa. 1990. *Domestic Violence: The Criminal Justice Response: Studies in Crime,* Law & Justice, Vol 6. Newbury Park, CA: Sage Publications.

———. 1992. *Domestic Violence: The Changing Criminal Justice Response.* Westport, CT: Auburn House.

Byrnes, A. 1989. "The "Other" Human Rights Treaty Body: The Work of the Committee on the Elimination of All Forms of Discrimination Against Women." *Yale Journal of International Law* 14:1.

———. "Women, Feminism and International Human Rights Law—Methodological Myopia, Fundamental Flaws or Meaningful Marginalization?" Unpublished manuscript on file with Beasley and Thomas.

Cahn, Naomi R. 1991. "Civil Images of Battered Women: The Impact of Domestic Violence on Child Custody Decisions." *Vanderbilt Law Review* 44:1041.

Campbell, Jacquelin C. 1992. "If I Can't Have You, No One Can: Power and Control in Homicide of Female Partners," in *Femicide: The Politics of Woman Killing,* eds. Jill Radford and Diana Russell. New York: Twayne Publishers.

Cardozo, Benjamin. 1930. *What Medicine Can Do for Law.* New York: Harper.

Carr, Wilbert and Harry Wedeck, eds. 1940. *Latin Poetry.* Boston: D.C. Health.

Carraway, G. Chezia. 1991. "Violence Against Women of Color." *Stanford Law Review* 43.

Casebeer, Kenneth. 1989. "Running on Empty: Justice Brennan's Plea, the Empty State, the City of Richmond, and the Profession." *University of Miami Law Review* 43:989.

Charlesworth, H. 1991. "The Public/Private Distinction and the Right to Development in International Law." *Australian Yearbook of International Law* 12:322.

———, et al. 1991. "Feminist Approaches to International Law." *American Journal of International Law* 85:25.

Chaudhuri, Molly and Kathleen Daly. 1992. "Do Restraining Orders Help? Battered Women's Experience with Male Violence and Legal Process." In *Domestic Violence: The Changing Criminal Justice Response,* ed. E. Buzawa. West Port: Auburn House.

Chinken, Christine and Wright Shelley. 1992. "The Hunger Trap: Women, Food and

Development." SUNY Buffalo Proceedings from the Third Biennial Symposium on New Feminist Scholarship.

Chodorow, Nancy J. 1978. *The Reproduction of Mothering: Psychoanalysis and the Sociology of Gender.* Berkeley: University of California Press.

Chrystos. 1986. " 'What Did He Hit You With?' The Doctor Said." In *Naming The Violence,* ed. Kerry Lobel. Seattle: Seal Press.

Cixous, Helen. 1983. "The Laugh of the Medussa." *The Signs Reader: Women, Gender and Scholarship,* ed. Elizabeth Abel and Emily Abel. Chicago: University of Chicago Press.

Cott, Nancy. 1977. *The Bonds of Womanhood: "Women's Sphere."* New Haven: Yale University Press.

Clark, Natalie Loder. 1987. "Crime Begins At Home: Let's Stop Punishing Victims and Perpetuating Violence." *William & Mary Law Review* 28:263.

Cobbe, F. P. 1881. *The Duties of Women.* London: Williams and Norgate.

Cohen, Jane Maslow. 1989. "Comparison-Shopping in the Marketplace of Rights." *Yale Law Journal,* 98:1235–1276.

———. 1992. "A Jurisprudence of Doubt: Deliberative Autonomy and Abortion." *Columbia Journal of Gender and Law* 3:175–246.

Coker, Donna. 1992. "Heat of Passion and Wife Killing: Men Who Batter/Men Who Kill." *Review of Law and Women's Studies* 2:71.

Colby, Kimberlee Wood. 1982. "When the Family Does Not Pray Together: The Religious Rights Within the Family." *Harvard Journal of Law and Public Policy* 5:39.

Cole, Susan. 1989. *Pornography and the Sex Crisis.* Toronto: Amanita Publication.

Collins, Patricia Hill. 1990. *Black Feminist Thought: Knowledge, Consciousness and the Politics of Empowerment.* Boston: Unwin Hyman.

Consultation Report. 1991. *Report of the Consultation on Women and Human Rights.* Washington DC: Women in Development/Human Rights Watch.

Cook, R. 1990. "International Human Rights Law Concerning Women: Case Notes and Comments." *Vanderbilt Journal of Transnational Law* 23:779.

———. 1992. "International Protection of Women's Reproductive Rights" *N.Y.U. Journal of International Law and Policy* 24:645.

Copelon, Rhonda. 1988. "Unpacking Patriarchy: Reproduction, Sexuality, Originalism and Constitutional Change." In *A Less Than Perfect Union: Alternative Perspectives on the U.S. Constitution,* ed. J. Lobel, New York: Monthly Review Press.

———. 1990–1991. "Losing the Negative Right to Privacy: Building Sexual and Reproductive Freedom." *New York University Review of Law and Social Change* 18:15–50.

Corimer. ?. 1986. "Coming Full Circle." In *Naming the Violence,* ed. Kerry Lobel. Seattle: Seal Press.

Cornell, Drucilla. 1991a. *Beyond Accommodation.* New York: Routledge.

———. 1991b. "Sexual Difference, the Feminine, and Equivalency: A Critique of MacKinnon's *Toward a Feminist Theory of the State.*" *Yale Law Journal* 100:2247 (reviewing Catharine A. MacKinnon, *Toward a Feminist Theory of the State*).

Côté, A. 1991. *La rate au coeur: Rapport de recherche sur le traitement judicaire de l'homicide conjugal au Québec.* Québec.

Cover, Robert M. 1983. "The Supreme Court 1982 Term. Foreword: Nomos and Narrative." *Harvard Law Review* 97:4.

Crenshaw, Kimberlé. 1988. "Race, Reform and Retrenchment: Transformation and Legitimation in Anti Discrimination Law." *Harvard Law Review.* 101:1331–1387.

———. 1989. "Demarginalizing the Intersection of Race and Sex: A Black Feminist Critique of Antidiscrimination Doctrine, Feminist Theory and Antiracist Politics." *University of Chicago Legal Forum* 1989:139–167.

———. 1991. "Beyond Patriarchy and Racism: Black Feminism and Violence against Women of Color." *Stanford Law Review* 43:—.

———. 1994. "Mapping the Margins: Intersectionality, Identity Politics, and Violence Against Women of Color." *The Public Nature of Private Violence,* eds. Martha A. Fineman & Roxanne Mykitiuk. New York: Routledge.

Crnich, Joe and Kim Crnich. 1992. *Shifting The Burden of Truth.* Lake Oswego: Recollex Publishing.

cunningham, e. christi. 1991. "Unmaddening: A Response to Professor Angela Harris." *Yale Journal of Law and Feminism* 4:155–169.

Czapanskiy, Karen. 1991. "Volunteers and Draftees: The Struggle for Parental Equality." *University of California Los Angeles Law Review* 38:1415, 1459–1463.

Daro, Deborah and Mitchel, Leslie. 1990. *Current Trends in Child Abuse Reporting and Fatalities: The Results of the 1989 Annual Fifty State Survey.* Chicago: Nat'l Comm. for Prevention of Child Abuse.

Davis, Angela. 1989. "Slaying the Dream: The Black Family and the Crisis of Capitalism." In *Women, Culture and Politics.* New York: Random House.

"D.C. Court to Recognize Independent Tort of Spouse Abuse." 1989. *Family Law Reporter.* 15: 1501–1502.

Des Rosiers, Nathalie. 1992. "Les recours de la victime d'inceste." In *Common law d'un siècle, l'autre,* ed. P. Legrand. Cowansville: Éditions Yvon Blais.

"Developments in the Law—Legal Responses to Domestic Violence." 1993. *Harvard Law Review.* 106:1498–1620.

Dill, M. 1984. "The Constitutionality of the Feme Sole Estate and the Virginia Supreme Court's Creation of an 'Homme Sole' Estate in *Jacobs v. Meade.*" 19 *University of Richmond Law Review* 163.

Dinnerstein, Dorothy. 1976. *The Mermaid and the Minotaur.* New York: Harper and Row.

Dix, G. 1971. "Psychological Abnormality as a Factor in Grading Criminal Liability: Diminished Capacity, Diminished Responsibility and the Like." *J. Crim. L. C. & P. S.* 62: 313.

Dobash, Russell, P. and Ruth Emerson Dobash. 1979. *Violence Against Wives: The Case Against the Patriarchy.* New York: Free Press.

Dolphyne, F. A. 1987. "The Ghana National Council on Women and Development: An Example in Concerted Action." In *Sex Roles, Population and Development in West Africa: Policy-Related Studies on Work and Demographic Issues,* ed. Christine Oppong. London: James Currey Limited.

Don, T. 1986. *An Introduction to the Ontario Association of Interval and Transition Houses.* Toronto: OAITH.

Donaldson, M. A. and J. Gardner Jr. 1985. "Diagnosis and Treatment of Traumatic Stress Among Women after Childhood Incest." In *Trauma and its Wake: The Study & Treatment of Post-Traumatic Stress Disorder,* ed. C. Figley. New York: Brunner/Mazel.

Donnelly. J. 1982. "Human Rights and Human Dignity: An Analytic Critique of Non-Western Conceptions of Human Rights." *American Political Science Review* 76:303.

Douglas, Mary. 1966. *Purity and Danger.* Boston: Routledge and Kegan Paul.

Dressler, J. 1982. "Rethinking Heat of Passion: A Defense in Search of a Rationale." *Journal of Criminal Law and Criminology* 73.

Drucker, L. 1989. "Governmental Liability for "Disappearances": A Landmark Ruling by the Inter-American Court of Human Rights." *Stanford Journal of International Law* 25:289.

Du Plessis, Rachel Blau. 1990. *The Pink Guitar: Writing as Feminist Practice.* New York: Routledge.

Duclos, Nythia. 1990. "Lessons of Difference: Feminist Theory on Cultural Diversity." *Buffalo Law Review* 38:325.

Dupps, David S. 1991. "Battered Lesbians: Are They Entitled to A Battered Woman Defense?" *Journal of Family Law* 29:879–899.

Dutton, D. and S. L. Painter. 1985. "Patterns of Emotional Bonding in Battered Women: Traumatic Bonding." *International Journal of Women's Studies.* 8:363.

Dutton, D. G. 1988. *The Domestic Assault of Women: Psychological and Criminal Justice Perspectives.* Boston, MA: Allyn and Bacon.

Dutton, Mary Ann. 1992. *Empowering and Healing the Battered Woman: A Model for Assessment and Intervention.* New York: Springer.

Dworkin, Andrea and Catherine MacKinnon. 1988. *Pornography and Civil Rights: A New Day for Women's Equality.* Minneapolis, MN: Organizers Against Pornography.

Dworkin, Andrea. 1987. *Intercourse.* New York: Free Press.

Early, Gerald. 1988. "Her Picture in the Papers: Remembering Some Black Women." *Antaeus* 9 (Spring).

Eaton, Mary. 1991. *Theorizing Sexual Orientation.* Unpublished LL.M. thesis. Kingston, Ont.: Queen's University.

———. 1993. "At The Intersection of Sexual Orientation and Gender: Toward Lesbian Jurisprudence." Forthcoming in *Lesbian Legal Theories,* ed. Ruthann Robson. New York: Routledge.

———. 1994. "Abuse by Any Other Name: Feminism, Difference, and Intralesbian Violence." In *The Public Nature of Private Violence,* edited by Martha A. Fineman and Roxanne Mykitiuk. New York: Routledge.

Eisler, Raine. 1987. "Human Rights: Toward an Integrated Theory for Action." *Human Rights Quarterly* 9:287–308.

Ekland-Olsen, S. 1988. "Structured Discretion, Racial Bias and the Death Penalty." *Social Science Quarterly* 69:853.

Ellis, Mark Vincent. 1988. *Fiduciary Duties in Canada.* Don Mills: DeBoo.

Engle, K. 1992. "International Human Rights and Feminism: When Discourses Meet." 13 *Michigan Journal of International Law* 13:517.

Ensign, Diana J. 1990. "Links Between Battered Women's Syndrome and Battered Child Syndrome: An Argument for Consistent Standards in the Admissibility of Expert Testimony in Family Abuse Cases." *Wayne Law Review* 36:1619–1642.

Erickson, Nancy S. 1991. "Battered Mothers of Battered Children: Using Our Knowledge of Battered Women to Defend Them Against Charges of Failure to Act." *Current Perspectives in Psychological, Legal and Ethical Issues* 1A:197.

Expert Group Report. 1991. *Report of the Expert Group Meeting on Violence Against Women.* Vienna: Commission on the Status of Women (EGM/VAW/1991/1).

Fagan, J. 1989. "Cessation of Family Violence: Deterrence and Dissaution." I. *Family Violence,* eds. L. Ohlin and M. Tonry. Chicago: University of Chicago Press.

Faludi, Susan. 1991. *Backlash: The Undeclared War Against American Women.* New York: Crown.

"Family Violence Prevention and Services Act: A Report to Congress." 1988.

Farrand, M. 1911. *The Records of the Federal Convention of 1787.* New Haven: Yale University Press.

Faulkner, Ellen. 1991. "Lesbian Abuse: The Social and Legal Realities." *Queen's Law Journal* 16:261–286.

Federal Bureau of Investigation, U.S. Department of Justice. 1984. *Uniform Crime Reports for 1983.*

Feild, Hubert S. and Bienen, Leigh B. 1980. *Jurors and Rape: A Study in Psychology and Law.* Lexington, MA: Lexington Books.

Fineman, Martha. 1983. "Implementing Equality: Ideology, Contradiction, and Social Change, A Study of Rhetoric and Results in the Regulation of the Consequences of Divorce" *Wisconsin Law Review.* 1783:789.

———. 1988. "Dominant Discourse, Professional Language and Legal Change in Child Custody Decision Making." *Harvard Law Review.* 101:727–774.

———. 1989. "The Politics of Custody and the Transformation of American Custody Decision Making." *U. C. Davis Law Review* 22:829.

———. 1991a. *The Illusion of Equality: The Rhetoric and Reality of Divorce Reform.* Chicago: University of Chicago Press.

———. 1991b. "Images of Mothers in Poverty Discourses." *Duke Law Journal* 274.

———. 1991c. "Intimacy Outside of the Natural Family: The Limits of Privacy." *Connecticut Law Review.* 23:955.

———. 1992a. "Feminist Theory in Law: The Difference it Makes." *Columbia Journalism of Feminism & Law* 1:1.

———. 1992b. "The Neutered Mother." *University of Miami Law Review* 46:301.

———, and Opie, Anne. 1987. "The Uses of Social Science Data in Legal Policymaking: Custody Determinations at Divorce." *Wisconsin Law Review* 107.

Finesmith, B. 1983. "Police Response to Battered Women: A Critique and Proposals for Reform." *Seton Hall Law Review* Winter.

Finkelhor, D. 1986. *A Sourcebook on Child Sexual Abuse.* Beverly Hills: Sage Publications.

———, and A. Browne, A. 1985. "The Traumatic Impact of Child Sexual Abuse: A Conceptualization." *American Journal Orthopsychiatry* 55(4): 530.

Finn, Peter. 1989. "Statutory Authority in the Use and Enforcement of Civil Protection Orders Against Domestic Abuse." *Family Law Quarterly* 23:43–73.

———, and Colson. 1990. *Civil Protection Orders: Legislation, Current Court Practice, and Enforcement.* U.S. Department of Justice, National Institute of Justice.

Fishkin, James. 1983. *Justice, Equal Opportunity, and the Family*. New Haven: Yale University Press.

Flitcraft, Anne, William Frazier, and Evan Stark. 1979. "Medicine and Patriarchal Violence: the Social Construction of a Private Event." *International Journal of Health Services*. 9:461.

Florida Statutes Section 921.141(5)(h).

de Fonseca, Medeiros R. 1977. "Law and the Condition of Women in Brazil." In "Law and the Status of Women." *Columbia Law Review*.

Fox-Keller, Evelyn. 1985. *Reflections on Gender and Science*. London Yale University Press.

Fraser, A. 1983. *Looking to the Future: Equal Partnership Between Men and Women in the 21st Century*. Minnesota: University of Minnesota Humphrey Institute of Public Affairs.

Fraser, Nancy. 1990. "Struggle over Needs: Outcome of Socialist-Feminist Critical Theory of Late-Capitalist Political Structure." In *Women, the State, and Welfare*, ed. L. Gordon. Madison: University of Wisconsin Press.

Freeman, Allen and Elizabeth Mensch. 1987. "The Public-Private Distinction in American Law and Life." *Buffalo Law Review* 36:237–257.

Freud, Sigmund. 1930. *Civilization and Its Discontents*. New York: W. W. Norton.

Fridman, G. H. L. 1992. *Restitution*. Toronto: Carswell.

Friedman, Lee M. 1915–1916. "The Parental Right to Control the Religious Education of a Child." *Harvard Law Review* 29:485.

Friedman, Lucy N. and Couper, Sarah. *The Cost of Domestic Violence: A Preliminary Investigation of the Financial Cost of Domestic Violence*. Unpublished manuscript, New York: Victim Services Agency.

Frye, Marilyn. 1983. "To Be and Be Seen: The Politics of Reality." In *Essays in Feminist Theory* by Marilyn Frye. Freedom, CA: The Crossing Press.

Galanter, Marc. 1966. "Religious Freedoms in the United States: A Turning Point?" *Wisconsin Law Review* 217.

Garcia, Jane. 1991. "The Cost of Escaping Domestic Violence: Fear of Treatment in a Largely Homophobic Society May Keep Lesbian Abuse Victims from Calling for Help." *Los Angeles Times*. May 6:2.

Garwood, Alfred N., ed. 1991. *Hispanic Americans: A Statistical Sourcebook*. Boulder CO: Numbers & Concepts.

Gelles, Richard. 1980. "A Profile of Violence Toward Children in the United States." In *Child Abuse—An Agenda for Action*, eds. G. Gerbner, C. J. Ross, and E. Ziegler. Oxford: Oxford University Press.

———, and M. Straus. 1988. *Intimate Violence*. New York: Simon & Shuster.

Georgia Code Ann. Section 27–2534.1(b)(7).

Gilbert, Sandra M. and Gubar, Susan. 1979. *The Madwoman in the Attic*. New Haven: Yale University Press.

Giles-Sims, Jean. 1985. "A Longitudinal Study of Battered Children of Battered Wives." *Family Relations*. April: 205.

Gilman, Charlotte Perkins. 1899. *The Yellow Wallpaper*. New York: The Feminist Press (reissue, ed. 1973).

Goldstein, J., Freud, A., and Solnit, A. 1973. *Before the Best Interest of the Child* (revised ed. 1979).

Gondolf, Edward and Ellen Fisher. 1988. *Battered Women as Survivors: An Alternative to Treating Learned Helplessness.* Lexington, MA: Lexington Books.

Gordon, Linda. 1986. "Family Violence, Feminism and Social Control." *Feminist Studies* 12(3):453.

———. 1988. *Heroes of Their Own Lives: The Politics and History of Family Violence in America.* New York: Viking.

———. 1990a. "Family Violence, Feminism, and Social Control." In *Women, The State and Welfare,* ed. Linda Gordon. Madison: University of Wisconsin Press.

———. 1990b. "Response to Scott." *Signs* 15:852.

Gordon, Mary. 1985. *Men and Angels.* New York: Random House.

Greven, Philip. 1991. *Spare the Child—The Religious Roots of Punishment.* New York: Alfred A. Knopf.

Grillo, Trina. 1991. "The Mediation Alternative: Process Dangers for Women." *Yale Law Journal* 100:1545–1610.

Gross, S. and R. Mauro. 1989. *Death and Discrimination.* Boston: Northeastern University Press.

Grossberg, Michael. 1985. *Governing the Health: Law and Family in Nineteenth Century America.* Chapel Hill: University of North Carolina Press.

Hammond, Nancy. 1988. "Lesbian Victims of Relationship Violence." *Women & Therapy* 8:89–105.

Haraway, Donna. 1988. "Situated Knowledges: The Science Question in Feminism and the Privilege of Partial Perspective." *Feminist Studies.* 14:584.

Harding, Sandra G. 1986. *The Science Question in Feminism.* Ithaca: Cornell University Press.

Harkavy, Jeffrey M. 1982. "The Defending of Accused Homosexuals: Will Society Accept Their Use of the Battered Wife Defense?" *Glendale Law Review* 4:208–232.

Harper, Laura. 1990. "Battered Women Suing Police for Failure to Intervene: Viable Legal Avenues After *Deshaney v. Winnebago County Department of Social Services.*" *Cornell Law Review* 75:1393–1425.

Harris, Angela P. 1990. "Race and Essentialism in Feminist Legal Theory." *Stanford Law Review* 42:581–616.

———. 1991. "Race and Essentialism in Feminist Legal Theory," in *Feminist Legal Theory: Readings in Law and Gender,* eds. Katharine Bartlett and Rosanne Kennedy. Colorado: Westview Press.

Harris, Trudier. 1984. "On the Color Purple, Stereotypes, and Silence." *Black American Literature Forum* 18:155.

Harshaw, J. W. III. 1989. "Not Enough Time? The Constitutionality of Short Statutes of Limitations for Civil Sexual Abuse Litigation." *Ohio State Law Journal* 50:753.

Hart, Barbara. 1986. "Lesbian Battering: An Examination." In *Naming the Violence: Speaking Out About Lesbian Battering,* ed. Kerry Lobel. Seattle: Seal Press.

———. 1988. *Safety for Women: Monitoring Battered Programs.* Harrisburgh: Pennsylvania Coalition Against Domestic Violence.

———. 1990. "Gentle Jeopardy: The Further Endangerment of Battered Women and Children in Custody Mediation." *Mediation Quarterly* 7:317–330.

Herman, J. 1981. *Father-Daughter Incest.* Cambridge: Harvard University Press.

———. 1992. *Trauma and Recovery.* New York: Basic Books.

Higgins, Tracy. 1990. "Rethinking (M)otherhood: Feminist Theory and State Regulation of Pregnancy." *Harvard Law Review* 103:1325.

Hirsch, Susan F. 1994. "Interpreting Media Representations of a 'Night of Madness': Law and Culture in the Construction of Rape Identities." *Law and Social Inquiry,* eds. L. Frohman and E. Mertz. Special issue on women, law, and violence, vol. 19, No. 4.

Hobbes, Thomas. 1640. *The Elements of Law, Natural and Politic,* ed. Ferdinand Tönnies. London: Frank Cass & Co., Ltd. (1969).

———. 1651. *The Leviathan,* ed. C. B. MacPherson. New York: Penguin Books (1984).

———. 1682. *Behemoth, or the Long Parliament.*

Hodgin, Deanna. 1991. " 'Mail-Order Brides' Marry Pain to Get Green Cards." *Washington Times.* April 16: E1.

Hoff, Lee Ann. 1990. *Battered Women as Survivors.* London: Routledge.

Hoffman, Jan. 1990. "Pregnant, Addicted—and Guilty?" *New York Times.* August 19:6.

hooks, bell. 1981. *Ain't I a Woman?* Boston: South End Press.

———. 1984. Feminist Theory from Margin to Center, Boston: South End Press.

———. 1989. *Talking Back, Thinking Feminist, Thinking Black,* Boston: South End Press.

———. 1990. *Yearning: Race, Gender and Cultural Politics.* Boston: South End Press.

———. 1991. "Theory as Liberatory Practice." *Yale Journal of Law and Feminism* 4:1–12.

———. 1992. *Black Looks Race and Representation.* Boston: South End Press.

Horton, A. L. and J. A. Williamson. 1988. *Abuse and Religion.* Lexington, MA: Lexington Books.

Hotaling and Strauss. 1989. "Intrafamily Violence Outside the Family." In *Cessation of Family Violence,* eds. L. Ohlin and M. Tonry. Chicago: University of Chicago Press.

Hughes, Robert. 1992. "The Fraying of America." *Time* February 28:44.

Human Rights Commission. 1983. *United Nations Action in the Field of Human Rights.* New York: United Nations (ST/HR/2/Rev. 2).

ILC Yearbook. 1972. "Draft Articles on State Responsibility," II *Yearbook of the International Law Commission* 95–125.

Independent. 1991. "Judges nail 'lie' that husbands cannot rape." p. 3.

International Women's Rights Action Watch. 1992. CEDAW No. 11, August.

Irvine, Janice. 1990. "The Search for Shelter." In *Confronting Lesbian Battering.* ed. Pamela Elliott. St. Paul: Minnesota Coalition for Battered Women, Lesbian Battering Intervention Project.

Island, David and Patrick Letellier. 1991. *Men Who Beat the Men Who Love Them.* New York: Howarth Press.

Jack, Rand and Dana Crowley. 1989. *Moral Vision and Professional Decisions.* New York: Cambridge University Press.

James, J. and J. Meyerding. 1977. "Early Sexual Experiences and Prostitution." *American Journal of Psychiatry* 134:1381.

Jan E. Stets, *Domestic Violence and Control* (1988). New York: Springer-Verlag.

Jayawardena, K. 1986. *Feminism and Nationalism in the Third World.*

Johnson, Barbara. 1987. "Apostrophe, Animation and Abortion." In *A World of Difference.* Baltimore: Johns Hopkins University Press.

Johnston, Jr., John D. 1972. "Sex & Property: The Common Law Tradition, the Law School Curriculum and Developments Equalitize." *New York University Law Review* 47:6.

Jones, Ann. 1980. *Women Who Kill.* New York: Hold, Rinehart, and Winston.

———. 1986. "The Burning Bed and Man Slaughter." *Women's Rights Law Reporter* 9:295.

Kanuha, Valli. 1990. "Compounding the Triple Jeopardy: Battering in Lesbian of Color Relationships." *Women & Therapy* 9:169–184.

Karp, Leonard and Cheryl Karp. 1989. "Spousal Abuse." In *Domestic Torts: Family Violence, Conflict and Sexual Abuse.* Colorado Springs: Shepard's/McGraw Hill.

———. 1989."D.C. Court Declines to Recognize Independent Tort of Spouse Abuse." Family Law Reporter 15:1501–02.

———. 1990. "Victim of Battered Woman's Syndrome Recovers in a Civil Action for Battery and Emotional Distress." Am. Trial Law Ass'n L. Rep 33:314

Katz, J. 1988. *Seductions of Crime.* New York: Basic Books.

Kaye, J. 1967. "The Early History of Murder and Manslaughter." *Law Quarterly Review* 83:365.

Kelly, Andrea and Elisa Long. 1992. "Violence Against Women: Proposed Legislation." *Texas Journal of Women and the Law* 1:285–290.

Kelly, Liz. 1988. "How Women Define Their Experiences of Violence." In *Feminist Perspectives on Wife Abuse,* edited by K. Yllö and M. Bograd. Newbury Park: Sage Publications.

Kerber, Linda. 1988. "Separate Spheres, Female Worlds, Women's Place: The Rhetoric of Women's History." *Journal of American History* 75:9–39.

Kinports, Kit. 1988. "Defending Battered Women's Self-Defense Claims." *Oregon Law Review* 67:393–465.

Klaus, P. 1984. "Family Violence." In *Bureau of Justice Statistics Special Report.* Washington, DC: US Department of Justice.

Kline, Marlee. 1989. "Race, Racism and Feminist Legal Theory." *Harvard Women's Law Journal* 12:115–150.

———. 1992. "Child Welfare Law, 'Best Interests of the Child' Ideology, and First Nations." *Osgoode Hall Law Journal* 30:375.

Koonan & Waller. 1989. *Jury Selection in a Woman's Self-defense Case.* LC/SC CACJ/Forum. May–June.

Knudsen, Dean and JoAnn Miller, eds. 1991. *Abused and Battered: Social and Legal Responses to Family Violence.* New York: De Gruyter.

Kristeva, Julia. 1982. *Powers of Horror: An Essay on Abjection,* trans. Leon S. Roudiez. New York: Columbia University Press.

———. 1987. *In the Beginning Was Love: Psychoanalysis and Faith,* trans. Arthur Goldhammer. New York: Columbia University Press.

LaFave, W. and A. Scott, Jr. 1986. *Criminal Law* Sections 7.12 and 7.13. St. Paul: West Publishing.

Lahey, K. 1985. "Until Women Themselves Have Told All That They Have To Tell . . ." *Osgoode Hall Law Journal* 23:519–41.

Law Reform Commission of Canada. 1984. *Working Paper 38: Assault.* Ottawa: Ministry of Supply and Services.

Law, Sylvia. 1984. "Rethinking Sex and the Constitution," *University of Pennsylvania Law Review* 132:955.

Leeder, Elaine. 1988. "Issues and Myths Relative to Lesbian Battering." *Women & Therapy* 7:83–99.

Leo, John. 1992. "The Trouble With Feminism." *U.S. News and World Report.* p. 19.

Leonard, Leigh. 1990. "A Missing Voice in Feminist Legal Theory: The Heterosexual Presumption." *Women's Rights Law Reporter* 12:39–49.

Lerman, Lisa G. 1984. "Mediation of Wife Abuse Cases: The Adverse Impact of Informal Dispute Resolution on Women." *Harvard Women's Law Journal* 7:57–113.

Lesemann, Dana. 1991. "Who's Speaking? Who's Listening? Who Cares? Authority, Narrative, and Transformation." Unpublished manuscript.

Levine, Judith. 1992. "The Personal is the Personal." *Village Voice.* March 17:65.

Levinson, D. 1989. *Family Violence in Cross-Cultural Perspective.* Newbury Park, CA: Sage Publications.

Lewin, T. 1975. "Psychiatric Evidence in Criminal Cases for Purposes Other Than Defense of Insanity." *Syracuse Law Review* 26:1051.

List, Lawrence. 1963–64. "A Child and a Wall: A Study of "Religious Protection Laws." *Buffalo Law Review* 13:9.

Littleton, Christine. 1987. "Reconstructing Sexual Equality." *California Law Review* 87:1279.

———. 1989. "Women's Experience and the Problem of Transition: Perspectives on Male Battering of Women." *University of Chicago Legal Forum* 1989:23–58.

Lobel, Kerry. 1986. *Naming the Violence: Speaking Out About Lesbian Battering.* Seattle: Seal Press.

Loftus, Marilyn. 1986. "First Year Report of the New Jersey Supreme Court Task Force on Women in the Courts." *Women's Rights Law Reporter* 9:129–177.

Lokken, R. 1991. "Peru's President Defends Record on Human Rights," *Reuters Information Services–*AM. November 18.

Loseke, D. 1992. *Battered Women and Shelters: The Social Construction of Wife Abuse.* Albany, NY: SUNY Press.

Loulan, Joanne. 1987. *Lesbian Passion.* San Francisco: Spinsters/Aunt Lute.

MacKinnon, Catharine A. 1982. "Feminism, Marxism, Method and the State: An Agenda for Theory." *Signs* 7:515.

———. 1984. "Not a Moral Issue." *Yale Law and Policy Review* 2:321–45.

———. 1985. "Feminist Discourse, Moral Values and the Law—A Conversation." *Buffalo Law Review* 34:11.

———. 1987a. *Feminism Unmodified.* Cambridge: Harvard University Press.

———. 1987b. "Unthinking ERA Thinking." *University of Chicago Law Review* 54:759.

———. 1989. "On Consent and Rape." In *Toward a Feminist Theory of the State.* Cambridge: Harvard University Press.

———. 1991a. "From Practice to Theory, or What Is a White Woman Anyway?" *Yale Journal of Law and Feminism* 4:13–22.

———. 1991b. "Reflections on Sex Equality under Law." *Yale Law Journal.* 100:1281.

Macleod, L. 1980. *Wife Battering in Canada: The Vicious Circle.* Ottawa, Ont.: The Canadian Advisory Council on The Status of Women.

———. 1984. *Battered but not Beaten.* New York: Springer Publishing Company.

Maguigan, Holly. 1991. "Battered Women and Self-Defense: Myths and Misconceptions in Current Reform Proposals." *U. Pa. L. Rev.* 140:379–486.

Mahoney, Martha A. 1991. "Legal Images of Battered Women: Redefining the Issue of Separation." *Michigan Law Review* 90:1–94.

———. 1992. "Exit: Power and the Idea of Leaving in Love, Work, and the Confirmation Hearings" *Southern California Law Review* 65:1283.

———. 1994. "Victimization or Oppression? Women's Lives, Violence and Agency." In *The Public Nature of Private Violence.* Edited by Martha Albertson Fineman and Roxanne Mykitiuk. New York: Routledge.

Mahoney, Maureen A. and Barbara Yngvesson. 1992. "The Construction of Subjectivity and the Paradox of Resistance: Reintegrating Feminist Anthropology and Psychology." *Signs* 18:44.

Manuh, Takyiwaa. 1984. *Law and the Status of Women in Ghana.* Addis Ababa.

Marguiles, Peter. 1992. "The Cognitive Politics of Professional Conflict: Law Reform, Mental Health Treatment Technology and Citizen Self-Governance." *Harvard Journal of Law and Technology.* 5:25–63.

Massachusetts Supreme Judicial Court. 1990. "Gender Bias Study of the Court System in Massachusetts." *New England Law Review* 24:745–856.

Massaro, Toni. 1989. "Empathy, Legal Storytelling, and Rule of Law: New Words, Old Wounds?" *Michigan Law Review* 87:2099–2127.

Matsuda, Mari J. 1989a. "When the First Quail Calls: Multiple Consciousness as Jurisprudential Method." *Women's Rights Law Reporter* 11:7–10.

———. 1989b. "Legal Storytelling: Public Response to Racist Speech: Considering the Victim's Story." *Michigan Law Review* 87:2320.

———, et al. 1993. *Words that Wound: Critical Race Theory, Assaultive Speech and the First Amendment.*

Matthews, Nancy Anne. 1989. "Stopping Rape or Managing its Consequences? State Intervention and Feminist Resistance in the Los Angeles Anti-Rape Movement, 1972–1987." Ph.D. dissertation, University of California, Los Angeles.

McClain, Linda. 1992. "The Poverty of Privacy?" *Columbia J. of Gender and Law* 3:119–174.

McConnell, Joyce. 1992. "Beyond Metaphor: Battered Women, Involuntary Servitude, and the Thirteenth Amendment." *Yale Journal of Law and Feminism* 4:207–253.

McGillivray, A. 1987. "Battered Women: Definition, Models and Prosecutorial Policy." *Canadian Journal of Family Law* 6:15–45.

Méndez J. and Vivanco J. M. 1990. "Disappearances and the Inter-American Court: Reflections on a Litigation Experience." *Hamline Law Review* 13:507.

Michelman, Frank. 1990. "Private, Personal But Not Split: *Randin v. Rorty.*" *Southern California Law Review* 63:1783–1795.

Mill, John Stuart. 1869. *The Subjection of Women,* ed. Susan M. Okin. 1988. Indianapolis: Hackett.

Miller, Alice. 1981. *Drama of the Gifted Child,* trans. R. Ward. New York: Basic Books.

———. 1983. *For Your Own Good: Hidden Cruelty in Child-Rearing and the Roots of Violence,* trans. H. & H. Hannum. New York: Noonday.

———. 1990a. *Banished Knowledge: Facing Childhood Injuries,* trans. L. Vennewitz. New York: Meridian.

———. 1990b. *The Untouched Key: Tracing Childhood Trauma in Creativity and Destructiveness,* trans. H. & H. Hannum. New York: Doubleday.

———. 1991. *Breaking Down the Wall of Silence: The Liberating Experience of Facing Painful Truth,* trans. S. Worrall, New York: Dutton.

Miller, Sue. 1986. *The Good Mother.* New York: Harper & Row.

Minow, Martha. 1985. " 'Forming Underneath Everything That Grows': Toward a History of Family Law." *Wisconsin Law Review* 819.

———. 1986. "Rights for the Next Generation: A Feminist Approach to Children's Rights." *Harvard Women's Law Journal* 9:1.

———. 1987. "Interpreting Rights: An Essay for Robert Cover." *Yale Law Journal* 96:1860.

———. 1989a. "Introduction: Finding our Paradoxes, Affirming our Beyond." *Harvard Civil Rights-Civil Liberties Law Review* Volume 24:1.

———. 1989b. "Pluralisms." *Connecticut Law Review* 21:965.

———. 1990a. "Adjudicating Differences: Conflicts Among Feminist Lawyers." In *Conflicts of Feminism,* eds. M. Hirsch and E. Fox Keller. New York & London: Routledge.

———. 1990b. "Words and the Door to the Land of Change: Law, Language, and Family Violence." *Vanderbilt Law Review* 43:1665–1699.

Miss. Code Ann. Section 99–19–101(5)(d).

Mnookin, R. H. and D. K. Weisberg. 1989. *Child, Family and State—Problems and Materials on Children and the Law.* Boston: Little, Brown and Co.

Model Penal and Commentaries, Vol. 2. 1980. Section 210.6.

Mohanty, C. 1991. "Under Western Eyes: Feminist Scholarship and Colonial Discourses." In *Third World Women and the Politics of Feminism,* eds. C. Mohanty, Russo and Torres. Bloomington: Indiana University Press.

Mont. Code Ann. Section 46–18–303(9).

Morgenson, Gretchen. 1992. "A Whiner's Bible." *Forbes.* March 16:152.

Morrison, Toni. 1987. *Beloved: A Novel.* New York: Knopf.

Murphy, Jane. 1993. "Lawyering for Social Change: The Power of the Narrative in Domestic Violence Law Reform." *Hofstra Law Review,* forthcoming.

NAACP. 1993. *Death Row, U.S.A.*

Nagel, Thomas. 1975. "Libertarianism Without Foundations." *Yale Law Journal* 85:136–149.

———. 1991. *Equality and Partiality.* New York: Oxford.

Napier, C. 1990. "Civil Incest Suits: Getting Beyond the Statute of Limitations." *Washington University Law Quarterly* 68:995.

National Center on Women and Family Law. 1987. *Custody Litigation.* New York.

National Coalition Against Domestic Violence. 1990. "To the Lesbian Nation." In *Confronting Lesbian Battering,* ed. Pamela Elliott. St. Paul: Minnesota Coalition for Battered Women, Lesbian Battering Intervention Project.

National Institute of Justice, Department of Justice. 1986. *Confronting Domestic Violence: A Guide for Criminal Justice Agencies.* Washington, DC: U.S. Government Printing Office.

Nedelsky, Jennifer. 1989. "Reconceiving Autonomy: Sources, Thoughts and Possibilities." *Yale Journal of Law and Feminism* 1:7.

———. 1990. "Law, Boundaries and the Bounded Self." *Representations* 30:162.

New York Times. 1988. December 9:2.

———. 1989. February 2:25.

Nicholson, Linda. 1990. *Feminism/Postmodernism.* New York: Routledge.

Noddings, Nel. 1984. *Caring: A Feminine Approach to Ethics and Moral Education.* Berkeley: University of California Press.

North Carolina General Statutes Section 15A–2000(e)(9).

Note. 1978. "Adjudicating What Yoder Left Unresolved: Religious Rights for Minor Children After Danforth and Carey." *U. Pennsylvania Law Review* 126:1135.

———. 1985. "Victims Behavior in Sexual Assault Trials." *Social Problems* 34:4.

———. 1986a. "Actionable Inaction: Section 1983 Liability for Failure to Act." *The University of Chicago Law Review* 53:1048–1073.

———. 1986b. "To Have and to Hold: The Marital Rape Exemption and the Fourteenth Amendment." *Harvard Law Review* 99:1255–1273.

———. 1988. "Juror Misconduct and Juror Composition." *Golden Gate University Law Review* 18:589–631.

———. 1990a. Comment "Crossing DeShaney: Can the Gap Be Closed Between Child Abuse in the House and the State's Duty to Protect?" *Iowa Law Review* 75:791.

———. 1990b. "DeShaney and the Jurisprudence of Compassion." *New York University Law Review* 65:1101–1147.

———. 1990c. "Battered Women Suing Police for Failure to Intervene: Viable Legal Avenues after *DeShaney v. Winnebago County Department of Social Services*" *Cornell Law Review* 75:1393.

O'Brien, Edna, 1992. *Time and Tide.* New York: Farrar, Straus and Giroux.

Oberman, Michelle. 1992. "Sex, Drugs, Pregnancy and the Law: Rethinking the Problems of Pregnant Women Who Use Drugs." *Hastings Law Journal* 43:505.

Office of Policy Planning and Research, U.S. Department of Labor. 1965. "The Negro Family: The Case for National Action." [The Moynihan Report] Reprinted in *The Moynihan Report and the Politics of Controversy* eds. Lee Rainwater and William L. Yancey, 1967, p. 75.

Okin, Susan Moller. 1989. *Justice, Gender and the Family.* New York: Basic Books.

Okri, Ben. 1991. *The Famished Road.* London: Vintage.

Oku, J. N. 1990. *Equality and Responsible Parenthood in Ghana.* Paper presented to the International Seminar on the Equality of Women. Sarajevo.

Olsen, Frances E. 1983. "The Family and the Market: A Study of Ideology and Legal Reform." *Harvard Law Review.* 96:1497–1578.

———. 1985. "The Myth of State Intervention in the Family." *University of Michigan Journal of Law Reform* 18:835–864.

———. 1992. "Children's Rights: Some Feminist Approaches to the United Nations Convention on the Rights of the Child." In *Children, Rights and the Law*, eds. P. Alston, S. Parker and J. Seymour. Oxford: Clarendon Press.

Oppong, C., ed. 1987. *Sex Roles, Population and Development iln West Africa: Policy-Related Studies on Work and Demographic Issues*. London: James Currey Limited.

Orentlicher, D. 1990. "Bearing Witness: The Art and Science of Human Rights Fact-Finding." *Harvard Human Rights Law Journal* 3:83.

Ostrander, Susan. 1989. *"Feminism, Voluntarism and the Welfare State: Toward a Feminist Sociological Theory of Social Welfare."* The American Sociologist. Spring: 29–41.

Ostriker, Alicia. 1986. *Stealing the Language: The Emergence of Women's Poetry in America*. Boston: Beacon Press.

Pagelow, Mildred Daley. 1981. *Woman-Battering: Victims and Their Experiences*. Beverly Hills: Sage Publications.

Pateman, Carol. 1988. *The Sexual Contract*. Stanford: Stanford University Press.

Pence, E. and M. Shepard. 1988. "Integrating Feminist Theory and Practice: The Challenge of the Battered Women's Movement." *Feminist Perspectives on Wife Abuse*, eds. Kersti Yllö and Michele Bograd. Newbury Park, CA: Sage Publications.

Peterson, S. 1990. "Whose Rights? A Critique of the "Givens" in Human Rights Discourse." *Alternatives* XV 303:308–310.

Pharr, Suzanne. 1988. *Homophobia: A Weapon of Sexism*.

———. 1990. "The Connection Between Homophobia and Violence Against Women." In *Confronting Lesbian Battering*, ed. Pamela Elliott. St. Paul: Minnesota Coalition for Battered Women, Lesbian Battering Intervention Project.

Piercy, Marge. 1976. *Woman on the Edge of Time*. New York: Fawcett Crest.

Pinckney, Daryl. 1987. "Black Victims, Black Villains." *New York Review of Books*. January 29:17.

Pleck, E. 1987. *Domestic Tyranny: The Making of American Social Policy Against Family Violence From Colonial Times To the Present*. New York: Oxford University Press.

Porat, Nomi. 1986. In *Naming the Violence*, ed. Kerry Lobel. Seattle: Seal Press.

Preamble Law 54 for the Prevention and Intervention with Domestic Violence.

Proverbs 31:10–31, King James Version.

Ptacek, James. 1988. "Why do Men Batter Their Wives?" In *Feminist Perspectives on Wife Abuse*, edited by Kirsti Yllö and Michelle Bograd. Newbury Park, CA: Sage Publications.

Puerto Rico Women's Affairs Commission. 1991. *First Report on the Implementation of Puerto Rico Domestic Violence Legislation*.

Radford, Jill and Diana Russell. 1992. *Femicide: The Politics of Woman Killing*. New York: Twayne.

Radin, Margaret. 1980. "Cruel Punishment and Respect for Persons: Super Due Process for Death." *Southern California Law Review* 53: 1143.

———. 1982. "Property and Personhood." *Stanford Law Review* 34:957–1015.

Rapaport, E. 1990. "Some Questions about Gender and the Death Penalty." *Golden Gate Law Review* 20: 501.

———. 1991. "The Death Penalty and Gender Discrimination." *Law & Society Review* 25:367.

————. forthcoming. "Passion and Premeditation: Capital Domestic Murder in the Post-*Furman* Era."

Rasche, Christine. 1986. "Minority Women and Domestic Violence: The Unique Dilemmas of Battered Women of Color." *Journal of Contemporary Criminal Justice* 4:150–171, vol. 2, p. 4.

Raspberry, William. 1989. "If We Are to Rescue American Families, We Have to Save the Boys." *Chicago Tribune*. July 19:C15.

Rawls, John. 1971. *A Theory of Justice.* Cambridge, MA: Harvard University Press.

————. 1993. *Political Liberalism.* New York: Columbia.

Renzetti, Claire M. 1992. *Violent Betrayal.* New York: Sage.

"Report of the Gender Bias Study of the Supreme Judicial Court." 1989. *Suffolk University Law Review* 23:576–683.

Reproduction Rights Update. 1990. February 2:3.

Resnik, Judith. 1988. "On the Bias: Feminist Reconsiderations of the Aspirations of our Judges." *Southern California Law Review* 61:1877.

————. 1987. "Due Process: A Public Dimension." *University of Florida Law Review* 39:405–431.

Reynolds, Z. 1990. "My husband had the right to rape me," *The Independent,* p. 14.

Rich, Adrienne. 1976. *Of Woman Born: Motherhood as Experience and as Institution.* New York: Norton.

Richards, David A. J. 1980. "The Individual, the Family, and the Constitution: A Jurisprudential Perspective." *New York University Law Review* 55:1.

Richie, Beth. 1985. "Battered Black Women: A Challenge for the Black Community." *The Black Scholar* 16:40–44.

Rimonte, Nilda. 1989. "Domestic Violence Against Pacific Asians." In *Making Waves: An Anthology of Writings By and About Asian American Women* ed. Asian Women United of California. Boston: Beacon Press.

————. 1991. "Cultural Sanction of Violence Against Women in the Pacific-Asian Community." *Stanford Law Review* 43, No. 6.

Roberts, Dorothy. 1991. "Punishing Drug Addicts Who Have Babies: Women of Color, Equality, and the Rights of Privacy." *Harvard Law Review* 104:1419.

————. 1993. "Racism and Patriarchy in the Meaning of Motherhood." *The American University Journal of Gender & the Law* 1:1–38.

Robson, Ruthann. 1990. "Lavender Bruises: Intra-Lesbian Violence, Law and Lesbian Legal Theory." *Golden Gate University Law Review* 20:567–591.

Roiphe, Katie. 1993. "Date Rape's Other Victim." *New York Times Magazine* June 13:26.

Romany, Celina. 1989. *Colonial Crimes and Misdemeanors.* Unpublished manuscript on file with the author.

————. 1990a. *"Ellos/ellas y nosotros: Breve paseo por las autopistas y callejones sociales."* Hunter College *Center for Puerto Rican Studies Journal.* Spring: 101.

————. 1990b. *In the Matter of Privilege: The Intersection of Race and Gender in the Critique of Privacy.* An expanded version of a presentation given at the Jurisprudence Section, American Association of Law Schools. Unpublished manuscript on file with the author.

———. 1991a. "Ain't I a Feminist?" *Yale Journal of Law and Feminism.* 4:23.

———. 1991b. *"Indepencia sin feminismo, cronica de una muerte anunciada." En Rojo, Claridad.* Puerto Rico. May 24–30:16.

———. 1992. "Neither Here Nor There . . . Yet (Colonial and Gender Subordination)." *Callaloo (A Journal of African-American and African Arts and Letters).* 15.4:1034.

———. 1993. "Women as Aliens: A Feminist Critique of the Public/Private Distinction in International Human Rights Law." *Harvard Human Rights Journal.* 6:87.

Rorty, Richard. 1989. *Contingency, Irony and Solidarity.* Cambridge: Cambridge University Press.

Rosenfeld, Alan. 1989. "The Statute of Limitations Barrier in Childhood Sexual Abuse Cases: The Equitable Estoppel Remedy." *Harvard Women's Law Journal* 12:206.

Ross, Susan Deller. 1991. "Legal Aspects of Parental Leave: At the Crossroads." In *Parental Leave and Child Care: Setting a Research and Policy Agenda,* eds. Janet Shibley Hyde and Marilyn Essex. Philadelphia: Temple University Press.

Rossiter, Clinton, ed. 1961. *The Federalist Papers.* New York: New American Library.

Russell, Diana E. H. 1986. *The Secret Trauma: Incest in the Lives of Girls and Women.* New York: Basic Books Inc.

Savage, David G. 1990a. "Study Shows Racial Imbalance in Penal System." *New York Times.* February 27:A18.

Savage, David G. 1990b. "Young Black Males in Jail or in Court Control Study Says." *Los Angeles Times.* February 27:A1.

Schecter, Susan. 1982. *Women and Male Violence: The Visions and Struggles of the Battered Women's Movement.* Boston: South End Press.

Schneider, Elizabeth M. 1986a. "Describing and Changing: Women's Self-defense Work and the Problem of Expert Testimony on Battering." *Women's Rights Law Reporter* 9:195–222.

———. 1986b. "The Dialectic of Rights and Politics: Perspectives from the Women's Movement." *New York University Law Review* 61:589–652.

———. 1990a. "Battered Women: Reflections on Feminist Theory and Feminist Practice." Unpublished manuscript on file with the *Connecticut Law Review.*

———. 1990b. "Legal Reform Efforts to Assist Battered Women: Past Present and Future." Unpublished manuscript on file with *Connecticut Law Review.*

———. 1991. "Commentary: The Affirmative Dimensions of Douglas's Privacy." In *He Shall Not Pass This Way Again: The Legacy of Justice William O. Douglas,* ed. S. Wasby. Pittsburgh: University of Pittsburgh Press.

———. 1992. "Particularity and Generality: Challenges of Feminist Theory and Practice in Work on Woman-Abuse," 67 *New York University Law Review* 520–568.

———. 1994. "The Violence of Privacy." In *The Public Nature of Private Violence,* eds. Martha A. Fineman and Roxanne Mykitiuk. New York: Routledge.

Schuler, M., ed. 1992. *Freedom From Violence: Women's Strategies from Around the World.* New York: PACT Communications (UNIFEM).

Scott, Joan. 1990. Book Review. *Signs* 15:848.

———. 1992. "Experience." In *Feminists Theorize the Political,* eds. Judith Butler and Joan W. Scott. New York: Routledge.

Shelton, D. 1990. "Private Violence, Public Wrongs, and the Responsibility of States." *Fordham International Law Journal* 13:1.

Smith, Dorothy E. 1990. *The Conceptual Practices of Power: A Feminist Sociology of Knowledge.* Boston: Northeastern University Press.

Sonkin, Daniel Jay. 1987. *Domestic Violence on Trial: Psychological and Legal Dimensions of Family Violence,* ed. D. Sonkin. New York: Springer Pub. Co.

Span, Paula. 1989. "Women Protest 'Hedda-Bashing'; 300 Sign Response to Steinberg Case." *Washington Post.* March 13:B1.

Spelman, Elizabeth. 1988. *Inessential Woman: Problems of Exclusion in Feminist Thought.* Boston: Beacon Press.

Spivak, Gayatri. 1987. "Subaltern Studies: Deconstructing Historiography." In *Other Worlds: Essays in Cultural Politics.* New York: Methuen.

———. 1990. "Criticism, Feminism and The Institution." In *Post-Colonial Critic: Interviews, Strategies and Dialogues,* ed. Sarah Harasym. London: Routledge.

Standards for Services. 1990. *Standards for Services to Battered Women and Their Children.* Colorado: Women's And Children's Treatment Committee.

Stark, Evan and Flitcraft. Anne. 1985. "Woman-battering, child abuse and social heredity: what is the relationship?" In *Marital Violence,* ed. Norman Johnson. London: Routledge & Kegan Paul.

———. 1988. "Women and Children at Risk: A Feminist Perspective on Child Abuse." *International Journal of Health Services* 18:97.

Steinem, Gloria. 1992. *Revolution From Within.* Boston: Little, Brown and Company.

Steinman, Michael, ed. 1991. *Woman Battering: Policy Responses.* Cincinnati: Anderson.

Stepan, A., ed. 1989. *Democratizing Brazil.* England: Oxford Press.

Stephen, James Fitzjames. 1991. *Liberty, Equality, Fraternity, and Three Brief Essays.* (1873). Chicago: University of Chicago Press.

Stone, Lawrence. 1977. *The Family, Sex and Marriage in England 1500–1800.* New York: Harper and Row.

Stordeur, R. and R. Stille. 1989. *Ending Men's Violence Against Their Partners.* Newbury Park, CA: Sage Publications.

Strauss, David. 1989. "Due Process, Government, Inaction, and Private Wrongs." *Supreme Court Review* 2:54–86.

Straus, Murray. 1979. "Measuring Intra-family Conflict and Violence: The Conflict Tactics Scales (CTS)." *Journal of Marriage and the Family* 45:75–95.

———, Gelles, Richard J., and Steinmetz, Suzanne K. 1980. *Behind Closed Doors: Violence in the American Family.* Garden City NY: Anchor Press.

Straus, Murray and Richard Gelles. 1987. *Costs of Family Violence: U.S. Public Health Report* 102:628–641.

———. 1986. "Societal Change and Change in Family Violence from 1975–1985 As Revealed by Two National Studies." *Journal of Marriage and the Family* 48:465–479.

———. 1990. *Physical Violence in American Families: Risk Factors and Adaptations to Violence in 8,145 Families.* New Brunswick, N.J.: Transaction Press.

Suarez-Orozco, M. M. 1990. "Speaking the Unspeakable: Toward a Psychosocial Understanding of Response to Terror." 18 *Ethos* 3.

Summit, Roland. 1983. "Child Abuse Accommodation Syndrome." *Child Abuse & Neglect* 7:177–93.

Suleiman, Susan Robin. 1985. "Writing and Motherhood." In *The (M)other Tongue: Essays in Feminist Psychoanalytic Interpretation,* eds. Shirley Nelson Garner, Claire Kahane and Madelon Sprengnether. Ithaca, NY: Cornell University Press.

Sullivan, Lawson. 1993. "Essentially Lesbian: Theorizing the Limits of Lesbian Jurisprudence." *Columbia Journal of Gender and Law,* forthcoming.

Sun, Myra and Laurie Woods. 1989. *A Mediator's Guide to Domestic Abuse.* New York: National Center on Women and Family Law.

Supplementary Homicide Reports, 1976–87.

Swigart, Jane. 1991. *The Myth of the Bad Mother: The Emotional Realities of Mothering.* New York: Doubleday.

Swinton, David 1991a. "The Economic Status of African Americans: 'Permanent' Poverty and Inequality." in *The State of Black America* 1991 ed.:

Swinton, David. 1991b. "Urban League Urges Action." *New York Times,* January 9:A14.

Symposium. 1982. "The Public/Private Distinction." *University of Pennsylvania Law Review* 130:1289–1610.

Taub, Nadine and Elizabeth M. Schneider. 1982. "Perspectives on Women's Subordination and the Role of Law." In *The Politics of Law: A Progressive Critique,* ed. D. Kairys. New York: Pantheon.

Taussig, M. 1989. "Terror as Usual: Walter Benjamin's Theory of History as a State of Siege." 7 *Social Text.*

Thomas, Dorothy and Michele Beasley. 1994. "Domestic Violence as a Human Rights Issue." In *The Public Nature of Private Violence,* eds. Martha A. Fineman and Roxanne Mykitiuk. New York: Routledge.

Thomas, Kendall. 1992. "Beyond the Privacy Principle." *Columbia Law Review* 92:1431.

Thomas, Mason P. 1972. *Child Abuse and Neglect—Part I: Historical Review, Legal Matrix and Social Perspectives." North Carolina Law Review* 50:293.

Thompson, Tracey. 1991. "Study Finds 'Persistent' Racial Bias in Area's Rental Housing." *Washington Post.* January 31:D1.

Timerman, J. 1981. *Prisoner Without a Name, Cell Without a Number.* Newbury Park, CA: Sage Publications.

Tong, Rosemarie. 1989. *Feminist Thought.* Boulder, CO: Westview Press.

Trescott, Jacqueline, 1986. "Passions Over Purple: Anger and Unease Over Film's Depiction of Black Men." *Washington Post.* February 5: C1.

Tushnet, Mark. 1986. "The Constitution of Religion." *Connecticut Law Review* 18:701.

Tyler, R. 1868. *Commentaries on the Law of Infancy and the Law of Coverture.* Albany, NY: W. Gould & Sons.

U.S. House, 100th Cong., 1st Sess. 1987. Hearing before the House Select Committee on Children, Youth and Families, "Women, Violence, and the Law." Washington DC: U.S. Government Printing Office.

UN Nairobi Report. 1986. *Report of the World Conference to Review and Appraise Achievements of the UN Decade for Women: Equality, Development and Peace.* Chap. I, section A "The Nairobi Forward-Looking Strategies for the Advancement of Women." New York: United Nations.

UN Report. 1989. *Violence Against Women in the Family.* New York: United Nations.

Unger, Roberto. 1976. *Knowledge and Politics.* New York: Free Press.

———. 1982. "Passion: An Essay on Personality; A Program for Late Twentieth Century Psychiatry," *American Journal of Psychiatry.* 139–155.

Unified Court System of the State of New York. 1986. "Report on New York Task Force on Women in the Courts." *Fordham Urban Law Journal* 5:11–198.

United States Commission of Civil Rights. 1982. *Under the Rule of Thumb: Battered Women and the Administration of Justice.* Washington, DC: The Commission.

Universal Declaration. 1948. Preamble to the *Universal Declaration of Human Rights.* G.A. Resolution 217 A(III) of 10 December 1948. New York: United Nations.

US DOS Country Reports. 1991. *Country Reports on Human Rights Practices for 1990.* Washington, DC: US Department of State.

Utah Code Ann. Section 76–5–202(1)(d).

Van Praagh, Shauna. 1994. "The Youngest Members: Harm to Children and the Role of Religious Communities." In *Public Nature of Private Violence,* eds. Martha Albertson Fineman and Roxanne Mykitiuk. New York: Routledge.

"Victim of Battered Woman's Syndrome Recovers in a Civil Action for Battery and Emotional Distress." 1990. *Association of Trial Lawyers of America Law Report* 33:314.

"Violence Against Women Act of 1991." S-15, 101st Cong. 1st Sess.

Volpp, Leti. (Mis)Identifying Culture: Asian Women and the "Cultural Defense," Unpublished manuscript on file with the *Stanford Law Review.*

Waits, Kathleen. 1985. "The Criminal Justice System's Response to Battering: Understanding the Problem, Forging the Solutions." *Washington Law Review* 60:267.

Wald, Kenneth D. 1992. *Religion and Politics in the United States.* Washington, DC: Congressional Quarterly Press.

Walker, Alice. 1982. *The Color Purple.* New York: Harcourt Brace Jovanovich.

Walker, Gillian. 1990. *Family Violence and the Women's Movement.* Toronto: University of Toronto Press.

Walker, Lenore E. 1979. *The Battered Woman.* New York: Harper and Row.

———. 1984. *The Battered Woman Syndrome.* New York: Springer Publishing Co.

———. 1989. *Terrifying Love: Why Battered Women Kill and How Society Responds.* New York: Harper & Row.

Wallerstein, Judith and Blakeslee, Sandra. 1989. *Second Chances.* New York: Ticknor and Fields.

Walt, Vivienne. 1990. "Immigrant Abuse: Nowhere to Hide; Women Fear Deportation, Experts Say." *Newsday.* December 2:8.

Warner, Rex. ed. 1955. *The Complete Greek Tragedies.*

Warren, D. M. 1973. *The Akan of Ghana: An Overview of the Ethnographic Literature.* Accra: Pointer Limited.

Wechsler, H. and J. Michael. "A Rationale of the Law of Homicide." *Columbia Law Review* 37:701.

Weinrib, E. 1975. "The Fiduciary Obligation." *University of Toronto Law Journal* 25:1.

Weisberg, R. "Deregulating Death." *Supreme Court Law Review* 1983:305.

———. "The Supreme Court 189 Term. Death Penalty—Aggravating and Mitigating Circumstances." *Harvard Law Review* 104:139.

Weisbrod, Carol. 1987–1988. "Family, Church and State: An Essay on Constitutionalism and Religious Authority." *Journal of Family Law* 26:741.

West, Robin. 1987. "The Difference in Women's Hedonic Lives: A Phenomenological Critique of Feminist Legal Theory. *Wisconsin Women's Law Journal* 3:81.

———. 1988. "Jurisprudence and Gender." *University of Chicago Law Review* 55:1.

Westra, Bonnie and Martin, Harold. 1981. "Children Of Battered Women." *Maternal-Childnursing Journal* 10:41.

Will, George F. 1986a. "Voting Rights Won't Fix It." *Washington Post* January 23:A23.

———. 1986b. " 'White Racism' Doesn't Make Blacks Mere Victims of Fate." *Milwaukee Journal* February 21:9.

Williams, Joan. 1991a. "Dissolving the Sameness/Difference Debate: A Post-Modern Path Beyond Essentialism in Feminist and Critical Race Theory." *Duke Law Journal* 1991–296.

———. 1991b. "Gender Wars: Selfless Women iln the Republic of Choice." *New York University Law Review.* 66:1559.

Williams, Patricia. 1991. *The Alchemy of Race and Rights.* Cambridge: Harvard University Press.

Williams, W. 1982. "The Equality Crisis: Some Reflections on Culture, Courts and Feminism." *Women's Rights Law Reporter* 7.

Williams, Wendy. 1984–85. "Equality's Riddle: Pregnancy and the Equal Treatment/Special Treatment Debate." *New York University Review of Law and Social Change* 13:325.

———. 1989. "Notes from a First Generation." *University of Chicago Legal Forum,* 99.

Wilson, E. 1976. *The Existing Research into Battered Women.* London: National Women's Aid Federation.

Wilson, James Q. 1969. "Violence." *Toward the End of the Year 2000,* ed. Daniel Bell. Boston: Beacon Press.

Wilson, M. and Daly, M. 1988. *Homicide.* New York: A. De Gruytard.

Winnicott, D. W. 1960. "The Theory of the Parent-Infant Relationship." *International Journal of Psychoanalysis* 41:585.

———. 1965. *The Maturational Processes and the Facilitating Environment.* New York: International Universities Press.

Wiredu, K. 1990. "An Akan Perspective on Human Rights." In *Human Rights in Africa: Cross-Cultural Perspectives,* eds. A. A. Na'im Abdullai and F. M. Deng. Washington: The Brookings Institute.

Women and Violence: Hearings Before the Senate Committee on the Judiciary on Legislation to Reduce the Growing Problem of Violent Crime Against Women. 101st Congress, 2d Session, 1991.

Women, Violence and the Law: Hearing Before the House Select Committee on Children, Youth and Families. 100th Congress, 1st Session 3, 1987 (Statement of Rep. George Miller).

Woodhouse, Barbara Bennett. 1992. " 'Who Owns the Child?'": Meyer and Pierce and the Child as Property." *William and Mary Law Review* 33:995.

Woolf, Virginia. 1984. "Professions for Women." *The Virginia Woolf Reader*, ed. Mitchell A. Leaska. Orlando: Harcourt, Brace Javonovich.

World's Women. 1991. *World's Women: Trends and Statistics, 1970–1990.* New York: United Nations.

WRP/Asia Watch. 1992. *Double Jeopardy: Police Abuse of Women in Pakistan.* New York: Human Rights Watch.

WRP/Helsinki Watch. 1992. "Hidden Victims: Women in Post-Communist Poland." *News From Helsinki Watch* 14:5.

WRP/Middle East Watch. 1992. "Punishing the Victim: Rape and Mistreatment of Asian Maids in Kuwait." *News from Middle East Watch* 4:8.

Wynn-Davies, P. 1991. "Judges nail 'lie' that husbands cannot rape." *Independent.* October 24:3.

Yllö, Kersti and Michele Bograd, eds. 1988. *Feminist Perspectives on Wife Abuse.* Newbury Park, CA: Sage Publications.

Zimring, Franklin. 1987. "Legal Perspectives on Family Violence". *California Law Review.* 75:521–539.

Zorza, J. 1992. "The Criminal Law of Misdemeanor Domestic Violence 1970–1990." *J. Crim L. & Crim.* 83–46.

Cases

Baehr v. Lewin. 1993. 852 P.2d 44 (Haw.).

Bailey v. Bailey. 1867. Mass Supreme Jud Court, Plymouth, 373.

Bailey v. Lewis. 1991. 763 F.Supp. 802 (E.D.Pa. 1991).

Baker v. Nelson. 1971. 191 N.W.2d 185 (Minn.); appeal dismissed for want of a federal question: 1972. 409 U.S. 810.

Balistreri v. Pacifica Police Dep't. 1990. 901 F.2d 696 (9th Cir.).

Barrere v. Barrere. 1819. Cases in Chancery (New York) 187.

Blake v. State. 1977. 239 Ga. 292, 231 S.E.2d 637.

Bowers v. Hardwick. 1986. 478 U.S. 1039.

Boynton v. Kusper. 112 Ill.2d 356, 494 N.E.2d 135.

Bray v. Alexandria Women's Health Clinic. 1993. 113 S.Ct. 753.

Brossard (Ville) v. Québec (C.D.P.). (1988), 88 C.L.L.C. 17031.

Brown v. Board of Education. 1954. 397 US 483.

Browning v. Corbett. 1987. 153 Ariz. 74, 734 P.2d 1030.

Bruno v. Codd. 1977. 90 Misc. 2nd 1047, 396 N.Y.S.2d 974 (N.Y. Sup. Ct.), rev'd on other grounds, 64 A.D.2d 582, 407 N.Y.S.2d 165 (N.Y. App. Div. 1978), aff'd, 47 N.Y.2d 582, 393 N.E.2d 976, 419, N.Y.S.2d 901 (1979).

Buenoaano v. State. 1988. 527 So.2d 194.

Burdine v. Amperse. 1866. 14 Mich. 90. 92.

Burr v. Burr. 1842. 10 Paige 20.

Cannaday v. State. 1984. 455 So.2d 713.

Carlson v. Illinois. 1980. 404 N.E.2d 233, 79 Ill.2d 564.

C.D.P. c. Ville de Repentigny. [1986] D.L.Q. 95 (S.C.).

Coffman v. Wilson Police Dep't. 1990. 739 F. Supp. 257 (E.D Pa.).

Coker v. Georgia. 1977. 433 U.S. 584.

Commonwealth v. Shoemaker. 1986. 359 Pa. Sup[er. 111, 518 A.2d 591.

Crocker v. Finley. 1984. 99 Ill.2d 444, 459 N.E.2d 1346.

Daly v. Derrick. 1991. 281 Cal.Rptr. 709 (Cal.App. 6 Dist.).

Dandridge v. Williams. 1970. 279 U.S. 471.

DeRose v. Carswell. 1987. 242 Cal. Rptr. 368 (Cal.App. 6 Dist.).

DeSanto v. Barnsley. 1984. 476 A.2d 952 (Pa. Super. Ct.).

DeShaney v. Winnebago County Dept. of Social Services. 1989. 109 S.Ct. 998.

Doe v. Bolton. 1973. 410 U.S. 179.

Douglas v. State. 1991. 575 So.2d 165.

Dudosh v. City of Allentown. 1989. 722 F. Supp. 1233.

Ellsworth v. City of Racine. 1985. 774 F.2d 182 (7th Cir.).

Estelle v. Gamble. 1976. 429 US 97.

Evans v. Eckelman. 1990. 265 Cal.Rptr. 605 (Cal.App. 1 Dist.).

Fead v. State. 1987. 12 Fla. L. Week 451, 512 So.2d 176.

Frame v. Smith. [1987] 2 S.C.R. 99 at 136; 78 N.R. 40.

Freeman v. Ferguson. 1990. 911 F.2d 52 (8th Cir.).

Furman v. Georgia. 1972. 408 U.S. 238.

Georgia v. Hamby. 1978. No. 3478 (Ga. Superior Court, April 12).

Godfrey v. Georgia. 1980. 446 U.S. 420, 100 S.Ct. 1759.

Gray v. Reeves. (1992), 64 B.C.L.R. (2d) 275; [1992] 3 W.W.R. 393; 89 D.L.R. (4th) 315 (S.C.).

Gregg v. Georgia. 1976. 428 U.S. 153, 100 S.Ct. 1759.

Griswold v. Connecticut. 1965. 381 U.S. 479.

Hammer v. Hammer. 1987. 418 N.W.2d 23 at 25. 142 Wis.2d 257 (Wis.Appl.).

Hill v. Hill. 1806. Oct. Term (Mass) 150.

Hodorowski et al. v. Ann Ray, Mary Ellen Burns and Texas Department of Human Resources. 1988. 844 F.2d 1210 (5th Cir.).

Holmsted v. Director of Public Prosecutions. 1946. A.C. 588.

Hynson v. City of Chester. 1990. 731 F. Supp. 1236 (E.D. Pa.).

Illinois v. Buggs. 1986. 493 N.E.2d 332, 112 Ill.2d 284.

In re Guardianship of Kowalski. 1986. 382 N.W.2d 861 (Minn. Ct. App.).

In re Guardianship of Kowalski. 1986. 392 N.W.2d 310 (Minn. Ct. App.).

In re Guardianship of Kowalski. 1992. 478 N.W.2d 790 (Minn. Ct. App.).

In re Jacobs. 1989. 444 N.W.2d 789 (Mich.).

In re State ex rel. Black. 1955. 283 P.2d 887 (Utah).

Johnson v. Johnson. 1988. 701 F.Supp. 1363 (N.D.Ill.).

Johnston v. Wellesley Hospital. [1971] 2 O.R. 103; 17 D.L.R. (3d) 139 (H.C.).

Jones v. Hallahan. 1973. 501 S.W.2d 588 (Ky. Ct. App.).

Jurek v. Texas. 1976. 428 U.S. 262, 96 S.Ct. 2950. 49 L.E.2d 926.

Kennedy v. Kennedy. 1878. 73 N.Y. 369. 374.

King v. Victor Parsons & Co. [1973] 1 All.E.R. 206 (C.A.).

Lac Minerals v. International Corona Resources. [1989] 2 S.C.R. 574.

Lawrence v. Lawrence. 1832. 3 Paige 388.

Lindsey v. Normet. 1972. 405 U.S. 56.

Luster v. Price. No. 90–0115–CV–W–8 (W.C. Mo. July 5, 1990) (LEXIS, Genfed library, Dist. file).

M.(K.) v. M.(H.). [1992] 3 S.C.R. 6; 142 N.R. 321; 96 D.L.R. (4th) 289.

M.(M.) v. K.(K.). (1987) 11 B.C.L.R. (2d) 90; 35 D.L.R. (4d) 222 (S.C.B.C.); rev'd (1989). 38 B.C.L.R. (2d) 273; 61 D.L.R. (4th) 382 (C.A.).

Manu v. Manu. [1959] Ghana Law Reports, 21.

Marsha v. Gardner. 1991. 281 Cal. Rptr. 473 (Cal.App. 2 Dist.).

Mason v. Mason. (1831) Cases in the Vice Chancellor's Court, 278.

Matter of Farley. 1991. 469 N.W.2d 295 (Mich.).

Maulden v. State. 1993. 617 So.2d 2998.

McMillan v. State Mutual Life Assurance Co. of Am. 1990. 922 F.2d 1073 (3d Cir.).

Meiers-Post v. Schafer. 1988. 427 N.W.2d 606 (Mich. App.).

Merton v. State. 1986. 500 So.2d 1301 (Ala. Crim. App.).

Metro Broadcasting. Inc. v. FCC. 1990. 110 S. Ct. 2997.

Meyer v. Nebraska. 1923. 262 U.S. 390.

Moreland v. State. 1990. 552 N.E. 2d 894.

Mormina v. Ville de St-Léonard, J.E. 87–950 (Qué. S.C., 1987).

Muhammed v. City of Chicago. No. 89–C–6903 (N.D. Ill. Jan. 14, 1991) (LEXIS, Genfed library, Dist. file).

Muller v. Oregon. 1908. 208 U.S. 412.

Nearing v. Weaver. 1983. 295 Or. 702. 670 P.2d 137.

Norberg v. Weinrib. [1992] 2 S.C.R. 224; 6 W.W.R. 673.

North Carolina v. Stanley. 1984. 310 N.C. 332, 312 S.E.2d 393.

Osei-Koom v. Osei-Koom. [1967] Ghana Law Reports, 274.

Osland v. Osland. 1989. 442 N.W.2d 907 (N.D.).

Québec (C.D.P.) c. Québec (Ville). [1986] R.J.Q. 253, rev'd [1989] R.J.Q. 831 (C.A.), leave to appeal to S.C.C. refused (1989), 103 N.R. 160*n* (S.C.C.).

Palmer v. Palmer. (1828) 1 Paige 276.

People v. Forman. 1989. 145 Misc. 2d 115. 546 N.Y.S.2d 755 (N.Y. Crim. Ct.).

People v. Groff. 1987. 71 N.Y.2d 10.

People v. Jernatowski. 1924. 238 N.Y. 188, 144 N.E. 497.

People v. Liberta. 1985. 64 N.Y.2d 152, 474 N.E.2d 567, 485 N.Y.S.2d 207, 1020 (1985).

People v. Winters. July 1823. Decisions in Criminal Cases, Clinton Oyer and Terminer, 10.

Perkins v. Perkins. 1809. Massachusetts Nov. Term. 68.

Perry v. Perry. 1831. 2 Paige. 501.

Phillips v. State. 1982. 250 Ga. 336, 297 S.E.2d 217.

Pierce v. Society of Sisters. 1925. 268 U.S. 510.

Plessy v. Ferguson. 1896. 163 U.S. 537.

Preston v. State. 1984. 444 So.2d 939.

Prince v. Massachusetts. 1944. 321 U.S. 158.

Proffitt v. Florida. 1976. 428 U.S. 242, 96 S.Ct. 2960, 49 L.E.2d 913.

Quisenberry v. State. 1987. 319 N.C. 228, 354 S.E.2d 446.

R. v. Lavalee. (1989) 44 C.C.C. (3d) 113 (Manitoba Court of Appeal).

R. v. Lavalee. (1990) 1 S.C.R. 852.

Regina v. Mawbridge. 1707. Kel. J. 119.

Reynolds v. United States. 1878. 98 U.S. 145.

Richardson v. State. 1992. 17 Fla. L. Week S241, 604 So.2d 1107.

Roe v. Wade. 1973. 410 U.S. 113.

Santos v. State. 1991. 16 Fla. L. Week. S633, 591, So.2d 160.

Santosky et al. v. Kramer Commissioner of Ulster County Department of Social Services. 1982. 455 U.S. 745.

Sauveteurs et victimes d'actes criminels—9 [1990] C.A.S. 46.

Sauveteurs et victimes d'actes criminels—24 [1991] C.A.S. 116.

Seaboyer v. R. [1991] 2 S.C.R. 577.

Singer v. Hara. 1974. 522 P.2d 1187 (Wash. Ct. App.).

Stager v. State. 1991. 329 N.C. 278.

Stanley v. Illinois. 1972. 405 U.S. 645.

State v. Greene. 1989. 324 N.C. 1, 376 S.E.2d 430.

State v. Hadinger. 1991. 573 N.E.2d 1191 (Ohio Ct. App.).

State v. Huffstetler. 312 N.C. 92, 322 S.E.2d 110.

State v. Moorman. 154 Ariz. 578, 744 P.2d 679.

State v. Rider. 1984. 449 So.2d 903 (Fla. Dist. Ct. App.).

State v. Riley. 1982. 649 P.2d 1273 (Montana).

State v. Wacaser. 1990. 794 S.W.2d 190, 105 S.Ct. 1224, 469 U.S. 1229, 84 L.Ed. 2d 366.

Stephens v. Zant. 1983. 462 U.S. 862.

Thurman v. Torrington. 1984. 595 F. Supp. 1521 (D. Conn.).

Tyson v. Tyson. 1986. 727 P.2d 226 (Wash.).

Villars v. Provo. 1989. 440 N.W.2d 160 (Minn. Ct. App.).

Wiley v. State. 1918. 19 Ariz. 346, 170 P. 869.

William Brook's Case. 1821. The New York City Hall Recorder. 66.

Williams v. State. 1986. 494 So.2d 819 (Ala. Crim. App.).

Wisconsin v. Yoder. 1971. 406 U.S. 205.

Youngberg v. Romeo. 1982. 457 U.S. 307.

Contributors

MARIE ASHE, currently a member of the faculty of the Suffolk University School of Law in Boston, Massachusetts, has written extensively about legal regulation of female gender and female sexuality. Her work includes: "Zig-Zag Stitching and the Seamless Web," 13 *Nova Law Review* (1989); "Inventing Choreographies: Deconstruction and Feminism," 90 *Columbia Law Review* (1990); "Abortion of Narrative: A Reading of the Judgment of Solomon," 4 *Yale Journal of Law and Feminism* (1991); "The 'Bad Mother' in Law and Literature: A Problem of Representation," 43 *Hastings Law Journal* (1992); and " 'Bad Mothers,' 'Good Lawyers,' and 'Legal Ethics'," *Georgetown Law Journal* (1993).

MICHELE BEASLEY received her law degree from Georgetown University Law Center in 1991, where she focused on jurisprudence and feminist legal theory. She has published a number of written works, including articles on abortion, human rights, and domestic violence. While at Georgetown, Ms. Beasley represented battered women seeking Civil Protection Orders in D.C. Superior Court. Ms. Beasley is also a former staff attorney for the Women's Rights Project of Human Rights Watch, where she investigated abuses against women. While at the Women's Rights Project, she conducted a fact-finding mission to Kuwait to investigate rape and abuse of domestic servants in Kuwait. The report of that mission, *Punishing The Victim: Rape and Mistreatment of Asian Maids in Kuwait*, was published in August 1992 by Human Rights Watch in New York.

Ms. Beasley currently practices corporate law at the firm of Chadbourne & Parke and is a member of the Women's Commission on Refugee Women and Children. Ms. Beasley has researched and spoken extensively on the issue of war crimes on behalf of the Women's Commission.

NAOMI R. CAHN is currently an Associate Professor at the George Washington University National Law Center. From 1988 to 1993, she was the Assistant Director of the Georgetown University Law Center Sex Discrimination Clinic, where she supervised students representing victims of domestic violence. Her work has focused on issues concerning the representation of women and family in legal ethics, in theory, and in practice.

JANE MASLOW COHEN is Professor of Law at Boston University. Her teaching and research interests include property; family law; health care and bioethics; law and literature; and feminist and interpretive theory. Before entering law teaching, Professor Cohen practiced law, with an emphasis on family law. She is a graduate of Wellesley College and the Yale Law School.

KIMBERLÉ WILLIAMS CRENSHAW (J.D. Harvard; LL.M. Univ. of Wisconsin) is Professor of Law at U.C.L.A. Law School and Samuel Rubin Visiting Professor of Law at Columbia Law School. She has lectured and written extensively on civil rights, Black feminist legal theory, and race and the law. She is a founding member of the Critical Race Theory workshop, coauthor of *Words That Wound: Assaultive Speech and the First Amendment* (Colorado: Westview Press, 1992), and the coeditor of a forthcoming volume, *Critical Race Theory: A Reader*. Her work has appeared in *Harvard Law Review, National Black Law Journal, Stanford Law Review,* and *Southern California Law Review*. She serves on the governing board of the Law and Society Association and the Society of American Law Teachers. A specialist on legal issues confronting Black women, she assisted the legal team representing Anita Hill.

MARY EATON received her LL.B. and LL.M. from Queen's University in Canada. Following her first round of studies, she worked as a prisoners' rights advocate and later served as a clerk to Madam Justice Bertha Wilson of the Supreme Court of Canada. She is currently a J.S.D. candidate at Columbia University, where she has been awarded an L.L.M. Her work focuses on lesbian issues and law, and she has both written and spoken extensively in this area.

MARTHA ALBERTSON FINEMAN is the Maurice T. Moore Professor of Law at Columbia University in the City of New York. She is a 1975 graduate of the University of Chicago Law School. She clerked for Luther M. Swygert of the Seventh Circuit Court of Appeals. Professor Fineman began teaching in 1976 at the University of Wisconsin Law School. In 1984 she developed the Feminism and Legal Theory Project at Wisconsin. The project is now located at Columbia Law School, and is devoted to fostering interdisciplinary feminist work on law and legal institutions. In addition to numerous articles and book chapters on feminism, family law, the regulation of intimacy and sexuality, Professor Fineman is the author of *The Neutered Mother, The Sexual Family and Other Twentieth Century Tragedies* (forthcoming 1994) and *The Illusion of Equality: The Rhetoric and Reality of Divorce Reform* (Chicago 1991). She is a contributor and coeditor of a number of collections of papers from the Feminism and Legal Theory Project, including *Reclaiming the Colonized Category: Mothers in Law* (forthcoming 1995) and *At the Boundaries of Law: Feminism and Legal Theory* (Routledge 1991).

SUSAN F. HIRSCH is Assistant Professor of Anthropology at Wesleyan University in Middletown, Connecticut. She received her Ph.D. in Anthropology from Duke University. She has written about the influence of Islamic law and Islamic courts on shaping gender relations in colonial and postcolonial coastal East Africa, with particular attention to the language of marital conflict and disputing. She is coeditor of *Contested States: Law, Hegemony, and Resistance* (forthcoming from Routledge).

MARTHA MAHONEY is an associate professor at the University of Miami School of Law. A former labor and community organizer, she was a founding member of the San Francisco Women's Health Collective, did support work for United Farm Workers boycotts, and worked in garment and microfilm factories. Her master's thesis in history at Tulane University focused on race, economic development, and public housing in New Orleans. She graduated from Stanford Law School in 1989 and has been at Miami since 1990, teaching courses on land use, race and class, domestic violence, and on developing solo or small firm law practice in the public interest. She has published articles on domestic violence, sexual harassment, and race and feminist theory.

ISABEL MARCUS, Ph.D. (Pol. Sci), J.D., is a Professor at the School of Law (State University of New York at Buffalo). She has taught previously at the University of Texas (Austin) and CUNY Law School as well as at universities in The People's Republic of China and Poland. Her recent work includes the development of an interdisciplinary Domestic Violence Program at SUNY Buffalo.

JOAN MEIER is an Associate Professor of Clinical Law at George Washington University National Law Center, where she directs the Domestic Violence Advocacy Project. Professor Meier has worked, litigated, and written about domestic violence for approximately ten years, including extensive legislative and policy advocacy with the D.C. Coalition Against Domestic Violence. Her research and writing focus on domestic violence, family law, and criminal procedure. She is currently working on a book, *Criminal Law and the Family* (with Naomi Cahn), and an article on the interdisciplinary teaching of a domestic violence clinic. She graduated from Harvard University and University of Chicago Law School.

ROSEMARY OFEI-ABOAGYE is completing her Doctorate in Jurisprudence at Osgoode Hall Law School in Toronto. A Ghanaian woman who has studied in North America, her research straddles the concepts of two essentially disparate regimes and brings a rich diversity to American jurisprudence. Her postgraduate research has been on the interdisciplinary subject of domestic violence in Ghana and the ways in which its incidence and eradication compare to studies done on the phenomenon in Canada and the United States. She is presently studying the relationship between formal equality provisions and cultural norms. She is the first Director of the Equity Access Program and a Scholar-in-Residence at the Faculty of Law, Queen's University, Canada. Ms. Ofei-Aboagye holds a Bachelor of Law from the University of Ghana and a Master of Law from Queen's University, Canada. She is also a member of the Ghana Bar Association.

ELIZABETH RAPAPORT is currently associate professor of public policy and philosophy at Duke University; in January, 1995 she will join the faculty of the University of New Mexico School of Law. She has taught philosophy, law, public policy, and women's studies at universities including Boston University, Brown University, University of Southern California, and the University of Sydney. She will be teaching courses on criminal law, legal ethics, jurisprudence, and advocacy. She is a graduate of Harvard Law School, and has a PH.D. in philosophy from Case Western Reserve University. Her current research focuses on gender and the death penalty and on jurisprudence. She has written about ethics, politics and a range of gender issues.

CELINA ROMANy is a poet, painter, journalist, and feminist theorist and activist in movement for women's human rights. She is also a Professor of Law and Co-Director of the International Women's Human Rights Program at City University of New York Law School.

NATHALIE DES ROSIERS, (LL.B.) Montreal, (LL.M.) Harvard, is a member of the Quebec Bar and the Law Society of Upper Canada, and an Associate Professor, University of Western Ontario. She has written articles for Mr. Justice Chouinard, Supreme Court of Canada 1983, and practiced in the litigation department at Lerner & Associates, from 1985 to 1987. She was Assistant Professor, University of Western Ontario, from 1987 to 1993. She teaches in the area of Constitutional Law, Administrative Law, Law and Social Welfare, and is Commissioner of the Ontario Law Reform Commission, from 1993 to the present. She was a member of the Premier's Constitutional Advisory Committee, from February 1992 to October 1992, Representative of the Public on the Attorney General Consultative Committee on Limitation Periods, from 1989 to

1990, and Secretary and Director of the Report of the Canadian Bar Association Committee on Limitation Period, from 1988 to 1989. She has published "Les recours de la victime d'inceste" in P. Legrand, dir. *Common law, d'un siècle, l'autre* (Yvon Blais, 1992); and "Discretion in Social Assistance Legislation" (1992) 8 Journal of Law and Social Policy, 204.

ELIZABETH M. SCHNEIDER is Professor of Law at Brooklyn Law School. She has written and lectured widely in the areas of civil rights, women's rights, and violence against women. In addition to the article reprinted in this volume, her writing in the area of domestic violence includes "Particularity and Generality: Challenges of Feminist Theory and Practice on Woman-Abuse" 67 *New York University Law Review* 520 (1992); "Violence Against Women and Legal Education; An Essay for Mary Joe Frug," 26 *New England Law Review* 843 (1992); "Describing and Changing: Women's Self-Defense Work and the Problem of Expert Testimony on Battering," 9 *Women's Rights Law Reporter* 195 (1986), "The Dialectic of Rights and Politics: Perspectives from the Women's Movement," 61 *New York University Law Review* 589 (1986); "Equal Rights to Trial for Women: Sex Bias in the Law of Self-Defense," 15 *Harvard Civil Rights— Civil Liberties Law Review* (1980), and a report for the Ford Foundation, *Legal Reform Efforts to Assist Battered Women, Past, Present and Future* (1990). She teaches Women and the Law and Civil Procedure, and has also been Visiting Professor at Harvard Law School since 1989, where she has taught Gender Discrimination, Civil Procedure, and Battered Women and the Law. She is working on a book on violence against women and feminist theory and practice which will be published by Harvard University Press and a casebook on domestic violence. She is a graduate of Bryn Mawr College and New York University Law School and has a master's degree in political sociology from The London School of Economics.

MARCIA SELLS is the Assistant Dean and Dean of Students at Columbia Law School, her alma mater. She first worked as an Assistant District Attorney in the Kings County District Attorney's office where she tried rape, domestic violence, and child abuse cases. During her last year as an ADA, she trained first-year Assistants. Ms Sells spent two years at Chadbourne & Parke, where she litigated securities, trademarks, and products liability cases. She has served on the New York City Bar's Committees on Sex and Law and Recruitment of Lawyers, and now serves on the Special Commission on Minorities and the Courts. Ms. Sells has also served on the Governor's Task Force on Rape and Sexual Assault, and is co-editor of *Women, Know Your Rights,* published by the NY State Division for Women.

DOROTHY QUINCY THOMAS is currently the Director of the Women's Rights Project of Human Rights Watch, in Washington D.C., a project designed to monitor and denounce state-sponsored violence against women and gender discrimination worldwide. She has extensive experience in international human rights and has lectured and published extensively on women and international human rights.

SHAUNA VAN PRAAGH, B.Sc. (Toronto, 1986), LL.B. (Toronto, 1989), LL.M. (Columbia, 1992) is a 1993/1994 Boulton Fellow at the Faculty of Law of McGill University and a continuing candidate for the J.S.D. (Doctorate in Law) degree from the Columbia University School of Law. She has taught at the law faculties of Columbia, King's College London, and McGill. In focusing on issues raised by the children of religious communities, Ms. Van Praagh's doctoral research and writing intersects and draws upon the areas of constitutional law, family law, and feminist legal theory.